CIVIC WAR AND THE CORRUPTION OF THE CITIZEN

CIVIC WAR & THE CORRUPTION OF THE CITIZEN

Peter Alexander Meyers

THE UNIVERSITY OF CHICAGO PRESS

Chicago and London

PETER ALEXANDER MEYERS is a political theorist and
professor of American Studies at the Sorbonne Nouvelle
in Paris. He is originally from New York City. Contact him at
http://www.civicwar.org.

The University of Chicago Press, Chicago 60637
The University of Chicago Press, Ltd., London

17 16 15 14 13 12 11 10 09 08   1 2 3 4 5

ISBN-13: 978-0-226-52208-1 (cloth)
ISBN-10: 0-226-52208-3 (cloth)

Library of Congress Cataloging-in-Publication Data

Meyers, Peter Alexander.
 Civic war and the corruption of the citizen / Peter
Alexander Meyers.
    p. cm.
 Includes bibliographical references and index.
 ISBN-13: 978-0-226-52208-1 (cloth : alk. paper)
 ISBN-10: 0-226-52208-3 (cloth : alk. paper)
 1. September 11 Terrorist Attacks, 2001—Influence.
 2. War on Terrorism, 2001–3. United States—Politics
and government—2001–4. United States—Politics and
government—20th century. 5. Cold War. I. Title.
 HV6432.7.M486 2008
 973.931—dc22

                              2008009639

♾ The paper used in this publication meets the minimum
requirements of the American National Standard for
Information Sciences—Permanence of Paper for Printed
Library Materials, ANSI Z39.48-1992.

FOR ALEXI

The Constitution of the United States establishes . . .
the Army [which] serves as a repository of its national
values and embeds them into its professional ethos.
Proper subordination to political authority, loyalty,
duty, selfless service, courage, integrity, respect for
human dignity, and a sense of justice are all part of the
Army's identity. . . . Moreover, the people expect the
military to accomplish its missions in compliance with
national values . . . and reserve the right to reconsider
their support should any of these conditions not be
met. . . . The responsibility for the conduct and use
of military forces is derived from the people and the
government. . . . In the end, the people will pass judgment on the appropriateness of the conduct and use
of military operations. Their values and expectations
must be met.

"THE AMERICAN VIEW OF WAR,"
Army Field Manual FM 100–5 (1993)

All you that are enamored of my name
And least intent on what most I require,
Beware; for my design and your desire,
Deplorably, are not as yet the same.
Beware, I say, the failure and the shame
Of losing that for which you now aspire
So blindly, and of hazarding entire
The gift that I was bringing when I came.

EDWIN ARLINGTON ROBINSON, "Demos I" (1920)

Contents

Acknowledgments

As a matter of theory and method this book develops the view that no one acts alone and that action cannot be what it is without the presence of others. The same is true for thinking. I grew up in New York City and by the natural inclinations of my polis I find myself talking with everyone, everywhere, all the time. I cannot name my hundreds of interlocutors in the public sphere since September 11, 2001, but I want to thank them for both complicating and clarifying the scene I have tried to bring before you.

Still, many names are vividly in mind. Three outstanding people—Craig Calhoun, Andrew Feffer, and Harvey Goldman—prompted me to write this book, and through ongoing dialogue and encouragement they have mightily contributed to whatever merit it may have. I am further privileged to have shared in the erudition, generosity, and patience of Peter Brown, Daniel Cefai, Dominique Colas, Owen Fiss, Tony Grafton, Carla Hesse, Stan Katz, Ira Katznelson, Nan Keohane, Franck Lessay, Paolo Napoli, Josh Ober, Kim Scheppele, Joan Scott, Allan Silver, Yan Thomas, Joan Tronto, Nadia Urbinati, and many others who, given the way these things go, will undoubtedly present themselves to my memory once this book is in print; I am sure that I will be issuing apologies and additional thanks for years to come.

My thinking was further aided by discussions with colleagues following talks I gave at Columbia University, Pomona College, Princeton University, the University of California at Los Angeles, the University of California at San Diego, and several meetings of the American Political Science Association.

Presentation of material from this book in the Columbia University Seminar on Studies in Political and Social Thought, and subsequent discussion with some of its members, significantly advanced my thinking. I am grateful to University Seminars at Columbia, led by Robert Belknap, for supporting publication with an award from the Warner Fund.

I never cease to be fascinated and inspired by my students in France and the United States, and those with the fortitude to read this book will see our dialogue continued here. I found particularly illuminating conversations with students in the Army ROTC program at Princeton.

For years I exchanged ideas with Dan Menaker and the late Fifi Oscard about the increasingly precarious balance between writing for the citizen and writing for the bookworm; in a sense this book continues those conversations.

I could not have finished or even conceived this work without the extraordinary support, patience, and collegiality of the Institut du monde anglophone, under the leadership of André Topia and Marie-Christine Lemardeley, and the Université de Paris III–Sorbonne Nouvelle, with the concurrence of the French Ministry of Education. This involved my nomination for several years to the Centre national de la recherche scientifique (CNRS) and the Centre de théorie du droit, directed by the estimable Michel Troper. I am profoundly indebted to these institutions and to the people of whom they are composed. In the United States, the Department of Politics at Princeton University under the leadership of Helen Milner appointed me first as visiting fellow and then as visiting professor. Astonishing vivacity and fellowship at the School of Historical Studies of the Institute for Advanced Study in Princeton sustained me as I brought to a conclusion the project that had begun, thanks to Craig Calhoun, under the auspices of the Social Science Research Council in October of 2001, when my first notes appeared on their Web site. A further development of my thinking appeared in an essay published by the New Press in 2002.

Doug Mitchell of the University of Chicago Press noticed that my immediate reactions to the events following September 11, 2001, needed to be spelled out in more detail and he set about providing an opportunity for me to do so. Under his patient tutelage, albeit to his astonishment, what was projected as a brief pamphlet grew into three distinct but interrelated books. Although most of the present volume had been written by the summer of 2004, its publication was delayed when I tried to bring it to a wider audience more quickly than the workings of a university press would allow. Although most readers of the manuscript praised it highly, apologetic editors were overcome with the anxiety that their consumers could never think clearly enough to see themselves as citizens and thus, as I argue in these pages, as responsible for the amplification and misuse of power. Following this unfortunate adventure the inimitable Doug Mitchell welcomed me back to the University of Chicago Press, offering another brilliant reading of the manuscript and provided me with anonymous reports that improved it immensely. I count too among my blessings the way Joann Hoy applied her meticulous hand to my sentences, as well as the oppurtunity to work with Mary Gehl, Isaac Tobin, and Tim McGovern. Laura Bennett created the index.

My active political life started when, at the age of eight or nine, I assisted in my little way in the electoral campaign of New York State Assemblyman William F. Passannante, and I began a lifelong conversation with my mother, Joan Simpson Burns, and my father, Alfred Lee Meyers, about the civic world and our place within it. My mother's activism continues to this day and her reading of these pages has contributed important insights to them.

I am what might be called a born-again humanist, baptized over and over again every day by the love and courage and intelligence of my wife, Effie Rentzou. This book is as much her gift to me as it is my gift to her.

Note to the Reader

This book is part of a trilogy with the common title *Democracy in America after 9/11*. While the volume you are holding, *Civic War and the Corruption of the Citizen*, is the first of the three, it was written last. In these pages political problems of institutions and power are treated in terms of the historical development of symbolic forms in relation to the position of the Citizen. The second volume articulates the theory of politics presupposed by this one; under the title *The Position of the Citizen* it spells out basic conditions that make civic life possible, showing how politics creates a distinctive type of human relationship in space and time through the use of speech. The final volume, *Political Pathologies of the Citizen*, returns again to the American landscape of politics and history to illustrate ways in which a democratic regime can develop against itself. Thus the trilogy as a whole argues that power-constituting symbolic forms (part 1) are shaped by conditions of possibility for politics (part 2) that may nonetheless operate in antipolitical ways (part 3).

Port of Entry

Roles we play in society are forms of relationship with other people. They can be identified with some precision. Actions of and reactions to a Mother or a Child clearly differ; a Soldier is not the President and the President is not a Soldier. Of our many and overlapping roles, *Citizen* is the one that makes everyday life with others possible when no higher authority takes charge. Although it is the motor, and the heart, of democratic societies, Americans devote little time and less attention to specifying and caring for the role of the Citizen. More than any other of the many facts with which you have become familiar since September 11th 2001, this one is drawing us towards crisis.

Most of what comes to mind when you think of politics—those politicians, Congress, the White House, the perpetual return of elections—is just its shadow. Politics is first and foremost the activity of the Citizen. I do not mean by this *your* many and various *personal* activities, but rather what happens when any person, including you or I, assumes the role of the Citizen and we allow ourselves to be constrained by that role in order to gain its benefits. A subtle or imperceptible shift or slip can bring us into this character, can bring us into the political world.

The history of the word provides a compelling clue to its significance: the Citizen is the type of person who "lives in the city." Less strictly but more precisely speaking, the Citizen takes full possession of those facts that appear most clearly in cities but that, in the modern world, characterize a wide range of human relationships in many different settings.

And what are these facts? That we do, and must, live together, not just one day, but every day; that this *we* is plural, and cannot be composed of reiterations of the same, and thus is, like a city, spread over space and

time in a complex order or organism that, if unified in perfect and perfectly stable consensus, would cease to exist; that within this plurality of
humankind each, for better *and* for worse, depends on the others; that,
wherever on the earth this "city" appears, from within its relative kind
of space—a space more like the spontaneous and flexible formation of a
team than like the field on which the team plays—problems necessarily
arise and often take the form of conflicts over power, which is to say, since
power is never one thing, conflicts over *differentials between powers*;* that
of the limited options we have for responding to the incessant problems
of everyday life, politics begins with the use of language and the turning
away from violence that entails, and it proceeds through the negotiation
of differences between conflicting parties; that however metaphorical
the "city" of the Citizen may be, it always involves more than the imagination of a single person or head-on conflicts within pairs or between two
factions, and includes in an unpredictable mix the additional forces of
fluctuating third parties.

From these facts it should be immediately clear that not all of what
any person does is political and that no one is everywhere and at all times
a Citizen. To act as a Citizen is, if *fortuna* permits us this, an option for
when trouble comes knocking; sometimes we choose this role, sometimes
we fall into it. It is just as easy, indeed easier, to fall out of it.†

That is the sense of the word *politics* as used in this book. The antithesis
of politics is war, if by *war* is meant nothing but the brute experience of
mass violence.

However, as a matter of social and historical fact politics and war are
related in complex and ambiguous ways: yes, people fight when dialogue
breaks down, or negotiate to end battles, but it is also true that modern
states have been built on warmaking capacity, revolutions have overcome
elites weakened by war, equality has flourished in times of emergency,
and so forth.

It is the complementarity between politics and war, the agonizing
entanglements of these two very different types of human relationship,

---

* Thus the intimate affinity of politics with the topics of inequality and justice.
† All of these very general considerations will be spelled out in the sequel volumes of *Democracy
in America after 9/11*. At that stage I take into account the contradictions inherent in all social
roles, although I eventually drop that vocabulary altogether and show that what one does to be
properly called "citizen" is to position oneself with respect to others in social space in particular
ways.

that will lead our attention in this book. When the Citizen is called to ready for war, to make it possible, to make it, both sides of the equation are transformed. New types of war correspond to new positions for the Citizen.*

A double transformation of this sort is occurring today at the center of American life. Almost no one has taken the full measure of this fact or assessed its impact on the constitution of power in democracy.

The book you have in your hands is not a comprehensive history or theory of these ongoing transformations of the American political land-scape. It is a diagnosis, and it runs along intentionally narrow lines, the way a cardiologist would refrain from comments about the brain. In the following pages, every inspection and speculation is conducted with ref-erence to the special characteristics and outlook of the Citizen. At each turn the guiding intention is to articulate some aspect of the position of the Citizen, a position that you, dear Reader, might imagine and adopt as your own.

The story begins, as we are, in medias res, in the middle of things. That is the one sure feature of political life. Dancing, as it were, on the land-slide of events, you, should you be a Citizen, have only what is at hand, meager resources and flawed beliefs, the beat of everyday life, with which to position yourself.

The author of this book is not, cannot be, an expert in *your* life. Or even in *our* common life. The special knowledge here concerns conditions that make the role of the Citizen possible, that sustain it, or that destroy it utterly. Thus has the imperative *should* been scrupulously excised from these sentences. Only *you* can know what *you should do*. Where the Mor-alist would in the following pages insert his smug and chastising prod, a different voice appears.

It is because we have knowledge of politics, of the nature of political relationships that constitute the role of the Citizen, that I am authorized to write not that *the Citizen should* but that *the Citizen had better* do this or that. The *better* is measured by the most basic facts of political life, the possibility of living in splendid plurality, living with a dominion of words over violence. How minuscule and mighty that hope.

You can choose otherwise, but *you had better* know what it means to live with that ramifying and sometimes irreversible choice.

---

* This does not diminish the specificity of the political.

With everything here tuned to project a way of thinking you might imagine and adopt as your own, and in that way with fresh vigor position yourself as a Citizen, it is natural that the topics brought forward for consideration gravitate towards *what people say*.* That is because *speaking to one another in public* is the single most important activity of the democratic Citizen. *Speech* is what positions us. *Speaking* is how we carve out our positions. Indeed, it is not an event or events *as such* that reshape American democracy. The political effect of every incremental change or explosive novelty depends on how events are seized upon, reacted to, represented, and deployed; effect grows out from the significance with which events are endowed and the frames of interpretation that connect them to other facts of our lives. Blindly or with insight, by cool habit or with heated anger, events are woven into the fabric of history by the energies and actions of the Citizen. In this process, nothing bodes more clearly for defeat than bad interpretations.[†]

A forest of bad interpretations looms around us. Did, as they say, "everything change on September 11th"? Obviously not, for we live in the same world, and the old facts of political life are still with us. What about the chicken-or-egg question incessantly posed: "Is terrorism about 'us' or 'them'?" It evades the primordial experience of the Citizen, which is his or her relation to other citizens, and thus we had better see "September 11th" as the symbolic field in which a particularly noxious future for America has been emerging. And when they tell us it is "natural to be afraid"? We should hesitate again, for now as always our fears, the needles of terror, depend on what we believe about the past and what we hope for the future. Perhaps, as they say, "America is still the land of opportunity," but can it be so when war gives a free hand to public and private opportunists? And when fingers are pointed towards an "imperial presidency" grown again under the Bush administration? We had better respond that the power of the Executive matters less in absolute terms

---

* In the following pages you will find an abundant use of quotation marks. I differentiate between the majority of words for which I take direct responsibility and the expression of the social fact that common ways of speaking and recalling words appear in the public sphere. To mark this social fact I occasionally place quotation marks around a single word and thus urge you to hear a voice that is familiar but anonymous, and not my own.

† Bad interpretations are sometimes also malicious ones: the claim that "weapons of mass destruction" threatened the United States in 2003 was for everyone but the ones who told the lie a bad interpretation.

than in relation to its constitutionally defined counterparts and counter-powers; the complicity of Congress has been an even deeper scandal of the first decade of the new millennium.

While the Citizen is a role and a form of relationship, a position vis-à-vis others, it is also an interpretive framework. What I mean is that to position oneself as a Citizen is to adopt a particular way of seeing the world and one's own place within it. This interpretive framework is not a superfluous benefit that one gains in addition to taking on the role. Just as *being* a doctor is constituted by seeing, thinking, and acting like a doctor, so being a citizen is constituted by distinctive ways of seeing, thinking, and acting.

The potentials inherent in the position of the Citizen derive from the additional social fact that these political modes of perception, cognition, and activity are relatively stable over time and, crucially, shared in common with others. Like the language we speak, the role of Citizen is larger than any individual and outlives each of us because it belongs as much to others as it belongs to any person who lives in and through it. No one alone can be a Citizen; the role of the Citizen is channeled and delimited on all sides by others. How the potentials of the Citizen are realized depends on the times in which one lives.

A, perhaps *the*, central feature of our times is war. A book that offers diagnosis for the position of the Citizen must therefore find adequate ways to draw connections between America's experience with war and the opening and closing of potentials manifest in the position of the Citizen. Many obstacles stand in the way. The forms of and occasions for war have multiplied. As a social practice war is increasingly open-ended. These and other new circumstances are deeply related to ongoing and long-term transformations in American society.

Of course, not everything can be taken into account. The first task is to discover what is essential to the political diagnosis I undertake here. While other writers have examined dimensions of war *that bear on* the position of the Citizen, the leading concern of this book will be to balance such considerations by focusing on features of war *that may be seized, deciphered, and engaged by* the Citizen.

In many or most other times and places, war tangles together social roles: Citizen, Soldier, Bystander, Victim, and other types constantly cross paths; it is not uncommon for one person to alternate vertiginously among several of these roles.

In the United States the experience of war has for a full century and a half been decisively different: among us, only soldiers have been touched by or delivered military violence, only soldiers have stood by the field of battle, and only they have been maimed or laid low in its roiling fury and wake. In our country today, the Soldier may be a Citizen, but the vast majority of citizens are not soldiers.*

Thus when an American says *we have decided to go to war* or *we are at war* or *the war is the challenge of our generation* or *we need to escalate or withdraw*, that *we* does not have its finger on the trigger or its boots on the ground. The subject in such sentences is the fabric of life among citizens, where each of us every day goes to work, to school, to the market, *and to war.*

What to make of this fact? This is a central topic of this book. We may be relieved to see on one side a "politics of war" as the clear province of the Citizen and on the other side the violent clash of armed forces, the "warfighting" of the Soldier. In the United States, these roles and their operations remain relatively distinct.

The problem here lies in how we evaluate this distinction. Most of us suppose that the Soldier's experience exhibits the real identity of war, and that the great mass of socially ordered human energies and resources is just its system of supply.

But as a matter of political fact, as something that citizens live and can lay their hands on, *our war occurs right here, right now, in repetition and design that generates and permits the pursuit of violence elsewhere.*

This fact, which I will demonstrate later, is bound to irritate subscribers to common sense. Even those familiar with centuries of debate con-

---

* In 2002, 1.2 million people were on active military duty in the U.S. armed forces. In 2004, the total number of military veterans in the United States was 24.5 million, or 8.5 percent of the population; one-third of that total served in Vietnam and half as many served in World War II; although I do not have precise numbers, it is safe to assume, given the foreign basing strategy of the American military (702 bases in 2003; Department of Defense, *Base Structure Report*), that a substantial number of these people did not see combat. The other group with high potential for having direct experience of military violence is foreign-born residents of the United States. Census Bureau figures (Y2000) for foreign-born residents from sixty countries where they might have been party or witness to the violence of war suggest an upper threshold of about 7.9 million people who might not fit within my assumption, or just over 2.86 percent of the total population (277 million); about a quarter of these date from World War II or the Korean War. This calculation is extravagantly rough and the real figure is likely to be very substantially smaller. The rate of naturalization of the foreign-born population (about 37 percent in 2000) is not relevant here, given my broad and nonjuridical definition of the Citizen.

cerning the republican citizen-soldier, the modern professionalization of armies, or the tightening military-industrial weave of the social fabric by "total war" will be taken aback by this radical observation.

So let us be clear. The stark analytic apparatus that guides this book is meant to push thinking this way: *real* war is not immediate violence but rather a form of politics; politics is an active relationship among citizens; war is thus a certain modality and inflection of the way *we live together*; since the nineteenth century in the United States, this war-as-a-way-of-life no longer necessarily depends on armed forces local or expeditionary battling it out somewhere in the world; the operations of the Soldier have become an occasionally catalytic but generally auxiliary fact; therefore the paradigm for American war in the twenty-first century is not—as so many assert in abetting the "Bush Doctrine"—World War II but rather the Cold War; that is why what is happening to democracy in America after September 11th had better be understood as *a continuation of the Cold War*, even as this occurs under the amazingly successful covering myth that "the Cold War is over."

In correspondence with these facts, war will be considered in this book almost exclusively as something that *happens to and among citizens* and *happens to us where we live*.

This fact and perspective has no proper name. Although it is the property of the Citizen it is not *civil war*; indeed, one of its most striking characteristics is the appearance of *civil peace*, an uncanny consensus and absence of conflict. Nor is it a reiteration of the *total war* that ground populations into and with the pervasive machinery of industrialized warfare in the twentieth century.*

Civic war—a mongrel name suggesting a neoplastic attraction of opposites in which the political facts of the Citizen come to serve exactly that devastating form of human relationship they were meant to avoid—is what we had better call our object of inquiry. My imposition of this odd invention is, I insist, prerequisite if the Citizen is to get anywhere in thinking through the new political landscape of our time.

The scene studied in this book appears at the intersection of basic conditions of political relationship and the growth of *civic war*. Within

---

* The language of "total war" that entered our vocabulary in the first half of the twentieth century does not adequately address the phenomena discussed in this book; I say more about this in chapter 3.

this space, at once chaotic and rigidly constraining, we will imagine the Citizen inserted. More precisely, this book adopts the perspective of the Citizen so inserted, so chaotic, so constrained, and from that position attempts to reinvent guiding political questions of our time.

What, dear Reader, would you ask in that position? With what words and deeds, fellow Citizen, would you reply?

Every question is provoked by an event and reiterated with its repetition. The path of inquiry here begins, likewise, with an event, the attacks on the World Trade Center and the Pentagon on September 11th, 2001.

We will distinguish from other effects the initial shock and, in the first chapter, follow its transformation into fear and terror.

The next step, where terror is made into war, is articulated in chapter 2.

We will then see, in chapter 3, how enormous expansions of the power to make war in the twentieth century occurred within an even more encompassing constitutional development: the growth of general emergency powers. Indeed, when viewed from the perspective of the Citizen, war powers *are* emergency powers. The latter are applicable throughout society, and this is a major mechanism by which even an expeditionary war is made into a *civic war*.

The larger purpose of this third chapter is to bring to light ways in which war feeds on emergency and emergency on war. Within this circular relationship between war and emergency the question of violence returns. What is the function of violence in American *civic war*?

Chapter 4 responds by pointing to ways in which violence—the fact and its representation—blurs boundaries that normally define social roles and common beliefs. It is a vehicle for highly exploitable modes of confusion and disorder. Violence suspends disbelief. In the specific experience of the Citizen—who encounters combat neither as Soldier nor as Victim—the function of war's violence is to maintain the high-pressure immediacy of emergency. Therefore violence—whatever its sources and purveyors—sustains the powers invoked in the name of emergency.

Pundits and politicians told us then and still repeat that the "end of the Cold War" paved the way for the "new world of September 11th." Chapter 5 will make clear that nothing could be farther from the truth: characteristic patterns and political pathologies of the Cold War continue as essential and even amplified features of the American scene today.

By the beginning of chapter 6, the major pieces of the puzzle—for it is a puzzle to ask by what sort of questioning one can position oneself as a Citizen in America today—will be on the table and begin to fit together. The emerging picture is not the one anticipated by even the most vocal critics of the "war on terror" and its well-catalogued excess.

Although President Eisenhower famously pointed to a new "elite" of power and "military-industrial complex" born of the Cold War, neither he nor those who have drawn out implications from this insight went far enough. The specifically *political* significance of these changes of society, institutions, and belief remain to be identified.

The danger for the Citizen is not primarily the erosion of constitutional rights here and there descried by dissenters. This erosion is a painful and important symptom; it is not the root cause of democracy's disease after September 11th.[1]

What is the deeper problem? To bring it into view, we will have to acknowledge that civil and political rights are not a simple or unambiguous good. Although they are necessary for the operation of any modern democracy, they are also accompanied by costs. Some costs can be paid with money—as when enforcement agencies like the Department of Justice are armed with the means to sanction and police social interactions—but the most intractable costs arise from the way that rights operate within the field of politics more generally. Any appeal to rights as a way out of or remedy for conflict has inherent in it a basic paradox.

On its face, a right is a defense against the abuse of power. At the same time, it takes power to make a right effective. There is in this sense always the lurking possibility that application of a right will need to presuppose the solution of the problem it is meant to address. Rights sometimes depend on the powers they seek to control.

From case to case there are ways to manage this paradox. In multiplying powers a cautious political system can refer the defense against one power to another power. At best, this ensures that no entity is the "judge of its own acts," following the ancient principle that "no man may be a judge in his own case."

But nothing can dissolve this paradox altogether. When big questions arise the paradox presses us with urgency. And it is in just such situations that the more fundamental problem comes into view. The *most* infectious political virus is a steady reduction of many powers to few, of multiple powers to just one, which, when it wants to transgress rights or justice or decency, meets no effective opposition. In a moment we shall find the proper name for this tendency.

You will want to say, if common sense has its steady grip upon you, that it is just this terrible prospect of uninterrupted power that must draw all our attention and energy to rights, and that it is imperative to reinforce an unbreachable wall of *right*, the Citizen's ultimate line of defense. And, indeed, only the foolhardy would deny that when power runs rampant the Citizen must move quick and bold to the defense of rights under attack.

Nonetheless, the paradox of rights complicates the significance of both the attack and the defense against it. It provides an interpretive frame within which the "abuse of executive power" and the "assault on our rights" had better be understood.

For, however grave this situation may be, however much spying and lying and free-handed arrogance may roam the land, *what counts more against democracy are encroachments not on the rights but on the powers of the Citizen. What counts most is abdication of those powers by the Citizen*, even while our energies and vitality remain nonetheless and always the spring of the powers applied, here and there unchecked, against us.

Nowhere is the necessary vigilance in favor of rights so tragically misleading as it is in the great discursive game, the master formula of contemporary common sense, that cajoles us day in and day out to find a balance between "liberty" and "security," to unhappily but unavoidably trade one for the other.

It takes a citizen to see that "liberty" and "security" are not opposites. To speak of "trading" one for the other obscures a much more important fact: when national defense collides with democracy, the challenge is not so much to liberty as to "publicity," or "publicness."*

Thus, while few failed to notice the Bush and Cheney administration's obsessive attachment to secrecy, most have misinterpreted this offense. The major problem is not violation of a "right to know" (as a general fact, there is no such right).

For the Citizen, what matters more is that American constitutional democracy generates its most fundamental power by making things public. *Publicity* serves to amplify diffuse human energies into the political

---

* The general fact of publicness is properly called *publicity*; in this book, I do not use the word in the narrow sense of self-promotion.

power of the Citizen. *Publicity*, not liberty in the abstract, is therefore the essential mode for balancing the powers of the other constituents of the constitutional order and its administrative State. *Publicity* had better be the primary concern for anyone who, as Citizen, aims to impede the degeneration of democracy.*

It is here that the most sinister demon of "September 11th" casts its shadow over the American republic. Terrorism is not its source. It is more basic than the erosion of our rights. Even extravagant abuses of power and rampant corruption—to be expected in times of war, *military* or *civic*—pale by comparison. The most fundamental and insidious threat is *monocracy*.

This word—born in the palaver of the French Revolution, hashed out by luminary figures like Sieyès and Tom Paine, carried home and spread about by Thomas Jefferson, familiar to his generation but not ours—names the aspiration to or achievement of a form of government in which just one power is decisive. It is the black hole of political life. Nothing is more dangerous to democracy. *Monocracy*, with its common complement *civic war*, is the second characteristic feature of our times.

Now, every American is educated to see the vaunted genius of our Constitution. A machinery of different functions—executive, legislative, judicial—is supposed to play one kind of power and its interests against the others, checking the growth of each and balancing all together. This "separation of powers" multiplies them. It requires, generates, exalts pluralism. It impedes monocracy.

But the democratic project of our national constitution and character extends beyond the "branches" of government. Citizens—our energies and dreams—are the essential power that underpins the others. It is the Citizen who, by adding or withholding support, ultimately modulates and transforms public and private powers alike. The balancing wheels and checking levers of a watch are no metaphorical match for this; what the Citizen disposes is metamorphosis, where the grounds of action become at turns rock or magma, concrete or quicksand, welcome beach or foundering shoal. This process, this power, is complex almost beyond imagination. It varies with every scene of our actions, every association

---

* Thus, in this book I will not make much use of the familiar and heated but not very illuminating terms "liberty versus security" in which much debate has been conducted.

and faction, every capacity and incapacity to believe, to judge, to strive, to resist.

You know that many have called this the *sovereignty of the people*. But to do so begs every important issue and draws the veil of one pithy and impressive phrase over the true nature of political life; it deflates the potentials of the Citizen—*your* potentials—in the process. *Sovereignty* once looked—in the seventeenth century—like just one thing because there was so often one king. Even then it mistook the person for the social fact of his power. Applied to the flux of everyday life among citizens, the idea of *sovereignty* makes an even bigger mistake: it urges us, if only for a dangerous and decisive moment, to see the essentially plural as one. *E pluribus unum* proclaims a monocracy of many, the stern communitarian face of the "tyranny of the majority."

It is, however, the special case of Executive power that will occupy the major part of our attention in this book. Again *sovereignty*, with its image of sword and scepter, is a falsifying name for this power. Thus you will find in the following pages, as a subplot of the main story about the position of the Citizen in the moment of *civic war*, a search for different concepts and language, a search for alternative ways to figure the constitution of power.

In whichever hands the title or reins of power are held, one of its primary tendencies, like monopoly in the economic sphere, is towards consolidation and the elimination of rivals. As a fact not of personal ambition but of system, this tendency is towards the elimination of "checks and balances." When barriers are weak, power surges forward in a rising tide. With each monocratic advance, the rebuilding of levees is more difficult.

Where is the breach? Where does *just enough* become *too much*? On this key point the inexactitude of political diagnostics taunts us. There is no rule or measure to indicate the tipping point into monocratic power. Everything depends on the imprecise and undependable judgment of the Citizen. Judgment serves not just the tenor of analysis but also, because what we lean into and pull back from depends on our beliefs, as the motive for action.

Monocracy grows from bad judgment, where fanatics are admired, where complicity is rewarded, where the conformist is a hero, where megalomania and stupidity are hidden from view. Closed societies experience monocracy as usurpations of power; it is something the strong take from the weak. In an open society, monocracy is a self-destructive sort of gift that citizens give to those who, behind extravagant praise, despise them; it is a convergence of many factors into a pervasive and unchecked form of agreement in favor of the few.

The hope and the flaw of democracy is that it boils down, not to "the Will of the People," but to the judgment of the Citizen, which is to say the capacity of each person to size up a situation and pitch his or her energies one way or another. The list of impediments and constraints in this practice is as long as a lifetime. This book, in its own eccentric way, urges engagement in your own life; lived as it is, this is almost bound to bring you to the position of the Citizen. For every day is something new. Thresholds for action are constantly shifting ground. In the weave of lives lived together with others, the power of the Citizen is as simple as it is unpredictable: Shall I let *this* pass—or shall I stand against it? Is *this* abuse, *this* lie, *this* outrage, the one that will bring me into the street—or will I avert my eyes, my ears, again, and close my door?

Such a possibility of resistance to power in any form is the most elemental substance of our constitutional "separation of powers." The failure of citizens to hold back the tide of monocracy, to sap its strength and inflect its flow, is the most fundamental sort of political corruption. Every other venality and arrogance can be tolerated today only if tomorrow or the day after something or someone will raise itself up to oppose them.

In the end, only the Citizen can make effective this oppositional— "checking and balancing"—role. Abdication from it is the *corruption of the Citizen*. The specific development and new shape of this corruption since September 11th is the subject of this book.

1. From Shock to Terror

On September 11th, a novice French videographer named Jules Naudet stood at the corner of Church and Canal in Manhattan. His camera pointed west. The subject, a firefighter, was attracted by a loud noise overhead. He looked up. Nearby, Captain Dennis Tardio said to himself "Where is he going?" and added "Nobody flies this low over Manhattan."[1] In the space of the next few seconds, Naudet adroitly swung his camera around and followed the low-flying jetliner downtown. Another firefighter, Ed Fahey, saw "all the guys just . . . lookin' up at it, and . . . every one of 'em was tryin' to control the plane with their bodies." So there they were, on the corner, "tryin,' you know, they seen it, and they were tryin' to steer it with their bodies." The plane stayed its course. Then, with the cadence of that day, "it just vrroomshh. . . . the roar was just like it was almost inside you, and then when it hit the building, the feeling . . . was like someone took the air and sucked it out of my lungs and my head just became so light-headed, my knees buckled, and it felt like a dream as I seen the plane crumple into the building, just disintegrate . . . pooom."[2]

Perhaps "the terrorist attack on the World Trade Center was the most documented event in history."[3] Yet only Jules Naudet recorded its onset, as the hijacked Flight 11 from Boston penetrated the torso of the north tower and engulfed it in flames. His video camera preserved two sorts of information. It collected an image. It also registered Naudet's own reflexes. The edges of the frame became instantly the needle of a meter. That machine measured Naudet's reaction before it could be clouded or tempered by what came next. It did so more precisely, one may believe, than if another Jules Naudet had been filming him at the same time.

On the screen. The fireman looks up. He turns back to the lens. The camera leaves him. It pans smoothly to the left. Two quick beats. Then the inexorable impact. Fire and cloud mushroom around the column. The camera lingers. There is a slight wavering. Two long seconds now. Naudet starts the zoom in. Five seconds tick. We inspect deep inside the inferno. The lens, the camera, the eye pulls back for a wider view. He has some difficulty handling his instrument. Still, it is trained steadily on the target.

You can feel Naudet's immediate reaction in the movements of the image. He is not afraid. Sense his astonishment, redoubled, perhaps, by curiosity, urged on, perhaps, by professional ambition.

From around the frame unimaged voices enter the scene. Quick caws to be repeated throughout the day counterpoint into a chorus of amazement. "Holy shit!" "Oh my God!" The voice is as always a first line of defense. Then the leap. Within minutes the firefighters of Ladder 1 are on their truck. They are rolling downtown. "Everyone we was passin' was lookin' up; it was like the world just stopped."[4]

As the destruction unfolds recording devices are turned on all over New York. The pace of image making accelerates. Jules's brother Gédéon picks up another video camera and heads out on foot from the Ladder 1 fire station on Duane Street. "I remember slowly walking down to the World Trade Center." "What really stick," the angular French voice recounts, "in my mind is passing by people, feeling them, feeling their astonishment. The eyes saying 'this is not happening.'"

From those first moments and throughout the day, a human tide floods two ways. Surge towards the site seems almost greater than the flow away. The outward movement is not flight, really. The procession is orderly. People seem suspended; their faces show astonishment. Disbelief.

As the specter of death descends on this newly disfigured Manhattan, it is met with sympathetic grief. A young woman surveying the scene from the shore of Staten Island is stony-faced until she mouths the words "it's horrible." Then she begins to cry.[5] It is more than fear. Tears of sadness and rage seem to burn the hearts of bystanders everywhere.*

Then the leap carries the firefighters inward. They "felt the mood that we were going to put the fire out; everyone seemed to be confident."[6] Jules, with his camera, understood, after almost nine months living with

---

* N.b. that someone watching television is a spectator, not a bystander.

Ladder 1, that "it was going to be a long job; it was going to be a tough job; [but] they'll put it out"—he recalls in a future tense where nostalgia for hope lingers—"that's what they do."

What fears the fellows of Ladder 1 had were pointed and specific—"secondary explosion or possibly a second plane"—but, as their Captain Tardio would recall, "I never in a million years feared those buildings comin' down, never." Jules and the camera stayed with them. Now in the lobby of the north tower he "was seeing the look on them. It was not fear, it was 'what's going on?' Disbelief."[7]

No one knows what it was like in the inferno or on the floors above. Reports from elsewhere inside the building do not tell primarily of panic. Some people are leaving their place in the elevator for others. One person slows his pace to escort a blind man from the building. Telephones are transmitting love to a spouse, a child, a friend. Photographs record an orderly descent in the interminable stairways.[8] Into this humanity Ladder 1 ascends. Jamal Braithwaite carried his gear up more than twenty floors and remembered "there were some casualties, there were several people with their hair singed, skin hanging off [but] nobody was panicking; it made the evacuation a lot easier."[9]

From the floors above, out of reach, out of hope, people were jumping. A veteran of the fire department arrived on the scene and thought, "How bad is it up there that the better option is to jump?" On the street more bystanders. Aghast. Crying. Helpless. No one can know the emotions of those who chose to dive. Many seemed to perform a dance of uncanny purpose and grace.[10] A steeled act of "will."

Yet, if human beings have a supreme faculty, an asymptotic approximation to their God, it is not, for all its freedom and creativity, the "will." It is encompassing memory. For, although life is always *right now*, through memory *right now* becomes a lifetime. And while time has inexorable dominion over life, mercilessly ripping us out of the *now* or casting us back into it, with memory we are granted a power to negotiate time back.

How formidable, then, must be the shock that batters memory into silence or makes it run amok? That stops time—the map of *living* itself—dead in its tracks? That comes on the heels of sudden death to take away our breath and foreshadow wholly the end of time? That shock, that complete astonishment, is the antagonist of time, the disorienting guide of disbelief, the arrow pointing nowhere to turn.

On September 11th you know the earth stood still. Then it groaned and turned over. In the next moment, even as the victims died, the clock ticked again for the Citizen. It was in that next moment, as we were thrown back into time, that the tight fist of fear began to close.

You will have heard and may believe that "fear of the unknown is, of course, the most powerful fear of all."[11] This is exactly wrong. It takes a great deal of knowledge to be afraid. Think of the ignorant infant who, for the first time, reaches with curiosity towards the flame. Think of what flames have taught us.

The pieces of how human reactions unfold fit together into a puzzling picture. The part of fear does not stand alone. It is based on what one believes. Beliefs arise from past experience. Past experience does not go away with the next ticks of the clock. It remains present and effective as various sorts of memory.* Thus, as fear stands on belief, it stands on this all-too-human relationship to time. Fear out of time is inert.

Still, not even the most phobic person fears only the past. Fear must have a current motive too.† What moves fear is one's own need or desire to act, to take a step forward. The difference between the *need* and the *action* is important. The need is present; the action future. The need is a situation calling for response; the action transformation of that situation. Beliefs inform the relation between the need and the action. Imagination, taking the form of plans or intentions or desires, projects us towards what has *not yet happened*. Time unfurls as we go.

As survivors, or as readers of a book, we may stand back from the event and organize these elements into a story, a line of narration. It often runs like this: Once upon a time, I had certain beliefs about my situation; then a problem arose and I needed to act; my action responded to the problem, and, well, from there things took a turn for the better or for the worse. What is missing here? The implicit emphasis on tidy rational calculation obscures the additional facts that bring fear in. Fear enters to bully me because, at some moment, some *now*, a representation of all the elements takes shape. The pieces of the puzzle all come together in my imagination. The image may be uncertain but still vivid. As it includes all the parts, and I am one of the those parts, I place myself in the middle. I

---

* Memory may be registered in habits, dispositions, emotions, images, words; its relation to the forms and modes of history is a different question.
† Strictly speaking, memory is also a current motive; this degree of precision is not helpful here.

fear this representation and this scary representation is my fear. This is why fear cannot stand back, why an inventory provides small solace.*

Such an image effectively poses a question: *Will my response to this situation suffice?* While the imagination may represent things that are unquestionably real, the direct object of fear is always a projected image of what is not yet and may not arrive.

Action—unlike reflex behavior—keeps us in the flow of human time. With the *need* or *desire* to act, the future, or the love of the future that is *hope*, becomes a force in the present. There is no fear aside from action, outside the flow of time, no fear for those "coldly indifferent to the future."[12] Thus what we fear is not the unknown, but the missing part, a part defined by the vast constellation of what we know but which our imagination cannot quite master. The arrow in the quiver of fear is not a lack of information, but what we take to be the probability that our capacities will fall short of what we imagine is coming for ourselves. "It is a necessary incentive to fear that there should remain some hope of being saved from the cause of . . . distress."[13] As fear "is an inconstant sadness, born of the idea of a future . . . thing whose outcome we to some extent doubt," it cannot exist except as mingled with hope.[14]

What sort of hope lingered on as the clock ticked again? As another plane, banked to cut like a knife, sliced its way through the south tower? Gédéon Naudet recalled it this way: "When the second plane hit, that's when you could see fear, you could see it in everybody's eye." As he walked with his camera the few blocks from the firehouse to the World Trade Center, "the entire world was there. . . . different colors, different languages." He saw that "they were all looking at the same thing and talking about the same thing and reacting the same way."[15] What could one think? "At that moment, anything seemed possible." Maybe "the end of the world was comin'." Things no one could have imagined just moments before appeared on the mental screen: "There was going to be more planes coming in, there was going to be bombs going off. . . . [Maybe] they just had us surrounded."

An imagined future overflowed with horrors. It entered experience. Each possibility exacted its quotient of hope. Such a surfeit of hopes does

---

* What converges in this representation are all the parts that appear to me, not all the parts identifiable to an external or post hoc reporter.

not allay fears. It amplifies them. There is no inverse proportion; because fear is ultimately related to capacities, the multiplication of hopes is taxing, exhausting in its implausibility. Fear escalates.

However, it does not escalate equally. For each type of person a different process sculpts fear from shock. Focused attention, belief, capacity, habit, and other factors can inhibit or protract this process. New events may circumscribe it altogether. The clock had turned more than an hour while Captain Tardio had raced to the north tower, climbed thirty floors up and thirty flights down, evacuated the building, and now stood on West Street watching as the second collapse began. Even then, experience overtaken by experience, he "was frozen for a second or two, actually frozen . . . in amazement." He thought, "This can't be happening; this can't be coming down; the Twin Towers coming down?"

So did Gédéon Naudet actually see, as he thought he saw, everyone react in the same way?* How could that be, if what bridges the gap from shock to fear is one's experience? The answer is that even if we cannot account—and may not need to account—for the special parts of each individual's experience, people's lives are often similar enough for patterns to emerge. These patterns produce social types. In this respect one firefighter has more in common with other firefighters than with other citizens.

The Firefighter with professional expertise has, of course, become knowledgeable about fires. He has also trained his body in a certain way. He has inculcated relevant habits and reflexes. Moreover, because a fire will go its own way, or "get out of control," the Firefighter must also develop the flexibility that action requires. He must train himself to foresee possibilities and apply his judgment in a crisis. Imagination—projective future orientation—is the faculty required for this.

The Citizen uses imagination in a different way. While the Firefighter's imagination is stocked with images that respond to specific hopes that proliferate as the fire progresses—Can I get through this door? Can I pull the child from under the bed? Can I make my way out of the building?—the Citizen's imagination is applied with a higher degree of open-endedness or uncertainty. Due to its generality the Citizen's hope is complemented by an amorphous and sometimes debilitating fear.

---

* Naudet's own experience is suggestive. He passed along the same street three times on September 11th: the first time, people were looking up at the towers; the second time, they were running away; the third time, after the collapse, the street was almost empty. He says he was really scared only the third time.

This difference between two types of reaction—the Firefighter's and the Citizen's—emerges from past experience. Each has been led up to the event along a particular path through time. But the path does not end there. Experience continues in the event. Something is added in the present. A crashing plane, a falling building: everything enters the mix of experience. These additions have a double effect on the imagination. Adding information, they create a new sense of menacing possibility. At the same time, they defeat prior expectations.

For some, the multiplication of surprising events urged a shift from one interpretive category to another. Before they thought "accident"—after they thought "attack." Mayor Giuliani recounted it this way: only when "the police told me that a second plane had attacked World Trade Center 2 [did I] conclude obviously it was a terrorist attack."[16]

For most people, however, as new experience spoke against old experience, passive assumptions—"tall buildings don't fall down"—were supplanted by active hopes—"I hope these buildings won't fall down." Fear entered into action as a complement to these particular hopes. Although no one expects lightning to strike, the conviction that it cannot strike twice in the same place is even stronger. When the second plane found its mark, a much larger horizon of hope opened up and, with it, an exponentially greater range of fear.

Past and present experience meet in the mind or the body of the individual. But not only there. On September 11th, the transformation of shock into fear was catalyzed by social interaction. I want to be more precise and call this social *interreaction*. Again, variations in effect illustrate the different positions in which real people found themselves. The position of the Firefighter and the position of the Citizen are not the same.

Observations from lower Manhattan call to mind a well-known "herd effect." If one person starts to panic and run, so do those around him. We often ignore, however, the fact that such effects are not specific to fear. In general, emotions are affected in a wide range of ways by the presence of others. Smiles, laughter, whistling, and the like are contagious. The point here is this: when no one ran, no one ran. A sight profusely documented on that day was the massive and deliberate march away from "ground zero." Crowds that stop, mill, migrate, or make haste are all modulated by social interreaction. Without the presence of others, one may not react at all: one friend who lived facing east on City Hall Park spent the morning of September 11th without television and concerned primarily to shield her children from the dust.

The effect of being together was different for firefighters. Unlike the crowds of citizen-strangers, they had long practical experience as a group in relatively well defined situations. Firefighters operate and relate to one another within an explicitly ordered "division of action," which is to say they perform acts that are possible only when several people are involved and each brings something different to the whole.* Firefighters develop an art of using one another. They do this like a machine, or like acrobats, but also as emotional human beings. When "you start to feel your anxiety build up . . . take a deep breath, and you say, this is going to be all right, let's just keep going. . . . brothers behind, we're in this together, we're fighting this together, and we're going to do what we have to do." It takes a lot for this to build up, and it takes a lot for it to break down. And thus, when Damian Van Cleaf, on the twenty-second floor of the north tower, heard a Mayday on the radio, with Chief Pfeifer calling calmly for the evacuation of the building, he said to his "brothers . . . , 'Well, we're on our own now.'" For the first time, he "looked in someone else's eyes and saw fear, which you don't see with firemen." The effect was collective. "It was scary because it just never happened before," he recalled later.

> I was in some sticky situations, where once in a while maybe somebody I was with would get a little shaken up they would look at me and it would be like "Hey it's all right," because you kinda like depend on each other. But when you have eight or nine men in a hallway and you all have the same look that just tells you that somethin's not right . . . something wasn't right, because never is everyone scared.[17]

For firefighters, the fire is in the center. In politics the Citizen is always at the center. Nonetheless, the experience of the firefighters highlights something general about the way fear arises within a division of action. And since to be a Citizen is also to operate within a division of action, we

---

* Since modern talk about action tends to obscure the fact that at all levels of life we depend in one way or another on other people, I have introduced into political theory this disturbing neologism—the *division of action*—to express in a general way and to hold emphatically before our eyes the fact that all human action takes shape and force from a context composed of other human beings. This topic will be discussed at length in chapter 5 of *The Position of the Citizen*.

can draw from the experience of firefighters to suggest how citizens may find their way.

At every moment, a human being has prior experience. Whatever else this means, it also means that one always has potential grounds for fear. What constitutes—or fails to constitute—*my* fear is *my* history. Thus *my* fear is never an immediate instinct. It is a topic of and for action. *My* history is the exact location where *my* action intervenes.[18]

This is not to say that one chooses or determines one's own fear. Far from it. What I am saying may be confusing because most people think that *to act* and *to choose* are the same. If that were true, it would have to be that fear escapes our choices *in spite of* the intimate relation between fear and action. The facts point the other way. It is precisely because fear is related to action that fear is not entirely in one's control. If this still seems like a twisted thing to say, the example of the firefighters should help straighten it out. Our fears, like theirs, are often intricately entangled within a division of action, where action takes shape around our dependence on others. My action can only accomplish what some others—near and far, known and unknown—can sustain; to work, the act must be woven into the fabric of human plurality, the sum of varied contributions by various people. So this is the point: we never determine entirely our own fear because we never determine entirely our own experience, our own history, or even our own action.* Firefighters have organized their collective experience in a manner that accepts to an unusually high degree their characteristic division of action. This allows them to manage fear rather effectively. The Citizen in America is accustomed another way. We often avoid in practice and deny in belief—to an almost pathological extent—that we are and must be implicated within a division of action.† Thus it is not just that firefighters and citizens perform different tasks. The emergence of fear follows one route for the Firefighter and an altogether different one for the Citizen.

Our fear proliferates as an unintended consequence of our own actions. Without ownership, lacking organization, detached from purpose, one's fear becomes appropriable for the purposes and projects of others. This is a drama of strategy and contagion. It involves a large cast of character

---

* Only the most perverse reader will imagine this means that we are not responsible for our acts.

† The significance of this avoidance and denial will be shown in *Political Pathologies of the Citizen*, part 3 of *Democracy in American after September 11th*.

types: the Terrorist, the Victim, the Soldier, the Entrepreneur, the President, and so forth. Each type has decipherably different relationships to
the flow of events and their aftermath, about which I shall have more to
say in due course.

No experience we could wish for would bring steadfast order, or even
the Firefighter's equipoise, to the division of action among citizens. We
had better pray never to be trained on daily bombings or the unremitting
scourge of a shooting war at home. But, war or peace, the body of citizens
has a loose and extensive quality that must be, to some uncanny extent,
disorderly, undisciplined, unregimented. This is both a necessary and a
desirable feature of democratic political life. Nonetheless, it produces
risky consequences that it would be better not to ignore.

Concerning most of that which seeks to enlist the judgment of the
Citizen—disputes of all sorts from which we are invoked and invited to
act as *the public*—we have no direct experience. Where experts are called
upon to *solve a problem*, citizens are called upon to *lend their energies to
the solution of a problem.** This fact distinguishes citizens from firefighters,
but also from soldiers, from bureaucrats, and so forth. One key to this
distinction is the difference between what is specific and what is general.
Well-defined tasks and methods answer many questions of the Expert
before they arise as such. Citizens faced with particular circumstances
typically confront them in a general way, and this augments demands on
the imagination.

Fear rises and falls within each person. More important for the Citizen
than the barometers of pulse and anxiety is the way that fear ebbs and
flows within a division of action. It is because of our plurality and unavoidable dependence on others that *fear becomes useful*. I do not mean
that *my* fear is useful for *me*—however much that may be the case when I
start back from the flame.[19] What counts is how *my* fear becomes useful
for *you*, and *your* fear becomes useful for *someone else*.[†]

That fear develops from shock, that this development depends on
belief, that it is not automatic, these are just the preface to the story of
political life. What counts more is the next step. Just as fear arises within

* Sometimes this involves *withdrawing* one's energies. I use the word *publicizing* to refer to
this process by which third parties are implicated in two-way disputes; there will be more on
this point later in this chapter. The fundamental political significance of *publicizing* will be
explained in chapter 10 of *The Position of the Citizen*.
† As opposed, too, to the contagiousness of fear mentioned just above.

relationships with others, its appearance constitutes a new set of relationships with others as well. Ramping up hopes for the unattainable, opening paralyzing possibilities, dragging us hither and thither, focusing attention on the short term, decreasing resistance or skeptical hesitation—in these and other ways fear guides, motivates, or inhibits action. In effect, fear changes the balance of forces within a given division of action. This balance favors some; it is a deficit for others. It is a situation of unequal opportunity even as it allows for, even requires, the appropriation and redirection of human energies. This is how the fears of one or many can come to have potential value for others.

Thus fear is not only an impediment. It is useful. But for whom? After September 11th the magnetic answer to this question is that fear is useful for the Terrorist.

But useful for what? Utility aims at a goal. The Terrorist today is not an assassin, his purpose is not to kill this or that specific person. His *final* goal is not to make you or me jump back in fear. Nor is the *final* goal to instill fear in a group. The scene of the terrorist act is set in a more complex way. Insofar as the act is not merely narcissism staged for peers, it is addressed variously to American policymakers, American corporations, American allies, or perhaps to leaders in another nation.*

In any event, the Terrorist acts through the body of the Victim and the imagination of the Citizen. Terrorizing Americans is a brutal but indirect tactic. It is not enough to interrupt life and take lives. Fear has value for the Terrorist to the extent that it reconfigures the relationship between the Citizen and whatever Executive function bears on the Terrorist's final design.

There is a difference between the Executive and the function it performs. Look at it this way. After his explosion has died down, the Terrorist wants something—withdrawal of troops or support? a policy change?—to occur. That *something* cannot be moved the way a rock can be kicked aside or underbrush cleared away. It is a social fact. This means both that it exists within a division of action and that only particular agents or agencies are capable of bringing it about.† In most cases

---

* Of course there are terrorist acts that have nothing to do with the United States, but these do not concern us here.

† People often misjudge which person or agency has this Executive power in a particular situation, but that is a different issue. Implication in the division of action also means that Executive power is distributed within a social group or network; e.g. the Commander-in-chief is nothing without chains of command. The significance of this point will be clearer in chapter 6.

the Executive agency is a position in society with a spatial or symbolic location—in the White House, at corporate headquarters—but not identical with a particular person. Typically the Terrorist cannot reach the person who exercises the Executive function, but even if he could kidnap or assassinate the present president or CEO, those *functions* would be taken over by another person.

The Terrorist must therefore attack the Executive function where it takes shape and substance, within a far-reaching social division of action. The farther away from the center, the easier the attack. The Terrorist's efforts go towards transforming the supports that hold up his ultimate target. And again indirection is the rule. Fear is not directly or specifically useful for the Terrorist. Obsessive prime-time television shows like 24 notwithstanding, the Kidnapper and Hostage Taker and Extortionist are nearly extinct relics of old-style instrumentalist terrorism.* Today's Terrorist prefers unlimited and thus especially disruptive fear.

Complications multiply quickly in any effort to understand exactly what the Terrorist wins or loses by his act. Everything depends on the situation before the attack and the reaction to it. Does the Executive have stable support or not? Is the executive function debunked or confirmed by the attack, or both? Dozens of questions like this arise from our curiosity about terrorism, but they are distractions from the primary interests of the Citizen. These interests point along another line: after the attack a new situation emerges; everyone seeks to reposition themselves; all the emotions and reasonings ignited by the attack become useful resources; fear is such a resource. However, the utility of fear is not reserved to the Terrorist. It is also available *for the Executive.*

Where today's Terrorist thrives on *unlimited* fear, such fear is not useful for the Executive. Thus, as soon as fear appears on the stage of society, the Executive has a motive to balance it. If there is too much fear citizenenergies will be disruptively diffuse and reactive; if there is too little fear, citizens may not support new projects brought forward by the Executive. The Executive seeks to manage fear, to limit or channel it in particular ways, but not to make it go away altogether. This is how fear is made *useful* within the dynamic political life among citizens. It thus becomes a

---

* A ticking bomb or deadline provide cheap suspense; an attack "out of the blue" does not. Monocrats feed on cheap suspense.

value. This value may be brought to bear against the Terrorist, or, where opportunity seeking and opportunism abound, it may be brought to bear in favor of projects with scant connection to the Terrorist's attack.

Subsequent chapters in this book will map out the ambivalence between opportunity and opportunism and track the transfer of public emotion through partisan endeavors into the long-term tendencies of power. For the moment, we linger with the Terrorist. Imagine his method.

As a technical matter—concerning instruments and skills, logistics and networking—terrorism is an arcane science.[20] Viewed from the position of the Citizen, however, the basic rules by which the Terrorist turns fear to his own advantage seem rather straightforward. They can be reconstructed without any secret information or expert knowledge.

First, the Terrorist must know that shock and fear are not the same. He must design an event that will lead from one to the other. Not just any sort of shock will do. There are—from his point of view—"better" and "worse" victims.

Second, the Terrorist must learn some of the important beliefs and practices of the citizens he will attack through the body of the Victim. Only then can he know how, in the aftermath of the event he will stage, fear can be made to flourish. The more he knows, the less he will have to tend this flourishing with his own hands.

Third, the Terrorist must not seek to destroy the system he attacks. It is a machine mightier than any weapon—large or small—he may possess. He must *induce and accelerate a pathology* already potential in that machinery. He must make the system work against itself. This will have the additional effect of blocking reasoned and moderate response. Immoderate, hubristic response is inherent in the pathologies of democracy. One need only light the fuse.

Finally, while the Terrorist instigates his attack with an event, he must let the citizens he attacks carry his project to its conclusion. However towering and omnipotent the image of the Terrorist, he in fact is weak. The Terrorist comes in teams of four or five, buying an airplane ticket and a box cutter; he is one sickly human being in a cave in Tora Bora. Thus the Terrorist must rely on *our* energies and capacities to achieve *his* end. If that were not the case, he would attack directly. He would have no need to tell his victims "remain sitting" and "everything will be okay . . . [unless] . . . you try to make any moves."[21] The Terrorist cannot go it alone. Instead, he proposes *for us*, through the flamboyant and spectacular event, a new and perverted division of action.*

This list of rules—few here but potentially many more—imposes on the event careful and long preparation. When the event comes, it will bear a message in a code that can be deciphered by anyone. That message is not, however, its most important quality. Performance, not pronouncement, is essential. The primary function of the event is to shock. Whereas it was once perhaps sufficient to roll an invalid in a wheelchair into the sea or carry off eleven athletes in a helicopter to their death,[†] times have changed. Americans are now addicted to shock. The Terrorist knows that the threshold of effective shock is much higher than before. More and novel bang is required. This fact, together with the *cinematic culture*[22] from which it has emerged, joins the list of dispositions that will determine the reception of the event.[‡]

Terrorism is not a theme park. The "success" of the event depends on the transformation of shock into durable rather than disposable fear. On the one hand, this transformation runs on a single time line, pushed along by our beliefs and emotions and experience. On the other hand, the shocking event of the Terrorist constitutes a crucial ambiguity in our experience of time; it divides the social clock in two. From where the Citizen stands, shock is a suspension of time. It is the calendar that will always read "Tuesday, September 11, 2001." By contrast, the fear that emerges from shock links the present to past and future. In the apparent timelessness of shock the event compresses us into a reactive short term.

---

* This book is concerned, perhaps somewhat narrowly, with the specific type and facts of the terrorist attacks in the United States on September 11th, 2001. If suicide bombings in Iraq were primarily acts of terrorism, we might understand them in analogous terms both with respect to Iraqi citizens and occupation forces. However, suicide bombings in Iraq are, on the one hand, features of efforts to expel occupation forces and, on the other hand, tactics of civil war that deploy violence within the logic of highly localized antagonisms. When someone in the United States refers to these bombers as "terrorists," he or she either misunderstands the nature of the conflict in Iraq or is cynically attempting to assimilate the deadly and degrading form of life in Iraq to the experience of 9/11 and in that way generate support for the American adventure there and elsewhere. I do not address in this book terrorist acts committed by American agencies, although the difficulty of publicly naming them as such is an important part of the domestic political scene.

† Terrorists cast Leon Klinghoffer from the *Achille Lauro* into the Mediterrean in 1985; eleven members of the Israeli wrestling team were murdered during the 1972 Olympic games in Munich. Both events were widely represented and integrated into American political culture.

‡ These include several social pathologies—like the short-term orientation of action, a crisis mentality, and unchecked opportunism—that we shall consider in later chapters.

In this condition it is exceedingly difficult for citizens to grasp a crucial if odd fact: to live in fear is to be profoundly future-oriented. The Citizen is stopped *and* moving forward. But we don't *feel* that way.

At the same time, other social actors are fully aware that the clock is still ticking. The difference between these two experiences of time provides opportunities to sculpt shock into fear, or to manage the uses of fear. In this gap, the Terrorist, for one, moves his project forward.

The transformation of instantaneous shock into durable fear depends on another feature of the way the act is performed. The Terrorist must design the event so that, as it unfolds within the specific circumstances of contemporary American life, it will determine its own representation.

How can this be? Don't we, after all, experience the event and represent it in our own way? Yes. However, all this means is that the Terrorist is to some extent constrained by the instruments we provide him. The event must be chosen and shaped to fit with "our own ways." A particular *decorum* guides the process. If the Terrorist follows *our* rules, if *his* act is fit into *our* categories and practices and images, *we* will make it what *he* wants it to be. All this is at play when the Terrorist asks himself the pivotal questions: How do I draw their attention? What mechanisms will flood and overflow their imagination with representations commonplace among them? What will they fear *by virtue of who they are*?

Do not misread this. The strategic thinking of the Terrorist need not have anything to do with the all-too-familiar saying "They hate us because of who we are, not because of what we do." Meaningless catchphrases like this have often been used to justify ill-considered responses to terrorism, as if Al Qaeda , for example, had dropped from the moon and does not share in the intense and increasingly networked cohabitation of our planet. To see clearly what I mean here, keep in mind that to judge someone and to make use of what is predictable about that person are not the same; led by hate or love, when the gatekeeper opens the door every day at five you know you can walk through.

Thus the Terrorist must do more than just load his gun or even pull the trigger. He must do his deed in a way that will both harm the Victim and light fear in the Bystander. Imagination—informed by beliefs and dispositions we each have, nourished by our experience together—is what carries us from the moment of shock to the life of fear. In this fundamental sense the attack must take aim at the imagination. That is how it will unfold its perfectly real consequences.

The imagination features on the drawing board of the Terrorist for two reasons. The first is that his work does not end with the destruction of mighty buildings or human lives. With that it is just begun. What comes next is more important to the achievement of his final end. The second reason the attack takes aim at the imagination is that—as we have already seen—the Terrorist is not sufficiently armed for a direct military assault. Even with a nuclear weapon or a million doses of anthrax he cannot—as Americans once thought the Soviet Union might—annihilate or capture the entire people or territory of the United States. The preferred alternative is a relatively indirect attack. It employs means that can be mobilized only by capturing the imagination of the targeted population.*

In fact, several sorts of indirection are involved. The Terrorist undermines the Executive by destabilizing the everyday life of society through which human energies are fed into the Executive's policies and projects. This is not just the cutting of supply lines. The big payoff comes when the Terrorist can show that the Executive cannot do what the Executive claims it can do. This undermines political legitimacy.[23] Diminished political legitimacy—even the possibility of this deficit—pushes the Executive to reassert itself. Reassertion often occurs at the expense of the plurality and liberty of society. Thus the Terrorist event is repercussive. With one strike, ripples run from the Citizen to the Executive and back again . . . and again.

It may seem odd to speak of everyday imagination this way, as if what is projected in the human mind has measurable attributes like quantity, specificity, location, and so forth. This kind of thinking is sometimes applied to artists, writers, musicians, or other extraordinary individuals, but rarely to the Citizen. That is why I want to underscore the next point. Precisely because my aim is to survey the whole scene of the Terrorist's event and its aftermath, and to do so *from where the Citizen stands*, an ac-

---

* A similar situation can occur within so-called conventional warfare and its constraint by scarcity of resources; think here of the original British "terror bombing" of the Kurds in 1922, which reduced manpower needs by 85 percent and was applauded by the secretary of state for air, who was, as he put it, "convinced that by an extended use of air power . . . our Imperial prestige [can be] upheld with a minimum of expenditure both in lives and money" (cited here from www.nationalarchives.gov.uk, catalogue reference AIR 19/109). Other examples include the London Blitz (43,000 dead), Allied bombing of German cities like Dresden (total dead between 300,000 and 600,000), and of course the bombing of Hiroshima and Nagasaki (where the immediate death toll has been estimated between 110,000 and 275,000), which was justified as economizing on the costs of a massive invasion of Japan.

count of this imagination that is both finer-grained and more encompassing is essential here. For it is the Citizen's perspective that counts most for politics. We had better take into account everyday facts and the kinds of equality they impose on us, even when it comes to something as distinctive as imagination.

In fact, connections between the everyday and the extraordinary are unavoidable. Everyone recognizes that a Walker Evans or a Maya Lin, a John Hersey or a Toni Morrison, a Paul Robeson or a Jimi Hendrix, create representations of our national life that in one second are unimaginable and in the next unforgettable. It would be difficult to survey everything that goes into the effectiveness or constitutes the distinctiveness of such art, writing, or music. Whatever it is, however, ultimately depends on the way these works are received into everyday life. "Originality" is the name of a thoroughly social experience; everyone must recognize imagination just *there* where it lives among us. This same equation holds for all of civic life. The singular act of envisioning a national future remains sterile if the Leader does not capture the imagination of others. The political imagination moves within and incites the division of action.*

This everyday imagination cannot exist in one head. It must be distributed among many people through signs and symbols, images and institutions. It serves to guide our next step, to balance dependence among us, to affirm or deny our plurality, to adjust divisions of action, to ramp up our energies or reallocate them. The primary exponent of this imagination, the character who makes it effective in a democracy, is not the Leader but the Citizen. Thus it is precisely by focusing his attack on the imagination that the Terrorist attacks the Citizen.

What does it mean to *attack the imagination?* Isn't imagination a faculty of the mind? And as minds always inhabit individual bodies, isn't the only way to attack the imagination to attack an individual person? I want to suggest that these are not even the right questions, for in letting our thinking be guided this way significant effects of the practice of terrorism remain obscure.

Look again at the preceding pages. Three things are at stake in the way we understand imagination. The first is the basic ensemble of capabilities of the Citizen. The second is the disruption of those capabilities on the political stage set by the terrorist act. The Citizen's power appears as

---

* Let us call charisma, then, the maximum aptitude for decorum.

action but, viewed with a sharper lens, is crucially a matter of aligning or withdrawing energies from situations that congeal around and are represented to the Citizen as conflicts. In such moments of crisis (literally, from the Greek κρίσις, or "decision") the faculty that counts is judgment. What fills out judgment, what transforms it into a living practice, is a projective future orientation that traces the possible in each option along a vector of time. Imagination is thus the traveling companion of judgment; it is the armature of action.

Now, you will recall that earlier in this chapter I suggested that by contrast with the disciplined and practiced uses of imagination undertaken by other social types—such as the Firefighter—the Citizen's imagination is general and capacious. In the particular vitalizing imaginary that is *hope*, this benefit may be transformed into a dangerous cost: hope is an amplifier of fear. Here the Citizen is set reeling. As much as fear stems *from* the imagination, fear also plays *within* the imagination. The worldliness of fear—its entanglement with beliefs, with practices, with history—opens the imagination to the world, providing others with hooks into and handles on what each and every one of us takes to be an utterly personal, even bodily, experience of imaging consequences in the course of judging our way into action. Imagination is, then, a threshold with the Executive's power on one side and the Spectator's shock and awe on the other. The door is open.

Thus, in addition to the capabilities of the Citizen and their disruption, there is a third stake in the way we understand imagination. It is this ambiguity between and the connections among the various roles we find ourselves playing.

To keep all this in view, it may help to adopt another approach. A basic sense of the operation of language can provide an alternative paradigm for understanding how imagination works for the Citizen. It is obvious that each sentence one speaks is constituted from and consistent with a language, and that language is the property of no particular person, and that language exists before any given speaker is born and after that speaker dies. Something similar is true for the images of the imagination.

Now, this will not make sense if the word *imagination* brings to mind monsters or dreams. The function of imagination that concerns us here is each person's everyday capacity to project up the steps, around the corner, into the coming minutes or hours or days. When the phone rings we answer because we *imagine* that someone is calling. This everyday imagination is an extensive symbolic system. It includes an imaginary vocabulary of fear. The images of fear are not tested in a laboratory and then packed and shipped to the public; they work, increasing or decreasing in effect, precisely because they are in circulation among us. To interpret or read symbols is always to be apprenticed to other interpreters or readers.

Of the processes of circulation, all that one sees in everyday actions is a residual: this is the odd social fact that many people fear similar things in similar ways. Just as when you greet your neighbor he or she responds in kind, it is not by chance or simple nature that, on seeing flames, you and your neighbor both tend to have the same rather limited repertoires of actions. This is true in controlled circumstances: one can decide to turn on the stove or not, and it is not by personal habit alone that everyone turns on the stove in the same way. It is also true in improvised situations:* when terrorists knock down the Twin Towers, many people react in approximately the same way.

This is the right way for citizens to see their social environment. The key is to remember that just as each act is "divided"—which means, again, that it involves more people than just the "actor" and draws on situations that surround the "scene" of the act—it also involves sequences or phases. Imagination is a phase of initiation or adjustment. From that phase, the actions we undertake that make a difference move on: the "actor" moves from image to judgment, and from there to the production of particular effects. The imagination mimics images from within the circulation of our social environment; the "actor" is moved by differences between image and situation to make judgments, and to adjust or change position accordingly. The action is led forward through these phases. Imagination is often just one step ahead.

It is in this sense that what one does depends on what one imagines, and what one imagines depends on what others do. It should now be clear why an attack on imagination has high value for the Terrorist. With each tick of the clock, imagination is changing our way of life.

The successful Terrorist understands perfectly that most initiating images are thoroughly embedded in common sense. Here again the analogy with language may be helpful. Common sense is what tells us how to "do

---

* Improvisation is different from randomness and disorder.

the right thing," here and now. It is a big and vague feeling we share with others as we speak and signify and imagine. To take effect, however, common sense must touch down within a social landscape. This occurs in the form of specific commonplaces; these are patterned words and phrases, or images and sequences, that everyone uses to project their specific message or action and thus increase the probability of producing a specific effect.*

This process is circular. Commonplaces, each time they are effective, inflect and reinforce common sense, and orient many people in the same direction; at the same time, common sense serves as a kind of reservoir. It allows many people to grasp commonplaces, and this is what makes them effective.

My point is that *commonplace images* form a kind of language. They develop an aspect of common sense through an analogous process. Strong commonalities that appear from one person to the next—in actions, in reactions, in interreactions—are in significant measure consequences of this social distribution of imagination.[24] Images leave the body, the family, the circle of friends, the town . . . and then they return. They circulate, combine, are picked up or set aside; they are objects of imitation because they are useful, and they are useful because they are objects of imitation. Before the last century, this circulation of commonplace images was relatively narrow compared with today. Only a few things really "got around." In America, for example, many people knew by heart the lines and characters, stories and maxims of the King James Bible, and this constituted a widespread imaginary domain through which effective common sense was articulated and diffused. Today the comparable crucible of imagination is the whole technologically articulated public sphere, knit together with buzz and buying.[25]

To attack the imagination, and thus to make the Citizen the primary target of attack, the Terrorist's event must be as broadly and as fully public as possible. He has to "get the message right" and "get it out." It is not arcane psychology that permits the Terrorist to answer key questions like How do I draw attention? What will they fear? What triggers their imagination? It is practical knowledge of the public sphere; it is a kind of spectacle making and marketing know-how.

---

* The *commonplace* is a shared "space" in language but not a site of agreement; indeed it is the entry into and deployment of *commonplaces* that makes disagreement productive.

All this bears on one of the most perplexing questions today: How does one become a terrorist?[26] Does it depend on character and personal trauma, a biography of alienations and attachments? Since few pick the epithet "Terrorist" for themselves, could it be that *being one* is just an outcome of political contests in which one group tries to label another? That "naming games" are important is obvious, but the importance keeps changing, as names that provide an address for different social types become part of the way the people acting in those roles and against those roles are entangled in an array of forces.[27] "Freedom Fighters" sometimes become "Terrorists," fulfilling the role others have carved out for them. The fact is that the designation "Terrorist" is neither a matter of willful partisan opinion nor an objective status. It makes little sense to try to separate the question How does one become a Terrorist? from what seems like a prior question—What does one become when one becomes a Terrorist?

The Psychiatrist, the Voyeur, the Infiltrator, and dozens of others, will each have a way to answer this question. It is a drama of social types that the Citizen needs to consider in light of the broad social division of action that characterizes political relationships and in light of the way participants within that field produce the particular effects that makes them what they are—a Terrorist, for example. What I want to stress is that to become a Terrorist is to produce certain effects on or reactions in other people.* To be a Terrorist is to create a specific category of relationship with others. Whatever the distinguishing characteristics of this relationship, it—like every one of a long list of relationships, ranging from Father and Friend to Therapist, Lover, or even Victim—exists within the densely woven fabric of a whole life together with others.

Citizen is the relationship most thoroughly coextensive with this essential fact. In pointed contrast, *Terrorist* is an extremely narrow relationship. However, it has this crucial feature: the relationship that defines the Terrorist does not just bring together a small band of isolated destroyers; it joins that band to a much larger number of people who are extremely well connected. These people are Citizens.

At first these two groups meet at the margins. In an initial phase the Terrorist establishes a direct relationship with a subgroup of Citizens.

---

* It may happen that because everyone agrees that X is a Terrorist, he or she produces the requisite effect or reaction simply by walking down the street. Such demonization is an important part of our political environment, but it is not necessary to make it thematic here.

We commonly call these unfortunate people victims. Victims serve the Terrorist as entrée to the larger group of Citizens. A graph of the subsequent phases of the Terrorist's act would look like an inverted funnel or megaphone. The Terrorist exploits to maximum effect the extensive connections with others—let's call these *networks*—that inhere in the position of the Citizen. For the Terrorist the initial relationship with the Victim is instrumental and short-lived. His purpose is to move Citizens in a way that will transform the structure of the political relationships; the fabric of these relationships is the everyday life of the Citizen. In other words, the Citizen becomes a proxy within relationships—*our* national political life—in which the Terrorist, strictly speaking, has found himself unable to play an immediate part. One could say: the Terrorist cannot run for President, cannot lobby, cannot march on the Washington Mall. Nor does the Terrorist take direct aim at Leaders or Diplomats. It is through the Citizen that terrorism enters the political realm.

As the Terrorist enters the public sphere, armaments small or large are merely props. His most important weapon is dramaturgy. Whether or not "all the world's a stage," the staging of human relations is how things get done: the insertion of one's projects into exactly *this* time and place, deploying just *this* or *that* actor, appealing to precisely *these* Bystanders, Spectators, and so forth.[28] It is not enough to merely *will* an event, nor simply to *plan* it. Success is a matter of broad design. Dramaturgy is that design, a projective decorum manifest in the way the event is composed and unfolded in time and space. Dramaturgy is the predicate of reception, moving the event along to generate a certain type of relationship between actor and audience. It is the means through which the event eventually constitutes or cobbles together its own representation, how it enters the imagination, and how its initial shock is transformed into durable fear.

The Terrorist must foresee a narrative after the fuse is lit and the bomb goes off. He picks the time, place, and target with that narrative in mind. Because—it is crucial that we keep this in mind—*we* are the key weapon he uses against *us*, the Terrorist is not the sole author of the narrative. There are plenty of stories the Terrorist may imagine at his desk or in his cave that simply *cannot be told with the material of our lives*. Since his purpose requires that he implicate us in it, these stories cannot be told at all. At each moment in the unfolding plotline, some reflex or reaction of the audience must be the motive and force that drives the story to its next phase. The dramaturge calculates this reciprocal machinery.*

It is often sufficient for the dramaturge to write his script in broad strokes. Did, for example, the Al Qaeda teams expect to destroy their targets at exactly the same moment? This seems unlikely.[29] In any case, the ultimate sequencing of the event was an important part of its effect. When United Flight 175 slammed into the south tower, it imposed a particular type of interpretive framework on what American Flight 11 had done to the other building seventeen minutes earlier. A second conforming and confirming moment adds indelible new knowledge to support earlier suspicion. Once you have seen a scorpion in your room, *it is there* at bedtime, whether it is there or not. The two points in time create a vector or tendency in the imagination, directing the arrow's course, bringing certain hopes into view, setting on route particular fears.

The dramaturge knows, too, that we are always looking backward, always reshaping what we have seen to make it coherent with what we see now.[30] I will not allow that life is exactly like theater; it is impossible that each person has read the script and knows at every minute what has come and what is coming. Yet, as an event unfolds, it circulates back through every person implicated in the division of action, even through the actor who initiated it. As action is an ongoing process it constantly uses retrospection in a constructive way; the ongoing refiguration of interpretations weighs heavily on one's orientation towards the future. Hope—looking forward, embedded in time—cracks open possibilities for fear. This kind of circular process informs the design of the event along all of its parameters: the choice of location, the sequencing in time, the symbolism of its objects, the intensity and magnitude of the deed, the display of the attacker's virtuosity, and so forth.

The dramaturge can constitute an order only from available "materials." This order contains implicit or indirect instruction for the "actors," together with potential sanctions against those who derange the scene (the real or supposed Enemy-Sympathizer is, for example, someone who is punished for playing "out of role").† By way of this instruction—

---

* Actors like Al Qaeda play to more than one type of spectator and more than one public. We will remain focused here on the American Citizen as spectator.
† Think of the intense opprobrium against Susan Sontag, who, on suggesting that the dramatic composition of fear should be subject to more careful scrutiny, was viciously attacked by her fellow citizens in a way that must have delighted and encouraged Osama bin Laden.

part message, part template, part apprenticeship—subsequent representations of the event develop. What is *already familiar* in this unprecedented event is what makes possible its representation. The event needs only to unfold in a particular way and it will—so to speak, automatically—provide the key images and elements that will feed the story line the dramaturge desires. The catechism of the Terrorist's Apprentice is recited this way: repeated attacks may be repeated again, so do not act as though this was, like an earthquake, an isolated incident; it was a concerted effort to hijack four planes, and this may be expanded to forty or four hundred; to hit three targets in an hour requires a large organization and excellent coordination that will be reapplied; calibrated attacks on symbols of American power display intention and long-planned conspiracy that must be continuing; the apparent expense of the operation indicates vast resources in reserve awaiting new applications; multiple suicides signal fanatical and unremitting dedication that even foreknowledge cannot deter; and so forth.

All these fragmentary clues are provided by the dramaturge. They will be puzzled together by the Spectator. The Citizen will thus form the image of the Perpetrator *that the Perpetrator wants the Citizen to have of him*. This relatively consistent and well-diffused image is what Americans have come to fear.

If the Terrorist seeks to inspire this fear, he knows it is best to enact his drama on a suitable stage. He will not only devise an attack on individuals. He will not only take aim against the nation. He also targets the *city*. This is why the plan for the hijacked United Flight 93 failed to a significant extent when passengers forced the plane to crash in a field in Pennsylvania. It missed its mark in several senses.

Each of the intended targets—the Capitol or the White House, together with the World Trade Center and the Pentagon—had a different symbolic value. They also had something in common. All of them were in or linked with *cities*. In other words, these sites include concentrated networks of people and neighborhoods, and of capital, commerce, command, and communication. The city, like the Citizen, is an amplifier for the limited means of the Terrorist. In obvious ways, the city makes small means suffice for big destruction.

Less obvious but ultimately more important, the geographical city continues to be the primary residence and the persistent symbol of the citylike relationship that is politics.* To attack *the city*, therefore, is not just to get more "bang for your buck." It is a particular way to extend the consequences of an event over time and space. An attack on the city redirects the complex order of interdependence and plurality that *is* everyday life with others. It creates efficient pathways for the proliferation of new hopes and fears. It penetrates our defenses by reconfiguring with one blow the long-grown and fragile relationships by which the division of action is shaped and mobilized not just in favor of *this one* or *that one*, but the whole community.

Thus, to get at imagination, which is to say *to terrorize*, the dramaturge chooses the stage of the city. The face the city turns towards the world is what we call the "public sphere." The "public sphere" is the portal through which the Terrorist gains access to the sometimes apparent but often hidden conditions of political relationships that make up the position of the Citizen. Engagement with the "public sphere" may be necessary to create a spectacle, but it is not sufficient to the Terrorist's task.

These may seem odd and circuitous terms but they are corrective of some influential talk after 9/11. Predominant voices told us that "they attacked our freedom" or that "they tried to use our freedom against us." Perhaps. But such assertions refer us to just one side of a situation that is very much more complex. They also mistake our priorities. The political relationship is the condition of freedom, not the other way around. Thus, as it struck politics at its root, the wound inflicted by Al Qaeda was deeper than even the most avid defenders of freedom have understood. In retrospect of centuries to come, America's defeat and disgrace in Iraq will pale beside our national political suicide.

If political relationships are even more fundamental than freedom, we will have to have a fitting vocabulary to bring them into view. What is their primary vehicle in a modern society? Americans will almost by reflex point to elections. But this, too, is a mistake. The first thing that endangers political relationships is to imagine they are so sporadic. In fact, they arise, transform, and decay within everyday social interactions of widely various duration. Much more widespread than elections—indeed,

---

* While greatly transformed by time and circumstance, the word *politics* resonates with the Greek word for *city*—πόλις—from which it is derived. To be a Citizen is to amplify this resonance in ways we will come to later.

setting them up and encompassing them and giving them ground—are those active processes by which the surrounding community is drawn in one particular case after another into private affairs, and by which private matters become public ones. This typically occurs in a dispute between two parties where neither has sufficient purchase to advance their position. Then one or the other, or sometimes both, or perhaps their proxies, try to draw third parties into the dispute. They do this in an effort to change the balance of forces. They aim to produce a result that, in the limited context of head-to-head or toe-to-toe conflict, cannot be had otherwise. I call this act *publicizing*. The simplest definition of *publicizing* is just this: the implication of a third party in a two-way dispute. It is a crucial starting mechanism for a wide range of political activities and relationships in modern societies. Through the act of *publicizing*, one may constitute a *public*, which is to say a group whose involvement in an ongoing dispute changes to a greater or lesser extent the overall balance of forces at play.*

Those who think of, or from, the position of the Citizen rarely distinguish between the *publicizing act* and the "public sphere." You will see in a moment why I will emphasize it here. The former has a direct, constitutive relation to politics. The "public sphere" is something else. Its relation to politics is more complex. The "public sphere" is sometimes but not always a residual of *publicizing acts* or an institutionalization of their effects. But the Terrorist's indirection is intended to bypass exactly those moments when citizens are activated and directive of our own energies, the governors of our own "city." The Terrorist seeks to join and seize hold of social processes at the moment of the Citizen's passion, where shock unbinds the imagination, fear points the way, and a disorderly division of action runs amok in the streets.

The traditional vocabulary through which the "public sphere" is related to politics is rather different. It concentrates less on those actions which bring the "public sphere" into existence and more on the traits which make it a certain kind of "instrument" for action. *Public* in this traditional view is a near synonym for what is visible or common to everyone.[31] However, on its face this familiar idea is misleading. All its terms—

---

* In some cases even a "public" of one is sufficient to produce this effect. I will present the theory of *publicizing* in greater detail in *The Position of the Citizen* and in its entirety in study entitled *Why Is the Private/Public Distinction Important for Politics?*

"visible" and "common" and "everyone"—beg for further specification. By our nature, things appear to our eyes only within the limited range of sight. This is true no matter how our vision is technically amplified, multiplied, or extended. Only the most superficial features of our experience are literally *common to everyone*. Indeed, it is just those fundamental facets of the human experience that are universally shared—processes of the body and the mind—that are most likely to be classified as "private."

The fact is that in modern times the phrase "public sphere" has come to serve as a very diffuse kind of shorthand. It gestures to many different things at once. In general, the "public sphere" refers to some set of things that establish and sustain identifiable spaces—whether literal or metaphorical—in which another set of otherwise fragmentary, complex, or obscure features of everyday life appear to us as whole. As such, what occurs in such a "space" is taken to be useful by everyone who sees it that way. To this encompassing visibility is joined a sense of common entitlement. Thus certain kinds of rights—for example, freedom of speech—are said to be "public." Physical areas in the city that, for particular historical reasons, draw and accommodate the assembly of many people for civic purposes—for example, the Washington Mall—are called "public spaces." Technics that have taken over certain functions from these physical spaces and that seem to mediate human relationships in similar ways—for example, television or the Internet—are likewise perceived as "public" regardless of who actually owns them. The same is true of institutions—for example, the National Institutes of Health—that propagate values which are not immediately appropriable for the profit of particular individuals or groups. Administrative agencies exercising control of superfungible resources—for example, licensing and regulation of "airwaves" or national parks, but also of printed money, credit rates, and so forth—are officially "public." Even a certain range of corresponding citizen dispositions and capacities—for example, the desire to read newspapers or the ability to interpret broadcasts by C-SPAN—are thought of as aspects of "public spirit."

For the person who seeks a position as Citizen, surveying the "public" this way will occasionally be useful. But just as often it will be fruitless. Even such a long list cannot cover all potential elements of the "public sphere" or locate the right one at the right moment for action. More important here is that sometimes a traditional definition of the "public sphere" itself leads to immobilizing contradictions. Not everything in the "public sphere" can serve a politicizing function for everyone at all times. At some point the distinction between the "public sphere" as a resource for a wide range of actions—from commerce to evangelism—and the specifically political act of *publicizing* takes on particular importance.

Terrorism is such a point. This is not because it rises to the level of politics. Rather, the Terrorist's event is precisely meant to destroy political relationships altogether. It aims to allow the "public sphere" and its logics of "visibility" and "the common good" to run in reverse. It is just there, at the threshold between politics and the merely "public," that the Terrorist—as transformer of shock into fear—lays out his plot.

The dramaturgy of the "public sphere" can be excruciatingly extensive or effective. Here is what it does *not* necessarily involve: the active, interactive, dialogical elements of *publicizing* from which this or that *public* is formed, where particularity is of the essence. This is important because—contrary to what most people believe—the mere fact of entry into, or even the use of, the "public sphere" may not set politics in motion. That result is possible but not necessary. And some uses of the "public sphere" are antipolitical. And even when politics emerges in the "public sphere" it may become profoundly self-destructive.[32]

Here is the key contrast. In political relationships what counts is action. *Publicizing* is an active process; involving at least three distinct parties, it has a particular dynamic. The "public sphere" is something different precisely because it *may or may not* include *publicizing*. Typically it becomes just a resource, perhaps one among several. As resources are implicated within a division of action they vary as to *for whom* and *for what* they are resources. Unlike such resources as sunlight, air, water, and thousands of other things, what does not change about the "public sphere" when it is used as a resource is that it is composed of the energies of citizens. And the discomfiting fact is that human beings may be deployed by other human beings without being activated. Although all are tied together within a division of action, some manage to appropriate the energies of others in favor of their own projects. In this process relationships that are not political, or are even antipolitical, come to the fore. Outside of political relationships the role of the Citizen cannot exist. Yet what makes possible the Terrorist's imposition of shock, its prolongation through fear, and the production of its intended effects is the Citizen, who is tricked into a kind of political suicide, a suicide that is undertaken through the elements of politics but, at the same time, disintegrates them.*

Television allows for the most precise dramatic sculpting of shock into fear; it is the perfect instrument for this degradation of the Citizen. The Terrorist uses to maximum effect the machine that makes everything visible from a distance. While common sense is normally generated from active experience with others, the television conjures it up as spectators sit mesmerized, molded into a couch, before a flickering screen. Absent the *publicizing act*, without its interposition of a third party into two-way relationships, television nonetheless constitutes a kind of "public sphere." With three televisions for every four people in the United States, broadcasts from every nook and cranny of the globe are infused into millions of homes. This most important "public sphere" in America fits neatly the traditional definitions of the "public"—offering a seemingly universal visibility and making the visible common—yet simultaneously tends to privatize access to information and to individualize spectatorship by removing potential third parties from the networks of forces and the division of action within which problems and disputes occur.†

Whatever else television does to its adherents, for the Terrorist it provides an almost duty-free port of entry into everyday life. Television allows the Terrorist to inflect fundamental conditions from which political relationships emerge. It alters the position of the Citizen, however, without crossing the threshold of politics itself. Television may feed political relationships but it does not establish them. Television turns the Terrorist's event into general public disorder. This process is not *controlled* by the Terrorist but, if at all, by us.

More precisely, terrorism in the age of television produces a disconcerting mix of order and disorder. At the site of the attack everything known and familiar is disrupted. The present spectacle is intertwined with peril; bystanders react accordingly. All this changes with representation. In transmitting the spectacle, broadcast cameras filter out the danger. However shocking the image of a plane striking the World Trade

---

* This inherent "planned obsolescence" of terrorism may contribute to the Terrorist's increasing attraction to suicide.

† Note that collective spectatorship—even with immediate presence, such as at a sports arena or other mass gathering—may also fail to constitute political relationships. This is a major failing of the traditional way of thinking about the significance of the "public" for politics and why I have supplemented that vocabulary.

Center, the viewer with a television at home has, strictly speaking, nothing to fear from the precise thing he or she sees. The flames will not touch the viewer's skin. Indeed, in the horrible moment, there may even be something comforting in seeing images already imagined and concocted by Hollywood and, in that specific sense, somehow familiar.

For both those near and those far, the elements of shock and fear can be separated. The ticking clock of experience is what joins them together and that convergence changes over time. Nonetheless, the experience of the person at "Ground Zero" and the experience of the person watching television are not the same. The conversion of shock into fear occurs in different ways. With danger filtered out, the shock of the televised event is, so to speak, free-floating. It may be less intense, but it is also not contained by the very specific needs and urgency imposed on people in the *here* and *now* of an attack. Televised shock seems to the viewer to have wider and more immediate implications. It occurs "at home," in the same common visual space as C-SPAN, the Simpsons, and the Super Bowl. In this respect televised shock is more "productive." It is also subject to greater, faster, and more detailed manipulation. These effects, however, are not in the hands of the Terrorist.

Following the unfolding events on television is a contradictory experience. For millions of people, it is not the act alone but its combination with the camera that concentrates their "immediate sensorial attention" into the feeling of shock.[33] Images of death and destruction monopolize our senses because they monopolize in one instant all the means of mass communication. Yet even *this* incredible chaos is contained by television. Framed, commented, edited, interrupted, and persistently replayed, the representation of disorder seems to demonstrate exactly the opposite: a kind of orderliness in the "public sphere." The diffusion of a localized event—two planes destroying the World Trade Center— into everyone's everyday life seems to affirm—in some horribly inverted way—the vitality of the press, the media, the nation. The "public sphere" itself is bursting with life. Exactly that same obsessive broadcast of the news that brings us to the Terrorist's terror constitutes its apparent remedy: the newly pointed knowledge and angry unified resolve that derive from everyone everywhere seeing the "same thing" at the "same time." The scare quotes here are meant to remind us that one of the most consequential features of television experience is the way it brands images and image-practices and thus human sense perception as unitary and thereby as unimpeachable sources of evidence. In fact different channels broadcast different images (e.g. not every source presented images of the people who jumped) and only where the *time of the image* seized each viewer before the screen was the time of viewing approximately the same for each of them: the collapse of all this variety into one symbolic object known for its unity is a characteristic process in the formation of commonplaces. *America united!* was, of course, a preeminent exclamation after 9/11.

Such a new or renewed sense of unity or purpose may or may not be worthy of our pride. Either way, it disguises a second and more enduring disorder that the Terrorist can count on. The successful Terrorist-Dramaturge prompts Bystanders to the comfort of a false equation. The "public sphere," one has learned, is the heart of a democratic polity. However, this is only true *when the "public sphere" actually produces politics*. In fact, there is nothing inherently political about the commotion of commentators and self-inflated monologuists. The vehicle on which *politics* enters the "public sphere" is the speaking of citizens, one with another. *To speak* is not the same thing as *to be spoken to*, and to be spoken to is not the same as *listening*, something that is itself prerequisite to the transformative possibility of *good public speech*.[34]

This, again, is why the Citizen had better attend to the difference between uses of the "public sphere" and the act of *publicizing*. For good public speech is not a matter of harmony or harmonizing. Nor is it measured by orderly rules of debate or validity claims supposed to inhere in communication.[35] The primary political good in *public speech* is the relatively predictable if uncontrolled way in which it sets up conflict, changes the order of conflict, and releases new forces from within the division of action that help the Citizen resist a turn towards violence and away from politics. *Publicizing* is the characteristic form this process takes. It often seems extravagant, but it is, all things considered, an inclusive and democratic form of moderation. And it is precisely that form of moderation that the Terrorist seeks to suppress when he enters the "public sphere."

Thus the Terrorist, that dramaturge, does not enter politics. He uses the "public sphere" to push our democratic political regime to excess. As long as he can induce its inherent pathologies, others will do his work for him. "The media" simply "do their job." Whether in good faith or with the lust for profit, they abet the Terrorist.[36] They must bring us the news. An adequate representation of terrorism will always be astonishing. The

Terrorist harps on this astonishment. Astonishment suspends time, judgment, action, and words.[37]

More than words, more even than deeds, the Terrorist works with the power of the image to attack the imagination. Whatever televised anchors and pundits may say, however much they say, the *way they say it* accepts the image as constituted by the Terrorist-as-dramaturge. This, for a moment, for a day, or for a season, reduces the Citizen to speechless shock. While one often hears the complaint that our own media "put words in our mouths," the opposite is also true and far more important: "the media" becomes the instrument by which the Terrorist removes the words from our mouths.

If, in its dissemination, the bestial act imposes a consensus, it had better not be the dumb consensus of brutes. The animal *voice* of anguish, amplified, overwhelms all too fragile democratic practices of political *speech*. With the failure of speech and its specifically political properties, the doors of opportunism open for unchecked uses of power.

Certain peculiarities of television add to dumbing uses of the image. One of these concerns the way the image enters memory. Because the traumatic effect of shock varies with circumstances, those who witnessed the event directly and those who watched it on television, even if they recall more or less the same images, will experience that recollection in widely different ways. For the direct witness the image was mediated by present danger. This combination stays in the body. The television viewer, relieved of the pressure of danger, faces and is drawn into the image with an intensified curiosity. There is a kind of pleasure in this.[38] The bodily experience of memory for the television viewer includes this kind of attraction. It creates an interest in repetition that is almost entirely absent for the direct witness.

Earlier in this chapter we tracked the role that the unfolding order of events—the narrative path—plays in the constitution of future orientations; that is, how the addition of a second event to a first, and a third to a second, leads to the development of certain hopes and thus opens the way to complementary fears. Television, of course, largely alters how we experience this order of events. The Terrorist-Dramaturge zeros in on this fact. The experience of Bystanders on site is secondary for him, the experience of far-flung Spectators primary.

At "ground zero," the first and second planes struck the World Trade Center just one time each. Each tower collapsed only once. Television, obviously, obstinately, repeats. Within an hour, all television viewers had seen the towers fall a dozen times; within weeks, a hundred times.* Cut off from direct exposure to the event and to its danger, persistent repetition of the image becomes its own kind of duration. The event is enlarged: not only because it is diffused, but because it takes up more of the life of the viewer; not only because we are shocked over and over, but because we *are drawn towards the shocking* rather than backing away, and things that seem closer seem bigger. How many people actually *look away from* the omnipresent screens? Television is *for us* instrumental in making an instant into a moment, into a sequence, into a scenario, into a way of life, a new epoch.

In real time, the ninety or so minutes of the attack on September 11th were a very small portion of American history. In the timelessness of shock, drawn out by the time-filling capacity of television and other mechanisms of our culture, some part of every day is September 11th. Even now. And every day may become September 11th. This prolongation is where shock is transformed into fear. How can "time heal all wounds" when time itself becomes a festering wound?

It is not news that sometimes events are transformed into *historical moments* only well after the fact. An event one way or another continuous with the flow of its own time is later selected out, woven into the narrative of the nation, and then said to have been a turning point. This can be a long, slow, and intricate process. It was like that for the first centuries of our history. Few imagined the eventual impact of major technological innovations until they had long been worked into everyday life; the same is true even for visionary developments like the Erie Canal. Only generations after the event did Americans unquestioningly define themselves in terms of Columbus, the *Mayflower*, Valley Forge, or even the Constitution.[39] Only in the twentieth century did the Seneca Falls Declaration (1848) become the beginning of American feminism, or *Moby Dick* (1851) a Great American Novel. This gravity took time.

The opposite seems true today: everything appears in the "public sphere" as immediately "earth-shattering" or "epoch-making." Then the force of an old event can be revived pretty much overnight. Although by

---

* Around the second anniversary of September 11th a perspicacious Leon Wieseltier wrote: "The other night I saw the films of the destruction again, and I was shocked that they are shocking still." *New Republic* (September 22, 2003, 46). The same thing can be said today.

the close of the twentieth century the "only attack on American soil" had largely faded from American national self-conception, it had reentered everyday discourse months before 9/11 with the movie *Pearl Harbor*.[40] Just months later it was serving as a primary frame for interpretions of what had happened at the World Trade Center. That turn backward occurred on the very day when, we were told without irony, American history entered onto a whole new path.

Television and like technics complicate enormously the processes by which our experience as citizens is related to every other role we play in society. The "media" have paradoxically reduced the amount of *mediation*—steps, inflections, adjustments, negotiations, setbacks, reconsiderations, and so forth—involved in these processes. Citizens can do nothing without common sense, without its susceptibility to operate in political relationships. In the formation of common sense it matters how commonplace images enter the imagination. An image transmitted as perfectly formed packets of "information" lead us one way; an image shaped in dialogue and left fissured by conflict leads another way.[41]

As it turns out, for the Terrorist the characteristic feature of television is its *immediacy*. This is what serves all "propagandists of the deed" who want to "shock and awe" others into rebellion.* However much television may "stand between" the production and reception of signs, the tangible experience connecting the screen and the viewer is strangely direct and static. This is what makes television unreal, or lifeless, or sterile. There are no inherent stakes by which the event *as televised* is forced to develop over time.†

I admit that this is somewhat overstated. No human experience is utterly without mediation. Let us say, then, that television brings us the event with a large *quotient of immediacy*. On the one hand, this quotient is constantly renewed through repetition of the shocking image under the same circumstances of viewing; on the other hand, time passes and dilutes it.[42] The clock divided here seems the property of one person at a time, but it produces complex social consequences.

So, there is Jules Naudet, video camera in his hands, at the corner of Church and Canal. He is present at the event. Danger and the need to

---

* The former phrase was the motto of American anarchists who promoted assassination as prelude to general rebellion; the latter phrase was, of course, the motto of George W. Bush's similar program on Afghan soil in the fall of 2001.

† Mise-en-scène or narrativization is a contrived substitute for attracting attention.

act limit or channel his entanglement with it. The event is an experience constituted by particular choices and instruments, symbols and effects. The event itself allows only so many reactions. Jules and his adopted fire-fighting brethren can mediate the event—negotiate it towards something they can hope to overpower—quickly and in several ways. But they also recognize that the possibilities are limited. Its *presence* is a limit. This in itself is a kind of confidence, a basis for courage.

Once the event leaves Jules's camera, it becomes an entirely different kind of experience. One may be inclined to call this next phase of the Terrorist's design "representation" because we measure it against what we know to have happened at the corner of Church and Canal, and down those long blocks to "ground zero." For the Citizen, for this special role democracy must allow us to play, the word *representation* stands for evasion.* It recommends denial of just that experience that forms our common sense, congeals our commonplaces, stages our capacity for judgment, and shifts our positions with respect to one another. For Americans today, that key experience is an engagement with a screen. About this fact many derogatory things may be said. But here we focus on this: the Terrorist's event attacks the imagination of the Citizen; the interposition of this screen—with its shallow visibilities, close inspections, protections from harm, isolations, content-neutral conjunctions, and so forth—begs for repetition, a kind of social masochism. At first this forestalls mediation. Then mediation proliferates without limit. This is where the imagination and the world it constantly throws forward start to get out of hand.

A "representation" cannot be mediated by experience one has not had. When it comes to the images of September 11th, the vast majority of citizens lack any experience with the event itself. Nothing holds in check what the images can do to us, to the "city," to the "public sphere." Terrorism mixes its images with everything, and this profusion of untempered mediations constitutes a disorder of plenitude. The Firefighter's imaginative horizon is drawn tight by specific questions like "How shall I avoid the falling bodies or the collapsing building?" The Citizen's is not. The imagination steps and stretches by way of other images, and for the Citizen every image comes to seem relevant. The reservoir available for

* Representation in the sense of *representative democracy* is a very different topic; the relation between the two uses of the term is exceedingly complex and not relevant here.

this mix is mind-numblingly vast; you, dear Reader, can effortlessly find dozens of examples in the storehouse of your years apprenticed to television. Any comparable narrative line or structure maps itself onto 9/11 and turns 9/11 itself into the story it seems to be, transforming shock into prediction, prediction into hope, and hope into fear.

Television—that entire "public sphere" created by our experience with commonplace images, the sensory technics by which we receive these images, and the common sense that develops in that experience—cuts into us two ways. It is pure, direct, sensory, unadorned, *and* it is a mongrel mishmash of indirection and the imaginary. Given, as we saw at the beginning of this chapter, the extent to which fear is contingent on experience and belief, it would be difficult to concoct an instrument more perfect than television for the Terrorist's mix of immediacy and mediation.

In proposing that vast social processes are required to move the Citizen-Spectator from an initial shock to more durable fear, I have not distinguished one type of fear from another. But what attacks like those of September 11th seek to inject into the "public sphere" is not just *fear* but *terror*. And while the shift from shock to fear adds mediating beliefs along the way, the trip from fear to terror takes them away again. Terror is immediate fear.

The cultural environment of the United States seems perfectly suited to just this kind of additional misstep: addicted to shock and the short term, but inevitably alive within a durable web of dependence and plurality, living not in minutes but in lifetimes, we are eminently terrorize-able. Again television shows itself to be a perfect amplifier for this already dangerous mix.

Let me be perfectly clear. Television—the object, its programs, its social institutions—is not the origin of the Terrorist's terror. What happened on September 11th was not a dream. It was not a fantasy. People died. The criminal ring of nineteen, their masters, and their co-conspirators, are responsible. Some are still on the loose. It is clear that they or those they inspire will attempt to strike again on American soil. All of which is to say that there are good reasons for fear. Moreover, these people are ineluctable catalysts for American actions; it was and is impossible that we leave their challenge without response.* All this should be completely obvious.

---

* A morbid addendum here is that for at least the last thirty years those who tried to construct the motivating mental image of the Terrorist have never been very successful in America. Under

I state it so as to balance against an easy misinterpretation of what I have written in this chapter and how it relates to the purpose of this book.

My purpose is to give priority to the position of the Citizen. From that perspective, to suppose that terrorist attacks are primarily about "them" is utterly and entirely self-defeating. September 11th is about the American Citizen. Again, as long as we continue to swim in a sea of nonsense and sterile ideas it will be very easy to misunderstand what this means. I am not talking here about how past American policies, practices, or allegiances may have "caused" the attacks. This is in some sense or another indubitably true. It may or may not be important today. What I am saying is that *for the American Citizen*, the first and foremost fact about September 11th—the event, its rippling effects, and the aftermath that will unfold for a generation—is that it is about *us*.

This means we need to treat with utmost seriousness the fact that the Terrorist's drama is enacted—and, no matter how we pretend to export it, can only be enacted—on the American stage. This places the Citizen at the center. Our role in this drama must be recast accordingly. For, *no matter what the Terrorist does*, the way his event is received is the key factor in making the Terrorist's event what it is.

It is possible that the Terrorist's drama, once it infects the body of our public life, will run almost automatically to predictable conclusions. History offers many examples to suggest that no nation sees itself clearly in the mirror of its own times, or clearly enough to change this course. Still, I refuse to acquiesce in what I see: the demise of democracy in America, accelerated by the spectacle of September 11th. I remain convinced that some pieces from within the Terrorist's drama can still be seized hold of. The outcome of this story can be altered, if perhaps not altogether controlled, by citizens.

To confirm this belief, however, we will have to redirect our attention. Where and how terrorism originates is for now a distraction from what is even more important *for us*. The element the Citizen must discover abides in the processes through which the Terrorist's act is received into society. *We are that element.*

---

the Reagan/Kirkpatrick administration it was still possible to conduct a serious debate by contrasting the terms "terrorist" and "freedom fighter." Osama bin Laden revived the self-evidence and indisputability of the category "terrorist." In other words, he gave long-grown Right-wing pundits the means and the motive to construct a powerful new imaginary.

2. From Terror to War

Perpetual menacings of danger oblige the government to be always prepared to repel it; its armies must be numerous enough for instant defense. The continual necessity for their services enhances the importance of the soldier, and proportionably degrades the condition of the citizen. The military state becomes elevated above the civil.

ALEXANDER HAMILTON, *Federalist* no. 8 (1787)

In a flash, it was September 11th. A new epoch, a new world, they told us. But who decides this? So many things happened, so many forces were unleashed. The event multiplied. Each day it became harder and harder to see how the new day had actually begun.

Let this difficulty be a caution. You, reader, and I, writing, have since that date continued on our ways. The paths are familiar enough. That is why this book circles durable facts about human relationships and tugs at threads of old history. The past, long and short, remains hot with us. There is inertia in our institutions, our words, in the common ways we go about living. Could anything be more obvious? Even novelty depends on what we are given. Then it depends on a next step, on how we assume centrality in our own lives, on what we make of the fear-filled moment, and how accommodating that "we" remains.

Only for those who perished was the outcome of September 11th determined on that day. Yet, in the interval after, things and forces have been taking determinate shape. Each new development leads us towards a beginning that is further and further back in time.

Common sense should inspire the Citizen, like the buyer in the market. Be wary of the illusion of a "total rupture" or a "world turned upside down."[1] Such illusions may at times serve the interests of political progress; they may as well furnish the pleasures of psychological regression. But what is new is always long-brewed; by the time it is "new," it's old. And there is good fortune in this fact. The weapon with which to overcome Terrorist or Despot *is our past*. The best positions of the Citizen are configured by a common sense of continuousness. This sense is the armament of having been somewhere before and being now prepared to go forward. To believe the world or its present epoch is new is to believe the past destroyed.[2] Such beliefs put the Citizen in an impossible position—needing to create a world, rather than living in one.

Worlds old or new, however, have the same past—the same opportunities and the same nightmares. We cannot correct the past. Nor can we master the past from within a tidy space we call *the past*. Only one mastery—modest, imprecise, unsure—is allowed to us. It is the carefully thought-through step from our situation into the future. This moving ahead makes the past *something*, rather than oblivion. The great faculty of history, then, is reason: not because reason triumphs over all adversaries, but because it puts distance between us and our past, it permits us to extricate ourselves tentatively from the tangle of memory and dream.[3] Such distance is how we *choose our past*, how we take possession of it, close down obsessions, and move on. That is why, if the Citizen's world *is to change after September 11th*, we must first see exactly *how many essential things remained the same after September 11th*.[4]

Although it has been said a thousand times that September 11th was "not just another day,"[5] the challenge for the Citizen is to see it in just that way. Now mark my words: to say this is not to deny or diminish the tragic and terrible event. It is, rather, to insist that September 11th was part of our history, part of our ongoing world. For just as durability, consistency, and assuredness are characteristic of the way human beings live together every day, so, too, is the continuous outpouring of new things—terrifying or delightful, astonishing or mundane, momentous or fleeting. *Today* is where various *pasts* shake hands and come out fighting. That is what happened on September 11th.

The world, the canvas prepared for the Citizen before birth and pursuant to death, is continuous, even when one's life seems infinitely splintered. Bluster about "the end of history," so common a decade ago, was and will always be pseudo-eschatological nonsense.[6] *Do we live in a new world?* This is an ineffectual question. The Citizen had better ask: *What is to count as continuity and what as change? Who is to establish this? What, finally, is to be gained by such assertions? To whom will the benefits next accrue?*

One answer to these questions was spelled out in the preceding chapter. The Terrorist asserts, by the unprecedented audacity of his act, that the world has changed. At the same time, the Terrorist plays on the fact that the world remains the same as before. With this disorientation terrorism usurps our own energies and redeploys them against us.

Now to another answer. The Executive of the United States adopted a weirdly analogous posture. Almost immediately on that dreadful day and then after, the most visible and influential people around the president insisted that September 11th was a break in the flow of history, discontinuous with the past. Life "would never be the same after September 11th."[7] Gone, they said, as with the bombing at Pearl Harbor, was our naive sense of security.[8] We would henceforth live in a world defined by war. The war would be of an altogether new type, as we faced enemies without states, territories, or compatriots to whom we might address our response. It would be a terrorist war and a war on terrorism. The nation was now on "war footing," and the White House held a "war president."[9] "Old orthodoxies are obsolete."[10]

Who determines when the "past is dead" or "old orthodoxies are obsolete"? Those who defined the world as "new" were anything but unorthodox. The Executive was haunted by "Cold Warriors" returned from past administrations or revived after scandal,[11] guided by "Vulcans" and "neoconservatives" trained long before the 2000 election, and prompted by well-seasoned ideologues.[12] Policy advisers weaned on Vietnam, and then on the Soviet Union's "Vietnam quagmire" in Afghanistan (in which America played the dramatic role the Soviet Union had played in Vietnam),[13] had placed a plan for an American invasion of that country before the president on September 10. What exactly was it that had changed when it was enacted less than a month later?[14]

The fact of the matter is this: while vigorously promoting popular belief in discontinuity, the Executive exploited the general continuity of our beliefs and institutions and the specific continuity of its own people, methods, and aspirations.*

---

* That both the Terrorist and the Executive need the Citizen to enact their plans has nothing to do with the parochial concept of "moral equivalence."

The "new world," it was said, would be characterized by war. But when, exactly, did this war begin?

In very few respects was the message delivered by the terrorists in New York and Washington on September 11th imprecise. Yet it was not a declaration of war. Nor was it, in the early hours, received that way. President Bush told us that "today, our nation saw evil, the very worst of human nature. . . . These acts of mass murder were intended to frighten our nation into chaos." But the question—*Were these acts of war?*—remained open.[15] Flying airplanes into buildings containing thousands of people might have been "merely" criminal or immoral violence. The response of the Prince to "murder most foul" might still have been to "search, seek, and know how this foul murder comes."[16]

Within days murder was remade into war. The public words of President Bush, and corresponding action by Congress, began to qualify the attacks as *war*.[17] National goals and tactics changed with the name. A choice was made, as one particularly livid commentator wrote, not "to bring them to justice, but to bring justice to them."[18]

In the "autumn of war" the pundits went to work as if the way to conduct war was self-evident. Wasn't it enough that American power would be, as jingoistic country singer Toby Keith put it, unwittingly borrowing from Shakespeare, "unleashed"? Wasn't it enough to "put a boot in their ass"?[19] Wasn't the new American motto "whatever it takes"?[20]

Even bombs rained on Afghanistan did not decide what the war would be. The Executive pushed further. Others pressed forward. "If this be war," they said, let it be *real*—serious, tragic, unfair, dirty, carnal—war.[21] Since the homeland was attacked outside the rules of war, let us adopt a strategy of unruliness. Why should we heed Geneva conventions or any other restraint?[22] The thirst for revenge brought a facile consensus. Highbrow pundits like Professor Victor Davis Hanson and Dr. Charles Krauthammer led a cast of hawks.[23] Quick alignment with the position of the Executive was urged and secured. The majority of Americans followed the *Commander-in-chief*. "Whatever it takes."

Linger on this phrase. The "whatever" in "whatever it takes" must come from somewhere. The U.S. Constitution decrees that the president "shall take Care that the Laws be faithfully executed." The president can invite research, pardon, assign offices, break ties, host visitors, but he has few explicit powers to *originate* actions except in the role of Commander-in-chief.[24] This is an enormous incentive to shift projects under that rubric. Assignment of military funding decisions and the power to *declare* war to the Congress likewise moves the Commander-in-chief to shape his war projects in particular ways.[25] A *declared* war may diminish the power of the president; an *undeclared* war may increase it.

This enormous incentive appears in the following numbers. By 1971, only 5 of the 158 military actions engaged by the United States since 1789 had occurred under a declaration of war.[26] A hard-won and well-publicized *War Powers Resolution* was passed in 1973 with the intention to restore a balance of constitutional responsibility for the introduction of the "armed forces into hostilities." Yet even this left open the possibility that the president could bypass Congress in case of "a national emergency created by attack upon the United States."[27]

Thus after September 11th the Executive needed only popular mandate and opportunity, not authorization, to transform an act of murder into an act of war. The march up to reprisals was swift.*

As America attacked Osama bin Laden's Taliban hosts in Afghanistan, it became freshly clear that once set in motion our military machine would not easily be restrained. Scattered objections to the militarization of the conflict appeared. Some tried to turn back the clock. They insisted that, in fact, as de jure, no war had begun. Al Qaeda had better be tracked down like criminals and their supporters treated as co-conspirators. Among critics of an emerging "Bush Doctrine,"[28] detailed disagreements were overshadowed by one general conclusion: the blanket category of *war* should not be applied to villains without territory or state.[29] Criminal investigation would more effectively achieve our end—the elimination of Al Qaeda. Police-like operations, more than "smart bombs," would allow us to skirt skillfully around noncombatants.† By contrast, reliance on our planes-and-tanks technology would

---

* The president did, also, receive authorization in various ways; to a large extent it was superfluous; conformism to not obstruct was sufficient. The *War Powers Resolution* does require that, after the fact, troop commitments must be affirmed by Congress; the enormous "gray area" this creates was manifest in the debate in 2004 over John Kerry's position on the war in Iraq.

† This topos would slowly return to public discussion after President Bush declared that "major combat operations in Iraq have ended" (this is the title of the White House press release of the text of the speech he gave aboard the USS *Abraham Lincoln* on May 1, 2003) and "mission accomplished" (the White House made a banner with these words on it that was positioned behind the president as he spoke aboard the aircraft carrier); one might imagine that this would have provided nonpartisan support for distinguishing the invasion of Iraq from the "war on terror," yet public discussion and its opinions tended strongly in the opposite direction.

make it too easy for criminals to shield themselves behind a buffer of innocents.

Such objections did not have much traction in the fall of 2001. Nor did they gain in effect in the crucial months leading up to the invasion of Iraq. Even their most popular exponent, presidential contender John Kerry, largely downplayed his moderate adaptation of them.[30] Lingering shock and visceral patriotism contributed to this situation, as did concerted warmongering by the vast right-wing network rallied around the Executive.

But the failure of such objections to slow the movement to war also reflected our longer-term historical situation. The critics held to an old and, one might have thought, tautological distinction: war is war and peace is peace; soldier in war and police in peace.

This distinction is no longer sociologically apt. Since at least World War II the boundary between war and peace has eroded. We live today in a netherworld. While this fact is exploited in practice, it remains impenetrable to our thinking.[31] We shall see in a moment how this ambivalent situation bears on the position of the Citizen.

Now, in this light a strange fact appears if we follow events forward from September 11th. Whatever the degree of consensus or dissent, it seems that no one was quite sure when the war began, and this uncertainty cut across ideological lines. Did it begin that morning? That evening? With presidential addresses to Congress or to the nation? Or was it as late as October 7, when the first American bombers crossed into Afghani airspace? Or after? Or at all?

What we can say with certainty is that each different assertion aimed to configure the war in a different way and added to a conflict of positions that would continue long after September 11th.

Each of these positions asserted—as its point of contact with and against the others—the claims of *beginning*. I underscore here the special significance of claims of *beginning* because skepticism on exactly this point is, so to speak, a powerful method of democratic citizenship.* For, every *beginning* is largely *retrospective*.† As the clock ticked forward after

---

* This same skepticism is also well applied to claims of *tradition* and *eternal truth* . . . but that is better known than what I am urging here.

† The pattern here is like this: after an event at some Time$_2$ there is contest over what happened, continuity and discontinuity are asserted, and, by Time$_3$, Time$_2$ becomes a "beginning" based on the interpretation of its relation to a prior Time$_1$.

the attacks, the Citizen hoping to track his or her own position would have done well to follow the clues to the war . . . *backward.*

Everyone knew the perpetrator was Osama bin Laden.[32] Had he not declared war on the United States in 1996?[33] Had not President Clinton long considered that "we were at war with Al Qaeda?"[34] Had not CIA director George Tenet responded in like fashion?[35] Was this not obviously a continuation of the Gulf War?[36] Hadn't the incoming President Bush been briefed that "the main problem will be Al Qaeda"?[37] And even if the newly inaugurated president had ignored the obsessive pleas of Richard Clarke on the "Al Qaeda desk," had his "office of special plans" not designed an invasion of Afghanistan to lay hold of the enemy, waiting—as they said—for a "new Pearl Harbor" to accelerate that process?[38] The "new world of war" had, in fact, been beginning for a long time.

Does it matter for the Citizen when the war "really" began? In a sense that is perhaps not obvious, I think it does. Each competing account of the *beginning* does more than pinpoint a date on the calendar. It envisions a balance of continuity and change, it leads to a particular distribution of human energies and resources, it produces identifiable effects, and it registers gains or losses for different people. All of this bears on the position of the Citizen. All of this appears in, or is hidden by, the language in which the question—*When did the war begin?*—is answered.

In other words, each version of when the war began is the leading edge of a political contest. Behind that edge, shaping and shaped by the demands of politics, may be found certain prejudices concerning the essential characteristics of war. An account of *what war is* ties the Citizen to it, or separates the Citizen from it. Judgment, action, responsibility, conscience, and so forth—the engines of human experience—all come back to this point.

Start from the most common view of *what war is*, displayed in films like *Saving Private Ryan* or *We Were Soldiers*.[39] It holds that wars begin with the first shot, continue in a hail of bullets, and end when the soldiers reach the soil of home. Veterans recognize this image, decrying or applauding its verisimilitude. It has become the standard by which judgments are made and action is taken.

The problem with this view is simple: it leaves no place for the Citizen.* For reasons I will soon bring forward, it may even be rather injurious to

---

* Even if the republican ideal of Citizen-Soldier were still viable (it is not), that would also be squeezed out by this way of thinking.

the Citizen's interests. In reality, neither Soldier nor screen can separate the Citizen—as material or responsible agent—from the complex social process that is war.

Take another commonplace that immediately commanded attention and was repeated without much reflection after the attacks: "September 11th is our Pearl Harbor," or, as President Bush dictated to his diary that night, "the Pearl Harbor of the 21st century took place today."[40] The force of this expression quickened in the last months of 2001.[41] It was developed in rhetorically adroit polemics by avid militarist Victor Davis Hanson. It merits closer inspection here precisely because, at the same time that Hanson proposes to answer the question *When is it war?* his development of this analogy promotes a thicker account of what war is.[42]

Hanson's essay "Dates in Infamy" at first displays the image of "our Pearl Harbor" as a sign of continuity rather than change. This catches the reader off guard. Elsewhere, Hanson, like many others, had attached the image of "Pearl Harbor" to the topos "it's a new epoch." Here, instead, the two are initially separated.[43] This is intentionally misleading. By the last page of the essay the union will be made even stronger to show that "September 11 was not the end, but the very beginning."[44]

Hanson's parallel covers a lot of ground. Each attack was, of course, a murderous surprise. He focuses our attention instead on military capabilities: many more assets were left intact than were destroyed, including not only arms and supplies, but also commercial and infrastructural networks and territory; moreover, Al Qaeda was unable "to ruin the cultural, political, or economic life of a scarred New York"; if our enemies "bragged that we were either too wealthy, cowardly, or impotent to retaliate in kind," their bluster was no match for "West Point, GM, Cal Tech, Sears, the U.S. Senate, and the American Soldier"; we quickly took the war to Southeast Asia in the 1940s, and quicker still to Afghanistan in 2001, removing it from our homeland; immediately following both attacks, there was audacious planning "not merely to defend America, but to eliminate . . . fascism [and Al Qaeda] altogether and at once"; our "characteristically slow to anger culture . . . awoke from its slumber, tapped its arsenal of freethinking individuals, and then by consensus and law chose not merely to defeat but to eradicate its enemies."[45]

To this list Hanson adds similarities that are not, even within his wide compass, "merely military." The additions are nonetheless offered as characteristic of war. Boom and bust—in the two decades before Pearl Harbor and again in the 1990s—"had created a self-absorbed and then apprehensive America" and, recently, "after setbacks in Vietnam and Somalia . . . Americans were still unsure of their real power." Both eras "shared a psychological affinity with isolationism." Both infamous dates taught that "politically . . . [i]t really is folly to cut one's defenses in times of peace" and that "appeasement . . . is a prescription for disaster."

Easy enough to remark the apples-and-oranges quality of such comparisons.* And Hanson's polemic unravels if one asks what he supposes to have *ended* on each *beginning* date.

What I want to emphasize is a more revealing asymmetry between these dates of "infamy." At the moment Hanson writes, we know the consequences of Pearl Harbor, but not of September 11th. Thus, for all its angry but schoolmasterish matter-of-factness, the essay is precatory and the author a preacher. The reader is expected to take as accomplished fact an almost messianic wish. "Pearl Harbor" for the Japanese and September 11th for Islamists were "military blunders of the first order." This "similarity" is, of course, far from proven. Yet it is at the head of Hanson's list.

Overall, and apparently against its intent, Hanson's little diatribe does make clear a basic fact that concerns us here: war is not one thing, and it is more than a direct manifestation of a "savagery innate to all peoples at all times."[46] War is, rather, a composite social fact in which are intertwined systems of economy, society, law, and polity, along with traits of culture ("freethinking individuals"), disposition ("audacity"), and knowledge. This social fact is stretched out over time, constituting an abiding milieu within which citizens must position themselves.

Thus, whatever pundits may expound, the question *Did a new period of history begin on September 11th?* is of very limited interest. It is typically little more than a partisan ploy. We had better set this question aside. We had better reorient consideration of what happened on that terrible day through the personal experience of someone like you or me. For war or wars in course, wherever or whatever they may be, constitute a

---

* E.g. the basic difference in the enemy is brushed aside at the outset, nor does Hanson mention the difference between military and civilian targets, the different status of the territory attacked in response and its relation to the initial attack, the lack of planning for peace in the current struggle, the entirely different ideological climate, the oddity of the notion of "isolationism" in an "age of globalization," the unstated assumption that turns Vietnam into a "setback," etc.

sometimes near and sometimes distant part of the ongoing life of the Citizen. The Citizen had better ask, *How did my world, the world in which I have lived and in which I will live, change on that day and through the following ones?* The *person* who asks this question as a *Citizen* will worry at once about himself, his circle, and his nation. The rest may be left to future historians.

I have said that terrorism is not an event but a relationship.* It involves at least the Terrorist and the Terrorized, and usually a spectrum of parties who "mediate" between the two.† The relationship formed by terrorism overlaps with and is embedded within other relationships that, in turn, constitute one's everyday life together with others. The social fact of war is one of these wider relationships.

After September 11th, the links joining terrorism, war, and politics have become particularly animated. The Citizen must grapple with these shifting connections. By what means?

It almost goes without saying that we need "the most complete account ... of the events of September 11th, what happened and why."[47] The report of the 9/11 Commission attempted to establish such an account. Within the frame the commission set for itself, the report provides an impressive overview.[48]

However, findings by such commissions are almost always ambiguous in what they bring to the position of the Citizen. On the one hand, purposefully bipartisan commissions cannot move forward without consensus. On the other hand, the "commissioners' misplaced, though successful, quest for unanimity ... encourages just the kind of herd thinking now being blamed for [the scandal concerning WMD in Iraq]."[49] Moreover, because such reports aim directly to orient government policy they mirror the positions of the Expert, the Bureaucrat, or the Executive. These perspectives must be placed within wider frames if the Citizen is to make use of them. They are often in tension with the Citizen's interests and capabilities.

---

* Those who insist that terrorism is "merely a strategy"—by which they typically mean a neutral instrument that can be deployed by different people with different intentions and projects— usually miss the significance of the point I repeat here from chapter 1. Your enemy must behave a certain way, interact with you in a certain way, for a strategy to work at all. The strategy itself sets crucial conditions for this interaction, providing the enemy with material conditions that require appropriate response.

† Take the word *mediate* in its broadest sense: to stand in-between.

From the position of the Citizen, only the Citizen—drawing on whatever and normally insufficient resources are at hand—can give an authoritative account of what events mean for us. Only the Citizen handles the particulars of living together with other people ... *by doing it*. The Expert, the Bureaucrat, and the Executive may deal in technical minutiae but in so doing attend to *life together in general*. They aim to unify perspectives, whereas the life of citizens together inexorably multiplies points of view. Although "it is almost impossible to take effective action to prevent something that hasn't occurred previously,"[50] the agents of the State adopt—and are pressed to adopt, had better adopt—a posture of prevention. Such a posture is typically impossible for the Citizen. Once an attack draws the Citizen into a relationship with the Terrorist, his first position must be one of response. His second position is support for the actions of others. Only very rarely, and indirectly, can or do citizens today engage in meaningful preventive measures (i.e. something more than the strategic application of duct tape). And when they do, they step up from being Citizens to become Heroes.* Finally, the Terrorist's attack also draws the Citizen into new relations with the Executive, the Bureaucrat, and so forth, as well as with other citizens. It is a central purpose of this book to rethink the constellation of these relationships from the inside.

Against the background of the structured difference and interaction among these social positions, the report of the 9/11 Commission repeats a common mistake. It assimilates the position of the Citizen to the agents of the State. This, in turn, obscures the complex set of relationships initiated by the terrorist act. The Terrorist never faces a single unified *we*, but rather a society of many groups and interests always in motion. The State, or more precisely the Executive, may *lead* this movement but never controls it or represents it as a whole.[51] Thus, whether the widely accepted contention that "the terrorists exploited deep institutional failings within our government" is correct or, as Judge Posner has written, "overblown,"[52] it is in an important sense simply off the mark.†

I am, of course, not saying that the American government is or could be without some institutional failings. My point is that from the position of the Citizen, a position inherently difficult for an investigative body like

---

* This was the case for the passengers of Flight 93.
† The policy implications of this hamartia are enormous, weighing as heavily as it has, for example, on such institutional restructuring of the State as the newly created Department of Homeland Security.

the 9/11 Commission to grasp, the Terrorist constitutes a rather different sort of link to our political life. The Terrorist exploits the abiding milieu in which the problems of living together, and thus the questions of war and peace, are addressed.

This returns us to a central point of the preceding chapter. It is not so much the State as our own "public sphere" that the Terrorist turns against us.

To understand what it is about the "public sphere" that makes it susceptible to this kind of reversal, we need to focus on what makes it a "sphere" or a kind of space.* Except in a very limited, if momentarily devastating, way the Terrorist does not occupy our territory. The "public sphere" appropriated by the Terrorist is nevertheless a space of human relationship in which a world of persons and things at once holds us together and separates us. Its characteristic feature is not topography but balance. To think of this balance as a mathematical or physical *order*, perhaps as a complex equation or an intricate machine, is suggestive but inaccurate. The "public sphere" is an order of life and living, and thus of change and transformation. Each person, referent of innumerable "in-between" spaces, is affected by boundaries, forces, tensions, moments of saturation and emptiness, and a large number of other "factors." Potentials for *imbalance* lurk in the very structure of the "public sphere." Thus, as that structure is a human composite, the *need* to maintain balance is also part of it. Ongoing events, from problem to problem, from respite to respite, are intertwined with the "public sphere," moving it from balance to imbalance and back again, shifting between order and disorder.[53] Constituted this way, there is no single commanding position from which to set it right.

This means that the pivotal factor in maintaining order within the "public sphere" is not position but *time*. Each citizen, no matter how vigorously he mobilizes or manifests his views, has to let the events of which he is a part—but only a part—run their course. This is, paradoxically, the only way to be an *agent* of change. The "public sphere" is most likely to be well-ordered when the urgency of needs arising from problems corresponds nearly to the rhythm at which "publicizing acts" can be successfully undertaken.[†]

---

* Everything in this and the next paragraph is subject to qualifications expressed at length in *The Position of the Citizen*. The quotation marks around "public sphere" are meant to keep before our attention the complex shifting between dynamic and static senses of the word *public*.

[†] Again, "publicizing" is a technical term I have introduced into political theory to denote the implication of a third party in a two-way dispute.

The motive and arcane logistic of the Terrorist may elude us, but his strategy can hardly be obscure. President Bush was not wrong to say that the attacks of September 11th were "intended to frighten our nation into chaos and retreat."[54] Jordan's King Abdullah correctly told a *New York Times* reporter in the days after September 11th that "the terrorists are trying to break down the fabric of the U.S. . . . they want to be able to turn to your friends here and say, 'Look, this is all a myth.'"[55] Osama bin Laden has consistently displayed his plans.[56] "I tell you," he said shortly after September 11th in an explicit statement of the result he expected from his methods, "freedom and human rights in America are doomed. . . . The U.S. government will lead the American people—and the West in general—into an unbearable hell and a choking life."[57]

The Terrorist sees necessity as virtue. He always adopts a strategy of limited resources. Terrorism looks for a virus, something that, when launched into the "system," will wreak extensive havoc. Something that requires no further input. The extent of its malicious accomplishment is a function of how it exploits the organism into which it is inserted.

In other words, the Terrorist turns *us* into a weapon of mass destruction. And he turns that "weapon" against us. The process is simple. All he must do is to make everyday needs for security more urgent—or even *appear to be more urgent*—than the systematic rhythm of "publicizing" can handle. America—where so much is geared to the short term and where winners and losers alike seem to thrive on crises—is his perfect climate.

The machinery of the "choking life" envisioned by Osama bin Laden is composed of the most banal commonplaces: Americans live within a tense and shifting balance of liberty and security; an attack will increase the demand for security; the response to this new demand, in turn, will increase demands for liberty; liberty, once outweighed by immediate needs for security, will not be able to defend itself;* unsatisfied demand for liberty will increase the pressure on civil and political rights, which are, effectively, calls for more time in crisis situations. However, because rights are created and sustained by the State, this chain of events will enlarge one of the central paradoxes of modern politics: the State must act short and long term, responding at once to contradictory demands for *both* security *and* liberty.†

---

* This was Hobbes's great observation in the motto *bellum omnium contra omnes*.

† These issues will be taken up again in chapter 3.

Now, across the history of the American republic, this contradictory balancing act has not thus far produced encompassing long-term instability. I do not mean to say that arrangements have always been agreeable or fair to all; all I am saying here is that the whole system has rarely been severely disturbed.* But, even within that frame, and, perhaps, even more so in a future that will go outside that frame, the characteristic feature of perceived crises is that contradictory demands overflow their usual proportions. Balance fails. Every case becomes a pressing short-term problem.[58] What pushes a situation over into crisis is the replacement of a relatively small number of short-term problems by a larger number of short-term problems. Crisis lusts after time. The Terrorist is the miser of time.

This disorder is how the "public sphere" becomes an instrument for the Terrorist. An act of terrorism imposes at once, in a hundred different ways and for thousands of different people, one and the same question: "What, to be both safe and free, are we going to do today?"[59]

To be the immediate victim of a terrorist attack is to lose the opportunity to ask this question. Almost everyone else wakes up every morning with it in mind. The question is animated by the Terrorist but not spoken in a foreign accent. It occurs in the familiar tones of the Policeman, the Neighbor, the Judge, the Coworker, the President. Its effects ripple across all of society.

If Osama bin Laden foresaw America "choking," what "myth" is it that King Abdullah feared would be debunked?

In America, the song of ourselves is a great experimental mixing of peoples and the dream of unbound opportunity. This vision has sometimes been communicated to people beyond our shores who then slipped their shackles, entered the mix, and gave new voice to the American music.

The major "myth" of America abroad today, however, is something else. It is an image held up, in caricature or in dead earnest, by much of the world. It is not primarily about freedom or rights or "the American dream," although surely there are radical Islamists and other reactionaries who despise these things, too. The "myth" that King Abdullah and thousands of our allies fear will fall under the Terrorist's assault is the

---

* I use the neutral word *system* here to allow for the accommodation of American society with its decidedly undemocratic features like slavery and extraordinary inequality.

image of an untouchable omnipotence. It springs from our own narratives of undivided action—think of "the city upon the hill," "manifest destiny," "isolationism," "the world's policeman," "the only superpower," "unilateralism," and so forth.* The myth is evidenced by the global but never complete reach of our military, our corporations, our cultural products, and even our tourists. We assume so thoroughly this image for ourselves that it is largely invisible to us; indeed, the more we believe it, the more invisible it becomes.

At risk in the exposure of such a myth is not simply hypocrisy or contradiction. The myth concerns capacity. Capacity is always relative to circumstances. The Terrorist would force us to show what we can do—not in general, not in the image, but for real, *here and now*. Thus Osama bin Laden challenged America to prove its omnipotence.

George W. Bush accepted the challenge. He spit back hot talk about the "axis of evil," "crusade," "dead or alive," "no price too high," and the rhetoric of "whatever it takes." The tone was set in his first major address to the nation after the attack:

> this country will define our times, not be defined by them. As long as the
> United States of America is determined and strong, this will not be an
> age of terror.... The advance of human freedom ... now depends on us.
> Our nation—this generation—will lift a dark threat of violence from our
> people and our future.... We will not tire, we will not falter, and we will
> not fail.[60]

This speech presupposes remarkably precise capacity concerning wildly general, almost messianic claims: history, terror, freedom, and even the future are determined by "will," specifically *our* "will," *now*, which is inexhaustible. It is a manifesto of "undivided action."†

Moreover, there is not a new word in it. The project of the current Executive to make American power "unchallengeable" was thirty years

---

* America, of course, has other narratives that point to our inherent divisions, but often these too press towards a unitary conclusion, as in *e pluribus unum* or in the proliferation of "hyphenated" identities over the past two generations.

† "Undivided action" is related to the notion of the division of action introduced in chapter 1. These are not, strictly speaking, opposites; "undivided action" is an orientation, presumption, or assertion that features a strategic denial of the division of action but does not in fact escape from it.

in the making,[61] just as the larger project of an American omnipotence had been in the works for at least another generation before that.

Indeed, only willful ignorance could miss the continuity of President Bush's words with Cold War rhetoric and the triumphalism that returned to Americans after the demise of the Soviet Union. Once cards like these were on the table, our every danger and success would be measured by them. Any short hand will leave a lingering, residual threat. This is not only the language of hope and ambition, but the double multiplication of expectations and coincident anxiety.

Of course, the will-to-demonstrate-that-our-omnipotence-is-more-than-a-myth springs the trap set on September 11th in New York and Washington. The more that we try to control alone, the more the impossibility of total control becomes evident. Overreach creates a thousand new opportunities. At each turn someone else will show us up: even the "world's only superpower" simply cannot have all the capacities to which we have daily laid claim.[62] This is not because America is not mighty: it is because no success could be sufficient proof. Even the long-delayed capture of Saddam Hussein, what did it decide? Who swore that Osama would soon be in our grasp? What better gift, this promise, to an enemy whose resources have in many other ways been restricted: after September 2001 the Terrorist no longer needed to command armies or furnish his followers with suitcase bombs—it was enough for him *to hide* and we were cut down from giant to dwarf. That lesson has been hammered home. Suddenly our incapacities stood out; it became easy to see the disjunction between what we really can do—no matter how spectacular that is—and our trumpeted aspirations. We got scared. We got terrorized. We went to war.

Here the stakes of understanding war correctly—not as "dogs unleashed" but as a composite social fact—begin to appear before us in earnest. And it is here, too, that the purportedly national *we* that goes to war cries out for further specification.

Certainly, every individual responds to attack in a different way, but no *one* makes war by himself; there is no "private war."[63] Between the *someone* and the *everyone* stand dozens of different groups, identifiable by their common experience and interests, and each giving issue to a particular public persona.

These personae cover a wide range: Victim, Soldier, Enemy, Executive, Profiteer, and so forth, all the way up to the Citizen. Viewed from outside—in the manner of social science—each of these social types may appear as an actor, an entity with relatively predictable motives that moves within an identifiable field of relationships. However, these personae have additional significance *for* the Citizen. The Citizen must take counsel from but cannot for long cling to the aloof perspective of science. When it comes to politics the Citizen cannot stand outside but is always at the center. One's life with others is the key to the judgments *for action*. Thus, from *inside* politics, each type operates *for* and *through* the rest. All these personae become perspectives through which the Citizen can evaluate possible positions for him- or herself. Each type is an alternative imaginary "subject position" that tells us something different but not definitive about the relationship between war and everyday life, and the infiltration of terrorism into that relationship. Each type brings its particular and sometimes corrective sort of activism to the public scene.[64]

Such an exercise can go too far. Adopting, or giving too much weight to, a particular "subject position" can skew one's own position as Citizen. When the Citizen sees war exclusively through the eyes of the Victim, he goes astray. Representations of the Soldier's experience tend to distort the political scene as well.[65] "If you believe the doctors, nothing is wholesome; if you believe the theologians, nothing is innocent; if you believe the soldiers, nothing is safe."[66]

The question, then, is this: *Is there a comprehensive perspective on war that is not inherently misleading for the Citizen?*

The modern science of warfare achieved new insight early in the nineteenth century with the German thinker Carl von Clausewitz. "War," he famously wrote, "is merely the continuation of politics by other means."[67] I propose to you that this can be a powerful point of departure for thinking through the position of the Citizen.

The main virtue of Clausewitz's maxim is that it is based on an obvious fact. War is part of life.[68] However, what Clausewitz himself meant by politics is too narrow for our purposes. Writing in the 1820s, Clausewitz largely conformed to German common sense. He took the State to be the central locus of politics. There are good historical reasons for this, especially given his primary concern with the military aspects of *war*.[69] Focused on the State, and especially on its relationships with other states, Clausewitz may have meant little more than this: when negotiation and diplomacy fail, national leaders turn to troops and tanks to accomplish their goals. That this is clearly—if partially—true explains Clausewitz's persistent influence.[70]

At the same time, Clausewitz opens the door towards a more general view on the relationship between war and politics. He makes clear the absurdity of treating war as a "wholly isolated act, occurring suddenly and not produced by previous events in the political world."[71] It is self-defeating to imagine war as having a "single, ... perfect and complete"[72] solution that would remain uninflected by subsequent interactions.* A military man, Clausewitz was remarkable in adopting terms from philosophers (e.g. Kant and Hegel) only to assert against them a deeply pragmatic perspective. He demonstrated an unusually clear sense of the contingencies of real human action at the nexus of reason, emotion, and chance. In his view, no single perspective can encompass human action. Aspiration to the certainty of an "Archimedean point" imaginable only for an omnipotent God or sovereign is a losing proposition. Instead, Clausewitz shows that those who need to act with respect to war must calculate in terms of "probabilities," which is to say statements representing the way the world appears to those who actually live in it.[73]

These promising lines in Clausewitz's *On War* have often been obscured, occasionally by twentieth-century political thinkers who seem closest to him.[74] Therefore let me make my advice here explicit. Reading the maxim "war is the mere continuation of politics by other means," do not overemphasize the word *other*. In the relation between war and politics it is the *continuity* that counts most for the Citizen. The significance of this continuity depends on what *version of politics* is in play. Do not follow those who would turn Clausewitz's dictum around to suggest that in all politics the exceptional violence and play of force characteristic of military combat continue.[75] This way of thinking simply brings us back to old Thomas Hobbes—who taught that the politics established out of civil war was always haunted by its ghost, and reducible in the last instance to the sword of the sovereign. The interest of Clausewitz is exactly the opposite: the incessant priority he gives to politics. Thus, however clever it may seem, it is sterile to use *On War* to deny the most elementary distinction for the Citizen: politics and violence are two contrary forms of human problem-solving relationships.

---

* Two principles of reasoning that, it may be said, were violated by the Bush administration.

It remains important to illuminate one by way of the other. The complicating factor here is not that politics is "really" war and therefore violent. It is that war, while it applies violence in particular and devastating ways, only exists by virtue of relationships that are not themselves violent.* This complex relationship between war and politics is a major constraint on the position of the Citizen after September 11th. Can Clausewitz's insight help us to understand this? Can it be developed in a manner consistent with the everyday experience of politics today?

Historian Michael Howard points in a fruitful direction. War, he follows Max Weber in observing, "demands from the groups which engage in it a unique intensity of societal organization and control." The stakes are high. Despite images painted by Hobbes or portrayed in the figure of Rambo, no one can "go it alone" in war. People rise to the occasion by constituting new relationships with others. Thus it is essential to look closely at the way war "involves the reciprocal use of organized force between two or more social groups." These groups are "directed according to an overall plan or series of plans for the achievement of a political object."[76]

Howard seems to take a step consistent with but beyond Clausewitz. To pursue further this line of thinking about war is to both clarify and complicate the position of the Citizen. Yes, war is the continuation of politics, but it is also more than just a lifeless instrument to an end determined by political means. The groups that take up arms against one another must be seen as social organisms with highly articulated divisions of action. They are subject at all phases to internal processes of governance and negotiation.

This is the main point: this fact about warmaking groups and the implication of the Citizen within them means that they are neither led by, nor do they constitute, a central unitary will. Even a first step towards taking this point seriously suggests that various versions of politics must be considered as the Citizen thinks about war.

Certain historical facts tend to impede this move to a broader view of politics.† In early modern Europe, the activity of war linked parallel developments of nation-states and military power. All sorts of sovereigns knew what contemporary researchers have reaffirmed: "war made the State and the State made war."[77] This maxim is also apt—although in

---

* This is one reason why questions of responsibility in war are so difficult.
† I will deal with these in *Political Pathologies of the Citizen.*

different ways—to describe the first 150 years of the history of the United States.[78] Moreover, symbiotic relationships between the State and war are hardly things of the past. In some crucial respects the entanglements of State political institutions and actors with public and private power oriented around the military are today tighter than ever in America.

It is precisely within the way of thinking promoted by these historical conditions that Howard's emphasis on "social groups" is especially clarifying. He does not exclude the State from consideration, but neither does he limit attention to it. The State is one among a number of "social groups." Each of these groups, internally and in relation to the others, constitutes politics in a different way. These different versions of politics must be taken into account if we are to understand how war *today* is a "continuation of politics by other means."

This is true both for us and for our enemies.* Few have failed to observe that non-State groups can and do make war. Large numbers of regional or guerrilla armies have engaged in military operations around the world since World War II.† Private militias and militarized auxiliaries are thriving.‡ The warmaking capacities of global networks like Al Qaeda have come more fully into view since September 11th. It did not take long before we could see that these capacities have been further augmented by the American adventure in Iraq.

These observations are more complicated than they seem. It is worth noting that the proliferation of such "social groups" engaged in militarized activities depends in many ways on the State and its privileged relation to military activity. It is obvious that without transfers of money, weapons, and other technologies from States to ideologically oriented or mercenary private militias, these groups would find almost impossible the initial accumulation of resources necessary to undertake the very expensive enterprise of warmaking. The relatively recent conditions that make this direct reliance on States less necessary—for example, world

---

* Recognizing the inherent complexity of politics should, of course, change the value we give the idea that a "war against terrorism" is unprecedented because terrorists have no State. I will come back to this momentarily.

† While decolonization may often have been the motive for the formation of such groups, the fact that they were able to engage in military operations and the form those operations took have more to do with the Cold War. We shall consider this point below.

‡ A rare moment of effective local political opposition to lawless private American mercenaries in Iraq followed the Blackwater incident of September 16, 2007.

financial liquidity permitting massive private contracting of or donation to militarized extremists, the international drug trade, the black market in "surplus" weapons, and so forth—are nevertheless symbiotic with State activity—for example subsidized arms industries, the creation of astronomical profits through criminalization of drugs, covert support for guerrilla armies and drug traders, the use of public funds to pay private military "contractors" in places like Iraq, and so forth.*

However much "social groups" like Al Qaeda may ultimately depend on the State,† the need to come to terms with their existence suggests a perspective beyond the State. For the position of the Citizen this has a perverse effect. The image of equality in the arena of war—with one state balancing another—is often a condition of domestic stability; it allows for different versions of politics to flourish. The image of asymmetrical warfare—with an unstable, nomadic, and deterritorialized enemy ready to strike anyone from anywhere—presses the Citizen to make obsessive demands on the State, the only institution that seems fit to respond to terrorism.‡

To follow the line of inquiry initiated by Clausewitz and advanced by Howard in this direction may shed light on new kinds of war and new kinds of warriors. At the same time, however, it meets a major obstacle: it leads back to a version of politics largely outside the reach of the Citizen. I propose, therefore, to pursue the idea that "war is the continuation of politics" in a somewhat different direction. For this maxim also draws attention to how deeply war is integrated into everyday life.

This is where things get complicated. It is obviously true that for the Soldier on leave, for the Soldier's family, for the Veteran, for the Victim or Bystander, war is integrated into everyday life. My point is much more general and extends beyond these limited if important social types. It concerns the experience of war within the position of the Citizen. War occurs within the position of the Citizen primarily as a set of political relationships. To say this is not, as most people may be inclined to believe,

---

* There were more military "contractors" in Iraq in 2007 than the total of official American armed forces.

† The pivotal role of the American government in the career of Osama bin Laden—documented e.g. in Coll 2004—is well-known.

‡ This same pattern is not inapt to describe earlier phases of the Cold War. See discussion in chapter 3.

to misrepresent *what war really is*. Rather, it is entirely consistent with the essence of war as an encompassing human experience. This fact is especially important in twenty-first-century America.

It may be difficult to grasp exactly what I mean here. An initial aspect of it is rather simple. As we know with the intimacy of warm experience, Americans have not seen the other face of war—its oppressive violence—on our homeland since 1865.[79] This makes America unusual among modern nations. To observe this fact is, however, to underscore a rule that holds everywhere: violence is the essence of war only for the soldiers or the civilians who are under fire. Even for combatants and casualties, the majority of wartime is passed under threat, not in direct violence.[80]

So step away from the sites of battle. You will begin to see specifically political features of military bureaucracy. The intense application of social control required by war involves an extraordinarily fine division of action with a multitude of roles. Even when commands are backed by coercive military discipline an extensive use of speech oils the machinery of war. This speech serves more than just coordination. Command, prayer, conversation, confession, joke, insult, and even instruction on how to load your firearm create the "phatic communion" on which intense fraternal bonds characteristic of small combat units depend.[81] Language is always essential in the constitution of the social groups that wage war. This fact runs counter to wildly popular representations of war—such as Steven Spielberg's *Saving Private Ryan*—that despise words and set them categorically apart from the raw experience of violence. Such caricature of the Soldier's common sense is profoundly misleading. For the Citizen's *only* weapon is words.[82] The Soldier's experience is *citizenship plus violence*, not *violence minus citizenship*.

Take a further step back from the command relationships that join the Soldier to the military bureaucracy. What is war for citizens of the warmaking State? We are not on the battlefield, nor in the bunkers or the Pentagon, but at home or in school, at the factory or the office, in church or at the market. When we *go to war*, we *do not go anywhere*. And still the war *belongs* to us. For the Citizen, the difference between everyday life and the experience of war is not, so to speak, a change in kind. It is a redirection of our attention. It is "the continuation of politics by other means."

When this happens, the stakes vary with position. For the Parent or the Spouse, the well-being of the Soldier is at stake.* For the Citizen, at stake is the determination of purpose and ultimate control of specifically military social control.[83] For reasons psychological, historical, and pragmatic, citizens easily tend to evade the responsibility this implies. We act as if something deeply in our interest were nothing but a task for the Commander-in-chief. Democracies go this way; the *citoyen* loved Napoleon.

However, the fact remains: energies and constraints that compose war are widely distributed and highly politicized. Long before the momentous questions of democratic decision making come before us— Should *you* or *I* or *we* take part in war? If so, how?—the Citizen would do well to survey this field where war and everyday experience come together.[†]

The entanglement of the Citizen in social processes of warmaking appears in many forms. It is perhaps nowhere more paradoxical than in the assertion that *we have no choice*. While typically made by the Executive, this assertion conjures up an image of the intensely dangerous and violent experience of the Soldier or the Victim so as to mobilize support from the Citizen. Literally speaking, however, there is no human situation without choice (likewise, there is no human situation that is nothing but choice). Even in "total war" necessity is never unmitigated: a country invaded may assert the "necessity" to defend itself, but sometimes, in the face of overwhelming force, the better strategy is to relent. As Clausewitz observed, there is no final solution in war; with the asymmetry between attack and defense, invaders who hope to withdraw in quick victory may be decimated by lesser local forces who wait their opportunity.[‡] Complex social processes always issue in options.[§]

---

* Those who lose a loved one in war often justify their loss in terms of national duty, but at that moment they do not speak as Parent or Spouse, but as Patriot, often so as to sublimate the emotions characteristic of those other roles.

[†] I insist again that this complicates but does not undermine the basic distinction between violence and politics.

[‡] This is apparently what strategists of the Iraqi Republican Guard had in mind in the spring of 2003. After a brief wait, interpreted by President Bush on May 1 of that year as "the end of major combat operations," it became easier for the defenders to regroup and fight a dispersed occupying force rather than throw themselves on the lance of an invading one.

[§] All of which may, of course, be bad. We often say complexity inhibits choice, but the fact is that complexity also makes choice possible.

In any case, these considerations are distant from the immediate experience of the American Citizen. We have not faced invasion or occupation since the nineteenth century.

The political aspect of war appears again in claims that war must be restrained or follow rules. These claims may have pragmatic as much as ethical weight. Restraint in war serves to preserve the humanity of soldiers, to gain approbation or legitimacy at home or abroad, to assuage the faint of heart, to deceive the enemy, to conserve resources, to open negotiations for return of prisoners, and so forth. Restraint may be informal or systematic. It often proceeds through topical distinctions that motivate or facilitate pubic debate: wars can be declared or undeclared, just or unjust, conditional or unconditional, limited or unlimited, preemptive or preventive. Implicit in such distinctions are both the choices and the broad discursive field that give to war its specific shape.[84] In other words, everything that sets a limit on war reveals another of its connections to politics.*

Why, then, the abundance of descriptions of war, of America's current wars, as *necessary* or as *unlimited?* We will return to such claims below. For the moment, let me say only that once war is understood as entwined with politics, the steamrolling rhetoric of necessity becomes much less persuasive.

Likewise, the accusation that America has entered into an "unlimited" war becomes suspect. One may appreciate the sentiment behind this claim and still recognize that it is, on its face, false: nothing in human affairs is unlimited. It seems driven by an injudicious anxiety. It allows the speaker to evade responsibility for naming exactly what limits are operative and for showing how those limits work against some people and in favor of others. The Citizen who positions himself behind this accusation will be afraid of his own shadow.

Enlarge the frame further and we return to where we began this passage. Every perspicacious inquirer into politics has seen connections between democracy and war; few have missed the relation between modern warfare and the democratic State.[85] These correct but no longer sufficient observations make too close adherence to Clausewitz a risky business. Are we to be trapped between two untenable views, in which either war's violence appears as just a backdrop for bureaucratic intrigue, or the

---

* Likewise, legal constraints—from the Constitution to courts, statutes, treaties, international law—shape the actual practice of war. Note that evasion of this point is what led theorists seeking to make a categorical distinction between war and politics into extreme accounts of both.

State's control of awe-inspiring means of violence leads to a dangerously narrow view of politics?

After September 11th, the position of the Citizen may expand or contract with respect to the question of war. But it is nonetheless the position of the Citizen that determines what war will be.

Elsewhere I will argue in detail that citizens would do well to identify and identify with various streams of the American political tradition.* Here I want to underscore the following related point. As war is continuous with the unfolding of politics—even and especially at the level of everyday experience among citizens—the American political tradition is part of what citizens faced with war had better study. To approach and reevaluate our tradition, to transform it by positioning ourselves within it, there are basic questions we had better tackle head-on and with deep respect for our current situation. What does and does not count as war? When, where, and how should the Citizen choose to make war? Should citizens allow the Executive who makes war in our name to go unchecked or unchallenged? For how long?

These questions can be restated in terms that bear directly on the actions of the Citizen: *Which version* of politics does *this* war "continue by other means"? When we go to war, which aspects of our basic political life are furthered and which left behind?

Questions like these are answered de facto all the time. Somehow, somewhere, however, they had better come before the Citizen as reasons, as judgments, as responsible choices about *how to be an American.*

This is the real issue in *Democracy in America after 9/11* as a whole,† and against the background of events described in chapter 1 and the entanglement of war with politics articulated in this chapter, the approach to it can be restated with greater force. I am asking you to enter wholeheartedly the position of the Citizen and from that volatile and difficult perspective to see where things stand, and from within those narrow and frustrating constraints to think through our situation towards a new image of the future.

Every other approach known to me seems merely to reiterate the problems and draw us back into them. It is my hope instead that we

---

* See *Political Pathologies of the Citizen.*
† That is, the trilogy of which this book is the first volume; see "Note to the Reader" at the beginning of this book.

might advance by returning to an old, capacious, and ultimately simple view of politics. In this scene, citizens opt for speech over violence to struggle through everyday life together in a world where inevitably one problem is followed by another; in this process good actions thrive on and regenerate the plurality that is the essence of humankind; good citizens accept the division of action and distribute benefits accordingly, not in an arbitrary manner but by engaging in publicizing speech acts to mobilize support for projects as *we* weed out narcissistic and arrogant self-interest.

Let concerns such as these, rooted in the human condition, be the criteria by which the *character*—and to some extent the *goals*—of war are evaluated.

Measured in this way, the wars promoted by the Executive after September 11th are disturbingly paradoxical. They have been "continuations of politics" that are deleterious to politics. They are the bastards of an "antipolitics politics" prevalent in many aspects of American life. They have put us down hard on "war footing" and kept us in the flame. A nation long in that stance will always tend, as it were, to make war against itself. For it is never the Enemy who silences the Citizen, cuts off debate, shifts resources away from domestic needs, and so forth—no matter how much the language of *necessity* would make it seem as if the Enemy were the cause when the noose tightens around our collective neck.

In the normal experience of the Citizen politics takes various forms. Yet the common language of war today still tends to center politics around the State. This, in itself, diminishes the position of the Citizen. And it cuts off the key possibility of shifting strategically from one version of politics to another. An Executive that persistently employs the language of war to advance its projects multiplies this tendency rather than mitigating it. It is, for the position of the Citizen, doubly bad news.

While the basic question remains—*When is it war, and when not?*—we can now see that question in a strikingly different light. The conclusion I propose to draw from the preceding pages is this: what hangs in the balance here is *the form that politics will take*. That, specifically for the Citizen, is what *war* is about.

The war violence that smashes bodies with machines of death is a phenomenon utterly distinct from the political relationships among citizens. These are two fundamental and fundamentally contrary dimensions of human existence. Yet with increasing and alarming frequency they come together to form something new. This situation—so uncannily American—has no proper name. So, just as we refer to the fact that joins space and time without subsuming the one into the other as *space-time*, let us call the field where we live today with the precisely descriptive and pointedly sarcastic phrase *civic war*.

The old term of tragic continuing utility, *civil war*, speaks of what happens when the killing comes home. In the crisis of this American moment, we must divine, imagine, and carry on about the essentially political nature of war even for those who are never dyed in the rivers of blood and who, consistent with their nature *as citizens*, may never raise their hand against another of their own kind. The true political character of war needs its own name before the Citizen will see the growing ramifications of war itself. The oxymoronic juncture of *civic war* broadcasts this hope.

At first blush one may find this conclusion unsatisfactory or disheartening. This way of seeing the link between war and politics pushes yet farther from a single or fixed answer to the questions I have raised. Although I believe emphatically that citizens had better seek to know at which instant terrorists first attacked America or the moment our tanks rolled across a foreign border, even such precise information, should it be found, would not settle political conflict among ourselves. The best we can hope to take away from such debates and from the issues brought forward in this chapter is a sense of what is at stake when citizens haggle over such questions.

The good news is that the questions of war and politics are not like math problems or philosophical puzzles. An improved *sense* of what is at stake in the real circumstances of our actions *cultivates political judgment*. This is not negligible. Indeed, without political judgment democracy is lost. For the conflict of interpretations depends on the balance of political forces, and to retrace that conflict is to bring this balance into a clearer light. It points to where we can and should throw our weight. In this process the discourse of war configures the position of the Citizen. We had better look first to the field of politics and then to the field of battle, or *warfighting*,* to understand what about our world did and did not change on September 11th.

---

* This term of art for the application of violence in war seems to derive from the 1980s and is officially adopted in the *United States Marine Corps Manual FMFM-1* published in 1989. I will use it from this point on in contradistinction to *civic war*.

3. The Circle of War and Emergency

When the people of Himera had chosen Phalaris dictator and were on the point of giving him a body-guard, Stesichorus said to them these words—"A horse alone occupied a meadow, but a stag came and did much damage. The horse wished to avenge himself and asked a man if he could help to punish the stag. The man consented, on condition that the horse would submit to the bit and allow him to mount him, javelins in hand. The horse agreed to the terms and the man mounted him, but instead of obtaining vengeance on the stag, the horse from that time became the man's slave"—Then Stesichorus added "take care lest, in your desire to avenge yourselves on the enemy, you be treated like the horse. You already have the bit, since you have chosen a dictator; if you give him a body-guard and allow him to mount you, you will at once be the slaves of Phalaris."

ARISTOTLE *RHETORIC* II.20 1393B

If the President cannot perform an act which is necessary though illegal, then the law must be construed in such a way as to make legal every act which is necessary.

LUCIUS WILMERDING, "The President and the Law" (1952)

Justice Arthur Goldberg once borrowed a quip from debates about pornography to answer in brilliant earnest the question *Is it war or not?* He simply said, "I know it when I see it."[1] He did not mean thereby to exalt solipsistic judgment. This maxim implicitly recognizes that the speaking

I is part of a community and is fully apprenticed to its sense of decorum.* That is, such a self-evident judgment is only sufficient when others agree: "*I* know it when *we* see it." The hammering out of relevant concurrence takes place over long time and large space. This process—the formation of common sense—unfolds within the broadest compass of political life. It is an essential part of the power to make war.[2] We shall work back around to it in the following pages.

For now, let us confine the question *Is it war or not?* within a narrower sense of the political. The U.S. Constitution includes the prospect of war. At the brink of conflict, the Constitution's several explicit assignments of power stand out. Certain powers go to Congress and certain powers to the Executive.[3]

This *separation* of powers may be seen as *checking* each of them, but the latter does not follow from the former. In fact, the familiar phrase *checks and balances* is a tidy curtain drawn over complex and disorderly process. Despite widely spaced assignment these various powers overlap. And as James Madison observed, they must.[4] "The Constitution by no means contemplates total separation of . . . branches of Government."[5] At the most, it establishes "separateness but interdependence, autonomy but reciprocity."[6] Within the constitutional system a loosely bounded field comes into existence between Executive and Congress.

What goes on in this field? To claim that "the Framers regarded . . . checks and balances. . . . as a *self-executing* safeguard against the encroachment or aggrandizement of one branch at the expense of the other" would be deeply misleading.[7] Most "Framers" correctly saw the constitutional frame as composed of citizens.[8] And while Madison was prepared to "trace [the operation of] . . . opposite and rival interests . . . through the whole system of human affairs, private as well as public,"[9] the language Madison borrowed from Bernard Mandeville and Adam Smith did not have under his pen the economistic tone we associate with those thinkers today. No "invisible hand" guides political outcomes; the constitutional separation of powers is not a "machine that would go of itself."[10] Even if "the private interest of every individual may be a sentinel over the public rights," the result Madison envisioned at the level of government was in no way automatic.[11] Decisions in the intermediate field between branches of government—good or bad, favoring progress or degeneration—

---

* An apprentice is not a slave, and may with greater ease transgress or play with his form.

emerge from contest and negotiation, as every individual fights for him-
or herself and every citizen for his or her own position.*

Again, *Is it war or not?* With America under threat or engaged somewhere abroad in military operations this question is bound to arise with
regularity. Not just on the infamous days of Pearl Harbor or September
11th, but every day throughout many levels of society. Even as viewed
from a narrowly constitutional perspective it is a "political question."[12]
What does this mean?

The political field between branches of government is slippery. De
facto power to make war can shift with each incremental decision, each
time an office or officer assumes an answer to the question *Is it war or not?*
At times, however, the warmaking power will appear to fall almost entirely into the hands of the Executive. Although the constitutional frame
was designed to impede despotism, it allows this. Why?

The primary reason is that the Constitution does not simply generate
authority or authoritative decisions. Despite its appearance, it does not
assign preexisting powers.[13] The Constitution—one may say almost tau-
tologically—*constitutes political processes.* The ground of politics is always
a division of action.† *All* constitutional powers—large or microscopic,
explicitly granted or implied—exist within it.‡ More precisely, power issues from the division of action through political processes. Power is not
an "input." Nor can it ever project from a monadic source, like radiation
from a bar of kryptonite. It is *in the process* of their constitution that warmaking powers shift towards the Executive. This effect, too, needs to
be stated more precisely: as the division of action which constitutes the
warmaking power is reconfigured, it can become overwhelmingly coded
in common sense as *presidential.* This may qualify as "constitutional dictatorship," but not as despotism.[14]

---

* Obviously, conflict is also decisive *within* branches; witness not just the contentions of the
legislative process, but, e.g., the twisted path to major foreign policy in the administration of
George W. Bush. This fact does not bear directly on the discussion here.

† As mentioned earlier, the "division of action" refers to the fact that all acts are what they are
by virtue of the actor's situation in a world of other persons and things.

‡ This is true of all power relevant to politics. Specifically concerning constitutional powers:
because the Executive is led by one person, the constitutive role of political processes in presidential power is less obvious than, for example, the way even the most precise and explicit
grants of power to a multiple-member congress will issue from political processes. It is, I think,
clarifying to take Article 1 as the model for Article 2 and—as I have done here—for the relation
between branches.

Stay, for now, with the familiar image of a *balance of power*. Which shifts in the balance between branches of government would be constitutional and which not?[15] The alarming fact—which can be traced back to the division of action but which is not identical with it—is that no fixed rule can settle this oft-times urgent question. The threshold will depend on how numerous circumstantial conditions enter constitutional processes.

One of these conditions is the very question *Is this war or not?* For the Soldier or the Casualty there is usually just one response. The position of the Citizen yields something more ambiguous. Although the Citizen's appeal to the Constitution will always be fluid,* it is also bound to be most literal. The desire for principle—to end the regress of debate, to settle conflict without further conflict—is great. By odd contrast, those who enter the discursive zone of the Constitution through the narrow door of the law seek to expand debate, not to end it. The Citizen navigates in the passage between the safe harbor of principle and stormy process.

Although tensions around warmaking power have stretched across most of our history, they reached an important climax as reactions against the oppressive climate of the Cold War converged with an increasingly unpopular military adventure in Vietnam.† A moral opposition said it was unethical, a military opposition said it was impractical, a political opposition said it was unconstitutional. Although President Johnson had campaigned against Barry Goldwater promising peace, by his inauguration in 1965 escalation of the war was well under way. Just that year American engagement expanded eightfold.‡ The vocal minority seeking to end the war grew exponentially. We can assume that few listeners were surprised when, that July, one Mrs. Betty Compton stood as a "private individual" at a Wisconsin "town meeting" to say that "our policy is illegal, in the first place, because we are engaging in full-scale warfare without any formal declaration of war by the Congress of the United States."[16]

The logic of this claim seems simple enough: no one then, or as the number of American troops in Vietnam grew to more than half a million in the next three years, could reasonably claim that our presence there was anything but war, yet there had been no declaration of war, and therefore the use of our armed forces was an illegal abuse of power.[17]

---

* That is, the appeal will be more topical than juridical.
† On the Cold War as a system of domestic political culture, see chapter 5.
‡ From 23,300 to 184,300 military personnel.

This recurring popular view was regularly carried into federal courts after 1965.[18] It never passed the portal of the Supreme Court. Each rejection of certiorari tacitly affirmed an idea prevalent among federal judges: "The distinction between a declaration of war and a cooperative action by the Legislative and Executive with respect to military activities in foreign countries is the very essence of what is meant by a political question."[19] In other words, the objections to the war could not be settled as a matter of law; the conflict would therefore have to be fought out between the other two branches of government. As Justice Douglas dissented in each case—insisting that the question was clearly drawn and it was the duty of the Court to decide the constitutionality of the war[20]—the majority of his colleagues on the Supreme Court were unmoved. However, this view seems to have gradually shifted the approach of other judges. Federal courts after 1970 began to touch on the merits of Betty Compton's question.* The "political question" doctrine had justified their inaction, and they now came tentatively out from behind that screen. New decisions shed more light on the basic political processes involved in the warmaking power. Their position with respect to those processes still did not favor Mrs. Compton's view.[21] Whichever branch had taken the first step, once "Congress has ratified the Executive's initiatives by appropriating billions of dollars to carry on our military operation in Southeast Asia and by extending the Military Selective Service Act with full knowledge that persons conscripted under that Act had been, and would continue to be, sent to Vietnam," the process conditions for constitutionality are satisfied.[22] The Constitution does not render judgment. The practical outcome is determined by "concord" between Congress and the Executive, and this precludes even the Judiciary from settling the question with one decisive stroke.[23]

Is it war or not? When the direction of power centers on answers to this question, resulting "allotments" generally favor the Executive. Indeed, the "balance" can go very far to his side without negating the basic division of action and without turning the power thus constituted to despotism. How things go in this narrowly construed political realm depended then, as it depends now, primarily on the "attitude" of Congress towards the President.[24] In the 1960s that attitude was, long and by large,

---

* They found the courage to do this, however, only after troop levels were down by half from their peak.

concord or *agreement*. Once joined, from a constitutional point of view it no longer mattered what had brought Congress and the president together, or even that the pretext for congressional affirmation of the war—events supposed to have occurred in the Tonkin Gulf in 1964—was found later to be "fraudulent" and denied by new legislation.[25] The war was undertaken "politically" but—and this is the point—*within* the ample, and sometimes dangerously ample, framework set by the Constitution. Only a different *political* constellation would have made the war *illegal**—for example, if Congress had gone beyond the belated and superficial gesture of repealing the Tonkin Gulf Resolution to vote unequivocally to terminate hostilities, to withhold all funding, to interrupt conscription, and the Executive had continued the war with secret funds in collusion with the armed forces.[26]

To say that apparently unchecked warmaking power remains within the boundaries of the Constitution does not tell on which constitutional terrain it resides. Here the unusual way of thinking about war that I introduced in chapter 2—the *civic war* increasingly central to the experience of the American citizen—comes into view again. The idea that "war is the continuation of politics" allows us to connect immediate concerns after September 11th—the transformation of terror into war—with the most encompassing sense of politics to which I allude at various points in this book.[†] While the Citizen had better be interested in making clear the strong relationship between a civic-oriented representation of war—*civic war*—and the basic conditions of politics, I ask that for the next few pages you think in terms of the former without yet allowing the latter to retake the stage. Maintain for another moment the focus on aspects of constitutional politics. Problems within this narrower perspective will soon enough overflow its boundaries and it will become clear that a single version of politics is too precarious a basis for the position of the Citizen.[‡]

---

* Obviously, this point is made from the perspective of domestic and constitutional politics. For millions of Vietnamese or thousands of Americans killed in combat, proving the war to be without constitutional grounds would have been a meaningless exercise. From the point of view of international law, the legality of the Vietnam War was an important question for many groups of people, but it was not decisive in the context we consider here.

† *The Position of the Citizen* will elaborate this sense of politics in detail.

‡ The distinction and coincidence of multiple versions of politics is part of the American political tradition.

Consistent with the political character of war, the warmaking power is a political process. It does not issue from the authoritative decisions of one office. It is, rather, the result of many decisions, large and small, across variegated institutional fields. Viewed in light of the pragmatic question *What actually produces the effects we recognize as war?* this scene cannot be neatly divided into "branches of government," no less into distinct types of power. This complicates further the familiar vocabulary for thinking about the power to make war.

Now, one may admit that the constitutional assignment of war powers to one or the other branch of government is indistinct and nevertheless conclude that this does not much matter. It has often been said that the Constitution does not prohibit an orderly process of *delegation*.[27] Where time is short and action urgent, a balance may be achieved as Congress *delegates* its portion of the warmaking power—whatever that portion is—to the President.[28] The Vietnam period has been described in such terms. Perhaps we live in similar times?

What I want to underscore here is that appeal to an image of delegation is based on a view of power that is mistaken *in general*. Political power does not come in neatly bound packets that can be passed from one hand to another. All political power is a configuration within the division of action. It involves complex deployments of human energies; the emergence and direction of such energies are bound by beliefs and values, and these are ultimately constituted in language relationships. To map, as the Constitution does, the use of human energies according to the demands of different and often contradictory governmental functions like Executive and Legislative does not obviate the diffuse conflict inherent throughout and across these processes. Indeed, drawing precise boundaries often focuses and intensifies conflict. Thus, where *delegation* implies an initial clear-cut distribution, we have already seen that the Constitution sets Congress and the Executive within one fluid and shifting division of action, and it weaves deliberation over and application of warmaking power into irreducibly political processes. Even if the term *delegation* performs particular rhetorical functions within those processes, it is not an adequate description of them.

Once we are inside the enormously complex social fact of war, no single decision or command is capable of terminating ongoing contest at all levels. With every decision, conflicts shift ground. Conflicts are not so much remapped over the bright lines of institutional boundaries as relocated across tenuous thresholds of common sense.* This is where the position of the Citizen is contiguous with every other social role. Of course an official decision may change the formulation of a problem. But the practical effect that or any decision has on conflict—escalating or relaxing it, augmenting or diminishing resistance—depends on judgments made by citizens.[29] For the most part, these judgments are representations of common sense. That is, they are collective factors that change over the longer run, not in the instant of the decision. Every command must mobilize a vast army of loose discipline. The Constitution structures the relation between these two temporalities; it brings the institutional map and the thresholds of judgment into communication.

This fabric of judgment, energy, language, and institution is the background against which it may be said—more pointedly—that the Constitution is "an invitation to struggle for the privilege of directing American foreign policy" and that this is effectively "a *divided* power."[30] That is why it is never sufficient for one or a few congressional voices, no less a Mrs. Betty Compton or a plaintiff before the bar, to call a president out of bounds when he dispatches troops without a declaration of war.[31] An Executive action is only *really* out of bounds if those who object *successfully mobilize to win a vote—any kind of vote—against the President*. By so doing, they move the boundary of acceptable action back away from where the President is reaching to get his way. This takes his hands off resources. It interrupts his commands. It tarnishes his reputation. In the instance where no one can muster this kind of resistance, as was true during most of the Vietnam War, it would be just as misleading to say that alternative powers, like those of Congress, had been usurped by or delegated to the Executive as it is to say that the President has become a despot. Even when senators and representatives are deceived into agreement, as elected rather than hereditary officeholders, they remain responsible for their failure to impede destructive Executive projects.

Thus far I have emphasized the fluidity of the field between the Executive and Congress. But from division and conflict around the issue of war ensue moments of determinate result.† In practice, each such resultant

---

* This refers to the rhetorical "cement" that makes the State operative. N.b. that institutional boundaries are also ways of forming common sense.

† Not, as one is often inclined to say, *consensus*.

is a presidential power. On the one hand, it is a composite. On the other hand, it seems to emanate—in part because of the inherently initiative posture of the one who performs it—as a whole from "the authority of the President." This is more than just an appearance. The President's authority feeds back into "Congress's attitude towards the President." It nurtures particular agreements. Agreement gives the Executive yet more authority. So although the quantity of Executive power is composed within the constitutional division of action, it varies significantly with presidential ambition and reach.[32] As the President operates within a complex and fluid institutional and cultural setting, this striking fact emerges: his authority "is largely determined by the President himself."[33] As long as no one stands in his way. As long as Congress remains complicit.

To answer the question *Is it war or not?* one needs, therefore, to move eccentrically to another question: *Why does Congress agree with the President?* Assume for the moment that simple consensus is not the answer.* The motives of such agreement cannot be reduced to misinformation about gunboats in the Tonkin Gulf or "weapons of mass destruction" in Iraq.† Here we need to take another step—as I promised above we would—back towards a more comprehensive view of politics.

In 1966, Chairman J. William Fulbright and a handful of his colleagues on the Senate Committee on Foreign Relations found that "without there ever having been a national decision" or "a national commitment," America was in fact at war.[34] Looking back at the Tonkin Gulf Resolution, they aimed "to disassociate" themselves "from any interpretation that it was a declaration of war."[35] Their position implied a debate that the fait accompli made difficult; it seemed to many beside the point.[36] Fulbright of course recognized that the congressional majority was relentlessly in agreement with the "Presidential war." Thus he sought to broaden resistance to encroachment on and abuse of *his* powers within the frame of constitutional politics. The committee became a site of dialogue between *institutional forms* and *the judgments of common sense.* The process began with televised hearings of experts like

---

* The question would not arise if it was. On the "dog that doesn't bark" as a problem of politics, see *Political Pathologies of the Citizen.*

† Nevertheless, the purveyors of such misinformation continue to believe that it can be effective, as when in January 2008 the Pentagon promulgated a clearly false story in which Iranian boats were said to have threatened U.S. warships in the Strait of Hormuz (Porter 2008).

Secretary of State Dean Rusk, Lieutenant General James Gavin, General Maxwell Taylor, and former ambassador George Kennan. The nation heard authoritative alternatives to the President's account of *why we are in Vietnam*.[37] For the next five years, Fulbright's committee kept up a "frank and open discussion," refusing to ignore or "paper over . . . differences within the body politic."[38] By 1971 the central question before the committee had shifted dramatically from *Why are we there?* to *How can we get out?*[39]

Senator Fulbright's purpose, one might say, was not to demonstrate that the war *had been* illegal. He undertook to shift the thresholds of common sense and, in that way, form a new political constellation within which the war *would become unconstitutional*.

Caught in the tempo of minority resistance, the "powerful" Fulbright displays his incapacity. "If I knew how to bring what you have said . . . to the attention of the people, I would do it," but "I don't know how." The "only way I have . . . is to hold these hearings and to give the people an opportunity to see and hear you." He regrets deeply that he cannot ensure his witnesses wide exposure, but "only the office of the President has that capacity." Fulbright wreaks his frustration: "All I can do is give the opportunity" for *you* to speak.[40]

This is, of course, exactly the way to play the game. All the witnesses' voices became Fulbright's. Not surprisingly, the senator's true aptitude occasionally appeared on the scene. In 1971 committee member Claiborne Pell took a moment to admonish the young John Kerry, who had come to testify on behalf of the Vietnam Veterans against the War. "Chairman Fulbright," he said, "deserves a huge debt of gratitude from you and every one of your men" because until he opened hearings on the war in 1966 "the word 'peace' was a dirty word."* Not only did Fulbright take "public opinion at that time and turn it around," he created "the climate that produced President Johnson's abdication."[41]

Where Fulbright sought final effect, however, was in Congress. He counted on something that even the hardened cynic will allow—that senators and representatives are susceptible to "public opinion."† "Pub-

---

* In September 2007 a pathetically reduced John Kerry stood by as a young man who tried to question him about the war in Iraq was brutalized by police, "tasered," and carried off to jail.
† I use the word *susceptible* rather than the word *responsible* here so as to avoid a longer and more complicated discussion. Likewise, the phrase "public opinion" is used in the same loose and skeptical way I used "public sphere" above.

lic opinion" is not simply a set of propositions. It is a social fact that appears when propositions are brought forward for display in a certain way. "Public opinion" often stands outside politics. It enters political life when it corresponds with the specifically political speech act I have referred to as *publicizing*.*

As I wrote in chapter 1, the simplest definition of this publicizing is the use of speech to implicate a third party in a two-way dispute. This practice is a starting mechanism for a wide range of political activities and relationships in modern societies. Whether this occurs in the most local or the most global situations, publicizing is a crucial way to constitute a loosely bound group, a "public," whose involvement in an ongoing dispute changes to a greater or lesser extent the overall balance of forces at play.

I bring *publicizing* back into the story at this point to further qualify the description of how contest figures in the political relationship between branches of government. Recall that my first approximate statement of the intermediate field between branches of government paired contest with negotiation.† I now want to specify my shorthand use of the word *negotiation* in light of the *publicizing speech act*. Political relationships are rarely conducted directly between two parties in conflict. Yet we usually think of negotiation as an encounter between *I* and *thou* or as a subdued duel. Here I want to underscore the way that crucial alterations in the balance of forces between the two sides occur as one party or the other attempts to implicate a third party in the dispute. This is the essentially triadic structure of publicizing, and it recurs at every level: around the President's conference table, in the congressional committee or caucus, on a panel of peers like the Supreme Court, within and across the layers of bureaucracy, between agencies, among branches of government, and so forth.‡ It is important to emphasize this because it shows that, strictly speaking, politics is not a distinct sphere of activity; institutions and their societies are threaded through and through with politics.

---

* This is actually a rather complicated point: "public opinion" properly understood derives from *publicizing*; otherwise it is a misnomer for a range of things from common sense to politically sterile personal expression.
† See the fourth paragraph of this chapter.
‡ Formalized mediation is a different sort of process, starting from side agreements that come to the center in the practice of dispute. The process is depoliticized to the extent that key agreements, concerning e.g. the agenda or willingness to accept the result, are presupposed.

During the Vietnam War, the publicizing structure of action was particularly evident at the level of the nation as a whole.* In the early years of escalation, the President thrust onto the stage of "public opinion" propositions drawn from the ideological well of the Cold War. President Johnson's State of the Union address in 1965 and his first major policy speech concerning Vietnam, on April 7 of that same year, were perfect specimens of this kind of mobilization of common sense. This rhetorical fact exerted—indirectly, through "the people"—a range of pressures on senators and representatives that held a majority of them in line with the President. While I am not saying that other factors—like raw self-interest—played no part, the position of the President comes with a particularly potent conjuring force. In Justice Jackson's powerful words from 1952, "executive power has the advantage of concentration in a single head in whose choice the whole nation has a part, making him the focus of public hopes and expectations. In drama, magnitude and finality his decisions so far overshadow any others that almost alone he fills the public eye and ear."[42]

As the war continued, the minority in Congress needed to shift the threshold of common sense before common sense itself could be mobilized on behalf of the opposition to the war. Publicizing speech acts—including the Fulbright committee hearings—served as the starting mechanism for renewed contest with the Executive. The result clearly manifested the ultimate dependence of all constitutionally mandated warmaking power on *extrajuridical* but nonetheless *constitutional* factors.† The key would become the accelerating withdrawal of citizen support for the war.

Much of what I have written so far in this chapter points in the following direction. Despite the apparently self-evident constitutional clause (Article 1, § 8) granting power "to declare war" to Congress, that power may effectively shift to the Executive without any violation of the Constitution. Underlying this movement is the primary fact that all powers are constituted within a "division of action." Only sometimes, deriving from that fact, with reference to past conditions or future projects, or in the heat of an ongoing conflict, will one party or another interpret any

---

* N.b. that this way of constituting power is not inherent in democracy alone; it is characteristic of all regimes. Despite the generality of this fact, its manifestations in nondemocratic regimes, or even outside the United States, are not relevant here. It is well-known that the 1960s saw an extraordinary convergence of cultural resources in favor of publicizing speech acts.

† This hybrid phrase forecasts the broader view of politics to come; in the final analysis, I take the directed energies of citizens to be an essential part of constitutional politics.

momentary composition or deployment of the division of action under the rubric of *power checked* or *balanced* or *delegated*. For or against, only in one way can the Constitution determine if it is *war* we make in Vietnam or in Iraq or against "Terror," and what consequence that will have for the organization of power itself. That is by setting politics in motion and awaiting the result.

In that process, war, and therefore the responsibility for the future of war, derives from neither the unmitigated "will" of the Executive nor from the unitary voice of the Legislator. The division of action that leads towards war or away from it inevitably includes the Citizen. The Citizen's weight in this balance increases with his or her energy and voice, or decreases with passivity and silence.* Either way, the Citizen's responsibility remains.[43]

This returns us, along a rather different route, to *civic war* and a point passed over quickly above. War is not an external variable or input into a mechanical political system. To name *war*, to consider it, to lend oneself to or against it, is part of the fabric of politics.† Thus there is a strong relationship between the civic-oriented experience and representation of war and the basic conditions of politics. Nothing is more important for democracy than remembering that war is not just a "warfighting"‡ event. It is twice a *social fact* for the Citizen, once as concerns everyday life together with others, once when it presses on the experience of conflict.§

This perspective on warmaking power in constitutional politics would not bring solace to Mrs. Betty Compton. It does not deal a trump card to Congress. But it does support hesitation before a presumptuous Executive.[44]

Here the *antipolitics politics* of the administration of George W. Bush provides a telling example. For it is not only by presenting the current wars as *of necessity* and not *of choice* that the party of Bush denied the political character of war itself. They also insisted that the priority of Executive authority over political disagreement is a constitutional imperative.¶

---

* As opposed to the common view, *money* is more like energy than voice. The confusion of money with voice—as partly suggested by *Buckley v. Valeo* 424 U.S. 1 (1976)—impedes citizen judgment against corruption.

† As I have said elsewhere, this is not an affirmation of the Hobbesian commonplace.

‡ Again, this is the new term of art for direct and violent military engagement; see note at the end of chapter 2.

§ We shall not consider here how one's own and another's experience of war is deployed in political conflict.

¶ That they typically did so preemptively, anticipating resistance that had yet to fully materialize, only strengthens my point.

Dick Cheney laid down this apparently Hamiltonian line long before taking the office of vice president.[45] In 1982 Representative Cheney held that war is a type of decision "we look to the President to make ... [one that is] naturally made by a commander-in-chief rather than a legislative body." He added—true and ominous—that "the declaration of war is almost an outmoded concept."[46] In 1987, as he attempted to shield covert and illegal activities in Iran and Nicaragua from congressional oversight, Cheney asserted that "Congress must recognize that effective foreign policy requires, *and the Constitution mandates*, the President to be the country's foreign policy leader."[47] After 2001 this view continued to be a centerpiece of his administration. It is, obviously, an attempt to preemptively settle the very issue it raises. It has no decisive constitutional effect. Its force—which is all too real—is rhetorical.[48]

The Citizen—implicated in the political constitution of war at least through language and action as I have described, and in other ways as well—had better take as part of ongoing political contests any claim made by a branch of government to have definitive warmaking power. In positioning oneself in and around these contests, skepticism against all sorts of depoliticizing assertions (e.g. "this is a war *of necessity* and not *of choice*") is a first step. Even this seemingly small gesture is a positive drag on the effectiveness of such assertions precisely because their tacit aim is to move some people or to inhibit others from taking action. This simple stance, exceedingly difficult to grasp, is, almost immediately, if microscopically, repoliticizing. Without resistance, claims that depoliticize the direction of power easily advance and enter common sense. They are, so to speak, self-fulfilling prophesies.

This is another reason why, even in—especially in—the American constitutional regime, the political pathology of speechlessness is so dangerous. It mattered that Democrats and Republicans alike, first in 2001, then in 2002, then in 2003, and in every year forward, affirmed in law the delirious programs of the Executive. This was no delegation of power. It was a successful opportunistic use of the failed courage of a natural opposition.* For how power is—or fails to be—divided gains in importance when power is used. Shifts in the power to make war form opportunity. They are appropriable. They become extraordinary vehicles *for every kind* of project, no matter how tangential to the stated mission.

---

* We return to the topics of opportunism and abdication in the following chapters.

This familiar principle—the full force of which begins to come to light when war is understood as a social fact that "continues politics"—was perfectly evident to George W. Bush. He extrapolated it from his father's experience with a brutal clarity of vision reminiscent of vanguard communist leaders of the last century like Leon Trotsky. As Bush told an interviewer in 1999,

> One of the keys to being seen as a great leader is to be seen as a commander-in-chief.... My father had all this political capital built up when he drove the Iraqis out of Kuwait and he wasted it.... If I have a chance to invade... if I had that much capital, I'm not going to waste it. I'm going to get everything passed that I want to get passed and I'm going to have a successful presidency.[49]

In chapter 2 I traced the transformation of terror into war through a sequence of questions. *Is it war?* originated from the everyday experience of the Citizen. Recalling a principle first introduced in chapter 1—citizens live in the flow of history—shifted the question to *When is it war?* We pursued the popular analogy between September 11th and Pearl Harbor and, finding it profoundly misleading, shifted the ground again. Asking *For whom is it war?* brought to light a variety of "subject positions" inherent in the complex social fact of war. The position of the Citizen, which has priority in this inquiry, is informed by the other ones. A "position" is a social role and relationship, but it is also, literally, a location. Thus, to ask *For whom is it war?* is also to ask *Where is it war?* With this question we again crossed paths with topics from chapter 1: the Terrorist attacks the "public sphere" in which the energies and beliefs of citizens come together. That is where we should look first to understand the wars of September 11th. That is why I coined and insist on the idea of *civic war.* Orienting inquiry in this way reasserts the priority of the Citizen's experience and advances the central idea that war takes on specific characteristics when it is entangled with terror.* It brings forward, in turn, two minor themes present from the outset. The first is that war is a fluid social fact; its form and content are contingent on circumstances and depend on the perspective from which one encounters it. The second is that war

---

* This is why, despite certain overlaps between them, I insist on distinguishing *civic war* from "total war." I will revisit this point below.

is primarily a political constellation, in which the warfighting enterprise plays a spectacular and sometimes devastating, but nonetheless secondary, role. Within the set of relationships that constitute *war*, the Terrorist has posed a question *for us—What shall we do?* The answer is modulated by a further question—*What is at stake?*

It should be clear by this point that the inquiry has shifted away from the "enemy" and entirely to "our" side.* We may take stock of the interests and intentions of others, but the final measure of *our own action is our own life.* Moreover, there are no stakes in the past. Our people and buildings are already felled. What heads the list of stakes *now* is a self-image, a myth of America that people take personally, effective at home and abroad, without which concerted action requires self-defeating degrees of coercion.† In the experience of the Citizen this mythic common sense organizes the national division of action. But in the symbol and fact of the Executive, it has emerged since September 11th as a pathology of undivided action: "manifest destiny" reappears in the swagger of George W. Bush.⁵⁰ "Public opinion"—one (but only one) key collective representation of common sense—integrates these two opposing faces of the same historical moment. Thus we may return to the very first question—*Is it war?*—with a different kind of answer. Seen from the position of the Citizen—which is to say, from the center of everyday life together—war is not a fixed set of attributes (e.g. massive use of violence, transgression of borders, violation of or adherence to laws, etc.) but rather a pragmatic situation in which agency remains decisive.‡ To a large extent, outcomes in this situation pivot on the use and abuse of an image of national "will."§

Still, the answer to the question *What–when–for whom–where is war?* continues to divide naturally into two fairly distinguishable parts. On one side, it is a warfighting enterprise abroad; on the other side, it is a domestic way of life. Each has its specific means, discourse, subject positions, locations, temporality, and, finally, particular place within the constellations of political forces. To give priority to politics is not to exclude the military. It requires, however, that we interpret this realm of violence

---

*Arrival at this perspective is consistent with and justified by the argument in chapter 2.
† I actually think this self-image is too complex to state in one breath. But let's call it "Greatness" as a shorthand.
‡ Although certainly not in the sense that I or we simply get what we want, as or when we want it.
§ This is because where *agency* is decisive, the *self-conception of agency* is also decisive.

through the facts of the everyday life of the Citizen and not, as is so common, the other way around.

Unfortunately, this is where things get even more complicated. For the *version of politics* in play at any given moment is another major variable. What kind and context of political activity is or could be operative now?

We have seen in the first part of this chapter that to answer the question *Is it war?* is to set precisely this agenda. As we look further into this idea, it will be helpful, once again, to narrow the scope of inquiry. Our point of entry will be the vision expressed in the remarks by George W. Bush quoted just above. President Bush, here and elsewhere, made perfectly clear that the pivotal topic, the decisive obsession, of those who from January 2001 occupied the Executive branch is this: What becomes possible *with* war? This opportunistic perspective has a pronounced corrupting influence on the political division of action. And it has powerfully inflected the position of the Citizen after September 11th.

I have urged the Citizen to adopt a wide view of war, understanding it as *civic war*, a "continuation of politics." In this view, *war* is integrated in roughly the same way that *politics* is integrated within the range of relationships of everyday life. That is where it touches us; that is where we effect it or are affected by it. This connection through the Citizen to everyday life appears even within the narrow frame of politics that is directly organized by the Constitution. The sketch of *war powers* in the first part of this chapter aimed to make this clear. However, the distinction just formulated between the scene of expeditionary warfighting and the "home front" points in an additional direction.

The Constitution also explicitly and implicitly projects *emergency powers* that may be exercised "in the event that the nation is threatened by crisis, exigency, or emergency circumstances." These powers "are not limited to military or war situations."[51] Before the First World War, emergency powers in the United States were sometimes exercised in the manner of an open-ended Executive "prerogative." A justification for this was famously known to the Founders from the earlier writings of John Locke.[52] Over the course of the twentieth century such discretionary powers did not disappear. They were, however, increasingly channeled through statutes and constraints. The National Emergencies Act of 1976 now requires a formal declaration of emergency and delineation of the scope of application before emergency powers are brought to bear.[53]

Some "are continuously available to the President with little or no quali-fication." Others "exist on a standby basis and remain dormant" until the presidential declaration is made. Under emergency powers "the Presi-dent may seize property, organize and control the means of production, seize commodities, assign military forces abroad, institute martial law, seize and control all transportation and communication, regulate the operation of private enterprise, restrict travel, and, in a variety of ways, control the lives of United States citizens."[54]

At least provisionally, then, it may be said that there has been a shift from *exceptional* to *routinized* and more explicitly *codified* uses of emer-gency powers.* In this process the difference between *emergency powers* and *powers brought to bear in emergency situations* has been obscured.

In the remainder of this chapter, I will argue that this distinction should weigh heavily in efforts by American citizens to understand war as a "con-tinuation of politics" and thereby shape the position of the Citizen after September 11th. My argument will take us through pages that recall some relevant aspects of our history. This, in turn, will gradually bring us back into the discussion of the Citizen's experience of war and emergency.

Very loosely speaking, *war powers* bear on expeditionary warfighting and *emergency powers* bear on the "home front," or the context of civil society within which military action initiates, is sustained, and produces its political effects. How we experience and understand the relationship between these two types of powers shapes the position of the Citizen.

Although it has become common—by habit, history, or a certain Hobbesian logic—to suppose that *emergency powers* grow out from a more fundamental power to make *war*, I want now to suggest that the opposite is true and more important: *war powers* should be understood as a species of *emergency powers*.[†]

---

* We shall see that to refer to this as simply a shift from *extraconstitutional* to *constitutional* power would be to miss one of its most significant aspects. My objections to the language of "the exception" are sketched out at the end of this chapter.

† Keeping in mind, however, that *emergency powers* are not construed here according to the old image of the unified sovereign "will," but in recognition of the basic fact that all powers emerge within a complex division of action. In other words, everything said in the first part of this chapter about the issue of power from constitutional process should now be taken to apply to emergency powers as well. My point here also assumes that war powers generally coincide with emergency powers: while one can envisage a war that does not evoke emergency powers (the American invasion of Grenada might be seen this way), this would be a rare and uninformative exception.

Before I go on to show why this is so, let me say that there are good reasons to believe the opposite. At the end of World War II and the advent of the nuclear age it seemed entirely obvious that "war, public war, total war, is still . . . *the* emergency *par excellence*."[55] The structure of federal law, especially as it has developed after that period, points the same way. While chapters on "War Powers" and "National Emergencies" appear side by side in the *U.S. Code*, they are both under title 50—"War and National Defense."[56] This reflects a familiar consistency. Americans have often interpreted or justified *emergency powers* in terms of war.[57] The best-known example of this was the suspension of habeas corpus by President Lincoln during the Civil War. Initially Lincoln expanded state power over citizens by stretching the constitutional role of Commander-in-chief. His action has convincingly been called purely dictatorial.[58]

What happened next complicates the scene and will be important for events I relate in the following pages. In fact, Lincoln's action was not incompatible with the mixed character of *emergency powers*, which quickly reasserted itself. In 1863 Congress authorized the President to again suspend habeas corpus in his role as chief executive. The power was refined by the Supreme Court in 1866 in a decision that imposed some restrictions on Executive action; nonetheless, the power to suspend was generally affirmed in a separate opinion by the Chief Justice. Congress made further similar adjustments over the next decade.[59] While in each of these variations *war* appears to have been the motive or vehicle for emergency powers, some questions are in order. First, what is the relevant social fact of war, and what types of emergency activity does it precede? Was the point of departure for the suspensions, even in the larger context of a civil war, military crisis or a general change in the Citizen's relation to the body politic during wartime? These hesitations support the approach to *war* and to *war powers* I have already articulated. That should lead us in a somewhat different direction. Moreover, even when, as the Executive asserts itself under the banner of *emergency*, initiative and energy pass into the hands of the President, the power that results is nevertheless composite. There may be a monolithic aspect to Executive action, but even that typically serves by indirection the President's own projects. Charisma produces new public pressure that edges Congress towards cooperation. Occurring within constitutional processes such joint operations of the various branches may have a dictatorial tenor but they are not despotic.

Indeed, the most familiar milestones in the public history of broad emergency powers in the United States are not so much characterized by dictatorial Executive orders[60] as by infamous laws—from the Sedition Act of 1798 to the Espionage ("Trading with the Enemy") and Sedition Acts of World War I to the McCarran Act of 1950, with its provisions for declaration of an "Internal Security Emergency" and "Emergency Detention."[61]

This suggests the complex background of fact and common sense against which I now want to advance a more subtle genealogical version of my claim. Again, it concerns the relationship between *war* and *emergency powers*. After the Civil War, and with lingering memory of that devastating conflict, *emergency powers* shifted here and there into the metaphorical gap that joins *war* to other realms of social life. They did not, however, *need* war to operate. The last decades of the nineteenth century saw "an increasing tendency of society to breed crises."[62] These crises become the objects of emergency power. Nowhere was this tendency more present than in the proliferating industrial conflict that will serve as example here.*

Railroads, a swift ramp to the top of society for "robber barons," had become the nervous system of the nation. They were therefore also a lever for action by organized labor. During the "great upheaval" of 1877 President Hayes assumed unique authority to declare martial law. He dispatched troops around the country to battle striking railroad workers.† In each case he did so at the behest of state officials.[63] The strikes ended but the conflict continued. Consolidation of vast wealth and monopoly powers in the 1880s—especially in the form of "trusts" and "holding companies"—captured public imagination and sharpened demands for further federal regulation of the economy.[64] A comprehensive Interstate Commerce Act, focused on transportation, was passed in 1887, followed by the first federal labor relations law in 1888.[65] Two years later Congress passed with just one dissenting vote the very general Sherman Anti-Trust Act.[66]

Still, popular outrage against and resistance to Gilded Age hubris increased. So did social disorder. An accelerating depression in 1893 led to steep wage cuts. The first large-scale industrial union in the United States

---

* Note the rhetorically significant fact that responses to such conflict were often stated in terms of "industrial peace."

† In some places, local militias called to fight strikers had gone over to their side.

was formed under the leadership of Eugene Debs; the American Railroad Union grew exponentially in the following months. As the labor law of 1888 "failed in its purpose,"[67] a growing demand for "industrial democracy" exploded in 1894 in a wave of strikes. A "model" factory town just outside Chicago, ruled over by railroad-car manufacturer George Pullman, quickly became the center of national attention.[68] The federal government responded to the Pullman strike as they had in 1877. However, this time the state of Illinois refused to call on Washington. President Cleveland sent in troops anyway.

The restraint of Illinois's governor John Peter Altgeld had been intentional. While ready to use police and local militias to maintain public order, he, unlike most of his peers, had seen fit to tell his militia commanders that "it is not the business of the soldiers to act as custodians or guards of private property."[69] According to the governor, President Cleveland had acted directly against the interests and progressive public policy of the state of Illinois. Altgeld's forceful reaction illuminates this pivotal moment.

In a pair of telegraph messages to the President, Altgeld claimed that Cleveland was "in violation of a basic principle" of the Constitution: he had no authority to circumvent "local self-government."[70] "You calmly assume," wrote Altgeld, "that the executive can send Federal troops into any community in the United States at his pleasure ... under pretense of enforcing some law.... If this is the law, then the principle of self-government either never did exist in this country or else has been destroyed ... [for] it is also a fundamental principle in our government that except in times of war the military shall be subordinate to the civil authority."[71] Even if the crisis at Pullman was grave—and the governor had determined that it was not—the 1861 statute supposed to authorize federal intervention was "in reality a war measure."[72] Thus what especially concerned Altgeld was the field in which this novel power had been applied: "Federal interference with industrial disturbances in the various States is certainly a new departure, and it opens up so large a field that it will require a very little stretch of authority to absorb to itself all the details of local government."[73] If, as President Cleveland's actions suggested, "the executive is the sole judge, and nobody else has any right to interfere or even inquire about it ... then the executive can ... order troops to as many places as he wishes ... and have them act not under the civil officers ... but directly under military orders from Washington, and there is not in the Constitution or laws, whether written or unwritten, any limitation or restraint upon his power. . . . [H]is Will is the sole guide." Altgeld concluded that "this assumption as to the power of the executive is certainly new," and he "respectfully submit[ted] that it is not the law of the land."[74]

Altgeld did not prevail. Less than a year later, the Supreme Court upheld Cleveland's position against Progressives like Altgeld in the case *In re Debs*. With breathtaking directness Justice Brewer wrote that "the strong arm of the national government may be put forth to brush away all obstructions to the freedom of interstate commerce or the transportation of the mails. If the emergency arises, the army of the Nation, and all its militia, are at the service of the Nation to compel obedience to its laws."[75] This judicial alignment with the Executive, together with subsequent events, effectively showed that Altgeld's objections were out of step with the times.[76]

Nonetheless, Altgeld's objections go to the heart of the matter. The Executive *emergency power* was increasing precisely because it was gaining independence from *war powers* in the narrow sense of the term. What is important here, if we want to see the continuing relevance of this history for America after September 11th, is that, notwithstanding and indeed concurrent with this divergence, many continued to seek and find justification of *emergency* in *war*.

This story increases in importance as it continues to unfold in the early twentieth century. Similar legislation appeared without the sharp-edged rubric of emergency. The pattern of federal regulation of the railroads advanced. What had begun as a general concern with "just charges" in 1887 became in the Hepburn Act of 1906 authority to establish, following a complaint, a particular rate.[77] Four years later the Mann-Elkins Act required railroads to prove their rates were free from the effects of monopoly power.[78] In parallel with these impositions on commercial markets, the Erdman Act (1898) opened the possibility for federal arbitration of railroad labor disputes at the request of either capital or labor.[79] While certain provisions were struck down by the Supreme Court ten years later, a dissenting opinion by Justice Holmes foresaw legislation that would—at least briefly—favor unions.[80] For reasons we shall come to in a moment, the role of the federal government was cranked up when the Department of Labor Act of 1913 granted to the secretary of labor the "power to act as mediator and to appoint commissioners of conciliation in labor disputes whenever in his judgment the interests of industrial peace may require it to be done,"[81] and Congress gave the initiative for mediation of railroad disputes to the Executive branch.[82] Although there would be no general federal minimum wage laws until 1938, the idea was in the air, and Massachusetts passed the first state law of this type in 1912.[83] These laws, and others like them, set the ample stage of ordinary political life on which appeared developments in the relation between *war* and *emergency powers* especially relevant to our times.

In early September 1916, Congress passed the Adamson Act.[84] It established an eight-hour work day and fixed wage levels in the railroad industry. In this respect it seems to have grown directly from the trends sketched above: a relatively restrained but increasing effort by the State to find an equitable balance in power relations in the everyday work process. What makes the Adamson Act worthy of special attention here was its immediate context, to which the law itself did not explicitly refer.

In fact, the Adamson Act was a direct intervention by Congress into ongoing efforts by President Wilson to mediate a dispute between railroad owners and their employees. The dispute was clearly headed towards a national strike. A precedent for Wilson's involvement had been set, following the Erdman Act, when in 1902 President Roosevelt had personally tried to mediate a major coal strike.[85] Roosevelt had used as leverage against the mine owners—through the agency of J. P. Morgan— threats to send in the army and to "dispossess the operators and run the mines as a receiver."[86] But he did not follow through on the threat,* and the inviolability of private contracts in labor relations was soon after affirmed in decisions of the Supreme Court like *Lochner v. New York* (1905) and *Adair v. U.S.* (1908).[87] It was the Department of Labor Act of 1913 that reset the clock for Wilson and facilitated his intervention. When his efforts failed, however, Wilson called on Congress to settle the issue.

The Adamson Act was continuous with various vectors of Progressive political interest: widening the scope of economic regulation, sharpening Executive activism,[88] and asserting a new identification of the public good to include "quasi-public" entities like railroads.† If State

---

* In fact, Roosevelt was told by Attorney General Knox that seizure of the mines would be unconstitutional. We shall see in a moment how things changed.

† This is how Justice McKenna referred to the railroads in *Adair v. U.S.*

intervention in labor unrest had begun in a distinctly reactive mood in the nineteenth century, by the time of the Theodore Roosevelt administration it had become more balanced, or at least more ambiguous.[89]

The Adamson Act made no explicit reference to a general state of emergency or to war. Still, it illustrates the increasingly complex relation between the powers associated with these two conditions.[90] Here is why.

Several months after the Adamson Act came into effect the Supreme Court was called upon to review it. Now the explicit language of *emergency* entered the scene. Chief Justice White put in print what everyone knew. "The entire interruption of interstate commerce . . . was threatened, and the infinite injury to the public interest . . . was imminent." As "private right" had failed "to establish a standard by agreement," it was trumped by "the existence of a public right and public power to preserve" order. Thus, in the Court's view, State intervention in the workings of civil society was justified on *emergency* grounds *even in peacetime*.[91]

We have already seen that this separation of *emergency* from *war* was not an entirely novel position. I want now to highlight the ambiguity of this constitutional fact from another perspective. For, the shadow of war fell on this case in several ways.

One was very direct. In 1916 the Great War in Europe was exerting ever greater pull on Americans. German submarines were bringing the conflict closer to home. If President Woodrow Wilson's sharp response to the sinking of the *Lusitania* had temporarily eased the tension, his party's winning slogan in that year's election still reflected the preoccupation of the nation: "He Kept Us out of War."

Moreover, the Adamson Act followed forty years of heated industrial conflict. This conflict had often been played out in the language of "class warfare" and "industrial peace." In 1916 the image of girls in flames jumping from the high windows of Triangle Shirtwaist Company was still fresh. Wilson had first been elected in the aftermath of massive strikes in Lawrence, Massachusetts.[92] That terrible struggle, too, was vivid in memory. It had brought to national prominence the IWW* radicals who had inherited from the American Railroad Union the ideal of "one big union." Now news of the martyred Joe Hill—prominent IWW organizer, composer

* Industrial Workers of the World.

of dozens of popular labor songs, and author of a cartoon in the *Class War News* figuring an IWW submarine firing on the ship of "Capitalism"— filled the public sphere. "Red" Emma Goldman was at the height of her celebrity.[93] Progressivism—which seemed a middle way between wide extremes—was at its height, and "all four principal candidates in 1912—Taft, Wilson, Roosevelt, and Debs—were in some degree Progressives."[94]

Americans were living with two images of war, one international and the other domestic, which amplified the public feeling that a general strike in transportation would have devastating consequences. This is one way the effects of *war* channeled the application of *emergency* powers *even in peacetime*.

Let me underscore that I *am not saying* that these emergency powers *derived* from war powers. Indeed, my point is that we need two steps to see the complex interaction between *war* and *emergency* in American political culture. The first is to acknowledge the important respects in which *emergency* is prior to *war*. The second is to seek out how *emergency* is inflected by *war* in ways that make *war seem primary*. We are tracing here historical moments in which the independence of *emergency* from *war* becomes clearer to the historical actors themselves. This is not the final word. It will, however, bring us back to the point with which this chapter began: the experience of war for the Citizen is not determined by warfighting, but by how, at various levels, war is "played out" in everyday life, and how this "playing out" makes appeal to *emergency* a winning political strategy. This is a dynamic of *civic war*.

Now we can add that the shadow of *war* also fell within the law. Chief Justice White measured the significance of *emergency* in the instance of the Adamson Act against the experience of the Civil War. A decision of 1866—*Ex Parte Milligan*—had argued that even when justified on grounds of "rebellion" a suspension of habeas corpus did not imply that a citizen could "be tried otherwise than by the course of the common law." "Illustrious" founders had "limited the suspension to one great right, and left the rest to remain forever inviolable." Thus the *Ex Parte Milligan* decision of Justice Davis had concluded, "martial rule can never exist where the courts are open."[95]

Now it was 1917. Drawing on the common sense of his time Justice White extended an invisible bridge across two divides. We have just seen how, in one direction, it joined military and civic representations of war. In the other direction, it allowed for unchecked traffic between branches of government. As White drafted his decision for the case *Wilson v. New* he drew from *Ex Parte Milligan* the principle that "emergency cannot be made the source of power."[96] This may seem a clear directive against overreach by the Commander-in-chief. However, it was also pretext for an enlargement of congressional power in emergency situations at home. In White's words: "Although an emergency may not call into life a power which has never lived, nevertheless emergency may afford a reason for the exertion of a living power already enjoyed."[97] With regard to the Adamson Act the "living power already enjoyed" found its precedents in the events I have just sketched: the tandem growth of railroad legislation and Executive emergency power.

It is important to see that, up to this point, two vectors characterize the wider tendency. Immediately prior to World War I, the emergency power had to a significant extent drifted away from war and into a wider orbit. It followed the logic of political conflict in society. Nonetheless, the emergency power continued to be shaped by the gravitational pull of war in a variety of ways.

This drift was abruptly interrupted in April of 1917. The candidate who "kept us out of war" became the President who asked for and received a congressional declaration of war. He then brought about a decisive reconvergence of emergency powers and war powers.[98] On December 28, 1917, Wilson activated another "living power"—which is to say, congressional authorization on the books since August 1916—to nationalize the railroads for the duration of the "time of war" and its "emergency."[99] Six months later he followed the same model to place various means of mass communications under government control.[100]

There is a powerful inclination to take war—particularly *the Great War*, like the Civil War before it—as the true-pointing marker along the chronological path of change. This temptation should be resisted. War, as military and as civil practice, and war's system of political justification, are special facts rather than primary ones. War here and there overlays a longer and more continuous development of *emergency powers*. This development is often carried forward on other vehicles like nativism or class conflict or imperial ambition. Once having identified the priority of emergency for the position of the Citizen, however, a major qualification can be reintroduced: the periodic entanglement of the development of *emergency powers* with *war*, a fact of increasing frequency and decreasing distinctiveness, has been an essential feature of our history for almost a century.

After Armistice in the fall of 1918, the constellation of political forces entered a new season. While some of the powers exerted by the national Executive over public goods were ceded back to their private proprietors, the independent dynamic of emergency powers continued to assert itself.[101] Immigration may serve here as a barometer. With the advent of war in Europe, the number of immigrants to America dropped precipitously in 1915 (by about 75 percent). Slower immigration was subsequently reinforced by the Immigration Act of 1917. But American nativists were not primarily concerned with war. They identified foreigners as key sources of social and industrial disorder.* When immigration tripled in 1919 and then doubled again in 1920, this was viewed as a *peacetime emergency*. It led to passage of an Emergency Quota Act of 1921.[102] The essentially economic character of the immigration "emergency" comes into view when we consider that the famous decline in immigration that transformed America after the First World War only reached bottom in the years after the Wall Street crash of 1929.[103]

The 1920s roared forward. A decisive role for the national government was reasserted in the Railway Labor Act of 1926. Then, with the spreading Depression after 1929, emergency powers were increasingly applied towards social ends. Even before the election of Franklin Delano Roosevelt in 1932, emergency measures went well beyond regulation of prices and negotiation of the conditions of labor, aiming at more general response to the havoc produced by the "irrational exuberance" of capitalism.[104]

Here is something odd. I just wrote that we should not let *war* frame our understanding of *emergency*. Yet, by pointing to what happened *after the war*, that is exactly what I have done. It will help to see why this is not a significant contradiction if I now briefly revisit a claim I emphasized earlier in this chapter: the boundaries of the experience of war are different for each position in society, and thus every act and institution has its own rhythm. Apply this perspective to the Great War. Was it really more clearly delimited than the wars of September 11th?[†] Was the period of intense military and militaristic buildup between the sinking of the *Lusitania* (May 6, 1916) and the American declaration of war (April 6, 1917) really a time of peace?[105] Was the experience of the Citizen fairly

---

* This phenomenon was related to but wider than the "red scare."
† On the problem of locating the precise beginning of the wars of September 11th, see chapter 2.

narrated by the Soldier whose diary chronicled the death of twelve men five minutes before the bell-toll of Armistice and then the silenced guns five minutes after? Was it true, as Virginia Woolf wrote some days later, that "we are once more a nation of individuals"?[106] Should we suppose Executive *war powers* that continued after November 11, 1918, become *peace powers?*

The Citizen had better answer such questions from the perspective of politics. Political relationships are what sew simple and punctual events into the complex and temporally fluid social fact of war. If war powers and emergency powers can drift together and drift apart, it is because they are, so to speak, made of the same political stuff. Hard resources—weapons, money, and so forth—are not what count *for the Citizen* in the final analysis. Nor do these powers emanate directly from constitutional authorization. They are compositions of human energies, moved a certain way. What makes them powers of wide effect and worthy of formidable names like *war* and *emergency* is the remarkable consistency with which they can be mobilized—even against resistance.* This consistency is a function of the "cement" that holds together dependable connections among persons, which is to say relatively durable common sense and commonplaces.† It is with implication in speaking relationships that an urgent or dangerous matter in the everyday life of the Citizen becomes recognizable as *emergency* and can be "taken hold" of. In other words, it is through politics that emergency becomes a matter of power.

Later we will trace further developments in the shifting overlap between *emergency* and *war.* The pattern grows larger and, as Max Weber might have said, more "rational," at the same time that it becomes, as Freud might have said, more "irrational." The period leading up to and including World War II reiterates some of what we have already seen. It also sets in place conditions for the comprehensive infusion of war into society during the Cold War.

What these historical vignettes tell us depends, of course, on how we interpret our past and how we choose to live with it. A primary purpose of this book is to conduct interpretation and experience back to the posi-

---

* Although we think of these powers as "big," magnitude is actually a different issue.
† Commonplaces are both vehicles for and barriers against action; this fact will be considered in detail later in *Democracy in America after 9/11.*

tion of the Citizen. It will help to advance this purpose if I now restate, in slightly revised terms, some additional themes with which this chapter began.

The blurring of boundaries between war and not-war may be a general feature of modernity. It did not begin in the twentieth century. It found an early expression with the advent of a new type of war in revolutionary France.[107] Faced with military conflict in 1793, the executive body of government—the Committee of Public Safety—initiated mass conscription and a policy of "justice prompte, sûre, inflexible" known as "la terreur."* They promoted "a society every human element of which is involved in the struggle."[108] It has been said that such "politically ordered participation in the war effort of all personal and social forces" first occurred in the United States during the Civil War.[109] That conflict was carried out in fields and streets and homes on American soil. However, this was in itself no decisive novelty. War has always been and always will be all-encompassing in the zones—large or small, under siege or calling for "unconditional surrender"—where Citizen, Soldier, and Victim are one. Following common practice, we could call this fact by the phrase *total war*, which entered the vocabulary of political thinking in 1937.[110] This would be, however, imprecise in a way I think citizens do well to avoid. In a sense, it was the destructive "totality" of the American Civil War that obscured exactly what concerns us here. Remember that for decades after the surrender at Appomattox the Civil War continued to be fought locally on an almost daily basis. The fundamentally political character of that war has been more clearly reflected in the pervasive but essentially ad hoc consequences—up to contemporary debates over uses of the Confederate flag—of our failure to arrive at definitive national reconciliation.†

The key point obscured by the phrase *total war* is that *social* change is the primary factor tending to undermine the distinction war/not-war. The failure of this distinction is increasingly pronounced in the twentieth century and is only indirectly a function of war in the narrow military

---

* This is the famous phrase of Robespierre. Note the parallel between the breakdown of the boundary between war and not-war and the systematic integration of terror into popular government. In roughly the same period, political debate reflected increasing concern about the split between the social roles of Soldier and Citizen.
† The marker of "race" articulates this interminable war, total, perhaps, in mode, space, and, finally, time, but not well-described by its classification as "total war."

sense of warfighting. It is mainly due, rather, to acceleration of technological innovation and the industrialization of warmaking capacities. This particular form of economic development spurred the vast American expeditionary adventures that began in earnest with our entrance into the Great War in 1917.* The massing of armies was matched by widespread domestic mobilization. This disseminated a relatively immediate interest in warmaking to nearly every position in society and created a space of political opportunity containing high stakes and urgent motivations. By 1917 any substantial project of war needed to be forged in society. In turn, social projects could with profit be recast in terms of war.

With this general trend in mind I claimed, against one major tradition of political thought, that *war powers* may be drawn from *emergency powers* rather than the other way around. I suggested that to think clearly about how war bears on the position of the Citizen we had better give priority to *emergency powers*.

The effort to track consequences of the relationship between emergency powers and war powers is complicated by two additional themes. One is the proposition that we adopt a wider perspective on what counts as *war*. The other is the proposition that we understand *war as the continuation of politics* in light of various *versions of politics*. We will reenter this weave of factors in the coming chapters. Before that, we need to return our attention to the most fundamental of political facts: How does all this appear from within the position of the Citizen?

Here the priority is unequivocal but the distinction is not. *War* intrudes into the life of the Citizen as *emergency*. When the two overlap, it seems that striking images of *war* are what give shape to our experience of *emergency*.† When the two drift apart in time or space, we can see that *emergency* has its own inherent dynamics. Citizens tend to impose their personal experience of emergency on the image of war and then import that image of "war" into their experience to characterize emergency.

---

* I note the crucial "demographic" effect of technological change: a thousand men can kill a thousand of their kind with swords forged by a single man; a handful of men can kill thousands with a nuclear weapon made by thousands of people far removed from the scene of battle. This fact is at the origin of the vision of Donald Rumsfeld and others who want to use new technology to diminish the number of frontline soldiers necessary for "delivery."

† Notice that witnesses described Columbine High School as a "battleground" even though no battle can occur when just two cooperators have weapons and their victims do not. No one thought to call Harris and Klebold "crazed hunters" or "accelerated serial killers."

At the very beginning of this chapter I wrote that a more thorough answer to the Justice Goldberg question—*Is it war or not?*—would lead us back to the fact that warmaking power is grounded in politics in the broadest sense. We are still working towards a full development of that point and shall not complete it in this chapter. But having seen the circular relationship between *emergency* and *war*, and by giving, as citizens do, priority to *emergency*, we can now say that this first question really stands for a more basic one. The Citizen who asks *Is this war or not?* is effectively asking *What and when is an emergency?*

This paraphrase brings out the political moment of decision inherent in such questions when they are asked from the position of the Citizen. America's most original patriot, Tom Paine, would have called this *crisis.** The *crisis* begins not with an empirical determination of what is and what isn't an emergency, but as we ask ourselves, *Who decides* when and where there is emergency? This already implicates us in that decision. The *crisis* is reiterated as long as results of prior decisions shape our subsequent situation and force additional choices upon us.

The crisis in America after September 11th is clear: *What will be the position of the Citizen?* To approach this crisis, to make it a κρίσις from within which the Citizen can actually decide something, which is to say actually take a position as Citizen, I have braided together two lines of inquiry. One widens the view of war as a "continuation of politics." In this way war presents us with, and can be felt as, a *crisis of choice* rather than a *crisis of necessity.†* The other line of inquiry has illustrated with historical examples the way Americans have confused the issue of *emergency* with the image of *war.*

So *who decides?‡* At the root of all politics are judgments made by distinct persons. Each Citizen decides for him- or herself whether *his* or *her* situation is subject to *emergency.* While these judgments are necessary for politics, they are not political if they occur in isolation. At any given

---

* In the 1770s he followed the literal meaning of the Greek word κρίσις, which is decision.
†Even the necessity supposed in the maxim *salus populi suprema lex* must involve complex political choices; it has been rightly said, paraphrasing Thomas Jefferson, that "to pretend that the law of nature, the law of necessity, the law of saving our country when in danger, is law in the same sense as written law is to play with words." We return to this knot in chapter 6.
‡ Carl Schmitt's *Politische Theologie* proposes that the question *who decides?* (where decision is called for because no rule applies itself) points to the sovereign. I suggest here that sovereignty is of secondary concern in democratic politics; n.b. that "sovereignty" and "national sovereignty" are two very different issues.

moment an *emergency* is not what *I* say it is, but what *we* say it is.* This is true even if *I* am the king and even truer in a democratic regime. In each case, the determination will issue from political processes that range from everyday talk to the shifting combinations of the President, the Congress, and the People.

In other words, *emergency* is a social fact that encompasses our choices. It mutates over time because, facing problems, we attempt to "take hold of" our changing circumstances by using the language of *emergency*. This produces unending small concords and discords, which, in turn, determine whether *emergency*—the situation and the name—will become here and there effective or sterile. As this process transforms the situations in which we live, it leads to new constellations of common sense. These, in turn, expand or contract the *emergency* itself.

What *emerges* in *emergency* is not just a problem but also a potential.[†] As with the dialectic of fear and hope, no one faces the *crisis* of an *emerging situation* without sensing its potential and taking that into account. Both problem and potential are shaped and constrained by already existing circumstances. The context for *emergency*, especially when disputes arise over the collective response to *emergency*, is power, which is to say the use or alignment of human energies mobilized within a division of action by human speech relationships. Power always already has its forms. What the Citizen will count as an *emergency* will depend on his or her relation to the existing forms of power—including the desire to maintain or change them.

At this point tradition wants us to name two broad forms of power. *Normal powers*—spirit-persuading, energy-mobilizing, checking-and-balancing—are generated from within the constitutional system. Okay so far. But the temptation is strong to see around us a second kind of power that is not "normal" and thus, almost by definition, seems exceptional. Do we not sometimes find ourselves in a "state of exception" characterized by need for action that is overwhelming and immediate but of limited

---

* This social fact changes with circumstances and beliefs (including the assertion "*This* is an emergency"). To see how belief is central to this kind of social fact, think of how, despite its physical effects on people, cigarette smoking for centuries was not a public health emergency and then, suddenly, it was. Or think of the real consequences of the belief that a nonexistent nuclear weapons program in Iraq was more threatening than a real program in Korea.

† Only in and after the nineteenth century did the word *emergency* lose its primary association with a sense of opportunity.

duration? And do not such states stand outside the scope of the constitution? And isn't that what despotic *emergency power* is all about?

The answer to this last question is no. We have seen in this chapter something of how *emergency* really operates in political life in America. It would be largely mistaken to imagine *emergency powers* as simply reaction to particularly pressing problems rather than as complex long-term developments integrated into the everyday life of the nation at many levels. Moreover, it is important that the *topic* of *emergency* enters public discussion only when decision making is likely to meet resistance. *This too is the normal situation of politics.* Thus a claim like "this is an *emergency*" had better not be interpreted as mere description. It is also a justification in disputes about the course of action to be taken. Such disputes arise not only because we are not omniscient but because the measures proposed will always occur within an already existing division of action. Power, growing in the webs of human relationships, is not simply "wielded" in emergency; *power is at stake* as the response to *emergency* changes other things, and people seek to capture benefits from these changes. This energizes and amplifies the emergency itself. All of these are regular political processes.

This essential connection to power means that *emergency* will be conceived one way where sovereignty is unitary and another way where sovereignty is divided; one way in monocracy and another way where plurality reigns. The *raison d'état* of the king is not the same as the *emergency powers* of the constitutional President. It may be that in times when the image or self-image of the American president is modeled on a king, when in democracy the pathology of undivided action holds sway, citizens are misled into equating the two. But it remains our responsibility to recognize that this equation is false.

I want to make clear at this point my skepticism: I doubt that in real life the distinction between *normal* and *emergency* powers can ever have been as neatly drawn as professors, pundits, and partisans propose.[111] In the United States today, especially after September 11th, it has become almost impossible to set these boundaries. *Emergency* is determined and acted upon through the kinds of constitutional processes I described earlier in this chapter. The characteristic event of despotism, the arbitrary application of "will"—think here of George W. Bush's absurd and ultimately false assertion "I am the decider"—plays at most one small part even though the rhetoric of undivided action is disproportionately large.

These processes reach deeply into society and culture and are entangled with everyday speech relationships. They involve at all levels the vectors of opinion and common sense. This is what counts for power: when a shocked Congress changes its attitude towards the President, Executive power rises or declines; when fearful citizens add or withdraw support from representatives, the attitude of Congress changes; when the press calls the President the Commander-in-chief, military expectations and reflexes infest civil interactions; and so forth.

It remains that recent efforts to understand the origin and significance of emergency powers have sought a firm ground in the concept of "the exception." Before drawing this chapter to a conclusion, I want to say briefly why I think the conflation of these two very different phenomena is a mistake for the Citizen.[112]

When in the course of events the Citizen is compelled to ask *What and when is an emergency?* and to adjust his or her actions and allegiances accordingly, the answer had better not be "an emergency is when there is an exception." At best, that answer paraphrases the question. Worse, it is a trap; with the idea of "the exception" the Citizen anticipates an abstract but nevertheless neat and clear measure of the "normal" where, finally, none can be had. The only answer true to democracy, the only answer that accepts the responsibility of the Citizen, is this: *an emergency is what and when we say it is.* We simply do not need the theoretical language of "the exception" to identify emergency in the play of powers. We need, rather, the everyday languages of continuity and change, and a lexicon of civic values, to seek out what power will do for or against us.

In any event, emergency cannot be captured so easily. The logic of emergency and its pressures are tangential to the logic of exception from some norm. Both presuppose a particular position for the implicated parties and a certain stance towards change; an emergency is a relative acceleration of the time frame for action; an exception is a break with well-acclimated practices in which timing may or may not be at issue. In the everyday course of things *anything* can become an emergency while a much more specific and smaller class of things will count as exceptions. And despite this the precision of "the exception" is illusory. *It* cannot decide for *us* whether or not a particular use of power is acceptable. "The exception" inevitably points us back to the circumstances and motives, and thus to the persistent conflicts, that determine which *norm* defines—by contrast to it—"the exception" itself. Only in the event—which in times of war is especially unlikely or dangerous—that the *excepted norm* is uncontested will recourse to "the exception" settle any issue and clearly mark out what and when the emergency is.

When it comes to the affairs of civic life addressed in this book, we often imagine that the relevant norm, the norm from which we are wary of exception, is the legal or constitutional system as a whole. There are good reasons to operate this way. If one sees law as a clearly defined and relatively closed system, it is possible to rule out of bounds some uses of power simply by identifying as "exceptional" the situation that calls forth that power. By implication, whatever counts as "exception" is "outside" the law and must therefore be extraconstitutional. From this perspective, such exceptional emergency powers would be differentiated from *criminal* or even *unconstitutional* acts for an obvious reason: they are undertaken by entities generally authorized to make law and are covered by the reassuring belief that new authoritative assertions and acts will be of short duration and aimed at restoring the status quo ante.*

We could take this perspective further. Another clear and good reason for supposing that the law is a closed system is that we want to avoid minute-by-minute or case-by-case all-in contention about the validity of legal claims and the legitimacy of those who make and enforce those claims. The image of the "purely legal" appears before us as a confidence-inspiring source of order. This is often a convenient support for the "rule of law."

Even with these and other benefits, however, what appear as virtues in this view of law may turn into vices. Those who believe that law is a closed system, as well as those who need others to hold this same view, may be guided by complacency, habit, and self-interest and thus susceptible to insist on order above all else. This is especially pernicious where those who benefit from this order—which, now viewed from its other side, may stand as an impediment to change—are most vocal about its virtues; they push their arguments to extremes and the specter of a "slippery slope," where any allowance for politics in the Constitution seems to destroy it, commands the scene.

As there is no way to stop this kind of self-servingness, the Citizen had better accept it. Whether or not this commitment to law as a closed system is held in good faith, my point is that it can, and often does, emerge within a political context. It is not in itself any more malicious than other

---

* Whether or not such a thing exists in politics is another open question.

expressions of self-interest; however, its dangerous effects are multiplied where law's implication in political life is denied as a matter of strategy or ignorance. This is sufficient reason to view with a high degree of skepticism boundaries supposed to clearly set the constitutional system apart from the rest of political life.

All this is preface to a more important point. The facts relevant to the position of the Citizen after September 11th warrant a rather different view. Whatever one may say about the logical consistency of the body of legal rules, the key to the real operation of the Constitution is that it is an open system rather than a closed one. This does make it precarious in just the ways we might like to avoid, but it also makes it democratic. As the way in which we *constitute* powers and rules and decisions—which is to say, as a political way of life—the Constitution is inevitably fugitive and hard to pin down. Once measured by democracy, crisp and "self-evident" demarcations that in effect close the constitutional system—for better or for worse—must be seen for what they are: not neutral juridical facts but the residues and fuses of conflict or dispute. It does not follow from this that the claims and forces of the Constitution are willful or subjective. It just means that the effects and significance that emerge through the Constitution are objective resultants of the process of people living together and working through conflicts. To have a constitution is to push the occurrence of these changes from momentary events into the rhythms of ages, generations, lifetimes, and the greater arc of history.

Having said this, it now becomes possible to repeat a major theme of this book in new and adjusted terms: all these claims and disputes, together with the different ways of analyzing them, only arise before the Citizen where power is at stake. Politics is not a "virtual-reality" game. Even the language we use can become an occasion for the loss or gain of power. This is where, I suspect, appeals to "the exception" as a way to understand *emergency* tend away from the Citizen's sphere of influence.

Let us admit this much: by thinking through "the exception" one gains an image of emergency as a field of action. For "the exception" is not just a break with well-acclimated practices. It is, much more than that, an event that disrupts more or less self-executing rules.* This is why some have

* The use of this phrase, while in some sense apt, already suggests a commonplace, and in my view dangerous, resource we have for evading responsibility for our actions; this problem typically appears in democracy in the form of bureaucracy, but it may be a necessary by-product of the rule of law more generally.

seen in "the exception" a critical marker of sovereign power, the identity of the person or group who is really in charge. "The exception" seems to characterize a situation in which judgment determines everything.[113]

But this is not enough. What I have proposed and will insist on in the following chapters again cuts against this bias. We can agree that judgment *is* everything in politics. But where, in real life, is judgment *not* operative? This is the simplest of observations, but it weighs heavily against the reduction of emergency to exception. Do not get caught up here in sorting "good" judgments from "bad" ones. My point is that, whatever the quality of outcomes, at every level of the constitutional system all parties are constantly beset with either/or situations that they must feel their way through and come out of at the next step. This is judgment. It is the lifeblood of evolving human relationships. The democrat had better not too quickly pretend to constrict its sphere of operation.[114] And if such judgment is as widespread as I suggest, there is little place in political life for the notion of "the exception" to gain specific purchase.

How should we know, then, what is and what is not within constitutional bounds? The Constitution as a historical, cultural, and social fact is the process through which some topics or disputes are structured as political. Yet if we give credence to the view that "the exception" is where politics fully manifests itself, then we must come to the perverse conclusion that "the exception" is, somehow, inside the constitutional system. This is a clever but ineffectual paradox. It leads to anthropologically suspect formulations in which the "outside" is supposed, like a virus, to be imported into the system. As a logical matter, however, not just special laws but every new law could be described in this way. As a fact of history, it misrepresents both the genealogy of the Constitution and the practice of it. As political doctrine, it promotes paranoia and an abdication of responsibility for who we are and what the American polity has become.

The basic constitutional practice of multiplying and dividing powers embraces politics within the legal framework without pretending to master it. It allows us to acknowledge and live without existential anxiety within an open system. This multiplication of powers—which I shall soon refer to as *plurality*—at once breeds and gives order to limited conflict. Indeed, the living Constitution modulates the tensions and pressures and constraints of our everyday life into political relationships. It does this with astonishing variability. How far and in what directions plurality can go is the fundamental question of power in our democracy.

This is what is at stake when, from every single location in our collective life, we are called upon to answer for ourselves the questions Is this war? and What and when is an emergency? in the face of spectacular violence and fearmongering. The preceding pages have shown that these questions are not gratuitous. They reflect inextricable features of a tightening spiral that binds emergency to *civic war*. Emergencies do not occur in the philosopher's imaginary world of "the exception." The Citizen had better understand *emergencies* as events not outside civic life, but within it, at home, where *we* live.

The conclusion is that in the American system, as long as the Constitution is in place, there are no *emergency powers* outside its scope.* Dangerous enough—indeed, perhaps *more* dangerous because harder to identify—are the facts that the Constitution permits, and must permit: bad politics, failed courage, complicity, conformism, escape from responsibility, and a host of other political pathologies of democracy. There is no machine that makes things right. The tragic fact of *our* responsibility for democracy is that everything goes, either because *we*, in our unbounded perversity or ignorance, want it, or because *we* do not expend the energy to stop it.

Where I have written that the institutions and symbols of *war* are major factors in this complex process, it may have seemed as though I meant to say that the eroding boundary between war and not-war has opened the way to a perpetual "state of exception." These last few pages were aimed to clear away that impression. In effect, I am arguing the reverse, that the determination of *emergency*, its address, its effects, have been increasingly dragged within the compass of *normal* politics. This makes obsolete the idea of "the exception" for everyone but the solipsistic philosopher. The situation of emergency—not exactly new but finally recognizable for what it is—has made *war* a condition of possibility for all sorts of perfectly normal actions, no matter how odious or self-destructive they may be. The emergency of *civic war* in America has become a motor for the globalization of opportunism. It has made the already eroding field of politics less clear and more difficult to navigate.

It has also diminished the moral force of an accusation once ready at hand for muckrakers and debunkers, or for citizens like Mrs. Betty Comp-

---

* There are certainly illegal or criminal activities by agents of the constitutional system.

ton: *Desist, for your action lies "outside" the Constitution!** Failing this, we are deposited where we must undertake another sort of struggle. It is new only because, by common sense, invisible to common sense. It is to position ourselves as citizens. We are in a dark thicket; the rescue squads and SWAT teams are not coming; we will have to find our own way out. In this process, the Citizen had better keep in mind the distinction between *war* and *emergency powers*, even when the two become thoroughly entangled.[115] Armed with this admonition, we return in the next chapter to threads of our history with the hope of further clarifying its meaning.

---

* Contributing to a trend that involves other forces. We shall return to one of the consequences of this trend in chapter 6.

4. The Norm of Complicity and the Regeneration of Emergency through Violence

Unfortunately, in the modern state, with its great diversity of interests and opinions, due to the dispersion of technological and commercial enterprise, the act that comes closest to the totality of tribal festivals and the agape is the act of war. But modern war ("total war") itself is so complex, that we could hardly use it as our representative anecdote until we had selected some moment within war to serve in turn as representative of war.

KENNETH BURKE, *A Grammar of Motives* (1945)

In his first inaugural address, Franklin Delano Roosevelt announced that America would treat the problem of unemployment "as we would treat the emergency of a war." To meet the general economic crisis, he would "ask the Congress for . . . broad Executive power to wage a war against the emergency, as great as the power that would be given to me if we were in fact invaded by a foreign foe."[1] Roosevelt declared, and Congress immediately ratified by joint proclamation, a "state of emergency" with respect to "banking . . . and other purposes."[2]

Of course, not even a generation before FDR spoke in 1933, the American people had been involved in unprecedented warfighting adventure. Roosevelt invoked that experience to convey the new and dire predicament of the nation. *If you want to know what emergency is*, he seemed to say, *remember The War.* He used the image of war to enlarge the symbolically charged political field where civil society and the State intermingle. Like so many before and after him, he made *war* seem more fundamental than *emergency*, using the former to give significance to the latter.

We can now see how this is misleading. Start from the obvious fact. For the Citizen the experience of *war* is not direct involvement in warfighting violence. It is a composite social fact of a rather different sort. In most respects it is continuous with other features of everyday experience. In America, after September 11th, or after the invasion of Iraq in 2003, and now within the indeterminate span of the so-called war on terrorism, you and I go to work, to the house of worship, to the movies, to bed at night, and to breakfast in the morning . . . *and* we are at war. Although the guns and bombs and soldiers are not among us, it falsifies and demeans us to say that *there, in Iraq, there is a war*, or some other *over there, elsewhere*. These wars belong to us, they are American wars. Whether it appears clearly around us or not, whether we acknowledge it or not, war today is mixed together with all sorts of activities that make up the everyday fabric of experience in twenty-first-century America. *Civic war* is the proper name for this fact.

This poses an unexpected problem. The image most citizens have of war is entirely different. It derives from the moving image and its *cinematic culture*.[3] We imagine war as a theater of bullets and battles and mutilation. The expectations that form around this image make the Citizen's actual experience of war *as civic war* nearly invisible. Yet, as citizens, we cannot come to grips with the American reality of war if it is not delineated within our own experience. What would this involve?

The Citizen's experience of war takes shape in the midst of everyday life with others. War interlaces and animates with a special, heightened, and persistent quality the constantly repeated news, the workaday production of lethal hardware, the paper-shuffling of policy, the recruiters' roundup, anthems chanted and gossip in circulation, the price of oil and the value of money, the outfitting of the watchman and the guard, nightmare dreams, the drama of disaster, the video game . . . indeed, every last thing in society is more or less touched by war when war there is. Thus war for the Citizen is a sort of social contortion: away from battle, outside the unpredictable and the dangerous, the whole of the Citizen's war is a seamless unfolding continuity across the diverse and utterly normal day. And right *there*, like a proverbial red thread, is *emergency* running through it.

Just this cranked-up tension was manifest in President Roosevelt's speech. Seeking amplification in metaphor, FDR's words actually expressed a kind of tautological literalness. *You, my public,* he might have said, *will recognize the emergency if I call it war, because war is an emergency.* What he did not say is that the circle of war and emergency is lopsided. For the public, for the Citizen, *emergency* is the catalytic element in *war.* And *war* is not the only source of *emergency. War* is just one instance, one terrible and all too familiar instance, of a much more general phenomenon.*

Roosevelt's famous "bank holiday" did not take place on a battlefield. Yet his image was apt. As with the social processes that ultimately convey soldiers to battlefields, this *emergency* would involve intensive applications of State power on the domestic scene and narrowly purposive reconfigurations of civil society. And although the essentially political character of *war* is not featured in the image Roosevelt presents, his performance of that image in the field of politics made clear where the *emergency* was to be experienced by the Citizen. It had already come home.

FDR's action was not unique. It was rather a clear exemplar. It consolidated a long-growing trend. By the end of the nineteenth century, *emergency powers* were more and more often being directed towards social ends. When the Great War came, the *war powers* that had been invoked for action abroad became a springboard for new *emergency powers* exercised at home. At first the former overshadowed the latter. Under this cover, lines of demarcation between old emergency powers and the new ones were obscured. Thus opportunities for advancing political projects in the form of *emergency* continued to multiply. And what happened when the First World War came to an end? Appeals to *emergency power* persisted unadorned. Through the 1920s, claims of emergency were initiated independently of military need or reason.

Train your ear again on FDR's first inaugural address. What is striking today about that moment is the return of *war* as a pivotal political justification. FDR's words were spoken after more than a decade of *peace.* In that January of 1933, hard in the Depression, it should have been exquisitely clear that *emergency powers* are independent from the motivating

---

* A lot more could be said about the motives evoked when *war* is used as synecdoche for emergency. Think of the way FDR's words served to constitute hope for the suffering and the weak; as long as the Depression appeared to strike like an act of nature, action against it seemed fruitless; when FDR refigured the Depression as an enemy attack, people were ready to stand up and fight as much for their honor as for their bread.

circumstances of *war* to which they are typically ascribed. The new president's rhetorical move obfuscated exactly this fact. He achieved the following decisive result: the symbolic link to war decreased resistance to emergency powers and, in this way, increased their reach.*

When several years later the threat of renewed American involvement in armed conflict in Europe loomed large, President Roosevelt was effectively able to enter the new war without explicitly mobilizing the political support necessary for congressional authorization. Following the German invasion of Poland in 1939 he declared a state of "limited emergency." His order, approved by Congress, became the basis nine months later for the creation of the Office of Emergency Management; this office would itself become the umbrella for a wide range of administrative agencies.‡ In the spring of 1941 the emergency was reasserted under the term "unlimited." This was six months before Pearl Harbor and the explicit juridically effective declaration of war.†

In these and other similar measures FDR created precedents for working in both directions the circular relationship between *emergency* and *war*. As these new policies met with resistance, a specific kind of flexibility for navigating through political conflict developed around the nexus of *emergency* and *war*, where, in a pinch, each could be justified in terms of the other and no single argument (e.g. Betty Compton's "But we are not at war!") would serve to knock out either. This rhetorical machinery subsequently became a characteristic feature of the American political scene during what has been called—with a remarkable lack of irony—the "postwar period."

Before that, however, Roosevelt's America was confronted with the attack on Pearl Harbor. Through the First War Powers Act, passed in the

---

* We leave aside here the tangential motive to create a discourse about the failures of capitalism that did not name them as such; in this respect the metaphor of war was a way to cut socialists out of the public discussion.

† Ken Burns's film *The War* (2007) repeats what might be called the "September 11th theory of World War II," in which America awoke on December 7, 1941, from blissful ignorance of global events. Pretending to focus on local domestic experience, Burns's film bears a superficial and misleading resemblance to the project undertaken in this book. The crucial difference is that here we examine the structure and significance of politics for war, whereas from Burns one gets the impression that the only vehicle linking Hometown USA and "the War" was the troop transport and its only fuel was necessity. In his portrayal, democracy is something to be defended but not lived, and it appears as incapable of (for better or for worse) *choosing* to make war. This conveniently confirms the mythology George W. Bush has woven around Burns's viewers, but it is antithetical to the facts of our experience after September 11th ... and before.

days after December 7, 1941, the president was able to assume larger and more fluid *emergency powers*. These powers were to be applied across a wide range of society. Three months later the Second War Powers Act authorized the president to do whatever he deemed "necessary and appropriate in the public interest or to promote the national defense."[5]

Moreover, these new *war powers* effectively converged with *emergency powers* already in place. They merged into the growing network of Executive agencies largely under the auspices of the Office of Emergency Management. The comprehensiveness of the *war* itself, of its demands on social practices and institutions, inflated the opportunities inherent in *emergency*. The one turned into the other.

What comes into view here is a consequence of two long-term trends articulated in the preceding chapter. The first is the ongoing erosion of boundaries between *war* and *emergency*. The second is the Citizen's increased implication in the widening social fact of war. This second social-historical phenomenon has sometimes been referred to as "total war" because the technical and human means required to direct combat against the enemy's population and economic infrastructure (rather than just its soldiers) can only be mustered through the mobilization of the various capabilities of the whole attacking society.[6] I have already said that this description is misleading. To extrapolate so directly from the battlefield aims of mass industrialized warfare to conditions of life "at home" does draw attention to certain abstract social facts of contemporary warfare. At the same time, however, it obscures the concrete implication of the Citizen as such in these facts, and this is ultimately more important.

It is with the aim of so implicating the Citizen that we direct our attention here to a somewhat different shift: the return of war, in new garb, from the military to the civic realm. I have coined the term *civic war*—not to be confused with *civil* war!—to serve this end. It allows us to identify more precisely the ways war has become a decisive modality within the relationships that constitute the Citizen as a particular social type.

It makes sense to think of this as a *return* of war from the military to the civic because the military function in America has not always constituted its own distinct social realm.* The creation of standing armies

---

* Across time and cultures one sees an enormous variety in ways of integrating and distancing warmaking activities and civic life.

and the separation of the role of Soldier from that of Citizen, so hotly debated in the eighteenth century, became, as they were carried out in the nineteenth century, preconditions for the development of a modern industrial-bureaucratic military in the twentieth century. These historical facts of practice and belief continue to give rise to our common sense: we adhere to the image of a military separate from everyday life. But as a matter of social fact, *this common sense is false.** Moreover, it is dangerous, as it obscures the remaining, transformed, and, in key if unnoticed respects, ever more intense implication of nonsoldier citizens in war.

In this regard what seem like peripheral historical facts about the Second World War gain in significance. Surrenders by General Jodl and Emperor Hirohito on V-E Day and V-J Day in 1945 brought millions of Americans into the streets to celebrate the cessation of hostilities but did not terminate the *emergency powers* by which those citizens had come to be governed and more directly affected.[†] Thus, for example, nine months after the surrender of Japan, President Truman could continue to use in labor disputes powers granted specifically for the "war effort." Likewise, in 1947 the Supreme Court could allow—in *Wood v. Miller* (1948)—continuation of certain wartime rent controls to cover the return of soldiers to civilian life.[7]

Indeed, the Court's decision in *Wood v. Miller* presupposed the point to which I keep circling back: war and armed conflict map differently in time and space. *Civic war* has a form, qualities, and duration relatively independent from warfighting operations. A great deal depends on the valence attributed to this fact.

From and for the position of the Citizen, *civic war* is *real* war. Thus, the economic effects of demobilization were still part of the war, just as were, in retrospect, a long series of events leading up to Pearl Harbor. These ranged from the general economic effects of the arms buildup and the by-proxy militarization of the Lend-Lease Act to orders received by

---

*Although not central to the argument at this point, it should be noted that other important factors are at work here as well: the social imaginary of the military was crucially transformed following racial integration of the armed services, the abuse and end of conscription during the Vietnam War, the development of market-based recruitment (the so-called volunteer army), and so forth. As a consequence, the distinct military realm came to be mapped in new ways by social categories of race and class.

[†] Perhaps President Bush is more astute than he realizes in saying that "there will be no surrender ceremony on the deck of a battleship" in the "war on terror." Cf. the presidential address escalating the war in Iraq, January 10, 2007.

U.S. naval forces in September 1941 to "shoot" Germans and Italians "on sight."[8]

The fact that nothing and no one required the termination of *emergency powers* is decisive. This allowed the general administrative powers related to the war to be intentionally prolonged in statutes and executive orders. A series of maneuvers kept provisions of the War Powers Acts in effect through 1947. The state of emergency declared in 1939 and reaffirmed in 1941, a legal framework profoundly strengthened in its cultural effects by the military engagements that partially overlapped it, was not officially terminated until 1952. By that time various bridging measures and additional declarations of general emergency had in any event taken its place.[9]

Emergency powers, deploying the rhetoric of war, sometimes manifest in the politics of war, but in fact independent from military action, have in the course of the twentieth century metonymically stretched the spirit and motive of war across the whole fabric of society.

Here the position of the Citizen tells a truer tale. For the failure to assert or assume limits is more remarkable than the—literal—*emergence* of emergency in the first place. This durable arc of long-developed abdication appears with unusual clarity in the fact that the direct outcome of FDR's first inaugural address, that declaration of emergency in 1933, remained in effect for more than forty years.* It would be incorrect to call this an oversight. To the contrary, the general state of emergency was redoubled in 1950 when President Truman issued another such declaration. Only with the "domestic détente" of the 1970s and the scandals of the Nixon administration did this perpetual state of emergency become the object of serious debate. It was finally terminated by the National Emergencies Act in 1976.[10] But years of institution shape everyday practice, and since then the culture of emergency has for these and other reasons deepened its grip.

Laws get their hooks into society because laws do not enact or apply themselves. As romantic admirers of ancient republics like Montesquieu and Hegel insisted around the time of the American founding, law is not black ink on paper but rather an unwritten and unwritable matter of what the ancient Greeks called *nomos* and we call culture,[11] and thus

---

* At which exact points in time and space this fact produced effects is another question.

thoroughly entangled in the common sense that guides everyday life.* This social fact is perhaps most clearly manifest in the mysterious turning of the constitutional system as a whole.

In any event, this is why FDR's peacetime rhetoric of war is not a superfluous element in the story of real power. The rhetoric of war is a motive force in the circular process through which *war* and *emergency*, and the powers associated with both, feed off one another. The culture of emergency—and the corresponding expectation that the Executive should have ever larger and more precise powers—rises on the patterned quasi-syllogistic necessity that the word *war* advances: *if* this is *war*, then we *must*.

It should therefore surprise no one that FDR's rhetorical model was reiterated. The prolonged backdrop of war hot and cold after 1945 facilitated this development. Mounting the presidential stage for the first time in January 1961, John F. Kennedy inaugurated his term in office by reasserting in word and deed the "war against emergency" that had been so efficacious for FDR. The demand that the Citizen "ask what you can do for your country" had as immediate motive a solemn narrative in which, "since this country was founded, each generation of Americans has been summoned to give testimony to its national loyalty . . . [and] the graves of young Americans who answered the call to service surround the globe." The memory of war here serves again to stir the simmering emergency. With that gnarly Boston intonation, the president incites his "fellow Americans": "Now the trumpet summons us again—not as a call to bear arms, though arms we need—not as a call to battle, though embattled we are—but a call to bear the burden of a long twilight struggle, year in and year out, 'rejoicing in hope, patient in tribulation'—a struggle against the common enemies of man: tyranny, poverty, disease and war itself."[12] This by now tried-and-true reflexive topos of "war against war" could be applied with ease in favor of specific policy, even where citizens were steered safely into other motives, the advancement of higher ideals, and away from the base warlike intent of Kennedy's particular brand of emergency. Thus, for example, the president did not need to declare war

---

* Claims by these great political thinkers that law manifests the *ésprit* or the *Sittlichkeit* of a people were gestures back to ancient Greek νομος and Roman *mos* aimed to respond to countervailing new forms of legalism in eighteenth- and nineteenth-century Europe. I admit the peculiarity of calling Montesquieu "romantic" but insist it is in crucial respects an accurate characterization.

against the moon to make clear that the "race" into space would be essential if "we are to win the battle that is now going on around the world between freedom and tyranny," and that this would entail an unprecedented "degree of dedication, organization, and discipline" in which "every scientist, every engineer, every serviceman, every technician, contractor, and civil servant gives his personal pledge that this nation will move forward, with the full speed of freedom, in the exciting adventure of space."[13] On the spectacular stage of *civic war*.

Likewise, and closer still to Roosevelt's spirit, Lyndon B. Johnson furnished the rhetorical example of "war against emergency" that would set the tone for the generations up to 9/11. Far from any sort of military project, Johnson announced in his first State of the Union address in 1964 that "this administration, here and now, declares unconditional war on poverty." No one could doubt that the battlefield would be the homeland itself. Effectively mimicking both the Progressive Era and the New Deal, President Johnson turned a reemerging public discussion about the class structure of America around the image of war.[14] He spoke just months after the most successful terrorist attack on American soil in the twentieth century—the assassination of President Kennedy—and it seems plausible to say that Johnson thereby mobilized Americans' longing "for redemption through sacrifice."[15] The war metaphor served to "reduce the burden of proof," "isolate the opposition," and "sustain national interest."[16] The projects advanced under this rubric expanded to fill the space and possibilities created by the "declaration of war." This, again, was not merely the superfluous addition of words to the facts on the ground. "The rhetorical stance determined the direction of the policy" and "profoundly influenced the objectives of the poverty program."[17]

How can a constitutional democracy stand for such a durable and diffuse state of emergency and the forms of power that arise within it? Why didn't the postwar peace produce more debate about the uses of power and why didn't those scant debates produce more resistance to the emerging patterns of power?

To provide full answers to these questions, one would have to recount the various and complex processes through which American political culture after 1945 came to inhibit objections against enlarged Executive ambition, taking into account the pressure of growing international entanglements, the multiplication of long-brewed domestic conflicts, the

effects of new mass media, the retightening of paternal models of authority, the intensification of social and political bureaucracy, and indeed a
dozen other major social forces in full swing in "postwar" America. I want
to focus on just one theme here that, no doubt, overlaps with many of
these topics but remains nevertheless distinguishable from them. In 1974,
Senator Frank Church, attempting to survey the American scene from
the apogee of reaction against the presidency of Richard Nixon, gathered
up lines of thought from Clinton Rossiter's extraordinary book *Constitutional Dictatorship: Crisis Government in the Modern Democracies* (1948)
and held them against the background of the 140-page *Brief History of
Emergency Powers in the United States* he and his senate colleagues had
just commissioned from Library of Congress historian Harold Relyea.
Church drew from this the succinct conclusion that "emergency government has become the norm" in the United States.[18] Over the century of
development up to that moment, *emergency* and its corresponding use of
power had become part of regular politics and everyday life.

Thus we come again not just to the fact but to the problem of arriving
at understanding that is apt for the Citizen. In the last chapter we surveyed briefly and rejected the idea of "the exception." Another familiar
and related vocabulary comes to us from traditions of political writing
well-known to the Founders. Americans have often called upon a term
that was pivotal in the writings of John Locke and William Blackstone to
ask, Has the President expanded the *prerogative* to immediately enact his
"will"?[19] That is, Has the President stretched his part in the constitutional
balance, and fenced in the other parts, to shift it in his favor, thus making
it more arbitrary?

The notion of *prerogative* is not simple. Initially, in the ancient Roman
republic, it refers to a practice of popular government that designated the
first (*prae*) group to decide on new law (*rogo*, or question); in early modernity it points to a capacity of an absolute monarch in equivalent terms
but of a precedence or priority so distinct that we bystander-subjects
may not even discuss it;[20] later, framed by aspirations to the rule of law,
prerogative identifies an aspect of that same sovereignty but now relocated from the person of the king to the offices of the State.[21] In this last
phase, our phase, the persistent medieval assignment of *prerogative* as
"those rights and capacities which the King enjoys alone"[22] joins with
the need to justify such a power in modern constitutional terms. The
result most familiar to us is reflected in Locke's claim that *prerogative*

depends on "unforeseen and uncertain occurrences" that no law can cover and that require discretionary action by the Executive. This is an antilegalist constitutionalism, in which the preeminence of action over legislation is supposed to derive from a necessity that is both practical ("the emergency is upon us") and logical ("no law can predict all its own applications"), and necessity itself is measured by a norm with which, in principle, everyone could agree: *salus populi suprema lex*, or "the well-being of the people is the supreme law."[23]

This latest and in certain respects most extreme version of *prerogative* is the one we are prone to apply. It is the one that concerns us here. It suggests a perfectly familiar frame of reference within which to understand the ongoing transformation of our political culture. The approach to emergency powers through *prerogative* locates a background of American common sense, where individualist commitments—which may extend from the single person to the single sovereign to the single nation—are recognized as explanatory and power is modeled around a peculiarly modern image of "the will."[24]

This common sense is part of the very problem that must be brought to light if the Citizen is to understand his or her own position. Underscoring this here returns us to an issue narrowly sidestepped in chapter 1 when I proposed an unusual account of the Citizen's characteristic type of action and appealed to the idea that action is "divided" or "distributed" across networks of relationships. Now I want to put forward more vividly what is at stake. Without a clearer sense of this alternative view of action, we are unlikely to see how *war*, through the diffusion of *emergency*, modulates everyday political life, or how it gets its grip on each of us. Power is not simply the assertion of "will," and politics is not just the product of contradictions between one "will" and another. This again is why the language of *prerogative* is especially misleading.[25] It exacerbates a misunderstanding inherent in the single most important strategy offered to agents by the regime of individualism in America.* That strategy is the denial of the division of action and of the everyday interdependence that is its complement. Misunderstanding is inherent in that strategy insofar as it is taken at face value, as *description* rather than *strategic move*, as if to

---

* The fact that "individualism" leads to an empirically false description of human action does not mean that we do not appeal to it as belief and motive; this appeal is itself an additional social fact.

deny one's dependence on others is to *escape* from it, rather than to make use of it in particular ways. This gesture and the whole discursive edifice built upon it is profoundly antipolitical. Its terms cannot but confuse our analysis of politics.

This is a description of the fabric of society as it is woven or twisted under the exceedingly extensive set of circumstances we call *emergency* or *war*. These are not single events, or alien and inessential intrusions into normal life, or stains that come upon us and can be cleansed away. *Emergency* and *war* are patterns of human relationship, more or less prominent at one time or another, within the larger social weave.

It may seem that I am overly concerned about the choice of words with which to describe our *crisis*. But look at it this way. In the course of living one must survey one's surroundings. Terms are at once scalpels for cutting out a part of the whole and optics for seeing more clearly the part, the cut, and the rest. The Citizen is not the Sociologist.[26] It is one thing to describe in a general way—as I just have—a terrain of political relationships—the "fabric of society"—and another to enter and use it.* That is, if *emergency* and *war* are conditions of political relationships, *emergency powers* and *war powers* are ways of navigating through and making use of the fabric of society. The latter powers occur from within the former social facts; power is built on or through social relationships. Although we may read across centuries of debate that power is the basis of those relationships, or that power is the disruption of those relationships, such claims are false. To see power as prior or external to one's social situation is to lose all grip on reality just when clear-sightedness is most urgent.

And the issue here is power. In the United States, the constitutional order exemplifies facts about power that are much more general than any juridical document or legal practice can capture or represent.† The "separation of powers"—as doctrine, as institution, and as ideology—is not an imposition on power but rather a particular realization of its very nature and an attempt to use that fact against its own excess. "Checks and balances" may require categorically different parts (a "lever" here, a "gear" there) but is a practice framed by an almost Spinozistic politi-

---

* More precisely: both are modes of use, but with different ends, undertaken by different social types.

† N.b. that not only subsequent interpreters but even the Founders typically misunderstood this relationship, often supposing that power was only channeled or "checked and balanced" by the Constitution, rather than being *constituted* through it.

cal monism and disallows any sort of deus ex machina in public affairs.[27] Power—even apparently absolute or absolutist power—is never sui generis. All powers, including even the most immediate or brutal *emergency powers*, exist within some division of action. The division of action constitutive of Executive power cannot, ultimately, exclude the choices and acts of Congress. And, likewise, congressional power cannot, ultimately, exclude the choices and acts of the Citizen. Practices of choice like elections combine with (and gain their significance from) the fact that power at all levels draws positively and negatively on collective human energies. While these two implications of the Citizen in the constitution of power often follow very different logics, they both return us to the same fact. All constitutional powers arise within political processes. Wish and try as we might, these processes are never entirely circumscribed within the walls of the White House or the Pentagon, within the institutional boundaries of the presidency or Congress, or within symbolic orders like "inside the Washington beltway."

I really want to insist on this point when it comes to Executive power. For it is just this sort of power, personified in the President, concentrated by emergency, that seems simple and immediate. This false appearance is what allows those who issue absurd and rhetorically inept statements like "I am the decider and I decide what is best" to escape effective public criticism.[28] However, the sociological truth remains that all the President's powers arise within political processes constituted by the Constitution. The oddity here, of course, is that the scorn the President's self-description should have brought down upon him would have ultimately been misplaced. For no matter what outrage may issue now and again from the Executive branch of the American political system, the problem is not that the Commander-in-chief has become a king or an emperor. The expansion of one is inherently the failure of other constitutive powers. What counts, what actually transformed the "decider" into the Decider, was that practically no one save a few insipid comedians and the remarkable Keith Olbermann stood up to that declaration to call it by its proper name. When a Senator Byrd declares that "the President is not God," his words are not merely descriptive; he is admonishing his colleagues and constituents to *stand up against such pretensions, and precisely in so doing to prove them false.*[29]

Arguments about presidential "prerogative" typically derive from and point back to one source: the sense of injustice someone feels when subjected to the arbitrary decisions of another. But in many respects we are today in the opposite situation. Few in America seem to feel oppressed or "jerked around" by the willful, unjustified, and often incoherent fluctuations of the President's policies. In principle, abrogations of suspects' rights or broad intrusions into private affairs might touch anyone living within the reach of the State. Yet most Americans seem not to feel threatened by this possibility. Their attentions are elsewhere. Should we then say that a durable state of emergency has become possible because society is organized in a way that buffers most citizens from the direct pressures of arbitrary decision making?[30] If this were the case, however, it would just add another reason *not* to interpret our situation through the image of dictatorial *prerogative*. Simply, the image of a dictatorial "decider," no matter how vigorously promulgated by the President, obscures our attempts to reckon with the contemporary reformulation of *emergency powers*. We do best to set all such talk aside.

Where the *crisis* comes is not from dictatorship, "constitutional" or otherwise, but rather within the living constitution of democracy itself. To act through this crisis requires a different approach. Let us begin again with the following particularly apt observation made by Justice Jackson in the 1950s: "In the practical working of our government we already have evolved a technique within the framework of the constitution by which normal executive powers may be considerably expanded to meet an emergency."[31] The key to this "technique" is that Congress may, and often has, "granted extraordinary authorities which lie dormant in normal times."[32] More often than not such powers appear in specific emergency provisions of otherwise normal law.[33] They are dispersed, invisible, and inoperative until they are "called into play by the executive in war or upon proclamation of a national emergency." Through this constitutionally adept "procedure we retain government by law—special, temporary law, perhaps, but law nonetheless."[34]

This mutability may be seen as beneficial. "The discretion available to a Civil War President in his exercise of emergency power has been harnessed, to a considerable extent, in the contemporary period." Powers "available to the executive in time of national crisis or exigency have, since the time of the Lincoln Administration, come to be increasingly rooted in statutory law."[35] This is yet another reason why the individualistic "will"-oriented notion of "prerogative" misleads the Citizen: it tips us towards the view that "the buck stops" at the President's desk when in fact effects are being produced throughout the constitutional system.

Moreover, this mutability may also be detrimental. Might not the final result prove fatal, even by its very efficiency, when the originally uncoordinated outcomes of decades of diffuse deliberation converge instantly in the advent of unanticipated emergency circumstances? Even if such unplanned coordination were considered desirable, could a chief executive or Commander-in-chief anticipate and track exactly what had been unleashed as hundreds of widely scattered and previously unrelated laws that specify their own application under conditions of emergency suddenly stand, like an unfamiliar army, at attention? How, arriving with such speed and mass, could this new body of powers be checked? Would this not make political contestation less likely and more difficult? And would not caveat and objection lag ineffectually behind the Executive act?*

In the course of time the governmental "technique" to which Jackson refers brings emergency inside the rule of law and makes it a regular feature of the constitutional system. It highlights again the categorical difference between *emergency* and *exception*. It also makes clearer what is at stake in the everydayness of emergency.

The most straightforward and peculiar fact here is the maintenance of open-ended states of emergency. We noted FDR's remarkable declaration of 1933, and Truman's of 1950. Both lasted until 1976. They were overlapped and extended by others. We also saw that these emergencies were not primarily characterized by willful prerogative. The President's role in declaring emergency is limited to mobilizing the short-term and long-term complicity of Congress.

The *U.S. Code* clearly manifests this limitation. The President is authorized by legislation—the National Emergencies Act of 1976—to declare a "national emergency." However, "any special or extraordinary power" that devolves to the President as a consequence of this declaration must have prior authorization by an act of Congress (section 1621).† Thus Congress is a priori complicit in emergency powers by virtue of whatever laws it does or does not make before the desperate hour. Then the

---

* And so, our traditional terms fail again, for what sense can the word *prerogative* have when the Executive does not (and cannot) know exactly what it is "willing" by invoking an emergency. Even if this diffuseness of effects is subsequently accommodated within Executive strategy, the language of *prerogative* will obscure its significance.

† Any other powers in this situation would be either within the class of normal powers or, if not, and not additionally authorized by Congress, illegal.

complicity of Congress is regularly reiterated, as an active reaffirmation of the emergency is required from them every six months (section 1622b), and such a bill of confirmation or denial is prohibited from languishing in the process (section 1622c). Moreover, the President must state publicly which powers will be exercised (section 1631), and thus Congress cannot excuse itself by saying *we meant x* but *the President did y*. Every presidential order, rule, or regulation during national emergency must be recorded, indexed, and transmitted promptly to Congress (section 1641). In other words, an emergency is not, and certainly not for long, whatever the President points to and says, "I declare this an emergency" or "I am the decider." Likewise emergency powers do not extend to whatever, exercising an imagined "prerogative," the President chooses to do, even if it is "just this once," even if it is an "exception to the rule."

Now, what these sections from the *U.S. Code* intend is reinforcement of "checks and balances." Under certain conditions—which I refer to here as *complicity*—the effect is instead the amplification of one power.* This complicity is a characteristic feature of our times, and few admit how automatic it has become.[36]

The problem surfaced in a particularly indicative manner in 1952, when President Truman overstepped what I will now refer to as the *norm of complicity* and thus reinforced it. He presumed specific emergency power to be "inherent" in his office. Acting with reference to his own proclamation of "the existence of a National emergency" (December 16, 1950), Truman ordered the seizure of steel mills so as to prevent a nationwide strike by steelworkers during a war.[37] Moreover, he publicly took the position that the President could do whatever he saw as necessary. By not seeking the approval of Congress, by asserting that the "President is above courts," by implying he might "also seize the newspapers and/or radio stations,"[38] Truman offended the Congress, the courts, the press, and the people.[39]

When the steel companies brought suit against the government, the Supreme Court held that the President's order was invalid. Their decision in *Youngstown Sheet and Tube Co. v. Sawyer* was not a simple defense of private property rights.[40] In a series of concurring opinions the jus-

---

* Theorizing this issue the Founders inserted "virtue" of a specifically civic type as a stopgap; today this makes a nice campaign slogan but not an effective mechanism of governance.

tices rebuked the President for trying to do by himself something that requires collaboration with Congress. It is therefore typically understood as a landmark case regarding the doctrine of "separation of powers."[41] It may also be read as affirmation of what is clear by analogy from Article 4, § 4 of the Constitution, where in guaranteeing "to every state in this union a republican form of government" the whole of the United States is also called upon to "protect each of them . . . on application of the legislature, or of the executive (when the legislature cannot be convened) against domestic violence." This is, in my view, tantamount to saying that what it means to be republican is to grant priority to the legislature even in emergency. It is this priority that was reasserted at the national level in the *Youngstown* decision; it is this priority that requires us to point a finger at Congress today.

As far as we are concerned here, however, the key point is different. *Youngstown Sheet and Tube Co. v. Sawyer* erects no obstacle to the ongoing normalization of emergency powers within the constitutional system as a whole. Testing a limit of that process, the Court indicated in what form it would go forward. The Court affirmed the "technique" of government articulated by Justice Jackson.[42] The President was left with the power to identify general states of emergency; then, by declaration, he is permitted to bring into effect specific emergency provisions of statute law. Nothing ensures that the circumstances of this application will be the ones foreseen by the legislators who voted for these provisions.* Indeed, given changing circumstances within the long temporal reach of the statutory provisions, the purpose and result of particular applications are likely to be quite distinct from the nominal directives the President advances through the law. Such disjunctions will often serve the interests of the Executive office and those who hold it.

In *Youngstown* the Court effectively reaffirmed two social facts. The first is that emergency powers involve a division of action. In this the emergency power is just like every other kind. The President cannot have "inherent" authority to act alone because—notwithstanding the myths and pathologies of undivided action—that would contradict the nature of power. The second social fact—an often unnoticed corollary of power's

---

* Note that the declaration of emergency cannot be justified as an *Executive* function; it legislates what Montesquieu—a thinker beloved by our Founders—might have called "the spirit of the law." One corrective would be to amend the Constitution to assign not only the declaration of war but the declaration of emergency to Congress.

emergence within the division of action—is that recognition of a power can have the perverse effect of neutralizing it. Given the real constellation of constitutional beliefs and practices in the 1950s, the Court may have declared the priority of congressional authority but did so in the most minimal way, requiring only a rubber stamp for even the most aggressive uses of State power by the Executive. The language of the Court and the tenor of the times suggests strongly that the Court would have allowed Truman's purpose to be achieved by an act of Congress.

This connects with an additional aspect of the integration of emergency into everyday life. Whatever motive legislators may have—and they may have many—for including emergency provisions in a wide range of statute law, the result of such provisions has been an accretion of rapidly applicable means of social control in the hands of the Executive. The Executive can thus accelerate his actions. Now, the primary counterbalancing tendency at the disposal of the Citizen is what I have called the "publicizing speech act," or the implication of a third party in a two-way dispute so as to change the balance of social forces that dispute represents and continues. The operation of this force within the constitutional system, as a whole and at every level, inflects or modulates Executive projects. However, precisely those circumstances of deference to the Executive in emergency that accelerate Executive action also slow the effect of contrary assertions of citizen force through "publicizing." It is—I think—fairly easy to see that at crucial junctures the balance will change in favor of Executive projects.*

It may be admitted that even under such circumstances Executive power remains subject to "checks and balances" in the long run. But the *long run* provides recourse or solace only for those who can weather the storm. In the meantime, what changes in practice is the composition of power *within the Constitution,* which is to say *that which would be checked tomorrow is transformed today.*† Acceleration is one such transformation.

---

* Where certain publicizing acts can be accelerated (e.g. through the Internet) and beneficial results (e.g. ships stay in port, an election is won or lost) accrue, in time the process I describe here may be interrupted, although such short-term effects may also remain largely independent of the general trend to complicity with the Executive.

† We will see more clearly below that what constitutes power and what configures acts as legal or illegal are not always on the same map. It should be clear that some uses of power that emerge within the constitutional system are, and indeed should be, illegal; I will have a bit more to say on this surprising but not contradictory fact towards the end of chapter 6.

Accelerated Executive initiative is met by slower resistance, reconsideration, adjustment, and response. There is a time lag between the two. This margin of time becomes a field of opportunity for the Executive as he runs ahead of the rest of the political process. In such situations, recourse to the Supreme Court is not sufficient to "keep power in the hands of Congress if [Congress] is not wise and timely in meeting its problems."[43] The public cost of malignant use of this margin of time between act and reaction—like the polluting corporation that takes EPA fines as a business expense—can be astronomical. Exactly such opportunism around the invasion of Iraq has been funded by thousands of lives, billions of dollars, and the good name of the United States for generations to come.

Consistent with the unavoidably divided character of emergency powers, the perspicacious Justice Jackson affirmed that "a crisis that challenges the President equally, or perhaps primarily, challenges Congress." Even while observing the norm of congressional complicity in Executive adventure, Jackson recognized how dangerous that norm may be for the constitutional system. "We may say that power to legislate for emergencies belongs in the hands of Congress, but only Congress itself can prevent power from slipping through its fingers."[44] In the thrall of unprecedented Executive pretension, failing in the fall of 2007 to staunch the extraordinary military and political disaster still unfolding in Iraq, elected Democrats found themselves reduced to resolving—and thereby again belittling that word—that the august House of Representatives should condemn the "unwarranted slur" made by Rush Limbaugh against American soldiers who criticized the war; that courageous effort came on the heels of a Republican maneuver to "condemn an advertisement by MoveOn.org in The New York Times . . . that referred to Gen. David H. Petraeus as 'General Betray Us.'"*

We will soon consider in more detail how the historical and cultural situation in America after World War II bears today on the position of the Citizen (see chapter 5). In that context tight linkages between the normalization of emergency and the norm of congressional complicity stand in high relief and the combination of the two brings into existence powers that will be, at some crucial moments, irresistible.

---

* Reported by Carl Hulse in the *New York Times* on October 3, 2007. The ad followed a performance by the general in congressional hearings on September 11, 2007, reminiscent of Colin Powell's spectacle before the Security Council of the United Nations on February 5, 2003.

At this point, something else should also be clear. What counts in the normalization of emergency powers is not just the relation between the Executive and Congress. The position of the President with respect to the people is equally important. The concentration of Executive power in a single person is not just a matter of administrative efficiency. The fact that the whole nation has a part in choosing this one person makes the President, as Justice Jackson observed in 1952, "the focus of public hopes and expectations." No statement could name more concisely the legacy of Franklin D. Roosevelt. As Jackson also remarked, however, America after World War II was deeply afflicted with the political pathology of conformism, and the position of the President appeared in a new light:

> In drama, magnitude and finality [the President's] decisions so far over-shadow any others that almost alone he fills the public eye and ear. No other personality in public life can begin to compete with him in access to the public mind through modern methods of communications. By his prestige as head of state and his influence upon public opinion he exerts a leverage upon those who are supposed to check and balance his power which often cancels their effectiveness.[45]

Anyone who has observed himself, his friends, and his fellow citizens knows that the President does not in any direct way *create* public opinion; the President is not the *cause* of what we think or believe. Justice Jackson's point is that emergency powers involve more than simple negotiation between a (passive in this instance) Legislative and an (active in this instance) Executive branch of government. The adjustment between branches is a political process like other ones. "Publicizing," or the implication of a third party in the contest between them, can be decisive. The role of third parties in cases that bear on the highest prestige and authority of the President is played by the People in general and the various and shifting publics formed among them. The charismatic effect Jackson identifies weighs heavily here. The President has real advantages in this triangular process of "publicizing" because he can, as the saying so aptly goes, "command a public."

Where publicizing speech acts become a major factor, politics in the broadest sense has come into play. This politics overflows the relatively narrow frame of legal constraints that, for the purposes of clearer analysis, I have clung to the skirts of in this and the preceding chapters. This overflow is essential to one of the major lines of thought I develop in this book: the constitutional system in the United States is not limited to the branches of government, nor is it just a matter of providing a structure for the "rule of law." Only once a realm of citizen action, a political realm, has been formed can the Constitution be said to have accomplished its purpose. The "separation of powers" has no democratic meaning if it does not include the Citizen.[46] Moreover, it must be seen two ways at once: from one angle, with its own logic and time frame, "separation" pits one power against another to modify, delay, or cancel its effects; from another angle, again with its own logic and time frame, "separation" is a misnomer for a process of composition, as each "power" is always already a set of relationships with the others and the changing balance of the "components" is—as one advances and another gives way, as the effective boundaries shift in the process—identical with their transformation.

An obvious but nonetheless decisive implication of this wholehearted incorporation of the Citizen into the Constitution is this: the spirit and practices of emergency could not have come to define the field of politics without a profound transformation of common sense, which is to say a transformation in the widely distributed habits of practice and belief that hold society together. It is this wider shift, and not a purely juridical change, that is ultimately signified when we acknowledge with Senator Church that "emergency . . . has become the norm."[47]

Now, cultural reaction against this development may have taken various forms: a boisterous *antipolitics* in which everyone rails against "usurpers in Washington," a political deployment of *antipolitics* in which elected officials cannibalistically promote "privatization" to cut the bureaucratic supports from under Executive action. Democracy produces its own pathologies as internal and necessary features conduct the body politic towards a kind of self-destructiveness, and antipolitics is one of them.* But a somewhat different political pathology corresponds in a more potent way to the normalization of emergency. Once powers supposed to be divided are seen additionally as composed within a complex play of forces, the shifting balance towards the Executive sustained by the rhetoric of emergency must likewise be understood as involving failures of resistance.

Thus what I referred to above as the *norm of complicity* is more comprehensive than it seems at first. The cultural development that most com-

---

* Rather than being a simple preference for the "something else" of private life.

pletely effects—by failing to impede—the normalization of emergency, the production of an emergency-ordained-and-oriented common sense,[48] is the political pathology of uninflected speech, in which a sort of vociferous speechlessness seizes those situations in which actions, institutions, and legislation cry out for the corrective effect of public contest and negotiation. This is the context, our context, within which both extensive Executive powers and the loose and de-responsibilized authorization of such powers by Congress have ceased to raise indignation or resistance, or even serious questions, from citizens.[49]

We may now ask, *What motivates this critical abdication by the Citizen? By what lever does the President move the public against enacting resistance or against imposing constraints, and in that way exert "a leverage upon those who are supposed to check and balance his power which often cancels their effectiveness?"*[50]

The relevant answer here is, again, *war*. This is in part old news. The rhetoric of *war* has unparalleled *decorum*: it gets the "right" response from almost everyone; it pulls together all sorts of projects that are incommensurable under the rubric of *peace*. What is new is the way *war* is rooted more deeply than ever in *terror*. This multiplies the rhetorical force of *war* in the life of the Citizen.

Of course, other motives set the valence of the Citizen in the constitutional formulation of powers. But *war* has the greatest weight.[51] After September 11th, the call of *war* is what most easily silences the natural objections to presidential ambition and overreach.

Now we come again and squarely face to face, rearmed, with the effect produced as two great trends of the twentieth century intersect in everyday life: emergency government has become the norm, and the boundary between war and not-war has all but collapsed. As it has become more and more difficult to see when wars begin and when they end, a capacious zone of indeterminacy has emerged. In this zone we are pressed repeatedly to ask, *Is this war or not?* Ambivalence increases anxiety. It loosens the tethers on power. But what power is actually unleashed? If there is no clear *war*, there can be no clear *war powers*. The more general rule of emergency commands the scene. Against that backdrop, the image of *war*, precisely due to its indistinctness, generates even greater, enormous, opportunities. To dress domestic projects in the garb of war becomes a simple and common and increasingly unremarked political strategy. It runs the opposition down, and they "don't know what hit them." To appropriate the question *Is this war or not?* no less than to answer it becomes an exceedingly extensive and open-ended instrument for shaping domestic policy. More insidious still: the fuzzy boundary between war and not-war makes it easier to go to war *in order to* transform the political landscape at home. The Executive lies in wait for war, ready to take hold of the moment when it comes.[52] Carpe diem, seize the reins of the wilding that occurred on that New York September morning.

Listen again here to the voice of Justice Jackson. It resonates clearly today from the original moment of the Cold War. "Of course," he wrote,

> a state of war may in fact exist without a formal declaration. . . . but no doctrine that the court could promulgate would seem to me more sinister and alarming than that a President whose conduct of foreign affairs is so largely uncontrolled, and often even is unknown, can vastly enlarge his mastery over the internal affairs of the country by his own commitment of the nation's armed forces to some foreign venture.[53]

So we have come almost all the way around the circle we began in chapter 2. The struggle over who will decide—*Is this war or not?*—is of utmost importance for the Citizen. No authority—legal or constitutional, no less scientific, historical, or moral—provides definitive guidance. The Citizen must judge for him- or herself. The form and possibilities of how we will live together every day—in short, of politics—depends on how we answer this question.

Ask the question, in each instance where you are called upon to engage or abstain, *Is this war or not?* Let us assume this as a key maxim for citizen judgment and action in our time. Positive and negative answers each produce their own chains of reaction; if *it is war*, subsequent judgments and actions will be affected one way; if *it is not war*, subsequent judgments and actions will be inflected in other ways. The process of asking and answering this question has, in a certain sense, been the underlying motive of the present and the preceding chapters. My purpose has been to exemplify the kind of inquiry suited to the position of the Citizen in the United States today.

Now that thematic question—*Is this war or not?*—requires another pass by the position of the Citizen and a view from its specific perspective. We are drawn back to the nature of *war* as the "continuation of politics"* and the historical rearticulation of this social fact in the twentieth century as *civic war*. *Homeland, home front, town square, public sphere, Capitol, White House*, and numerous other scenes of civic engagement *in war* are not scenes of battle. To say this is to diminish but not disclaim the military warfighting aspect of war. It is to insist on the culminating point announced in the title of this chapter: the facts of the everyday life of the Citizen must be the starting point for understanding the realm of violence and its relation to politics.

That is to say, when we ask *Is this war or not?* the political answer to this question will not call forth the authorities of international law, nor will it feature the facts of troop expedition, weapons deployment, the intensity of combat, and so forth. Not even the body count. What will matter most is rather how such facts of warfighting are inserted into and shape the broader social fact of *civic war*, the circumstances of everyday experience that give motive and form to the acts of the Citizen.

This is the stage on which critical abdications by the Citizen do or do not materialize, and where the corresponding composition of *all* the constitutional powers takes shape.† It goes without saying that the potential for this corruption of the Citizen does not derive uniquely from the ways that warfighting operation are intermingled into civic life; indeed, the modern historical separation of the role of Citizen from the role of Soldier ensures this intermingling will be a source of tensions. It remains that the steady infiltration of military facts into civic life must be understood as a decisive factor in this sort of corruption for the following reason. The feature of war—any sort of war—that mobilizes citizens in civic life is *emergency*. Emergency—as material and symbolic pressure on experience—has a double effect. Although we may typically think of it as a motive to act, it often and at the same time moves those subject to it towards docility and deference. With this combined push and pull, an ambivalence inheres in *civic war*. The driving factor of emergency both activates citizens and channels our passive energies. The relative balance and applications of these two tendencies configures the political landscape of *civic war*. Call for "the defense of freedom" and the Citizen jumps forward; harp on the image of destruction and terror, and the Citi-

---

* See chapters 2 and 3 for development of this point.
† This is not to deny, of course, that other factors (juridical, institutional, ideological, economic, personal, etc.) influence the shape of these powers.

zen recoils in search of protection. Of course, the effects of discourse in politics are never this simple or direct. Nonetheless, add into this crude picture of social mechanism many more weights and levers and the type of balancing act that sets the political stage today becomes imaginable. If we are to have any hope of seeing how armed conflict actually enters into and transforms *civic war*, the realm of violence must be interpreted through the facts of the everyday life of the Citizen.

For the vast majority of citizens in the United States this insertion occurs by way of shocking representations of battlefield dangers that, as representations, have in fact been made safe, predictable, and subject to manipulation. This fact multiplies the importance of the interpretive practice I recommend for the judgment and action of the Citizen.

This is a very abstract description of what is ultimately a microscopic and gritty social process within which violence repeatedly lights the spark of emergency and catalyzes *civic war*.

Precisely because I have given so much attention to emergency powers it would be easy to misunderstand what I refer to in the title of this chapter with the phrase "The Regeneration of Emergency through Violence." So let me first exclude some familiar claims.

It would be beside my point to rehearse otherwise important arguments about violence in the origins or foundations of the State, about violence as a reserve and guarantee for State power, or about State power as a "monopoly of legitimate violence."[54] The tableaux one has grown to expect under such headings—citizens beaten down or terrified into submission—are belied by the very facts under discussion here. If American society were primarily controlled by this kind of violence, it would be absurd to unequivocally sustain, as I do, the conclusion that constitutional powers arise from such dimensions of political culture as citizen judgment and common sense. This is hardly a new point but one that seems time and time again to escape attention. David Hume pithily observed in 1742 that "nothing appears more surprising . . . than the easiness with which the many are governed by the few. . . . When we enquire by what means this wonder is effected, we shall find, that, as FORCE is always on the side of the governed, the governors have nothing to support them but opinion. It is therefore, on opinion only that government is founded; and this maxim extends to the most despotic and most military governments, as well as to the most free and most popular."[55] This maxim is apt today. One of the mysteries concerning the normalization of emergency powers in the United States is that it has so often been advanced without assertions of violence by the State against the Citizen. We did see in chapter 3 an extremely important exception to this: at certain pivotal moments in the century after the Civil War the State responded to industrial conflict by invoking emergency, then used emergency to apply violence against citizens, then incorporated for itself those expanded emergency powers. But it has been precisely in the situations where *emergency* and *war* converge—from the First World War to the present—that this kind of violence has become less and less necessary. Indeed, within an effort to think from and about the position of the Citizen today, to insist that latent violence is the final arbiter of all public questions seems obviously incorrect. It is certainly without significant overarching political effect.

This is a delicate and pivotal point, so let me be clear. I do not deny that in *other* respects State violence is a key social fact; I do claim that these otherwise enormously important aspects of the American scene are not essential to the transformation of politics registered in these pages. These issues can and had better be separated. For to insist that violence is not the ultimate arbiter of all public questions is not in the least to ignore or deny that a significant minority of people, citizens included, and occasionally identifiable groups or whole neighborhoods, are direct objects of State violence in America. The world and experience of the American citizen is shot through with activities and symbols of State violence; these include obvious things like the television show *Cops*, but also such dispersed things as the fact and image of prisons and the vast number of human beings whose lives are defined by them. Even the pervasiveness of guns in America works this way, the sheer symbolic presence of which is of incomparably greater importance than the actual number of times those guns are fired.* I admit that an account of all this would be worthwhile, and that it would sustain my culminating claim in this chapter, which I will come to in just a moment.

Before that, however, there is the more general point about the relationship between violence and political life: even the coercive use of violence against certain individuals or groups is not sustained as such

---

* The omnipresence of guns in the social imaginary may be a fact of high relevance to the acculturation of emergency powers; this point is too complex to discuss here, especially since common sense would have it (falsely) that what is symbolized by guns is potential resistance to State power.

through additional coercion. For example, while majorities do systematically allow police beatings or prison rape, it is not because they themselves
have been subject to some form of coercive violence by the State. Support
for violence typically arises from other social, cultural, or psychological
sources; some of these derive from experience with violence but many do
not. Such sources must include racism, sexism,* homophobia, arrogance,
inexperience, fundamentalist intolerance, and a host of others.[56]

One could go further and observe that the violence of the State, even
when the pretense to monopoly is not undone, may diminish rather than
amplify the State's own legitimacy. Under pressure of repeated violence
minorities may be more likely to resist (directly or indirectly)[57] than to
acquiesce in the devolution of constitutional politics through the dialectic of civic war and emergency described in this book. In other words,
those directly subject to the State's "monopoly of legitimate violence,"
insofar as they are relevant here at all, may provide a kind of exception
that proves the rule. The fact remains that most people who follow the
leadership of the Executive in emergency do not do so because they feel
threatened by the State.[58] It is neither fear of punishment nor the satisfaction of seeing transgressors arrested that undermine natural resistance to
the concentration of political power. The motive force is a greater fear
of something else.

We know full well that great fears may be ignited by the Terrorist. But
on that pretext such fears are enlarged by the Executive's use of the word
war. Whether or not that word is used metaphorically, its function *in
civic life* is to introduce, amplify, shape, and manage fear in the political
field. This rhetorical process, in turn, constitutes the politics of which the
social fact of war itself is a continuation.

All wars, even "wars of words,"[59] rely on such structuring references
to violence. Even if violence is not coterminous with war, the effects of
violence within the political field of war are usually overpowering. But in
what way?

It often seems, and has often been asserted, that a proclivity to aggression and violence is natural to the human animal.[60] Victor Davis Hanson—
the public provocateur we encountered in chapter 2—is only the latest
in a long line of writers who insist that this proclivity is the cause of

---

* I hesitate on this particular point because it is possible that sexism is inherently linked to
experience with violence.

war. No one can say whether this cartoon view contains some correct insight. For, the fact is that no one has ever seen a human being in a "state of nature." Human beings enter into proliferating relationships with other people from their birth, and these relationships cannot be separated from individual identity and motives. Human instincts and hormones, if they are behavioral in any meaningful sense, are always inflected by human relationships. This—and not the exception to it—is our nature.

It is, of course, just this relational nature that defines the position—every position—of the Citizen. Misguided followers of Thomas Hobbes may think otherwise, but they are wrong.* Or one may think the narrowness of Hanson's view excused by the fact that he studies an ancient world, a time before modernity deepened the complexity of the division of action. Yet this, too, is wrong. It ignores the dual role—Citizen *and* Soldier—at the core of ancient republics. The fact is that war has never been entirely about aggression, battle, or violence.

Those more cautious to see war not just as history but *in history*, in the developmental flow of human relationships over time, have been inclined to reverse the equation. The great historical sociologist Norbert Elias, for example, concluded that "it is not aggressiveness that triggers conflicts but conflicts that trigger aggressiveness."[61] Taken as a hypothesis concerning a fundamental question that can never be finally resolved, this at least changes, and changes profoundly, the picture before us. A conflict is always a relationship. It follows that society, with its civic realm, cannot be assumed to imply smooth cooperation. There is no founding moment of consensus, no "social contract" that makes, like some theological image of Paradise, everything all right. The fact is, in the words of French political theorist Pierre Rosanvallon, that "conflict and society are inseparable terms" and that "the acceptance of conflict lies at the heart of the process of the self-production of the social."[62]

To see things this way brings to the foreground another set of concerns that are confusing but nonetheless fundamental. For we have to keep in mind that *the political option*, the principle that opens the very possibility of politics, is to choose speech instead of violence when faced with conflict. To be a citizen is to lean away from violence with other citizens; with the increasing separation from the role of Soldier,

---

* And they have misunderstood Hobbes as well.

the Citizen may live an entire life without direct experience of war's violence.*

Thus an additional complexity of inquiry in pursuit of a position for the Citizen is indicated. War is a continuation of politics; violence is destructive of politics; yet, violence is also one persistent feature of war; the realm of violence must be interpreted through the facts of the everyday life of the Citizen; in what way, then, do the effects of violence enter, even capture, the political field without destroying politics altogether? We may ask this question in another way: there are two senses of the word *war*, one *civic* and the other *military*; what is the relationship between them?

In war, the human results of war's violence constantly intrude on the life of the Citizen. Some have sons and daughters who are returned dead, or disfigured, or transformed. The brush with war's violence reshapes character. The returned take up their citizenship in a new way, as do those who love or know them well. Mothers and widows and veterans vote, for example, and they remember their fallen and wounded sons and husbands and comrades when they do. These people may not be a majority of the population, but they exert great influence by writing books and making movies, by working for newspapers and teaching in schools, and simply by living every day together with fellow citizens. One way or another, they are reminders of what they have lived. They represent the violence of war. Their *presence* is itself a representation within *civic war* of that other *military* and *warfighting* side of war. Think of the aura of that slain soldier's wife at the market or in church. Remember how fellow citizens, from the first to last age, are mesmerized by the ones who have been directly touched by war's violence.

As they themselves function as signs of violence, those who have experienced violence often become the justification to make war. Thus one aspect of war feeds another: Do it for them! For the suffering survivors! For the memory of our martyrs! Let your anger rise before the weeping mother! Take an eye for an eye!

Many emotions are fanned in this recycling image of violence. The hero with his Purple Heart and the raging Rambo across the screen pump courage into the faint of heart. The motto "shock and awe"†—announced

---

* I will not speculate here on the impact this may have on the attraction to and practice of violence in other roles.

† This is, of course, effectively a terrorist motto in the sense described in chapter 1.

by the Executive in lieu of a coherent strategy for the invasion of Afghanistan in 2001—probably meant little for an enemy who never heard the name of the bomb that hit him but certainly bolstered pride and hubris on the home front.[63] Displays of overwhelming force show the Citizen it is "safe" to proceed further with the war.

Of all the emotions, however, the first raised by the representation of violence is fear. The violence of war has its initial effect on the position of the Citizen this way: it makes us afraid.*

I do not refer here to the terror felt, for example, by the citizens of Dresden when British and American bombs turned that town into an inferno in February 1945. Nor is it the terror of bystanders in Gaza or Damascus when Israeli rockets have taken down another leader of Hamas. My point here concerns how violence *there*—for example, at the site of an American expeditionary war—produces fear *here*—among us citizens.

However perverse it may seem, nothing suggests more clearly than terrorism how fear-producing effects of violence enter the political field without destroying it. It is an obvious but neglected fact that few are present at the scene of terrorist violence. The shock must make waves. To achieve his end the Terrorist both disorders our lives and *uses the order* of our "public sphere" to transform shock into fear, and fear into terror. It is, for instance, the media that broadcast *terror*, make predictable our response, allow the Terrorist to play us a certain way, and thus prolong his effect. Because fear always arises as a complement of certain types of anticipation or hope we are not afraid of the Terrorist per se but of the mental image of his future actions. We are dogged by *the threat*.

We, not *them*, move *terror* into *war*. And *war* is a reservoir of refreshed threat. The representations and the representatives of war's violence circulate among us. Perhaps the image of the Twin Towers falling will shock us for decades to come. But each day scenes of fighting in Fallujah or the presence of a wounded cousin in a VA hospital combine with common belief ("Iraq is a hot-bed of terrorists" or "The war in Iraq a key part of the 'war on terrorism'") and common practice (television, movies, news headlines) to keep vividly in mind *the threat*.†

---

* I have already shown—in chapters 1 and 2—that this is not a matter of instinctive reflex; fear is a social practice that builds on "immediate sensorial attention" or shock.

† N.b. that this belief is independent of whether there were or now are members of Al Qaeda in Iraq.

The continual regeneration of *the threat* is what makes this shift—*our* shift—from *terror* to *war* a prolongation of *terror* rather than a remedy for it. *We*, not *them*, accept *terror* into our *political life*.

In the process, *war*—entered into common sense and entwined with everyday experience as the paradigmatic instance of *emergency* I have described in this and the previous chapters—becomes a new and pervasive "frame of acceptance." We perceive the world as *war* and this symbolic fact structures action.[64] With *war*, future terrorist attacks no longer appear before us as simply possible. They are constitutive of our worldview. A world without terrorism ceases to make sense. Future terrorist attacks can be represented as necessary. The image of violence inherent in war purveys this necessity. This is frightening.

This is how violence enters the political field through the *image of war*. Why doesn't it tear politics apart?

While the effect I describe depends on actual ad hoc attacks by the Terrorist, it is frightening in a different and more systematic way. Unlike the immediate shock of September 11th, this fear is fit and acclimated within a complex and ongoing division of action. It is more structured and manageable. The Terrorist uses the "public sphere," but it is our transformation of *that use* into *war* that makes fear a constitutive part of the "public sphere."

Anything in the "public sphere" is ready for deployment in the constitution of political processes. It can, as we have seen from another angle, figure into the formation of the Executive powers of war and emergency. Just in using the State's "monopoly on legitimate violence" to increase security, the Executive grants credence to, even brings closer to home, the source of the terror it purports to assuage.

The State can never abolish all "illegitimate violence." But even broadcast aspirations to do so are suspect. Whatever its intent, violence by others can legitimate or serve as pretext for State action. This may involve the dispatch of armed forces. But not only that. That is, again, why we need a wider conception of *war*. For the *violence of war*—by *them* or by *us*—typically sustains fears that are functional within the everyday sphere of politics. Citizens feel protected by the State only if there is something from which to protect them.

Thus there are systematic incentives pulling in what seem like contradictory directions: to reduce fear and to amplify it, to dissolve fear and to control it. Only *enough* of the *right kind* of fear provides opportunity for power. The on-balance feeling of being protected is what undermines natural resistance to the concentration of power. As we have seen, the latitude sought and granted to power in times of war is broad. It extends, in the form of emergency, to all sorts of projects. And in the "system" constituted by America at war, our *civic war*, it is the Executive that most benefits from the increased terror produced by the violence of war. Think, for example, of how much everyone defers to a "war president" and how this alignment of energy and discourse overwhelms anyone who tries to oppose him.

One could go much farther in this direction. My main point, however, is that just as the Citizen had better adopt a more capacious view of war, an understanding of war as the "continuation of politics" in which several versions of politics are implicated would be well-served by more acute recognition of the symbolic role of violence in war. Indeed, for the Citizen, the crucial play of violence, *even during war*, is in the imagination. That is where emergency is regenerated. That is how violence becomes the wellspring not of the bursting pretensions of this new form of power but of the complicity that lets power take its own destructive course.

5. The Cold War Is Not Over

And this is happening in the face of the reality that the availability of
weapons of greatly increased lethality is growing. We all need to consider
where this risky trend could take us. In many ways, this war is different
than any we have ever fought. But in other ways, our situation today
resembles that of free nations in the early days of the Cold War.

DONALD H. RUMSFELD, address to 42nd Munich Conference on Security
Policy (2006)

Whatever war Americans are fighting today, a contest is ongoing to establish exactly when it began, how it continues, and when it will end. The
position of the Citizen is bound up in this struggle. Within the distensible
decorum of war, each assertion of continuity or rupture benefits different people in different ways. The claim *This is war* is being stretched
across the whole social field. It is made to touch on and thus refigures a
wide range of other, apparently unrelated, questions. Imagination is the
instrument of this stretching.[1]

Is this just metaphor? After all, FDR's *war on unemployment*, President
Johnson's *war on poverty*, President Nixon's *war on drugs*, or a dozen
other such "wars," up to and including the *war on terror* . . . these are not
real wars.

Or are they? For scores of pages now we, too, have tugged at the margins of the capacious symbol *war*, dragging it back to the "homeland"
from abroad, drawing it across the social terrain, mapping with it emergency, locating and relocating *war* in every nook and cranny of everyday
life. But I have made no pretense to settle the question *Is this war?* I have

aimed only to unfold that question as the Citizen might, and thus to reveal how in *civic war* the ambiguities inherent in the Citizen's experience themselves become motive forces in society, zones of untitled and thus appropriable effects around which plays for power succeed or fail.

Of this ambiguity the Cold War is an apotheosis. In no period of our history have citizens lived in greater obscurity concerning what the assertion *this is war* entails. In no period has this ambiguity weighed more heavily, wreaked more havoc, created more malign opportunity. Cold War is the paradigm of modern *civic war*.

There can be no doubt that the Cold War was more than a metaphor. The widely repeated commonplace that "it ended without a shot, it ended without anybody being killed" is literally false and deeply misleading.[2] The Cold War had definitive characteristics of what we think of as literal, military war: from the application of violence to the creation of a culture of preparedness and sacrifice, from the gathering of intelligence to geopolitical maneuvers, from massive investment in weapons to the integration of the military into economy and society.

Yet it is true that the Cold War was not decided by firepower on a battlefield.[3] It was "a long twilight struggle" punctuated by occasional détente or "springtime thaw." It was a war undeclared and often unspoken, largely covert and often fought on the ground of culture, a war of indirection and show rather than the "shock and awe" of direct assault. No mobilization of State and civil society has illustrated more clearly or with greater diversity the fact that war is "the continuation of politics by other means." The Cold War was a great machine that, over a period of decades, constantly reconfigured the division of action in American society and delimited the position of the Citizen. All this was fueled by imagination.

Shall we say, then, that, while not unreal, not fake, not something dreamed up by someone, the Cold War was nonetheless an "imaginary war"?[4] What would this amount to?

The Cold War must be understood in light of something that is true in general about human beings and a more specific fact about the modern American citizen. The first general condition is that imagination—our faculty for projective future orientation—is always operative in everyday life; it guides the next step, balances dependence, affirms plurality, adjusts the division of action, allocates our energies, and so forth. The second specific fact is that the experience of the American citizen has rarely unfurled in the space and time of battle.

In the Cold War, imagination ceased to be just one of several faculties of public discourse and became the primary one for a vast majority of Americans.* This shift allowed for the development of a new space of human relation. Anticipatory fear came to characterize the division of action at almost every point. The new circumstances of war conditioned this development.† For its intensity and long-lasting diffusion of enmity, the Cold War is comparable only with the Civil War. All the important action occurred within the "homeland" . . . but without battlefields.‡ Mobilizations of resources were initially demands placed on the imagination of the Citizen, a territory leaders constantly struggled to capture and hold. War factions exploited the "public sphere" as a crucible of socially distributed imagination. Common representations were built up and sent into battle on the field of common sense. Each worked with the imagination of the other to create or inflate resources. And the whole imaginary system of the Cold War revolved around a figure of terror, the *threat* of the weapon that was never used but remained vividly and ever present in imagination.

The "shot not fired," by means of which the Cold War was supposedly won, is, of course, the *atomic bomb*. Remember: neither you nor your parents have ever seen "the bomb," no less seen it explode. You have never experienced its physical force. Yet you are intimately acquainted with its powers. The word falls easily from your tongue. The effect is appalling.

Have even a handful of topoi in the history of humanity consumed as much attention? Like the ultimate creative power of God to which it has sometimes been compared, this destructive power has only been used once.§ By the time the Cold War had found its name, the image of nuclear weapons was already inscribed in every corner of the American mind. With this figure in mind, weapons tests and movements of battalions became tactical components in strategic attacks on the imagination.

---

* This fact fits within the broader transformation of the faculty of imagination since the nineteenth century, which is explained in my *Left Speechless* (forthcoming).
† Key features of the American mentality of Cold War exhibit this inflation of imagination; the messianic worldview symbiotic with the atomic bomb is an example, but so, too, is the so-called realism of strategic policy invention an imaginary consequentialism run amok.
‡ This is true for other "players" in the Cold War as well. By contrast, where tanks thundered in streets, the Cold War wrought something categorically different.
§ Literally, two American bombs dropped on Japan on August 6 and August 9, 1945, ended official combat in World War II, killed several hundred thousand human beings, and transformed the imagination of several billion more.

Not battle, but *threat*, not nuclear terrorists, but *nuclear terror*—in the old sense of a general existential fear brought upon the world by "the bomb"—moved the Cold War.[5]

It may seem that I am promoting an analogy between the Cold War and the position of the Citizen today. To put it that way is too weak. The Cold War does not merely suggest what kind of war we are in now. It is a key, perhaps *the* key, to our situation.

For to ask *What began on September 11th?* is also to ask *What ended before that day?* This question of continuity and rupture has been debated by Americans at every level of civil society and the State since then. Most people will insist that what paved the way for the new era of September 11th was the end of the Cold War. But what, exactly, had ended? How did it end? Or did it end at all?

The most widely held view is that the Cold War was essentially a geopolitical struggle between two "superpowers," the United States and the Soviet Union, conducted on the territory of others.[6] Almost by definition this would mean that the Cold War ended when the Soviet Union collapsed and the world was left with a single dominant nation.

Two consequences are supposed to have followed from the fact that the power of the United States was no longer checked by an approximately equal opponent. Americans came to believe they could act at "will."* Space opened in the international system for new conflicts and corresponding new strategies. For a variety of reasons, it is said, a significant portion of this space was captured by the Terrorist on September 11th.

In this common view, Cold War conflict was supposed to have been driven by Soviet expansionism, or by American expansionism, or by some combination of the two. To put it this way, however, is simply to enact in thought what the Cold War was supposed to have been in life. How illuminating is it, really, to add—as innumerable people followed President Truman in saying—that the struggle of the Cold War was between "alternative ways of life" or between the "false philosophy [of] communism" and democracy?[7] What is gained, really, by shifting reference from identifiable national entities to vague ideological commitments? Indeed, to think this way confuses the essential issues and makes even more vexing the question under scrutiny here: *Did the Cold War actually end?*

---

* The euphemism for which is "unilateralism."

Admit, if you like, that the Cold War was a matter of a particular "geopolitical" or "ideological" moment. Even if these views are correct, it does not follow that the Cold War had ended by September 11, 2001. No sword had passed, no surrender made, no treaty signed; and even had these events occurred, what, accustomed as we are to the fluid boundaries of other twentieth-century wars, would it prove?

In fact, these assumptions tend to disguise the many continuities between the decade, or decades, following World War II and the new wars of our moment. It is impossible that institutions, beliefs, and practices built up over several generations simply dissolve into thin air. They must persist, even if in so doing they often take on unexpected or perverse new forms. Recognition of this fact has in some quarters increased the search for precedents to the apparently new situation after September 11th, precedents that may shape or impede our continuing responses to it.

There are several common ways to reckon with the consequences of the Cold War today. One prevalent approach asserts that *by ending*, the Cold War created a vacuum that drew new actors onto the global stage. Another approach suggests that, even though the first one ended, our present international state of emergency is a *new Cold War*.[8]

The premise in both these views is wrong. Basic structures, programs, and personalities of the new wars after September 11th are ripe with the experience of the Cold War. There are important direct continuities on the sides of both friend and foe.* That the effectiveness of non-State actors has sharply increased should not obscure the fact that their game is being played by many of the same people with much of the same equipment. Across a wide range—from the CIA's education of Osama bin Laden to the formation of President Bush's foreign-policy group in the ranks of the Reagan administration or the substitution of Robert Gates for Donald Rumsfeld[9]—both progenitors and progeny of the Cold War are still with us. It is clear that more than analogy links the position of the Citizen today to this particular past.

Let me be brutally clear about what I am driving at here. I cannot adjudicate *for* the Citizen. But if we are to evaluate claims about our history *from* the position of the Citizen, we had better start asking questions like

---

* As there are continuities in the way American foreign policy transforms *friend* into *foe*, or vice versa.

How does the claim "the Cold War is over" help us to think through our current predicaments? Which positions and persons are favored by this belief and which disadvantaged?

I will recommend that to approach these questions we do well to reconsider the Cold War in light of what I have written in preceding chapters about America's modern experience of war. We had better focus on what the Cold War was *for* the position of the Citizen. This will require that we question or ignore many familiar narratives, or mingle them with new ones.

Whether the Cold War began in response to the Soviet occupation of Eastern Europe at the end of World War II (an "orthodox" view) or was primarily a Soviet reaction against an America reaching into "new frontiers" (a "revisionist" view), it quickly took on a life of its own within the United States. The Cold War was certainly a struggle over *communism*.[10] But as that word became a pivotal commonplace in American political culture, it had little to do with the ideology of the Soviet Union or the doctrines of Karl Marx. The word *communism* was astonishingly present in twentieth-century America, yet it had only the slightest institutional or ideological reality. This *dog that didn't bark* took its multiple meanings from how it was used within, and itself gave shape to, a capacious field of beliefs and contest in everyday domestic life. The negative proposition of *communism*—it is what we are not, it is the un-American or the not-yet-American—designated and ultimately justified the development of practices and movements that took *anticommunism*—like *antiterrorism* today—as opportunity for almost anything.*

My point here is this. In the everyday experience of American citizens, the Cold War was primarily a symbolic system operating within domestic political culture. It had powerful practical effect. This system was more basic to our political life than the conduct of foreign affairs that, in large measure, it determined. The principle features of this system were the threat of nuclear weapons and the feeling that the "American way of life" was under attack.

The trauma of World War II made Americans immediately susceptible to this growing, fundamentalist, and powerfully self-reproducing common sense. No one can doubt that it corresponded to and was fed by

---

* Paradoxically, these movements often developed the fanatical, authoritarian, or antipluralist tendencies they were said to be against.

certain international conditions. But I want to insist that for the Citizen the Cold War was to an astonishing degree independent from outside forces. It was thoroughly integrated into, and followed the local logic of, the everyday fact of living together with fellow citizens as that developed after 1945. From this experience—or, to say the same things in more precise terms, from this ongoing way of living together within a particular use of language—were constituted a view of the world, moral and political beliefs, institutions, artifacts of culture, and so forth. The Cold War was a powerful machinery orienting political conflicts and differences.

Many characteristic features of the experience of the Citizen during the Cold War continue today. How could it be otherwise? Every adult in the United States was born before the collapse of the Soviet Union. We are the grown children of the Cold War.* While most of us are not "Cold Warriors," we nonetheless have Cold War habits of thought and action. For, against, or agnostic, we are bearers of a primarily negative or antipathetic Cold War common sense. The positive—nota bene this means "in favor of," not "good"—significance of this common sense has only begun to define itself since the cloak of the Soviet threat has fallen away. It has grown out of the past sixty years of the American experience but now stands free from the symbolic object against which these same habits were developed.

I want to add here the following points. While my argument is not about geopolitics, neither is it oblivious to what happens outside American borders. I am not repeating the "revisionist" argument that domestic politics and especially capitalist economic interests drove American foreign policy after 1945 and that this fact was disguised behind rhetoric about the threat posed by the Soviet Union. That may or may not be true.

Rather, what I emphasize is that *the links of necessity and choice* between domestic affairs and the dealings of America in the world are primarily worked out *among us*, in the process of citizens positioning themselves. Politics does not "stop at the water's edge" because, properly understood, war, even America's expeditionary style of war, does not occur uniquely, or even primarily, outside our borders. The topology of warmaking may cut across the globe, but it is also inscribed within the details of our national, and even our local, life.

---

* I suspect that the same can be said even of immigrants to the United States in the postwar period, the majority of whom are from Latin America.

Absent from the Cold War was the everyday spectacle of battlefield carnage. The war took its place largely in the speech we use to accomplish the ongoing self-organization of society. Nonetheless, the Cold War exemplifies in great detail the essence of war as "a continuation of politics." Working on the position of the Citizen, war transforms what it continues. The Cold War manifested the decline of peace as the normal background condition against which clearly punctuated wars appear as events. It infiltrated war-readiness-without-mobilization into civil society. It is, in large measure, identical with the emergence of quasi-war as the norm.* In this process, September 11th was indeed an event of high importance *because it was a shocking amplification of existing trends*, not because it was a rupture.

We have seen pundits, prophets, and entrepreneurs advance themselves proclaiming that *the Cold War is over*. For the position of the Citizen this claim is utterly sterile. As others seize for themselves just the day, let the Citizen reach for a larger compass of our history. Let history proctor as we determine and pursue our national interests abroad. Let the historical continuity of politics be sought in real practices of human relationship, in the character of persons, in the forms of institutions. What is happening to us, what is at stake today, is this: *the Cold War persists*. It shapes the discourse and guides the conduct of politics at home. Now. The comprehensive cultural system that emerged in America over the course of the twentieth century continues its evolution. Nothing is more decisive than this fact for understanding the position of the Citizen after September 11th, its opportunities and pitfalls.[†]

The Cold War has typically been seen as a project of conservatives. This view derives, of course, from the conservative campaign to associate the domestic Left with the Soviet Union. It needs to be rethought for several reasons. Keep in mind that for the Citizen the Cold War—like other wars but even more so—was primarily an aspect of domestic political culture. Remember, too, that the *association with the Soviet Union* was drawn much more tightly by those on the Right than by American left-wing parties themselves. Finally, the symbolic system of the Cold

---

* This is why the question I am harping on in this book—"Is this or isn't this war?"—is actually a paraphrase of a wide set of practical questions that occupy a central place in political life.

† Not even the rise of jihadist Islamic fundamentalism, the shape of which movement is also largely a consequence of the Cold War.

War extended deep into common sense and cut across most political denominations.

The fact is that early purveyors of the Cold War, like the "brinksman" John Foster Dulles, were not so much conservatives as quintessential modernists bent on innovative transformation of American society. We will see what this means in a moment. I will then suggest how this modernist element in the mentality of the Cold War has resurfaced after September 11th, taking diverse forms in key players around the president. Once we have a sense of how the modernist worldview characteristic of the Cold War continues today, it can be shown that the most authentically conservative imperative present in *neoconservatism* is an aggressive antipathy to democracy. For trumpeting the false or even the true "spread of democracy" to others does not a democrat make.* In this respect, again, the Bush administration may have less in common with John Adams or Thomas Jefferson than with Leon Trotsky, exporter of revolution, who famously justified his tactics by saying "You can't make an omelette without breaking eggs."

Modernism—of the specifically political kind relevant here—revolves around the symbolic form and self-conception I have elsewhere referred to as the "new model will," the essential feature of which is to figure human beings as creating their own choices rather than merely having the faculty to freely decide between options that the world brings before them. The Modernist can imagine "the world to be annihilated," as that early modernist Thomas Hobbes did, because he or she can imagine creating a whole new world more to his or her liking from the ruins. The claims of the "new model will" started from an older theological logic of omnipotence and advanced it in secular egalitarian terms.[11] In modernist projects, appeals to the "new model will" justify strategic denials of both dependence and its division of action. Modernists at once exploit and minimize recognition of essential features of the political relationship like plurality and the publicizing speech act. They reach to take charge, to centralize control over everything, and for just that reason produce political pathologies when they engage in politics at all.[†]

---

* Democracies are not essentially charitable, but narcissistic.

[†] The very fact that it seems odd to refer to conservatives as "centralizers" is one reason why I promote a new vocabulary here. Their modernist impulse is masked by claims about privatization, free markets, philanthropy, etc. One may also point to the role of obsessive paternalistic control in the institutions of a free-market economy (the "firm" upon which the "market" depends; the absolutism inherent in the capitalist conception of individual property). We see

The arc of this modernist ambition is long. By 1800 the case for the "new model will" had been definitively articulated. This new symbolic form fostered the development of "more colossal productive forces than all preceding generations together." It would soon come to be broadly invested in culture and law.[12] By the century's end, it was fully manifest in the physical environment—from the pedagogically designed classroom to the planned and managed metropolis to the networks of canals and railroads across the whole nation—as modernists attempted to capture and channel through rational planning human energies amassed in great waves of immigration and urbanization in the decades following the Civil War.

It will take another book to catalogue the articulations of the "new model will," the effects they produced, and the further impact of those changes on the way human beings conceive themselves. It is enough to focus for now on the one great icon for all of this that, to our lasting misfortune, appeared at the end of World War II. For nothing accomplished and trumpeted the modern image of a human omnipotence more than the *atomic bomb*.

After two years of top-secret development and testing, the atomic bomb went public twice. Its destructive power was displayed to the population of Hiroshima of August 6, 1945. Its significance for American self-understanding was presented by President Truman sixteen hours later. Over the preceding month Secretary of War Henry L. Stimson had written the document Truman would provide to the press. Stimson, of course, had not seen the atomic bomb in action. Thus, from the very outset, imagination played the key role in constituting the cultural environment into which the bomb would fit and become a force in the everyday life of American citizens. Truman's press release conveys the following succinct message. The "atomic bomb . . . is a harnessing of the basic power of the universe. The force from which the sun draws its power has been loosed against those who brought war to the Far East." The United States, Truman implies, so overflows with power that we could devote "the tre-

---

this in a range of features from monolithic decision making (reflected in astronomical compensation rates and the starlike quality of CEOs) to the tendency to concentration. Likewise, evangelical philanthropy—as promoted by the Bush administration and as actually practiced in America—is an attack on plurality. We will return to this topic below. Of course, the "social engineering" projects of the New Deal and after were also modernist, but differed significantly in aiming to provide means that facilitate individual and collective self-determination.

mendous industrial and financial resources necessary for the project . . . without undue impairment of other vital war work." The "greatest marvel" is not the sheer existence of the atomic weapon but the fact that *we* made it and control its use, and with it we shall let forth "a rain of ruin from the air, the like of which has never been seen on this earth." "Atomic energy ushers in a new era" in which "it is not intended to divulge the technical processes of production or all the military applications, *unless or until some method of control can be devised that will protect us and the rest of the world from the danger of sudden destruction.*"[13]

This is a symbolic apogee of the arc of American ambition. It establishes the outlook of the Executive at the outset of the Cold War. And while Truman subsequently spoke of American attachment to internationalist projects like the United Nations, what appears here is a shockingly definitive statement of "unilateralism."

A wider-ranging comparison between our current moment and the early Cold War would be instructive. Then as now, we faced an unlimited war based on the possibility that the enemy could strike anywhere and anytime. We adopted a preventative posture involving ongoing war-readiness and characterized by intense secrecy and domestic security measures. We reorganized the armed forces around a new strategic situation and new weapons.[14] We restructured major parts of the military and national security bureaucracy.[15] Both moments were proceeded by a close election in which foreign policy played no prominent role.[16] A substantial part of our attention was directed to similar social issues—like "the family" and "the flag"[17]—and most people felt, somehow, these were related to the "war." All these changes were figured and refigured for the Citizen in a wider scene of words, images, and music.[18]

It would be easy to extend this list. However, I want now to underscore one additional and obvious fact: both early in the Cold War and after September 11th, *fear* came to occupy the foreground of our imagination.

What should the Citizen make of this remarkable and pivotal resemblance? A certain orientation follows if you believe the Cold War ended and we have embarked upon a wholly new era. Another way of positioning oneself would be recommended if these two historical phases in the political use of fear fit within a single framework.

Remember what George W. Bush wrote in his diary on the evening of September 11th: this is "our Pearl Harbor."[19] I have already shown why this analogy is flawed. I now want to point to another crucial fact *that this interpretive framework does not express.* In 1941 no towering sense of omnipotence was abroad in America. By contrast, in 2001 a decade of "cold war triumphalism" had brought to the Executive office persons of long-brewed ambition who saw nowhere in the world real obstacles to their power and their plans. In 1941 we were not "the world's only superpower."[20]

Why point to this difference to establish a similarity? As we have seen, fear is always companioned by aspiration. The size of the one is related to the size of the other. On September 11th an American sense of unimpeded omnipotence was caught up short. This worldview is a living legacy of the Cold War. September 11th does not mark its end, but rather its regeneration. It is a regeneration through violence.

If history ever has beginnings, the American bombing of Hiroshima was certainly one of them. The horrifying display of destruction created, so to speak, a pure reservoir of fear. Literature from nearly every nation in the next decades showed that this fear touched everyone in the world. At first, however, it did not weigh as heavily on Americans. Its instrument was in our hands. It would not, we imagined, be released from our grasp "unless or until," President Truman proclaimed, "some method of control can be devised that will protect us and the rest of the world from the danger of sudden destruction."

Subsequent events proved this view to be entirely wrong. On September 24, 1949, the *New York Times* headlined the first "Atom Blast in Russia." Until that moment, "free security" had shaped our national character and history.[21] Nuclear monopoly had prolonged this effect into the early era of postwar globalization. It now came to an end.

The existence of a single atomic weapon controlled by Americans had a particular strategic value. To realize this value in the political arena called for an appropriate rhetorical stance. Since few wanted to actually use the weapon, the atomic bomb had to be represented in order to produce its effect.* Many—like President Truman—favored an image of nuclear weapons as unstoppable means of destruction. For some, this image would ensure abstinence after the surrender of Japan. For those who

---

* The strategic impact of "the bomb" appeared first at the Potsdam negotiations with Stalin, immediately after the first successful test. This is the one case in which it would be used before being represented. Hiroshima was the original *signifiée*.

sought to extend American influence abroad, it would reduce the cost in lives and treasure.

Either way, representing the bomb and its masters as all-powerful would inspire overwhelming fear in our enemies. As long as we, too, were convinced of this power, and as long as we remained its sole owners, we could be relatively free from fear. "No one seemed too alarmed at the prospect" that the Soviets might develop their own weapon.[22]

The advent of the Russian bomb showed with stunning clarity the folly of this rhetorical stance. The apocalyptic image of nuclear weapons we had fostered turned against us when the "atomic terror" came home.*

After 1949, leaders in the American national foreign-policy establishment like Henry L. Stimson, John Foster Dulles, and George Kennan began to promulgate a different discourse. It would no longer be possible to dissolve all American fears about the bomb. Nor would it be desirable. Public policy required another approach.[23]

Thus America turned towards a "Cold War system of emotion management." Its intended purpose and eventual instituted effect "was to solve the problem of national will by confronting what was regarded as the most serious obstacle to American resolve in the face of nuclear attack: nuclear terror."[24] Against a background of this pervasive terror—the feeling that anyone, anytime, could deliver a devastating bomb anywhere—ongoing interventions by the State within civil society sought to constitute an effective balance in present feelings of fear. Simply, citizens should be afraid enough so that they would rally around costly and dangerous political programs but not so afraid that they would become altogether demoralized. The Cold War was a far-reaching "continuation of politics by other means." It was enacted primarily on the terrain of *civil defense* and became quickly the most extensive and intensive form of *civic war*.[25] Emergency powers were mobilized to effectively integrate fear into the everyday living together of citizens. Across an astonishing range of society and culture, every stripe of political opportunist drew on the immediate reserve of fear created by "the bomb" to drive forward their projects.

Is this vision of the Cold War plausible? It must seem at once impossibly precise—How could each person's fear be "managed"?—and

---

* This absolutist image of the power of nuclear weapons continued as a topos in discourses of peace and disarmament.

ineffectually vague—What real effect would these extraordinary feelings have on everyday life?

Yet reflect on your own experience after September 11th. At home, at work, at school, in the media and broader culture, your attention has been constantly brought back to dangers related to terrorism. Of course individual responses vary. Nonetheless, the timing, direction, and degree of what attracts your attention is orchestrated by "threat levels," public announcements, leaks of information, readiness programs, increased police presence, changing security measures in airports, and so forth. To a greater or lesser degree, your behaviors and beliefs fall into line with this information. Each instance may be microscopic. Together, like the humming of a great machine, they set the tone for living.

With this in mind, one may conceive more clearly how, during the early Cold War, the Cold War to which the next two generations of Americans would be apprenticed, the Cold War crucible of our current leadership, the management of fear was achieved through the instrument of omnipresent "Civil Defense" and omniscient surveillance.[26] The Citizen had better ask if and how we reiterate this pattern today.

Again, similarities between the two Septembers—1949 and 2001—are telling. One nation in the whole world with an atomic bomb held tight to the convincing amulet of its omnipotence. The history that haunts America tells us that everything went awry—not when the bomb was dropped on Hiroshima, but when the "nuclear monopoly" was broken.

"Monopoly," that familiar metaphor of ownership, does not express with clarity what was lost when the Soviet Union armed itself with the bomb. It is obvious that new considerations immediately entered the American strategic calculus. However, something else occurred in 1949. The claim to an omnipotence was split in two. This altered the American citizen's mental image of his or her own relationship to war and the basic distinction between offense and defense. When only one nation has nuclear weapons, a single offensive blow can decisively prove preeminence. Absent this possibility, long-brewed common sense tells us that defense should be the stronger position.* But against an enemy who possesses *what you believe to be an unstoppable, all-powerful weapon*, the defensive posture loses its key advantages. Defense ceases to be a source of security and becomes instead an amplifier of anxiety. Each measure to defend the

---

* Clausewitz, for example, identifies this as a general rule.

nation, none guaranteed and none sufficient, opens us to gnawing doubt. With this doubt, each measure taken becomes an opportunity to exploit fear, and fear becomes a ready vehicle on which the opportunists move to advance their projects.

After "the bomb," recourse to defense could no longer constitute an improved position or even provide a real sign of strength. Anxiety and nuclear impotence became motives for America to reassert a strategy of offense. However, in the new context the boundary between defense and offense was—to say the least—obscured. Even as the arsenal of weapons and "delivery systems" grew, a new and crucial strategy came to the foreground: spectacular bravado. An extraordinary kind of hubris was formalized in policy orientations described as "brinksmanship" and "mutually assured destruction." Americans trumpeted an aggressive readiness to "go all the way." A style reminiscent of the Terrorist's insinuated itself onto our public stage.

Thus, after 1949, the new mark of omnipotence was not simply the nuclear weapon, but the "will" to use it. Specifically, the "will" to stand down the Russian nuclear threat . . . "whatever it takes."

At the same time, claims to an omnipotence in the realm of defense required the occupation of everyday life. It played on the enlarged continuity between war and politics. It became the living legacy of civic war. A "national security State" developed.[27] This much is well-known. What citizens have noticed less is how this new configuration of State power grew through the administration of the "civil defense society."[28] In other words, civil society itself increasingly became the life-support system for institutions designed to constitute security without ever sending forth major military expeditions. In this way, the American political system—the comprehensive "cultural constitution"—evolved to accommodate the new norm of emergency.

These transformations had ethical consequences, which is to say they carried everyday habits and beliefs of the Citizen in new directions. Old designations of "liberal" and "conservative" fail to bring this ethical dimension to light. It involved, in a short span of years, a fundamental and contradictory shift. The awful "truth" established in 1945 was the equation of atomic weapons with Armageddon. The "Russian bomb" was greeted with the loud and broadcast claim that nuclear war would be "survivable." Faced with "the basic power of the universe" (remember the announcement by Stimson and Truman), who could believe this new bragging? The more it was advanced, the less plausible it became. Each person, each generation, asked themselves, "Who will survive?" They could not avoid the question "Why not me?"

Here, then, is a major story from the Cold War in America: the atomic bomb gave a fresh symbol to an older dream of omnipotence; from the beginning, the technical power of the bomb was the issue of and supplement to political pretensions; those into whose hands it fell relied on and took to heart the myth they made of it; with the loss of unique control they redoubled their efforts, aspiring to capture and control even the significance of that loss; if the bomb itself demonstrated omnipotence, only a new technology of communication could establish the desired meaning; reshaping the character and conduct of civil society became a universal intention of competitors for State power; the purpose of persuasion was to constitute the Citizen as the winning instrument in an apparently unwinnable war; this fine and imperfect balance, aiming to mobilize and delimit human energies and beliefs, produced a perfectly unexpected effect; *so convincing* was the double image of destruction and salvation that citizens learned to make demands on the State commensurate with the claim to an omnipotence; from the middle of this new kind of war, the Citizen saw it with new eyes—*everyone* must be saved, *no casualties* are permissible;[29] the nation began to tremble for the loss of one daughter or son; stakes that at first encompassed the whole world were reduced to the individual; once again, claims to an omnipotence generated a demoralizing political theodicy; to meet this demand, or to have this demand met, the Citizen again ceded his or her resistance to the growth of State power at the immediate emergency disposal of the Executive.

This line of development has been fraught with impossible and often violent contradictions. Indeed, one could call "the Sixties" the main event of the Cold War, and the recent return of public discussion about that decade may have been a functional prop or vehicle for the reinvigoration of the Cold War in its latest form as "9/11." In any case, this narrative cannot stand alone as history. What happened with "the bomb" extended and amplified ongoing changes in the nature of war and the status of emergency. It was entangled with other tectonic changes in our political life. Foremost among these changes was the emergence of viable claims of both civil rights and universal human rights. There was an uncanny overlap between the nuclear-age reimaging of destruction and salvation and the paradoxically diminished-and-enlarged role of the State in the emerging rights-centered politics of America.

It would take another book to trace the strange development of rights-centered politics in America and to spell out its significance for the political scene after September 11th. Wherever such a project might lead us, I want to state clearly the conclusion that serves us here: the version of the Cold War just sketched is what set the tone for September 11th, and it certainly did not end in 1989.

6. The Distemper of Monocracy

Une autorité monocratique quelconque, placée au centre d'un régime
public, tend toujours à passer la ligne de démarcation qui sépare la
surveillance générale de l'autorité active.

[Any sort of monocratic authority, when given the central position in
a public regime, always tends to cross the boundary line that separates
general attentiveness to the well-being of society from the active imposition of authority.]

Le Moniteur Universel (1789)

1. The Cold War Today

The lessons of Vietnam are few and plain: not to be hypnotized by the
word "communism" and not to mess into other people's civil wars where
there is no substantial American strategic interest at stake.

GEORGE KENNAN, "The Meaning of Vietnam" (1975)

Obviously, our current wars began sometime before September 11th. Of
course, processes already running, struggles already taking place, continued on that day. Yes, our historical path was inflected in some crucial
way. This sinister bend was not so much "the Pearl Harbor of the twenty-
first century" as a terrible repetition of that day late in September 1949
when American triumphalism after World War II was overthrown by the
first Russian bomb, and then again and again by subsequent events. Even
if we had in our own way become accustomed to the Soviet Union, the

"people's republics" founded some months later in China and East Germany came as shock after shock. That was abroad. What really struck home was news from the "homeland": Senator McCarthy's list and eventual accusations against the State Department; the arrest of "atomic spies" Fuchs, Gold, and Greenglass and then the national drama of the Rosenbergs; the assumption of war powers by Truman and the invasion of Korea; a doubling of the defense budget and the emergence of a new relationship between civil and military authority. And there was plenty more.[1]

Why underscore this comparison? Because the issue, for the Citizen, is not the momentary *shock* of an attack but the durable *terror*. Not because *terror* naturally leads to *war*, but because the American vocation since 1945 has been to make *war* out of *terror*.* If we think that "September 11th was not just a national security crisis . . . [but] a national identity crisis as well,"[2] it is worth asking exactly *which* identity was thrown into question and *how* this or another sense of national "self" was reasserted in the subsequent chain of events.

To a very large extent, liberals and conservatives came to agree on the Cold War. Does this mean that it thereby ceased to produce effects in domestic politics? Of course not. In fact, the opposite is true. General agreement about the significance of the Cold War became—to put it in this somewhat perverse way—the common ground of factional conflict in America, which was fought "between the passions and paradoxes of one and the same identity."† The Cold War set parameters within which long-standing and still-emerging domestic political battles would be fought. It became *a* (and at some pivotal moments *the*) primary American identification. Other claims on our attentions and aspirations took the backseat.[3]

At the advent of the 1950s, something like Thomas Hobbes's image of the world—conjoining managed uses of fear and aspirations to an omnipotence—increasingly defined the "homeland" in the United States. The icon of the age, the devil's realization of the Hobbesian dream, was the *nuclear weapon*. And it was only in 1949 that the meaning *for Americans* of nuclear weapons changed decisively. There again was that flash on the imaginary horizon. A red thread of doubt about America's omnipotence was inscribed into the unfolding history of our perpetual war. The specter of the *right kind* (meaning the *worst kind*) *of enemy* increased

---

* And then, in at least the particular way discussed in chapter 5, to make terror out of war.
† This is what Walt Whitman said of the Civil War.

our tolerance for ongoing sacrifice to the achievement of and control by military power. It decreased our tolerance for dissent.*

We cannot inventory here the entire iconography of speechlessness in the nuclear age; we can interrogate instances of its fallout after September 11th. Why did the nuclear synonym *ground zero* become the new name for lower Manhattan?† It was, after all, a site of crash and suicide, murder and demolition. Why was the argument for invading Iraq punctuated with the image of a "mushroom cloud"?[4] The world and a handful of worldly Americans knew even then that no "nukes" and likely no other "weapons of mass destruction" would ever be found in the depots of Saddam Hussein. Why did contender John Kerry agree wholeheartedly with incumbent president George W. Bush that nuclear weapons are—still and again—the most significant threat to American security?[5] Any veteran of the combat and politics of Vietnam, including America's most famous and now self-erasing dissenter, could see that the threat to the nation would be our own dumb and blind unilateral stumbling into another misguided military expedition.

To those who say Americans lost a certain naïveté on September 11th, ask what sophistication replaced it? What exactly is novel in an appreciation of or trembling before the threat of nuclear weapons? Or other "weapons of mass destruction"? To those who say that "realism"—the dismissal of domestic factors in international relations promoted by the disingenuous likes of Henry Kissinger—failed after September 11th, ask what true citizen was ever a "realist" when it came to his or her own country?[6] Why suppose that disillusionment or doubt regarding the myth of an omnipotence would evaporate naïveté, rather than enlarging its scope into armed rage? By what worldliness were 21,500 youth escalated to further fruitless sacrifice with 3,000 already dead in the president's war, the American war in Iraq?[7] *Unleashed* is a visceral and blinkered strategy, whether written by Paul Wolfowitz and Scooter Libby or sung by Toby Keith,‡ or reiterated in the post-Rumsfeld Rumsfeldian "new army"

---

* A fact that, not surprisingly, *increased* dissent in the next generation, with the extraordinarily ambivalent results over which we are still fighting today.

† In 1967, in reaction against obsessive "atomic terror," students at New York's Seward Park High School inaugurated an "underground" newspaper—*NeoDwarf*—with an image of lower Manhattan covered by concentric circles of a nuclear attack labeled "ground zero."

‡ Wolfowitz and Libby were authors of the "Defense Planning Guidance" of 1992. Toby Keith is a top-of-the-charts jingoist-militarist country-music singer.

language of the "surge." Perhaps the president's so prominent incapacity to speak the God-term of our century—*noo-kiul-lrr*—is symptomatic.

Think from the position of the Citizen: if the key to *our* Cold War was neither the Soviet *enemy* nor the Communist *ideal*, but rather the national experience of living every day in the shadow of "nuclear terror" and the belief that the "American way of life" was under attack, who will say for sure that the Cold War is over?[8] Even with the collapse of the Soviet Union and the decline of Communism a fundamental preoccupation with nuclear weapons and an American apocalypse continues. It has once again been cranked into high gear by official pronouncements and popular culture.

What if, now or tomorrow, we awake to find that the 1990s was not the dawn of peace but only a decade of *neo-détente?* Did, then, September 11th return the Cold War from recessive to dominant trait in American life?

To whom is it not obvious that September 11th injected a new type of shock, and a new type of life, into the persistent cultural system of the Cold War? The Terrorist today—with or without actual nuclear weapons or other "WMD"—has taken over the role played by "the bomb" in the 1950s. This role is not, like the one played by Communists or Communism, a political *agency* or an *ideological challenge* that could interact with or persuade our fellow citizens; and whereas Socialists and Socialist ideals were effective features of the times that produced earlier "red scares," no one in America today expects mass conversions to terrorism or a terrorist political party. It is the motivational or functional equivalence between "the bomb" and "the Terrorist" that joins the original version of the Cold War with its continuation after September 11th. Once again, shock has been transformed into terror, terror integrated into war, war diffused into politics, and politics recast as emergency.

While assertions of our exceptionalism may be traced back to the Founding—Hamilton proposed that "it belongs to us to vindicate the honor of the human race"[9]—the American claim to an omnipotence took the particularly pointed form so prevalent today only at the end of World War II. It mutated quickly. The point I stress here is that after 1949 omnipotence had to be proven in defense and not just in nuclear first-strike capabilities. Thus an ever greater task was conjured up, not just to call forth "the basic power of the universe" but to hold it in check.

This posture constituted forty years of arms race that would never have been sustained by the American people without a thoroughgoing transformation of political culture. While the stage was, no doubt, set by the circulation of sixteen million people (about 8 percent of the population) through active service in the armed forces during World War II, this transformation was not the collateral of war; *this new way of being neither Soldier nor Veteran but Citizen was itself the Citizen's experience of war.*

If the whole scene of "September 11th" is more Cold War, today we do not face the Soviet Union. Yet in what ways is the situation different or better? Even the old tranquilizing pretense that more and bigger weapons will protect us has been debunked. The attack, they say, is coming. In a cargo container. In a suitcase. Wrapped around a human waist. Under a postage stamp. Such prospects are run through the circuit of shock, terror, war, and emergency. They come back ripe.*

While real persons or events may or may not stand behind these representations, they are more than flashing pictures or night shadows. They emerge from the circulation within *civic war* as forceful justifications that become available for moving the social division of action. They are of unusually wide applicability. This application draws on and reiterates the shock value carried by the image of the Terrorist (as it was carried by the image of "the bomb"). But the durability of this effect, and thus its force as justification in ongoing public discourse, derives from additional factors.

What is the relationship between what these representations *do*—their capacity to shock and silence—and what they *are of*—the persons, events, beliefs to which they refer? How should they be classified and evaluated? If, as I claim, the image of the Terrorist enemy differs significantly from the Communist one, how so? While these questions merit closer attention than I can give them here, one observation is certainly in order. We are often told that the *ideology* we face today is something new, since Islamists, for instance, do not proffer propaganda in the manner of the Communists; perhaps in retrospect even the Cold Warrior could allow a certain amity with the Communist who "hated us" for capitalistic

---

* For example, a caller to C-SPAN (January 10, 2007) answered the question "Do you support the President's troop increase in Iraq?" with a brief narrative about Hamas paying "coyotes" $50,000 a head to smuggle Al Qaeda terrorists across the Mexican border to join thousands of their comrades in "sleeper-cells" in the United States.

behavior and not, like the Terrorist, "for who we are" or for something supposed to be essential to "Western Civilization."*

That comparisons in these terms are so familiar suggests how easily the topic of ideological difference seizes the mind of Americans raised on the Cold War. It is a reflex continued today, as when President Bush situated within "the decisive ideological struggle of our time" a decision to pour more American troops into the slaughterhouse of Iraq.[10] All such talk is, however, utterly misdirecting. First, because the Terrorist and the Communist not only have different ideas, but as social types they perform very different functions. And, as I indicated above, the symbolic equivalent of the Terrorist in the early Cold War was not the Communist but "the bomb." More important still is another interpretive mistake that emerges at this point. Even to inquire about *ideology* is to ignore a lesson manifest in the contemporary form that terrorism has taken: the freedom-constraining system of beliefs or the general worldview[†] of the Terrorist is of secondary interest to the Citizen when it is of interest at all. There may be something like an ideology that contributes to the aims and group coherence of terrorists, but it is only a problem for the Citizen by virtue of a more primary fact: the sheer act of terrorism and all that it entails.[‡]

By the late 1940s in the United States the significance of *Communism* was divided in a comparable way between what it meant for *them* and what it meant for *us*.[§] We may admit that Communism, unlike terrorism, has ideological content. Yet insofar as it appeared in postwar America—or even *could* appear, since ideology is a social constellation and not an individual belief[¶] —it is absurd to think of it as something

---

* It may be worth noting that one key charge against Communism—"Godless!"—has been met and we now have an enemy befitting an evangelical age.

† These two senses of *ideology*—as a fact about the impact of ideas in a common cultural field and as a sort of generally imposed mind control—have predominated in the use of the term since Destutt de Tracy coined it and Karl Marx adapted it to the second pejorative sense.

‡ The preceding chapters provide a relevant account of this.

§ What was happening elsewhere in the world is an entirely different matter; that Communism was a viable political position in places like Italy or Greece or Vietnam made its ideological claims a primary concern for citizens of those countries and a real concern for foreign-policy makers in the United States insofar as America sought to extend its growing empire to them. It does not undercut my argument here to acknowledge, in addition, that all this had an impact on the *civic war* taking shape as Cold War in the United States.

¶ That is, any number of devotees diligently studying the *Communist Manifesto* alone and in private does not an *ideology* make.

alien, as if Communist beliefs or ideas, like missiles, simply came spin-ning down one day in our midst. And thus the question that would, by analogy and continuity, shed light on our situation today is this— In what way did Communism belong to us after the Second World War?

Here it is important to reiterate a general point about ideology. How-ever it becomes effective and whatever its effects, ideology is always composed of representations. The importance of this fact was greatly amplified by the precipitous decline of any real social basis for Com-munism in Cold War America. Absent its persuasiveness or persuadable subjects, "we" confronted "Communism" in the primary form in which it occurred before us and in which it gained its real social force: as a figure of imagination, and within a whole lexicon of images, beliefs, and prac-tices that constitute our own "social imaginary."[11] For the Citizen, what counts about *their* ideology is primarily what it evokes *in us*.* In other words, one and the same term—*Communism*—served as a hinge between two radically different social facts. On one side there was the institutional and cultural cohesion of peoples elsewhere who understood themselves as Communists. On the other side there was the antagonist character in a narrative self-imagining of Americans. Each of these social facts had its own structure and developmental dynamics. As the Cold War infiltrated deep into American society, the connection between them diminished, I think it is safe to say, towards zero. Indeed, everyone knows that even the omnipresence of representations of "Communism" in America did not produce many Communists or more than a handful of spies or "de-fectors." What it did produce was a way of seeing and talking and living together among our fellow citizens. This "Communism" was woven into our common sense.

Cold War common sense was disseminated every day for decades in families and schools and books and movies and by almost every other means in American culture. Given the inherently slow turnover of ma-terial and mental culture, it is inevitable that—in one form or another, perhaps decreasing, perhaps increasing, but certainly in a slow-burning continual flux—the Cold War will continue for generations to come. It was no more ended with the cracking of Berlin's wall than was the Iraq

---

* Only in a political context does it matter that the planes that knocked down the World Trade Center were piloted by Islamists rather than, say, Martians.

War won with a shipboard declaration that "major combat operations . . . have ended."*

Rather, the Cold War, with its atomic iconography and phantasmagoric "Communism," continues as a constitutive social fact in American politics. It is one of the primary modes of the *civic war* through which and from which the development of this new kind of war infests ever more deeply our everyday life. The broad phenomenon of the Cold War—and the broader one, the century-long fact of *civic war*—has become such an amorphous feature of American identity that it passes today without a name. Nonetheless, with each decade since 1945 attributes of the Cold War have become available for reapplication to new circumstances and new purpose. This long-term development did not cease in 1989. Rather, it entered a new phase in which the formation of domestic political culture already in process for two generations began to operate with novel and surprising effect *behind the screen of the nearly unanimous proclamation of "the end of the Cold War."* Many people of good faith took this seriously; some naives among us still search—in vain—for the "peace dividend" that "should" have been "ours" to claim. Others—indeed, the very same Cold Warriors and "neocons" who have kept the pot boiling since 9/11—knew right away that, in effective service to their domestic political interests, the basic political game had not changed with the collapse of the Soviet Union.[12] That this phase of "domestic détente" may now be coming to an end, and their purposes of political conflict better served by insinuations of continuity than by declarations of rupture, has been signaled by such remarkable manifestos of neo-McCarthyism as Ann Coulter's *Treason: Liberal Treachery from the Cold War to the War on Terrorism* and Dinesh D'Souza's *Enemy at Home: The Cultural Left and Its Responsibility for 9/11.*[13] These propagandists, one may observe, seem to have had no problem identifying what is at stake for them in the "war on terror"—they exploit *civic war* to advance positions on "fundamental values and beliefs," especially as these pertain to the organization of social hierarchies and the distribution of social benefits. The primary strategy in this advance is yet another all-out attack on the so-called cultural Left. This assessment is, in its own limited and moronic way, more accurate than how the conflict

---

* President Bush aboard the *Abraham Lincoln*, May 1, 2003. The president introduced a certain irony into his own words retrospectively when—in his speech announcing the escalation of the war in Iraq on January 10, 2007—he added that "victory will not" involve a "ceremony on the deck of a battleship."

has sometimes been seen by those who are actually on the political Left and who have insisted that domestic "anticommunism" was the driving force of the Cold War. In fact, those who attacked "Communism" typically made that the justification for setting themselves against a whole spectrum of pluralistic democratic political values; Ronald Reagan was, by the content of his positions and the force they exerted on American political culture, the paradigm case; thus, to call this kind of position essentially "anticommunist" is to abet the politically self-defeating subsumption of a much wider range of values under that term.

This shifting vocabulary is indicative of the submergence and resurfacing of the Cold War over time. From its outset and for two generations, the rhetoric and practices of cultural conflict were an essential and explicit feature of the Cold War. In all its primary phases—McCarthyist nuclearism (1945–54), the apogee of Civil Defense (1951–63), the reactivist Sixties (1960–75), and Reaganism (1979–89)*—the Cold War as a fact of the American social and political landscape was experienced and expressed as a conflict between worldviews and ways of life. From McCarthy to Reagan, no astute observer could have doubted that the Cold War was synonymous with cultural conflict—even when that contest centered on the use of American military, economic, diplomatic, and "clandestine" power overseas. However, in the most recent phase of the Cold War—a period otherwise identified by almost all sides and factions as "the end of the Cold War"—it could not be named as such. Thus the familiar topos—Cold War—could no longer be relied upon as an adequate symbolic marker for the broad range of cultural conflicts to which it had previously referred. Roughly the same struggles, however, were continued under the alternate rubric of the "Culture Wars," a phrase that appeared and captured the public imagination concomitant with the

---

* This very rough division assumes that significant differences separate the following periods: (1) from the bombing of Hiroshima in 1945 to the public disgrace of Senator Joseph McCarthy in 1954; (2) from the founding of the Civil Defense Administration in 1951—in reaction to the Soviet nuclear weapon and the Korean War—to the advent of the Johnson administration with the assassination of President Kennedy; (3) from the shift in the civil rights movement towards student activism in 1960 with the founding of the Student Nonviolent Coordinating Committee and the lunch-counter sit-ins in Greensboro, North Carolina, to the final expulsion of Americans from and capture of Saigon in 1975; and (4) from the Iranian Revolution of 1979, which both opened political space for the emergence of Ronald Reagan as president and introduced Islam as a key feature of the Cold War, to the fall of the Berlin wall in 1989.

collapse of the Soviet Union.* In correspondence with this transformation of domestic political discourse, the "Culture Wars" at home continued to be projected onto the international scene, now as a "clash of civilizations," and this motto for international political Manichaeanism quickly became another functional substitute for "Cold War" after 1989.[14] In the wake of September 11th, and with ever greater explicitness after the invasion of Iraq, Americans have witnessed here and there a return to the language of cultural conflict that was essential in earlier phases of the Cold War. The likes of Coulter and D'Souza make this move in a way that aims, in atypically undisguised fashion, to reassert connections between the current political scene and its origins in the decades following World War II.† This is, perhaps, a desperate effort to reinvigorate domestic cultural struggle even as the military adventure in Iraq comes to naught. This return of the Right to a somewhat more defensive posture—symbolized as well by the hairbreadth shift to Democratic control of Congress in 2006—may constitute the opening of a new phase of the Cold War.‡

Whatever the terms, this kind of rhetorical flexibility is a crucial way in which the Cold War has retained a vehicular power, carrying forward the terror of September 11th into both the *military* and *civic wars* of our present and advancing the projects and ambitions that trail in their wake, just as it paved the way for the "global reach" and cultural explosion of the 1960s, which were its initial corollaries.[15]

While some actors and staging may have changed, essential processes of the Cold War have been resuscitated in chillingly straightforward if largely unnoticed ways. The struggle to appropriate its benefits and slough off its costs continues; rather than ending, or even diminishing,

---

* An indicative milestone is James Davison Hunter's *Culture Wars: The Struggle to Define America* (1991). Like so many key terms and tactics of the radical Right in the United States, this one seems to have been borrowed from the various Left notions of *Kulturkampf*, a phrase that first appeared in Germany as Bismarck, in alliance with the liberals, tried to assert state control over education after the First Vatican Council promulgated the "doctrine of papal infallibility" in 1870. Of course, the idea that the formation of beliefs—"education" broadly or narrowly construed—is an essential part of politics is as old as political theory itself and, in its most famous early version (Plato's various accounts of and responses to Socrates' teaching and its political context) encompasses the key and continuing struggle between philosophy and rhetoric.

† In this very general respect, and despite the apparently infinite quantity of nonsense they address to the public, their analysis has a kind of Alice-in-Wonderland inverted truth to it; they illustrate the continuity that before the Iraq War only lurked in the background.

‡ In which Hillary Clinton, hoping to reenact Camelot, might have found herself facing something more akin to the Bay of Pigs and the "Cuban missile crisis."

opportunistic uses of Cold War beliefs and representations have reached new heights.* It will remain, for the foreseeable future, the context within which the Citizen must position him- or herself.[16]

2. Today's Cold War in the System of Opportunism

There is no "after the Cold War" for me. So far from having ended, my Cold War has increased in intensity, as sector after sector has been ruthlessly corrupted by liberal ethos. Now that the other "Cold War" is over, the real Cold War has begun. We are far less prepared for this Cold War, far more vulnerable to our enemy, than was the case with our victorious war against a global communist threat.

IRVING KRISTOL, in David Brock, *Blinded by the Right* (1993)

Why would anyone want to resuscitate the Cold War? What possible motive? An idealist ideology seeking the export of freedom? The expansion of empire? Reaffirmation of an American "psyche" wounded by defeat in Vietnam? Or inflamed by terrorist attack? An evangelical calling? The desire for glory? Or fame? Or fortune? An attempt to distract public attention from scandal at home?

Such questions will be debated for years to come—that is, they will be debated once the scales have fallen from our eyes, once we see that the Cold War did not end but continues in another form, as the amplification of *civic war*. Such a debate around *the position of the Citizen* and *what politics has really become* in America will depend on our being able to take the ramifying experience of September 11th as pretext for a new interpretation of the Cold War, and then taking that revised understanding of the Cold War as a frame within which to interpret the forces unleashed among us on September 11th itself. Redrawing in this way the panorama of the last half-century, we—not just a casual "we" of scribblers but the real political "we" of unreconciled but mutually bound citizens—would bypass the necessity supposedly imposed upon us by our place in the international system to focus on the intense play of domestic forces that in

* Search your memory for the phantasmagoric idea of a "peace bonus" . . . not to mention the direct and indirect expenditures and tax cuts that drained away the largest budget surplus in U.S. history to pay for expanding the military and the "profitability" of military industries after 9/11.

fact determines the aims and aspirations of a free democratic nation. This is where the full realization of the unavoidably true motto "all politics is local" would lead us.*

To start down this path, I have developed in the preceding chapters a wide view of *civic war*, of war as a civic way of life, increasingly integrated through shock, terror, and emergency. Briefly dormant, perhaps, but now reawakening, the Cold War reveals essential features of the Citizen's experience of war today: battle and conquest are not war's center of gravity, and war is not clearly distinguishable from other aspects of society.

You will want to ask again: do not certain things we may easily observe weigh against these statements? For no one can doubt that America *continues to be engaged in warfighting*. And even if we grant, as we do with the concept of *civic war*, that the political and social environment prerequisite to military capability and intention is of the highest importance for the Citizen, the degree to which Americans, at first excited by the fever of adventure and revenge, soon became dissociated from the wars in Afghanistan and Iraq and remained remarkably unperturbed by the obvious failure of our intensive military actions in those countries seems to belie the assertion that war is not clearly distinguishable from other aspects of society, or at least to make from it a kind of blindness rather than insight.† Are Americans simply led by ignorance or narcissism?

To position oneself as a Citizen today, however, is to see first that these two points—war is a fact of society and society is shaped around war—indicate two aspects of the same phenomenon, and thus to see how radically different the facts of war may be for the Soldier and for the

---

* It was Tip O'Neill (1994) who said that. For the sake of clarity: no one can claim that relations with other nations are not full of danger, or that these dangers do not limit options; but to call these facts sources of "necessity" is to assume that the nation has, perhaps like an individual, a "desire" to "survive," and nothing is farther from the truth, a fact most recently demonstrated by the extraordinarily self-destructive but democratically determined U.S. national policy of invading and occupying Iraq.

† How combat in Iraq appeared to Americans by the time of the 2006 elections may be more complicated than it seemed at first to many interpreters. How it appeared with the tragically hubristic escalation of the war in 2007, and the toothless phumphering of those who had the power to put a stop to it, will be a topic of historical discussion for centuries to come. This discussion began on the wrong foot when, faced with exit polls that indicated the war as voters' highest concern, pollsters and pundits misunderstood this as a direct opposition to violence and military adventure. In fact it was metonymy for corruption. Thus did the vacuous word "change!" spring up everywhere across the political stage in 2008.

Citizen.* This is not simply a difference of interpretive perspective. If in Afghanistan or Iraq the primary effect of our warmaking has been death, in America it was a reinvigorated way of life. Every day since September 11th the "war on terrorism" has been reconfiguring basic structures of society and politics.

By *structures* I mean important common practices oriented through the physical and symbolic conditions of life in which, as a language is to speech, agents must invest themselves to increase the probability of producing the effects they desire. Financial markets and industrial production would be structures in this sense, but so would Catholicism, racism, or *the Constitution*.[17] Structures set parameters for social positions, and agents who adapt themselves to these parameters become to greater or lesser degrees, and in that time and place, social types. It is not a simple matter to identify the structures that give rise to the social type that is of primary concern to us here. The *Citizen* is involved directly or indirectly in practically all structures of society insofar as public problems or conflicts are constituted in conjunction with any of those structures; thus the position of the Citizen implies, as an inherent element of the structure that defines it and by comparison with other social types, an unusual additional degree of self-consciousness or reflexivity. From a potentially long list of basic structures that have been inflected by the "war on terrorism" I want now to direct attention to one that bears heavily on the political action of *positioning* oneself as a Citizen and that is relevant in the formation of intentions, in the actualization of projects through the division of action, and in providing frameworks for public judgment and justification. Let us call this structure *the system of opportunism.*

Something of a digression is needed to show how the system of opportunism enters the story at this point. It is obvious that in all forms of human life new and unexpected things occur. Each society and historical epoch has its predominant ways of attributing origins to novel occurrence. It may be identified with terms like fate, miracle, providence, divine intervention, cosmic order, and so forth. In the secular modernity of Western societies particular ways of synthesizing certain common attributes of these and similar symbolic forms have appeared. None—not even the quintessentially nineteenth-century notions of "genius" and

---

* It is well known that the Soldier's experience has more in common with "them"—the ones engaged in battle—than with "us"—the ones on whose behalf the Soldier battles.

"creativity"—has become more pervasive and persuasive than the anthro-pocentric doctrine of "the will" that took the shape we recognize today sometime around 1800.* The significance of the adoption of this old term (it had already been in use for centuries) to modern cultural circum-stances is not simply that it provides a common name for the capacity *to originate*. It is also a way to weave the fact of novel occurrence back within the frames of reference that define continuity and rupture in one's ongoing life with others. This second function—which we may refer to as *the strategic uses of "the will"*—and its wide ramification is particularly important within the political field.

We Americans, full-blown exponents of a European-born modernity, have for two centuries marked novel occurrence within the division of action with this previously unprecedented symbolic form. In a positive sense, "the will" situates acts within a social environment: when an ac-tion is labeled as *willed*, it, and its effects, are associated with a proper name, they belong to the one who *willed* them, fall under the actor's responsibility, can only be appropriated by that person,[†] and so forth. This much is obvious. What I want to suggest now is that the connec-tion between novel occurrence and "the will" is also made in a negative sense and that in key respects this is even more important. Often the new and unexpected cannot be easily attributed or assigned to an actor.[‡] The code of "the will" is then brought forward to say what *this occurrence* is *not*. From the *new and unexpected* we construct by antithesis the *untitled*, the *unowned*, the *free from responsibility*, the *appropriable*, and so forth. In other words, we systematically constitute—from the smallest things, a spill, and gestures, the uncivil slip, up to whole zones of our common life, the warming globe—*unintended consequences of action*. From one side, *un-intended consequences of action* are the negative complement of "the will." From the other side, *unintended consequences of action* are a complemen-tary or constitutive ground of opportunism. When the *fate* of the gods or the *chance* of nature gives way to the diffuse and amorphous field of

---

* Please note that the sign "will" (along with its translations) is not new, but the force and sig-nificance of it changes radically around 1800. I referred to this in chapter 5 as the "new model will." See Meyers 1995.

[†] With additional mediations (like contract, permission, sale, etc.) additional persons can ap-propriate the outcome of one's "will."

[‡] Indeed, failure to see that all action is divided—the "division of action"—is a major obstacle to identifying the subject of novel occurence.

unintended consequences of action, leaving, as Jean-Jacques Rousseau observed, humanity "abandoned to ourselves,"[18] opportunism ceases to be merely an occasional meeting with the aleatoric. It has developed into a system.*

The system of opportunism generates openings that are freely appropriable. But not by everyone. Even the *unintended* is a positional effect. It is most valuable for certain actors under certain conditions. Just as *war* is an encompassing condition that proliferates unintended consequences of action, it also constitutes wide opportunity for many actors in many positions. In war things get out of hand. And still, *some persons, as social types, are better positioned than others to exploit that fact.*

Consider how deep the exploitation of unintended consequences of action can go. At this point, it would be easy to recur to the language of intention. It would be precise and correct to say something like this: effects coded as "unintended" become free zones for the further operation of "the will." This however tells only part of the story. For, as we have seen, all action relevant to politics is divided. No act can be produced by one "will."[†] So even in or with reference to the moment of intention the whole discourse of "the will" does not reveal itself.[‡] This is why the Citizen had better keep some critical distance from it. In society—rather than in the philosopher's "possible world"—"the will" is not the primary attribute of the subject who acts.[§] Actions are always combinations of faculties, dispositions, and circumstances articulated over time in space. In this process, "the will" serves as a coding device. It demarcates two complementary phases of acts, the intended and the unintended. This code has practical effect beyond the combinatorial impulse. In relations among persons, it upholds or demolishes boundaries, attaches and

---

* This systematic production of unintended consequences of action is the primary condition for the uninterrupted operation of Will-ful action. That is, in the structured practice of opportunism, unintended effects are constantly being exploited intentionally (and producing further unintended effects, etc.).

† Even God needed something on which to operate his Will in the creation of the earth; cf. Genesis 1:1–2: "In the beginning God created the heaven and the earth. And the earth was without form, and void; and darkness was upon the face of the deep. And the spirit of God moved upon the face of the waters" (King James translation).

‡ Note, too, that the notion of "intention" (*intentio* in Latin) completely changed its meaning in the modern era.

§ Strictly speaking, as "will" was understood in and after the nineteenth century, it was not an attribute at all.

detaches "handles" by which one may seize hold of passing events. "The will" is the door that lets us in or keeps us out, and by letting one in keeps out the other.

Within the system of opportunism such practical symmetries inherent in "the will" are present in some circumstances but not in others. Where an intention is stated, or at least statable, it is, paradoxically, easier to identify what constitutes the unintended consequences of action, and thus to see the whole staging of the act within the web of human interdependence.

We now need to consider another important type of actions. These derive from similar facts of human experience but cannot be positively represented in terms of intention.[19] For the relevant particular example here, I draw your attention to acts in which *emotions* have a clear and decisive catalytic effect. This class of acts is of high importance for the general economy of action and the system of opportunism that is symbiotic with it.

Emotions are how one *is affected*. This appears in the ancient Greek word *pathe*, from *pathos*, or "what happens," as it does in the Latin *patior* and the English *passive*, or *patient*, the person to whom "*it* happens"— whatever *it* is. No one, we say, can *will* him- or herself to be happy or sad; a person falls into these states in the course of experience.[20]

How these facts of our experience gain significance and serve or impede our projects depends on additional and deep cultural factors. Where, as for Americans, the modern discourse of "the will" is firmly in place, a particularly interesting potential opens for actors. That is, emotions can be mapped as unintended consequences of action. Nevertheless, they are not like other such synonymous effects. Emotions have no complementary intentional component. What I mean is that unlike when one steps forward and trips, where the first phase is clearly identifiable as a condition of the second, sadness, for instance, that attracts pity has no aim in this direction.* The *tripping* can be precisely labeled as *unintended* because the *stepping forward* is presumed to be *intentional*; by contrast, even when we identify pity as an *unintended* (welcome or unwelcome) consequence of one's sadness, the connection asserted is vague because the initial state *cannot be intentional*. The symbolic boundaries created

---

* There are, of course, neurotic deployments of emotion in this way, but then the status of the emotion *as passive* comes into question and another, more complex, dynamic takes hold.

in the ratio between intended and unintended cover a wide spectrum as in the increasing specificity from allusion to suggestion to proposal to promise to contract: the more precise the intention, the more exact the delimitation of the unintended;* indistinct intentions multiply the latitude of the unintended, increasing potential space for appropriation by some actors and decreasing the effectiveness of those who attempt to react to them. Where emotions reign, where markable intention dwindles towards zero, the unintended consequences of action abound, and the potential uses to be made of them know no limit.

Even as one's emotions become available for appropriation by others, those emotions appear to stand outside the division of action, indeed outside the sphere of social interaction altogether. An act that is piggybacked onto the vehicle of other people's emotions comes before us almost like a fact of our nature.† What emotions lack are those "handles" that appear in the intentional phases of action and that third parties seize hold of when called to make specific judgments about propriety, accountability, responsibility, and so forth. Emotions offer a free ride and long carriage.

So return to September 11th. The planes strike the World Trade Center. Thousands are killed. No one *intends* to get angry. It just happens. Who, by being angry, intends to sanction no-bid contracts for Halliburton in Iraq? Or to reelect George W. Bush president of the United States? Rather, what happens in the next phase of action is that some people apply their "will" to capture the disorderly unintended. It is an opportunity. General anger is made use of. It is mobilized on behalf of specific projects. The selection of *which* projects is a function of position within the *system of opportunism*.

Where the unintended is shaped and shadowed by an intention it becomes a certain kind of vehicle. It can be deciphered, retraced, and foreshortened. If confronted with the simple fact of having *voted* for George W. Bush, one can say, "It was not my intention that America should invade Iraq." Confronted with the scene of full-fledged anger it is not

---

* A contract is a notoriously effective tool for showing precisely what one can do, in the next phase of action, outside its terms.

† This coupling of emotion/nature plays a role in many older—ancient, medieval, early modern—frameworks for understanding action; one needs to be cautious, however, as the significance of the term *nature* changes over time, and especially after the eighteenth century. Note, too, that several generations of feminist scholarship have made clear how culturally and historically deep has been the symbolic assignment of nature to women.

appropriate to say, "It was not my intention that America should invade Iraq"—not because it *was* my intention, but because the very category of intention *appears inapplicable*. Emotions cause the *decorum* of judgment and justification to fail.* But—and this is a crucial point—the failure of *decorum* is a kind of disorientation within the division of action; not everything falls apart. With the persistence of some aspects of order—for example, identification of the *unintended* itself—openings for unimpeded opportunism are created.†

Now a difference between the appearance and reality of emotions is key. Emotions seem natural or instinctive; certain uses of human energies seem, for example, to follow inexorably the vector of fear. This is illusory. In fact, the force and direction and issue of emotions depend on belief and the presence of others, on experience and history, on position in social time and space. Even the most idiosyncratic responses to emotions arise from one's personal history with others (e.g. the tendency to retreat or attack when angry). The consequences of this fact multiply with the widening circles of society. These are topics we covered in the first chapters of this book and they concern us again here.

If emotions are not to be trusted, it is not because they are antithetical to reason. Nor is it because they are inconsistent. Indeed, precisely insofar as we experience emotions as immediate and automatic, they often seem too consistent.‡ This appearance is opposite the truth: emotions are dangerous because, on the one hand, they are thoroughly entangled in social relationships and thus especially subject to manipulation, and on the other hand, they are typically experienced or identified in privacy and thus buffered from everyday critique that could bring to light their social elements.

There is no straight line from fear, especially generalized fear, to the effects it sustains. But something powerful happens when fear is treated

---

* It complicates matters unnecessarily here to acknowledge that there is a *decorum* of emotions as well—but there is.

† It could be argued that all order in civic practice is, "in the final analysis," *decorum*, and that a categorization of ordering and disordering elements that compose the general fact of time-space-symbol adjustments within human groups (viz. *decorum*) would provide greater precision for understanding the system of opportunism. The attempt here to locate a common generator of intended and unintended consequences of action is a start in that direction.

‡ This belief—not the fact of human relationships, which are supremely complex—is what makes the one-size-fits-all advice of a Dr. Phil seem "just right" each time it is spoken. It was a sign of David Hume's insight that he understood emotions as more consistent than reason.

as just an unintended consequence of action. It becomes a zone of or resource for the unfettered advancement of particular projects as it—together with the human energies mobilized by it—is appropriated for the purposes of further actions.

The opportunist does not say "Citizens! Lend me your fears!" He operates through the beliefs that make fear, in every case, what it is. The large tendencies of belief distributed across whole groups of people constitute common sense—where "common sense" is understood in the properly rhetorical denotation as the practical/symbolic nexus of personal and social experience. Where opportunism has become systematic, the opportunist accomplishes his goal indirectly.* He makes what he can of fear through appeal to common sense. As it behooves him, too, to generate more fear, to shape fear in his favor, this he does by working to inflect common sense itself.[21] The situation is perverse, of course. The opportunists of our time insist that they are there to allay fear.[22] At the same time, both what is to be allayed and the allaying response to it are calibrated to fit the advancement of the opportunist's designs. Fear becomes a renewable resource with applications in specific "sectors."

Now the plot thickens. As a spring of political fear, the Cold War offers a deep reservoir of emotional allegiance and power accumulation that has ebbed and flowed since the first use of "the bomb." It has been constantly refreshed by more or less explicit programs of "emotion management." Today, in the latest incarnation of the Cold War, "the Terrorist" serves as the functional equivalent of "the bomb," even as nuclear weapons continue as metonymy for danger. Whichever way the "war on terrorism" treats the Terrorist, that war is relentlessly staged for and brings on stage the Citizen. The "war on terrorism" revises and extends the Cold War's way of shaping political life through the management of citizens' emotions.

If the Citizen is to have any hope of finding a new political position, the Cold War, the "war on terror," the war in Iraq, as unusual and distinct from one another as each may seem, must all be considered not as exceptions to "real war" but as wars that are normal within the long-developed and now-achieved frame of reference I have called *civic war*. Despite the typical representation of such wars, they do not begin as

---

* He does not, for example, wave a gun in your face, wait for you to be afraid, and then relieve you of your wallet.

duels, and they certainly do not continue that way. Whatever the aims of a single combatant or group, no one makes war without mobilizing the division of action in favor of their design. This fact alone—with its uncertain arousal of human energies—is a great vehicle for other apparently unrelated projects. It is the field in which opportunism takes command. As extensive support is required for war, boundaries erode and mobilizing that support becomes part of war. Emotions like fear, anger, and arrogance fire this mobilization. These are fundamental resources. Of course they are located in persons.* But just as belief—manifest in the social fact of shared language and other symbolic systems—mediates emotions, these emotions circulate. Emotional beliefs congeal as common sense.† The common sense of emotion—as cause, as prolongation, as motive, as effect—carries many people easily in one direction. The greater the ambition of the opportunist, the more he or she will seize upon this fact. For such efforts the image of war is efficient. War institutionalizes momentary feelings like terror and, expanding them across society and over time, provides continuity sufficient to the secondary opportunistic purposes it is brought to serve. At certain points, and with increasing frequency, the secondary purpose becomes the primary one.

The process works in another direction as well. The social project of war is of significant duration and cannot emerge from inconsistent emotions. Fear is again the clearest example. It often seems that fear for the safety of oneself, one's place, and one's people is an unshakably fundamental motive.‡ The fact is somewhat different: fear must be constantly fed or refueled. To find its way past politics, the violence of war requires, and then itself promotes, a sort of perverse inverted mirror of the slogan "keep hope alive." War exploits fear not as an individual fact but as something that has been invested in the form of common sense and thus depersonalized. However, it is exactly this bodiless type of fear that dies

---

* And, as we have already seen concerning fear, personal sources are neither spontaneous nor individual.

† The "public sphere" is the body of common sense; it is where the opportunist gets a foothold. See chapter 1 for a comparison of the Terrorist's and the Executive's redirection and deployment of *our* "common sense."

‡ I am not convinced that one can have fear *for* a subject; fear is always *of* an object, even when that object threatens another. One often hears talk of the Hobbesian premise that fear of death is the primary motive for survival; this falsifies Hobbes's view and, more importantly, misses the fact that people fight for themselves because, even when it is pitifully bad, it may be that "life is the sweetest thing."

out as seasons change. Such fear—one could say by definition—is remote from each person's everyday experience. Thus, even if fear is perpetually motivating, it must be perpetuated over and over again to sustain the project of war.

Likewise with anger. Anger looms, perhaps, largest in war as revenge. But while one obsessive person may harbor fantasies of revenge for a lifetime, for how long will the whole "body" of a people lust to avenge one person's loss, one family's loss? Even in a culture of martyrdom or blood feuds, the resilience of vengeance typically depends on changing costs and circumstances and a symbolic economy among the living, not the dead.[23]

And how often is arrogance, in its social proportion as the unison chant for conquest, so insistent that it does not incite its own erosion when the first dead warrior-children are returned to their mothers in a box?[24]

What makes war—durable, extensive ordering of the division of action and the imaginary life of society that it is—rise up from these emotions is their mixture. They become combined as subject positions are divided. Executive arrogance, Victim anger, Soldier courage, and Citizen fear form a mighty quartet. Those who suffer no risk, who, indeed, figure themselves with the omnipotence to overcome or account for all risk, have motive to build such an alliance, fueling fear after fear and holding up the body of the martyr.

This suggests something important about the "fear management" discussed in chapter 5. The public adjustment of emotional impetus is not only accomplished through the transmission of information or the structure of institutions. Nor should we expect to find it a foolproof system of direct control. Such management involves more than simple constraint. It is a staging of relationships, a play of passions and interests, which opens—for example, in the symbolic form of "unintended consequences of action"—new space and sparks new energies. The opportunist is a dramaturge. He does not seek to micromanage interactions. Rather, he positions his players on stage to appropriate these new social facts as they emerge.

The Terrorist uses our "public sphere" to make war against us.* Consider again why this works. However impenetrable our battalions,

* See chapter 1.

however protected or invisible the processes by which the Executive constitutes war and brings the Soldier and the Bureaucrat on stage, the underlying layer of social control that sustains and constrains the operations of the State is diffused throughout the "public sphere." Touch on that abiding milieu—in which the problems of living together, and thus the questions of war and peace, are addressed and directly engage the energies of citizens—and the body of the people will turn to serve your ends.* In other words, the Terrorist enters war through its "continuation," which is *politics*.

To this we must now add a fact difficult to swallow. When the Executive reenters politics through war, he passes through the same door as the Terrorist. Domestic actors, too, find opportunity in war's name and in its violence because the prospect of war extends and makes more manageable fear in society, fear that invigorates their far-flung projects.[25]

This symmetry between the Terrorist and the Executive is sometimes direct: just as in the particular instance that President Reagan employed Osama bin Laden in the role of surrogate against the Soviets in Afghanistan, so in the general fact that "they" use "us" and "we" use "them."[26] Forget for the moment the gruesome details—from "shock and awe" to Abu Ghraib and Guantánamo—possible in that symmetry. Focus instead on a part of it that revolves around the position of the Citizen.

The Terrorist depends entirely on "us." If he does not attach his project—through shock, for example—to our everyday lives as they converge in a "public sphere," his project will not advance. By contrast, none of our positions—as Executive, as Soldier, as Bureaucrat, and certainly not as Citizen—depends on the Terrorist. We could hold any one of those positions in a world without terrorism. The Terrorist and the Executive are symmetrical, however, when both, with whatever motive, in an opportunistic mode, operate with and on the same "material." That "material" is, so to speak, us.[27]

---

* As this involves energies and practices, it is a misnomer to simply call this "legitimacy."

3. *Civic War* and the Monocratic Tendency

Not that the monocrats & paper men in Congress want war; but they
want armies & debts: and tho' we may hope that the sound part of
Congress is now so augmented as to insure a majority in cases of general
interest merely, yet I have always observed that in questions of expense,
where members may hope either for offices or jobs for themselves or their
friends, some few will be debauched, & that is sufficient to turn the decision where a majority is, at most, but small.

THOMAS JEFFERSON TO JAMES MADISON (APRIL 3, 1794)

Of the several motives there may be to resuscitate the Cold War, the
one I want to focus on here, a particularly powerful and iconic one, has
been nurtured in the political culture of our constitutional system. It is
to be found in the function of the Executive. It has emerged from the
flexibility and reach of the Executive as that branch of government has
gained greater access to enlarged emergency powers. This enlargement
of power has an effect on the Executive as an office. Officeholders easily
develop, so to speak, an addiction to their own extensive authority. This
is not a primary narcissism, but a secondary and social one that occurs
within the division of action that characterizes the office and its powers. The Executive grows accustomed to the deference of others. Since
by deferring others do not remove themselves—which is to say, remove
their force and bridging effect—from the network of divided action, the
proper name for this key social fact is complicity.* This complicity el-
evates the authority of the office—which is to say, the unimpeded social
energies at its disposition.†

Consensus is, we like to pretend, a natural reaction to terror; in constitutional politics, where divided power is essential, consensus is complicity in the tending to monocracy. Against this background, then, however
many possible responses to terrorism there may be, it is now—in the arc
of a century to the point of September 11th—to the advantage of the

---

* See chapter 4 above.
† The complicit, conversely, gain satisfaction from the Executive's augmentation; a version
of this logic is spelled out in Hegel's *Phänomenologie des Geistes* in the famous section called
"Herrschaft und Knechtschaft."

Executive to respond to terror with war.* The fact is that terror makes for "good" war. I do not mean that in responding to terrorist attack defensive military actions are "just." That question—debated hot and wide after September 11th—is of a different order. Rather, what I mean is that war, the particular sort of war that develops around symbolism, weapons, and institutions that all have terrorism "in mind," serves to an unusual extent a wide range of the independent purposes of the Executive. The Terrorist hands the Executive a functional instrument to open wide political opportunity and to decrease substantially resistance to projects that—viewed from near or far—seem to have no relation to the vehicle on which they advance most swiftly.

The Cold War began at the nexus of the archetypal modern terror and twentieth-century warfare; it perfected them both.[†] It constituted a profitable and durable domestic system. The question for the Citizen, then, may not be *Why make terror into war?* That is nearly obvious. The Citizen should ask, rather, *Why would anyone expect the Executive to respond to terror in any other way? What forces are in play—what systemic "checks and balances"—that could prevent the Executive's return to the deep well of the Cold War?*

The Executive is an advantage-seeking machinery.[‡] The symbolic and institutional frameworks of the Cold War cranked up that machinery over a very long period of time. The combined result—the Executive office in our particular moment of America's political constitution—has been an enlarged field of opportunity, which is to say an allowance for especially profitable opportunisms at the service of both that office and those complicit with its aims and advances. In chapter 4 I asserted that the president's role in declaring emergency is limited to the capacious and complex task of mobilizing the complicity of Congress. Now we see,

---

* That—even more than the logic of "give them an inch and they'll take a mile"—is why, as the blunt statement of policy goes, "we do not negotiate with terrorists."

[†] I think it is probably a mistake to confuse the Jacobin model of terror (which was in some sense the paradigm for the Stalinist regime) with the symbolic form of "the bomb" and its effect on the political culture of the United States. I am similarly inclined to believe that the two other crucial models that thoroughly implicated terror in the American political scene—the attempted genocide of the indigenous population of North America and the deep institution of slavery—retained their significance in the twentieth century primarily in the (flawed and unequal) construction of rights and not in the formation of powers.

[‡] Always keeping in mind that this seeking often proceeds indirectly, e.g. by gaining the complicity of counterpowers to allow for the expansion of one's own (typically operating with the formal pattern described above as the appropriation of unintended consequences of action).

again contrary to the institutional presumption of "separation of powers," that congressional complicity is not only what I called it before—a *norm*—but also an *interest*.

Earlier in this chapter I suggested how the system of opportunism emerged through processes differentiated by "the will" and its intentionality. I am not saying here, however, that forays into or results from the enlarged field of opportunism are always or even regularly intentional; opportunisms often reap blindly the benefits of position. If Harry Truman, Lyndon Johnson, and George H. W. Bush entered this field one way, Dwight D. Eisenhower, Ronald Reagan, and George W. Bush engaged it in a different manner and with greater effect. These latter three presidents gained enormous success in their attempts to reconstruct American politics by building complicity within the larger civil society, where, by contrast, presidents like Richard Nixon and Bill Clinton failed because they faced the intense and to some extent organized opposition of society. The time and position in history of the president and the character he brings to his projects modulate considerably the tendency of the Executive office we track here through *civic war*.[28]

Citizens will always have an interest in who wins and loses in each case. The greater concern for the Citizen, however, and the central concern of this book, is with the ways in which that new system of opportunism, as social environment for the Executive and as the primary material for its acts, tends to reduce the many contending powers that compose democracy. It advances a logic of monocracy. The most republican spirit strains to slow its pace. The monocratic drive—as it seeks to consolidate unitary power—is against contestation and effective checking powers. This drive is a losing proposition for the Citizen, yet it cannot advance without *our* complicity.*

Hand in glove with monocracy an amplified sense of omnipotence takes to the stage. I have suggested some ways that this sense was heightened by the atomic means and political circumstances of the Cold War. In the dialectic of political culture that pushed forward through the

---

* I will use the term *monocracy* in its most literal and general sense: it derives from the Greek words for "single" (μόνο) and "power" (κράτος). Infrequently mentioned as a political regime, the term seems to have appeared in France in the 1780s. Having adopted it—we may suppose, as one needed only to read the *Moniteur*, a paper of wide circulation from which items were occasionally translated by the *European Magazine* and the *London Review*—during his time there, Thomas Jefferson went on to express with that word his relatively narrower but nonetheless intense opprobrium for Alexander Hamilton, the Federalists, and kings everywhere.

1950s, the claim to omnipotence itself brought unexpected risks to its claimants in the form of raised stakes and new demands. Even *la servitude volontaire* burdens the powerful with unanticipated responsibility. In the 1960s, liberation from an authority that exposed itself as antipolitical had to become—because that authority was a form of "popular rule"—the liberation of the self.*

Things do not always run this way. Sometimes, where a single source of power goes unchecked, the monocrat can diffuse such inherent obstacles to his or her own hubris throughout the division of action: errors and responsibility can be shunted off onto others, foreign or domestic; before a public attuned to the cinematic image and not the oratorical voice, the monocrat can contradict himself with impunity. Then the appeal of an omnipotence continues to grow for both the pretender and his public.

War feeds in direct ways this process of accretion. And no one in the political field gains from war more *justification to claim omnipotence* than the Executive.†

If this invokes for you the image of a Commander-in-chief at the head of a mighty army, think again. An army may serve monocratic ambition but is not itself such a power.‡ Armies are complex institutions composed of many internally contradictory forces. Witness five years of don't-ask-don't-tell–type conflict between Secretary of Defense Donald Rumsfeld and the generals over the composition of the forces that should stand behind and locate the "point of the spear."[29] By contrast, what I want to stress here is the impact of the Executive on the everyday life of the Citizen. This typically derives less from the deployment of armies than from—to give just a few examples—a federally mandated "bank holiday," privatization of the police, or tax cuts amounting to an astronomical 2 percent of the gross domestic product[30] of the entire nation.§ At each such step, the sign of the monocrat is aspiration to an omnipotence. In effect, his power comes down to just this: *Can I do what I want? Who will stand in my way?*

In general this means that increases in power are always relative to counterpowers. What matters is whether an assertion is held back or is

---

* Whether for better or for worse, no one should be surprised that a kind of chaos ensued.
† It is important to keep in mind here what we saw earlier: the real power of the Executive in wartime derives from "emergency powers," of which the "war power" is just one.
‡ I made this clear in chapter 2.
§ Which is to say, FDR's declaration of national emergency in 1933, the ongoing transformation of policing institutions since the 1980s, and George W. Bush's tax cut of 2001.

channeled by the projects and energies of other people.[31] In monocracy all powers tend to converge; it is a swiftly rising river flowing one way.

Monocratic power need not be absolute to produce the pretension that it is. And the pretension itself adds a distinctive type of force. For example, a president at war evokes common sense to justify his claim to an omnipotence—"I can stop The Bomb," "I can stop The Terrorist." He is, after all, *the President*. A compliant Congress allows the Executive free rein and his claim gains credence. They need not literally grant him a power; the rhetoric of war leaves open the path for him to claim power freely, and in so doing in fact to exercise it. This prospect is clear to the Executive and he loves it. He knows that "a mere demarcation on parchment of the constitutional limits of the several departments is not a sufficient guard against those encroachments which lead to a tyrannical concentration of all the powers of government in the same hands."[32] But neither is civic virtue sufficient guard. In the logic of the Executive the cunning President exploits not just fear but citizen patriotism and courage to settle the question *Is this war?* in the affirmative and thus, almost always, in his own favor, and typically in favor of his office. Should the American Congress ever again declare a war, our newspapers might as well print it on an inside page. But when the President proclaims *This is war!* he incites citizens and draws us into the complicity that feeds his claim to power. That proclamation itself reorients common sense. That is, it reorients the way the Citizen uses judgment to find a position. Public justification that leads judgment to follow the President is a real mobilizing power.[33] This, in itself, increases the force of Executive claims on monocratic power. The effect grows further with the irruption of political pathologies.*

The special value of war for the Executive was weirdly manifest in the final months of the 2004 presidential campaign. At a "town hall" meeting in Iowa, Vice President Cheney admonished his audience: "It's absolutely essential that eight weeks from today, on November 2, we make the right choice, because if we make the wrong choice then the danger is that we'll get hit again and we'll be hit in a way that will be devastating from the standpoint of the United States . . ."[34] It would have been shorter but no more blunt to simply say that *if you vote for John Kerry, you will die.* Although one may be surprised at how few objections were

---

* The final volume of *Democracy in America after 9/11* will identify a group of political pathologies of the Citizen.

raised against this extreme rhetoric, I do not think many took or were expected to take this literally.[35] Dick Cheney, like most in his president's inner circle, had aimed at and achieved a less direct effect. Such statements stretch by increment the limits of common sense; they normalize everything they frame. Cumulatively, over time, they create a "normal" audience *for themselves*. Even if during an electoral contest such attempts are met with some protest, they stake out a space for symbolic action during the subsequent administration of the country. They form part of the "mandate" and "political capital" claimed by the victor.[36] As long as hot contest after overheated rhetoric can be avoided—that is yet another effect of the rhetorical stretching—motives for resistance are dispersed and Executive pretensions enlarge yet again.[37]

Vice President Cheney's provocative assertion also conveyed a broader message that, like it or not, harmonizes with American common sense. War belongs to the Executive. It is the turf of those presently in office. Thus, what the vice president said was less a demand for consistency—as in "don't change horses"—than an assertion of property right. This is effective speech. It draws capacious lines. Anything construed as inside the boundaries becomes the dominion of the proprietor. He is monarch of the domain. War shifts again, in this phase of action, out of civil society and within the province of the State. Resistance, moves that could check power, lose their political character. Objectors are made over as trespassers. One says, "He is the president and we must follow," and whatever advice or advisers may come forward, the "recommendations" are passed "to the president" and then "it's up to the Commander-in-chief."*

Once again this is a bridge across which powers that seem in retrospect entirely unrelated to war accrue to the Executive in wartime. This fact itself should be suspect. Of the four black-letter constitutional sources for presidential power only one—the "Commander-in-chief" clause—refers explicitly to military activity.[38] And even this is, in the context of *civic war*, susceptible to stunning misinterpretation: the President is not a military figure, but the civilian overseer of the military; the President is not, as George W. Bush would have us believe, the "Commander-in-chief" of society, for in American constitutional democracy there is no

---

* Essentially identical comments were made by dozens of members of Congress and everywhere in the press; this is drawn from a press release from Senator Patty Murray (D-Washington), December 6, 2006.

such position; citizens, including and especially those in Congress, are not subject to the President's "will" in a chain of command.[39] The other three constitutional sources of Executive power are more encompassing, civil in tenor, and support the priority of emergency powers over war power.* Intermingling the civil and military in this way—the way of *civic war*—puts into effect a presumption, through the vehicle of war, that all emergency should become the sole province of Executive power, and that the Executive should be the "Commander-in-chief" of society.

I think this would have surprised even the original American "monocrat" himself, Alexander Hamilton, who saw clearly that "it is of the nature of war to increase the executive at the expense of the legislative authority."[40] For elsewhere the Constitution asserts that while guaranteeing "to every state in this union a republican form of government," the whole of the United States "shall protect each of them ... on application of the legislature, or of the executive (when the legislature cannot be convened) against domestic violence."[41] This suggests by compelling analogy that to be *a republican form of government* is to grant priority to the legislature *even in emergency*.† It is intertwined developments of state and society in the twentieth century that have undermined this priority and allowed the Executive to reposition accordingly.

So it is that at least since the inauguration of FDR the public sense of propriety accords to the President the reins. An "unlimited" war opens the prospect of unlimited Executive power. The effect is not so much the result of open-endedness in time but of the widening colonization of political space by monocracy.

Both those who seek to abet and those who seek to impede this trend often fail to notice an additional effect. As these advantages accrue to the Executive, complementary constraints on his power inevitably do begin to emerge. Perhaps not from direct resistance but at least from eccentric self-interested contest. For each time the Executive, aiming to justify the application of his power, points to a particular fact or situation and says, "This is a matter of war," he also determines, by contrast, untitled spaces for opportunistic actions by others.‡ This ordinary effect is multiplied

---

* As discussed in chapter 3. The President's other powers appear in article 2, section 1.1 ("executive power"), section 1.8 ("preserve, protect, and defend"), and section 3 ("faithfully executed").

† See the discussion of the *Youngstown* case in chapter 4.

‡ As Spinoza said, *omnis determinatio est negatio*.

where the stakes are high. The more the Executive reaches through the measure of war, constituting a climate of war, the more things escape his grasp and the more significant that escape appears—*especially to him.*

This is a pivotal moment in what may be called the dialectic of monocracy and omnipotence. When no one is watching, everyday disorder may not upset the sovereign.* During wartime in America, with no battlefields in the homeland and our populations spread across a continent, increases in disorder occur but are limited in effect. By contrast, *attention* to disorder increases exponentially. Likewise, the opportunistic appropriation of disorder ramps up sharply. *How* things *appear* to get out of hand—which derives from the new demands placed on the Executive by the People and by the Executive himself—constitutes a constraint on Executive action.†

In the early Cold War democracy itself was this *appearance of disorder.* The pathology of speechlessness produced a fever. Few objected to the investment of undivided decision-making power in a nuclear president. Dean Acheson—secretary of state and, it may be mentioned, analog of Condoleezza Rice‡—set forth the emerging common sense of the nation: "We are in a position in the world today where the argument as to who has the power to do this, that, or the other thing, is not exactly what is called for from America in this very critical hour."[42] Cold War architect and fellow adherent of the Democratic Party George Kennan was even more blunt in expressing a "distaste amounting almost to horror for the chaotic disorder of the American political process."[43] It must be acknowledged that in this context a minority still clung to the idea of politics against monocratic administration, as when Republican senator Robert A. Taft asserted vigorously that—*please note this carefully*—a *bipartisan* foreign policy is "a very dangerous fallacy threatening the very existence of the Nation." But even this tame and institutional allowance for the democratic play of interests was disallowed by those who could see the validity of its logic. Cautious conformism prevailed over deep insight when Taft's colleague Arthur Vandenberg§ allowed that bipartisanship was risky but could be

---

* N.b. that if sovereign bodies exist—this would include everything from the one king to the many people—they may have attributes like pride or vanity.

† This is the logic that will pressure the first president after George W. Bush to "stay the course" in Iraq, any promises to quickly withdraw notwithstanding.

‡ In the second term of President George W. Bush. Whether Acheson would have encouraged, as Rice did in July 2006, an unchecked invasion of Lebanon by Israel is another question.

§ N.b. that Taft and Vandenberg were both Republicans; even if their positions reflect the ten-

made less so as long as it only locked in after foreign policy had been "to-tally debated."[44] One need only ask, "When did the debate on Iraq end?" and "How long does bipartisanship last after the true facts have come out?" to see that the issue of democracy is not settled by such posturing.

Now consider again this familiar sequence: the terrorist attacks on September 11th left Americans in shock; our "public sphere" turned shock into fear; this constituted an appearance of heightened disorder; that unintended consequence of *our own actions* was opportunistically appropriated as a basis for warmaking; President George W. Bush—reiterating a ratio perfectly recognizable from the early Cold War system of "fear management"—at once played up the threat *and* insisted that the "war on terrorism" would be won, at once fabricating a threat of *our* "mass destruction" by Al Qaeda and Iraq and proffering himself stead-fast in the face of the Enemy.* That is, simply, President Bush used the symbolic form of war to extend his own power by giving it an indefinite object. This is what the phrase—repeated time and time again by Bush and the central players and propagandists in his entourage†—"whatever it takes" really amounts to: while the President would have us believe that by borrowing these words from workers at "Ground Zero" he iden-tifies with them, even patterns his actions on theirs, this effective bit of language is the height of cynical opportunism; the significance of that phrase "whatever it takes" is utterly altered when it moves from the angry mouth of one private person ready to contribute his individual energies and courage to a collective project and into the mouth of a leader en-trusted with all that comes together from an energetic and courageous people; the political actor must always take an impersonal position. "The constitution . . . is not a suicide pact" may mean that quick unified action

---

sions of working with a Democratic president, those positions also underscore how profoundly different the internal dynamics of the Republican Party and its position in the political process are today.

* President Bush's tautological reasoning in preparation for escalating the Iraq War in 2007 was an iteration of this same form. He described his thinking this way: "And so then I began to think, well, if failure's not an option and we've gotta succeed, how best to do so? And that's why I came up with the plan I did." Interview with *60 Minutes*, January 12, 2007.

† The 244 instances of the phrase "whatever it takes" at Whitehouse.gov (accessed October 2007) do not begin to show the centrality of this topos to the advancement of President Bush's image and programs; in addition to being constantly reiterated by all the leading members of Bush's party, "whatever it takes" was the theme of pivotal Bush/Cheney ads in the 2004 presidential campaign.

by the President is sometimes warranted but it also means that even with this dispensation the President may not lead the collective life-sustaining forces of the whole people into national suicide.[45] Any *person* may sacrifice him- or herself for the nation; no one may sacrifice the nation.

Within the political process, however, the *form* adopted by the president turned into a constraint *on him*. From September 11th forward, George W. Bush had repeated incessantly with slogans like "whatever it takes" and "dead or alive" and "bring it on" that the "war on terror" is "winnable." Then, during the summer of 2004, under pressure of the presidential election campaign, the circumstances of public discourse changed. In a rare and almost realistic response to facts President Bush attempted to retrench from his earlier position. Just before the Republican convention at the end of August an interviewer asked him once again, *Can we win the war on terror?* The president answered this way: "I don't think you can win it."[46]

This was not simply a lapse or mistake. It is obviously, even trivially, true. By the time the president spoke, however, the rhetorical train set in motion by him and his counselors had already left the station. President Bush's audience had long since adjusted to his triumphalist tone and terms. Hubristic language was in high demand. His opponents could not but adopt it as well. So minutes after the interview a cry went up from Democrats. They attacked Bush for *not being the proper leading character of the drama he himself had authored and in which they had invested, had had to invest, in order to defeat him.*[47] In one decisive moment Democratic candidate John Kerry, the War Hero, took over Bush's role.[48] He insisted that, of course, we could and would win the "war on terror"—"Absolutely."[49]

In short order a constellation of forces, located around the symbolic form Bush himself had wholeheartedly adopted, forced the Executive back into the "right" position. White House spokesman Scott McClellan immediately went to work "clarifying the President's remarks."[50] By the next day Bush was again on script. He proclaimed before the annual convention of the American Legion that "we meet today at a time of war for our country, a war we did not start, yet one that we will win. . . . in this different kind of war, we may never sit down at a peace table, but make no mistake about it, we are winning and we will win. . . . We will win by staying on the offensive. . . . We will win by spreading liberty."[51]

This small linguistic whirlwind exemplifies some of the systematic incentives we have seen that press the Executive to seek more power through war. The more he does so, however, the more power tends to escape him. This is not to say that the office is immediately weakened in any absolute sense. It is the new expectations, and in their wake some old ones, that are necessarily frustrated. What I want to emphasize here is the Executive's reaction on being entangled in this ambivalent process. In the present instance this "relative deprivation" did not lead the Executive to humility but to ever more outrageous pretension.[52] The tightening spiral draws down.

4. Two Poles of Power: Monocratic Omnipotence and Jeffersonian Justification

They see that nothing can support them but the Colossus of the President's merits with the people, and the moment he retires, that his successor, if a Monocrat, will be overborne by the republican sense of his Constituents, if a republican he will of course give fair play to that sense, and lead things into the channel of harmony between the governors & governed.

THOMAS JEFFERSON TO JAMES MONROE (JULY 10, 1796)

The wars of September 11th were initiated in reaction to terror but they revivified a brooding aspiration to an omnipotence. It went forth unhindered by reality, setting for itself the highest marks. When that aspiration began to fail it was not abandoned or inflected. It was redoubled. The unimaginable ignorance and self-destructiveness in each phase of America's policy in Iraq is as near to a pure example of the corrupting sinkhole of hubris as we are likely to see. Yet, as events have over and over again made clear, this hubris is not merely personal—Bush or Cheney—or even cabalistic—Rove or the Straussians. *The motive force here is the cultural logic of the Cold War*, reinforced by the blinkered psychological composition of those schooled in it. In other words, it is an action-guiding worldview that spans constitutionally separated powers and thereby makes that separation ineffectual.

It may be observed that especially under electoral pressure—where elections are not primarily the machinery of decision or political survival but the recharge of the symbolic system on which everyday politics feeds—the aspiration to an omnipotence reentered the public sphere with a vengeance. During that notable period in August 2004, before the national convention of the Republican Party, it had been widely predicted that the vice president, said to be a driving force behind the president's grand designs, would be jettisoned in the wake of the administration's evident failures.[53] There had been no "weapons of mass destruction," no trace of Osama bin Laden, no early or unbloodied exit from Iraq, and so forth, and only by the measure of subsequent years would we realize that the news could be worse. Instead, Dick Cheney, disgraced by the facts, was covered with laurels by his clan. And the obsession with control and denial that famously characterized the early Bush administration, incredibly, spiked up.

One particularly representative move in this direction was utterly consistent with the posture of the Cold War. Muddying again the distinction between offensive and defensive war, President Bush sought to out-Kerry Kerry, who was seeking to out-Bush Bush: "The best way to protect this homeland is to stay on the offensive."[54] This line—repeated roughly four times in the first presidential debate—may or may not have raised a scary prospect for enemies abroad. Viewed from the position of the Citizen it was an opportunistic reconstitution of fear in the political domain.

Opportunity and purpose are not the same. No matter how much fluid boundaries—between war and not-war, between offense and defense, and so forth—create opportunities, those opportunities still stand apart from the disposition and capacity to seize upon them. With one president

> there came, . . . whether by weird historical accident or by unconscious national response to historical pressure and possibility, a singular confluence of the job with the man. The Presidency, as enlarged by international delusions and domestic propulsions, found a President whose inner mix of vulnerability and ambition impelled him to push the historical logic to its extremity.

This, of course, was Richard M. Nixon, who "not only had an urgent psychological need for exemption from the democratic process . . . [but] also boldly sensed an historical opportunity to transform the Presidency" and consolidate its, and therefore his own, powers.[55]

While entrepreneurial spirit may be good for America, opportunism is not. Everything depends on the difference between these two postures, and that difference depends on *where the actual practice of power tends.*

If this seems like a simple formula for a brutal fact, you may not yet have fully grasped a major if often tacit theme of this book. For the tendencies of power—which is to say power itself, since power only exists as a modal feature in the living movements of human beings—occur within the division of action, making power both a composite fact and always one among several, and depend thus on the presence of countervailing powers; and, in tending this way or that, power has no fixed boundaries or quanta, but further depends for its shape and magnitude upon the human judgments that send action and social reaction crawling or spinning this way or that, that organize and inflect in each instant the divisions of action through which all tasks are accomplished or fail; and which judgments, further, are not merely applied in the spirit of ethical maxims—*What should I do?*—but as assessments of the use of social space constituted in every real and present division of action, and as instigation to the extending acts that allow or debar, dispose or disorder the appropriations of that space by others. It is this *judgment* that cuts between the opportune and the opportunistic and in that way marks the rise or decline of power.

Concerning the tendencies of power President Nixon showed us a certain direction. Steps taken by President Bush tell a perilously similar story.[56] For, in the first election debate with John Kerry in 2004, the incumbent president pictured not us but the Terrorist on the offensive. He again acknowledged the privilege of that position: "The enemy only has to be right once to hurt us." Then came the familiar implication that defense makes entirely different demands. On this point, however, he did not settle the balance of defense and offense or the question of how one may be turned into the other. He drew a conclusion that was strictly speaking irrelevant. It was nevertheless extraordinary and revealing. He said that, to protect ourselves, "we have to be right one hundred percent of the time."[57]

Here monocracy and omnipotence are fused. They constitute something authentically dangerous, the symptoms of which are widely discussed collateral consequences of a "war on terror." One is inevitably correct to be concerned about the infringement of rights, the prospect of "unlimited" war, and like topics that have occupied the public attention. But this Executive position touches on something more fundamental.

Why would someone present himself as assuming the demand to "be right one hundred percent of the time"? This is, obviously, impossible for any human being. The most cursory historical review of American foreign policy makes it a tragic joke. To assume this demand is to abandon the political "art of the possible" and enter another realm altogether, in which learning from experience, improvement, regret, magnanimity, and recompense are undesirable and even unimaginable. This antipolitics is not the only direction possible for American power or even for the powerful in America. What is its origin and motive?

The moment of nuclear monopoly—after Hiroshima but before the Soviet bomb—offered the Executive a taste of a new kind of power. Then the intervention in Korea gave birth to an "indiscriminate globalism," and it became difficult "to reconcile the separation of powers with a foreign policy animated by an indignant ideology and marked by a readiness to intervene speedily and unilaterally in the affairs of other states, [or] with an executive branch that saw everywhere on earth interests and threats demanding immediate, and often secret, American commitment and action."[58] In brief, as the domestic power of the Executive increased in parallel with the growing hegemony of the United States in the world system, how could the impulse to an omnipotence not be inherent in the leading office of the "world's only superpower"?

But foreign policy is only one resource for domestic projects; the link between them is not automatic.[59] The Executive office tempts the officer to ask himself, *Who will stand in my way?* When other "great institutions" of the American political process like "Congress, the courts, the Executive establishment, the press, the universities, public opinion" fail "to reclaim their own dignity and meet their own responsibilities,"[60] the answer to such presidential musings is—*no one; no one will stand up against Executive power.* This is almost sufficient motive to extend it. And it is then that concentrating forces like the terror of "the bomb" or the bombs of the Terrorist gain their full sway. It is then that war becomes a way of life, *civic war*, and the regime tends towards monocracy.

What metric gauges this tendency? How much deference or complicity or abdication is too much? Where is the threshold between the opportunity of emergency and the opportunism that corrupts not just the individual but a democratic political system?

The answer to this question is as simple as it is obscure: the boundary line between the opportune and the opportunistic is just where the Citizen positions him- or herself. More than anything else this *situation* determines the limits of power. Frustrating and difficult and tragically insufficient as this fact often is, it is only the judgment of the Citizen—*our* judgment—that makes the difference. Of the many factors constitutive of that judgment two come to the foreground here that may seem different but are in fact interrelated. One is attentiveness to the Constitution in all its forms. The other is the character of the President.

It is impossible for the Citizen to know the inner soul of the occupant of the Executive office.[61] We must take the President as a public character. The ejaculation of moralist clichés or fidelity to a spouse are irrelevant. The Citizen's first measure of presidential character is *attentiveness to the Constitution*.* This measure can only be applied with some hesitation, after each event, since it implicates not merely the suspicion but the whole and many-sided issue of deference, complicity, or abdication. All this had better be the object of our judgment.

The only way the President can prove himself worthy of deference, and the only way we may defer to him without abdicating the powers the Constitution allows us, is if the President himself insists that *we hold him responsible* and insists that *we defer not to the authority* of his office but to the appropriateness of his acts.† The corrupt Executive does not dedicate himself to such public rituals of responsibility; he seeks to evade them. The Citizen must demand the opposite, and the First Citizen or primus inter pares—for that, and not "Commander-in-chief," is the proper name for the constitutional executive—must demand it of himself.

At the outset of the American republic this view was common sense. It foresaw two phases of Executive action. Congress had barely opened its doors for business when in 1793 Representative William Findley acknowledged that any person charged with administration—"an executive officer,... the general of an army or the admiral of a fleet, and, though more rarely, even a financier"—could by terrible necessity "be induced

---

* Call this "republican virtue" if you like. In pre-Socratic Greece, the condition that made the polis a polis—*homonoia*—was, as Barbara Cassin (1995, 239) has written, that "one swears ... to be persuaded by the laws." This deep recognition is reiterated in the secular ethical writing of the great follower of Rousseau, Immanuel Kant, from whom admiration or attention (*Achtung*) before the law becomes the key figure of ethical life. But as a political matter Americans have never needed to follow the reductivist philosophy of Kant; love for the law and dedication to the rule of law was already, in the late eighteenth century, inherent in the revolutionary spirit of Tom Paine and present, as Marvin Meyers might have said, in the mind of the Founders.

† Demands that we respect an office per se tend to relieve officeholders of the need to win respect. There seems to be a corollary between the "decline" of qualities that should win respect—wisdom, honesty, public interest, courage, responsibility—and emphatic demands for this respect for the *office* of the presidency.

to depart from the authorized path of duty."[62] The statements of Representative James Madison Broom sixteen years later show the continuity of this view over a generation and across partisan lines:* "there may be circumstances under which it might be the duty of a public officer to depart from the laws."[63] It is fair therefore to take Thomas Jefferson as exemplifying the widely held understanding of that time on this point:

> A strict observance of the written laws is doubtless *one* of the high duties of a good citizen, but it is not *the highest*. The laws of necessity, of self-preservation, of saving our country when in danger, are of higher obligation

and there would certainly be circumstances that constituted "a law of necessity and self-preservation, and rendered the *salus populi* supreme over the written law."[64]

Such language will seem entirely familiar to you after September 11th. Yet its real meaning is utterly foreign to us. For the validity of an appeal to the well-being of the People over the mandate of the legislature required, in Jefferson's view, a second phase of action:

> The officer who is called to act on this superior ground, does indeed risk himself on the controlling powers of the constitution, and his station makes it his duty to incur that risk. . . . The line of discrimination between cases may be difficult; but the good officer is bound to draw it at his own peril, and throw himself on the justice of his country and the rectitude of his motives.[65]

The tone here resonates in many of Jefferson's writings. These particular lines were written to John B. Colvin, a well-placed pamphleteer for the Republican cause. Jefferson knew that in writing to Colvin his initially private words would find a broader public.[66] Producer and propagator of great words, Jefferson was also a voracious consumer of them, constantly borrowing in the way, we assume, he absorbed *monocrat* from

---

* Findley was born in Ireland in 1741, moved to Pennsylvania in 1763, was elected to Congress first as Anti-Administration and then Republican candidate, and was generally a supporter of Jefferson. Broom, by contrast, was thirty-five years younger and a Federalist from Delaware.

the *Moniteur universel* in France.* And indeed the phrase he articulates here seems not to be his own, but something he has taken over from his Republican colleague, the representative from Massachusetts Barnabas Bidwell, who declared that an officer might have to engage in "acts not provided for by any law" and that "[i]n such a case he must act under a high responsibility, and throw himself upon the justice of his country."[67] That Jefferson might have heard these words spoken or read them in a newspaper like the *National Intelligencer* underscores this crucial point.[†] This approach to Executive action in emergency "was accepted by every single one of our early statesmen."[68] The officer who thus steps outside the law to "take the responsibility upon himself"[69] had better "embrace the earliest opportunity to explain the matter and obtain a justification whilst the recent feeling arising from the occasion advocates his cause in the public mind."[70]

This phase of public truth telling, recognition, and responsibility was in Jefferson's understanding fit for all sorts of exigent situations, not only military action. The event through which Jefferson had almost unimaginable impact on the future of the United States—the Louisiana Purchase—was also conceived by him in just this way. "The executive," he wrote, "in seizing the fugitive occurrence, which so much advances the good of their country, has done an act beyond the Constitution," and the legislature, too, risking "themselves like faithful servants, must ratify and pay for it, and throw themselves upon their country for doing for them unauthorized what we know they would have done for themselves had they been in a situation to do it." This, Jefferson continued,

---

* From age seven for twenty years Jefferson followed rhetorical tradition and systematically collected the material of language in commonplace books. He practically codifies this social construction of common sense when he writes to Isaac McPherson on August 13, 1813, that "if nature has made any one thing less susceptible than all others of exclusive property, it is the action of the thinking power called an idea, which an individual may exclusively possess as long as he keeps it to himself; but the moment it is divulged, it forces itself into the possession of every one, and the receiver cannot dispossess himself of it. Its peculiar character, too, is that no one possesses the less, because every other possesses the whole of it. He who receives an idea from me, receives instruction himself without lessening mine; as he who lights his taper at mine, receives light without darkening me."

† This newspaper was edited by Joseph Gales and provided a key source for his compilation of the *Annals of Congress*. The process of circulation of this topos may include earlier uses of it by Jefferson himself, as in the famous but more distinctly private letter he wrote to John C. Breckinridge on August 12, 1803.

is the case of the guardian, investing the money of its ward in purchasing an important adjacent territory; and saying to him when of age, I did this for your good; I pretend to no right to bind you; you may disavow me and I must get out of the scrape as I can.

To this plea and justification he adds a most eloquent description of high political motive, one almost unimaginable to us today: "I thought it my duty to risk myself for you."[71]

In other words, Jefferson and his perspicacious contemporaries knew perfectly well that however much one may be obliged to act according to the "law of necessity," *it is no law.*[72] Yet emergency, that "fugitive occurrence," must always, in some sense, be accommodated. It is therefore the *accommodation* that must be brought *within* the constitution. And, as the constitution is the political distillation of the general sociological fact that all action is divided, *necessity* must also be fit within the division of action. The Founders had a relatively clear and commonsense way to obtain this Stoic posture. Their two-phase approach was based on the occasional fact of exigency and the oldest maxim of human justice—no one may judge his or her own case.* *Now* the Executive must determine if an emergency exists; *after the fact* some other agency—perhaps the legislature, perhaps the people, but certainly not the president himself hidden behind an armor of secrecy—must determine if the Executive was correct. This pivotal second moment of judgment cannot be accomplished without deference, humility, or even acquiescence on the part of the Executive.[73] Moreover, "[f]or this final and crucial condition—the need for ex post approval—to apply" the Executive must proceed with "open and public acknowledgment of the unlawful nature of such actions and of the necessity that called for committing them in the first place."[74]

Since the middle of the twentieth century, this second critical phase, the one that "will confirm and not weaken the Constitution by more strongly marking out its lines,"[75] has often been blocked by a spreading pathology of undivided action, the systemic hubris of office cultured within *civic war.*† In this case, where the president refuses to demand

---

* And, likewise, made their approach commensurate with the Athenian and Roman models that informed their understanding.
† It tends too much to obscurantism and ideology to simply refer this back to the failure to claim or impose responsibility. Note another sign of the pathology of undivided action: today this assignment or assumption of responsibility within the structure of action is strictly applied only

our judgment and indeed sees no reason for it, the Constitution provides the mechanism of impeachment to force the issue into the space of politics. In other words, the second corrective phase after power is stretched beyond its normal limit may be initiated by other agencies within the system.[76]

5. Phases of Communication: Secrets, Lies, and Publicness

Without publicity, no good is permanent; under the auspices of publicity, no evil can continue.

JEREMY BENTHAM, *Political Tactics* (1791)

The political pathology of undivided action and its perverse corollary of denied and evaded responsibility were manifest in essentially monocratic tendencies of the administration of George W. Bush. These tendencies appeared well before his first presidential inauguration. Bush's initial actions proclaimed clearly that the most contentious election in living memory did not merit reconciliation or mutual adjustment.* To the contrary, programs across the board that had been sponsored by President Clinton were, for just that reason, blocked and reversed. Concerted efforts closed access to public documents, suppressed lines of public information, reasserted an extreme "executive privilege," shut down internal "leaks" and dissent, and so forth. Even deep conservatives and avid supporters of this president objected that "a veil of secrecy has descended around the administration," adding that "the American people do not and should not tolerate government by secrecy."[77]

That secrecy is, in certain circumstances, a part of government no one will deny.[78] It has also been clear from the beginnings of the Republic forward that those public officers who could would push to cover information injurious to themselves and their projects. On balance, however, it was relatively easy before the twentieth century to find well-placed advocates of Woodrow Wilson's view that "government ought to be all

---

to *challenges to power*, in the form of "civil disobedience," and not to institutionalized power. Did, for example, Dick Cheney offer to be judged for war crimes when no "weapons of mass destruction" were found in Iraq?

* His own statements—like "I'm a uniter, not a divider"—notwithstanding (interview in *Salon*, May 6, 1999).

outside and no inside. . . . Everybody knows that corruption thrives in secret places, and avoids public places, and we believe it a fair presumption that secrecy means impropriety."[79]

To many Americans today this view will sound almost ludicrous. Living experience weighs against it. An intensifying motive for secrecy is bound up in the changes traced in the preceding pages: the new societal form of war, *civic war*, with its tightening circle of war and emergency, with its heightened representation of terror, and so forth. The motive has gained in effect as these changes have been integrated into a commonsense system of public justification, deploying with ever-greater frequency immediately effective commonplaces like "national security" and "executive privilege."[80] Efficient means for enlarging secrecy have emerged from the rationalization of information, a process ranging from formal and permanent systems of security classification to the digitization of massive quantities of data.

Although the "secrecy system" in American government has deep roots in our history, it came to full bloom in the early phases of the Cold War.[81] What had begun as "a legitimate system of restriction grew after the Second World War into an extravagant and indefensible system of denial."[82] While the word *nation* has been in more or less continuous use for two millennia,* it seems to have first been combined with the word *security* by George Washington.[83] Nonetheless, it was only after the advent of the nuclear age that a Hobbesian paranoia under the rubric of *national security* became the center of gravity for a whole political culture. Over the course of the 1950s, "the national-security consensus swallowed up unwritten as well as written checks on executive supremacy in foreign affairs."[84]

It was to an important extent because of this "national-security consensus" and the associated obsession with secrecy that Executive supremacy in foreign affairs became such a fruitful resource for domestic projects.† Linkages between the two are manifest clearly in the claim of *executive privilege*.

If by *executive privilege* is meant only that the President keeps some matters to himself, the practice is no doubt as old as the Republic. How-

---

* By "continuous use" I refer to terms that spring directly from the Latin *natio* as used in a political sense by, e.g., Cicero, who writes of the *eruditissima Graecorum natio*.

† I mention here only publicly "owned" projects; the same applies in spades for the many private "free riders" on (oxymoronic) public secrecy.

ever, the fact that the expression itself did not enter the administrative lexicon until 1958 is telling.[85] As a comprehensive and explicit doctrine, woven into and made effective by a larger cultural context, *executive privilege* is an artifact of the Cold War. Institutional structures created by the National Security Act of 1947 were pregnant with it. A threshold was passed when, in 1954, Dwight D. Eisenhower "made the most absolute assertion of presidential right to withhold information from Congress ever uttered to that day in American history."* The novelty in his claim was its extension of the protective cover of secrecy to everyone in the Executive branch. Whereas "the historic rule had been disclosure, with exceptions, the new rule was denial, with exceptions." Eisenhower's directive "ushered in the greatest orgy of executive denial in American history."[86]

Claims of *executive privilege* are just the tip of the secrecy iceberg, a juncture at which just enough information becomes visible to provoke reaction from interested parties. Hidden from view, a broader contest for information—between positions structured by the Constitution and among citizens of every type—continued unabated over the two decades following Eisenhower's innovation. Even as it was forced into the light by counterpressure—famous examples include the "free speech" movement in 1964, the Freedom of Information Act in 1966, the Pentagon Papers in 1971, and the general cultural attention to "hypocrisy" with its revival of Progressive-style "muckraking" journalism[87]—the machinery of official secrecy pressed forward.

Few imagined how far this process could infiltrate into everyday life. Then the curtain rose on the drama staged by Richard M. Nixon. Watergate became the icon of presidential overreach cloaked in secrecy. For a time. The administration of George W. Bush offered itself as a contender. Less than two years after September 11th, it could plausibly be argued that the pretensions of the Executive had gotten "worse than Watergate."[88] By the end of 2005 the depth of the problem of secret government in the United States had been confirmed by the unauthorized publication of the NSA's practice of illegal wire-tapping. The extent of the problem, by its very nature, remains unknown. In retrospect it seems clear enough, however, that President Bush, whose personal and political biography ran parallel to the "culture of secrecy," had, like the circle around him, a

---

* It seems ironic today that Eisenhower invoked this new sense of *executive privilege* to defend his administration from the attacks of Senator Joseph McCarthy.

"fetish for secrecy" long before occupying the Executive seat. "It became only more obsessive after 9/11."[89] And, because the conditions for enacting that obsession had changed, more effective.

Here as in so many other instances, important interpretive mistakes and misplaced priorities derive from a failure to distinguish between the life of the person and the exigencies of a social role—be it Executive or Citizen. In personal relationships lying is an odious thing: lies demolish trust and lead one to misjudge one's place in the division of action; lies disrupt affirmative fusional feelings one gains with transparent communication and, as such feelings are a source of self-worth, undercut that as well. In private, lies are a kind of narcissism that friendship will not abide. As an ethical matter, lying has the potential to wound deeply. Now, because every person has experienced the ill effects of a lie, it is easy to feel that lying is likewise the worst offense for the public figure. While natural and explicable, this transfer of attributes from personal to political relationships is a mistake of the first order, and I want to insist upon it here. The social positions that arise within the field of political relationship and become the vehicles for public conduct have structuring parameters that are quite different from subject positions like Friend, Sibling, Parent, and so forth. Of course, some public figures—for example, the Journalist—must seek and convey the truth if they are to act in character. But for the Executive, the Legislator, or even the Citizen, truth telling is a secondary matter. This is not denigration but social fact because in these cases other features of the political relationship are more important. This does not mean that truth is unimportant, but rather that in these social positions one is brought to truth indirectly, in an interrogative form. The first thing to be expected from someone who engages others as Executive, Legislator, or Citizen is that they will act in conformance with the role they assume. These roles have several constitutive features, but the one that concerns us here is *publicness*. That is, to act from one of these subject positions is to thematize and to exploit, as a set of constraints on one's own possibilities and the possibilities for others, the way the role itself is situated within a highly reflexive division of action. *Publicness* is a series of open doors through which a variable set of others can have an impact on one's actions; *publicness* is therefore also the necessity of taking these others into account if one is to act at all. The effect of publicity is "checking"; the greater the publicity, the more persistent this shaping, constraining, or blocking pressure. The eventual effects of such "checking" are material constraints on action. Yet the process itself is mostly driven by interrogation, by a questioning from many angles and the consequent implication of third parties in two-way disputes. In this process truth—effective truth, truth that gets things done, not abstract "universal" truth—has the chance to emerge. Without this process we have no grounds on which to expect public actors to give priority to a personal dedication to truth, or even take an interest in it. Thus publicity is the primary framework within which the fact that truth is secondary in politics must be understood. Truth seeking in politics, or more precisely a fairly reliable tendency towards truth, occurs as a social fact rather than as a personal or moral one. Morality, it may fairly be said, demands that one tell the truth. Politics comes at truth through the mediation of a special form of social interaction, and although it is of secondary concern at any given moment, the tendency towards truth turns out to be a necessary function of the other factors that are primary. What appears to be the looser and more flexible of the two paths is ultimately more sure. Obviously, neither guarantees that the truth will carry the day.

Again, the properly democratic presidential form of truth telling is not the exposé or the State of the Union message; it is the demand to be judged, the confession of love of country that manifests itself as love of the highest law, the Constitution, that realization of the division of action in a political form, where no one is above the law and no one a judge in his or her own case. A "war President"[90] who *does not call for his own impeachment* has already failed in his duty.

It should come as no surprise that there are public analogies to the private effects of lying. Trust is important, likewise decorum, or the capacity to situate oneself effectively within the relevant division of action; the political equivalent of fellowship and love is not "community" but legitimacy in its very broadest sense; the Citizen's self-worth is not immediate pride (that is chauvinism) but a mediated social emotion one might call "republican spirit." But as a political matter, lying scoundrels only scar the surface of democracy. In the Citizen's expectations from and interactions with other public figures, the probability that they will lie (and that one will need to lie oneself) is high and to be counted upon. It needs to be figured into all calculations and adjustments. Such figuring is yet another constitutive feature of the position of the Citizen. Publicness is what guides judgment because it is the precondition for measuring whether or not a person is acting in conformity with the role they have assumed; in this way publicness is—to give just the most common example—the precondition for election and recall. Conformity (or not) with a role supplies additional major parameters with which others in corresponding roles may size up the environment; this is a fundamental source of trust, decorum, legitimacy, and republican zeal.*

Must we be more blunt? Politicians lie.[†] All that matters is what happens next, which is to say how the constitutional system orders itself around this fact. This bifurcation is inherent in public action and it is of crucial importance. While one must always go forward—that's what action is—something is invariably lost in so doing, on the path not taken and in what is left behind. To go back, to act as if one had not acted, would be to undermine the character of action itself—its irreversibility, risk, and reward. Trying to relive the past we destroy the future; trying to have everything we are left with nothing. These are banal but inexorable facts that are offset somewhat by other human capacities precisely because the clock does not stop. To learn from mistakes, to change course, to forgive, and to convict—these are openings for a perfectly secular redemption. They haunt each moment at the threshold of courage.

Any account of political action that does not include these two phases is not merely incomplete. To believe that once the die is cast the hand of fate is forever closed is to prompt at once timidity and recklessness. Nothing could be more dangerously misleading.[91]

The corrective function that trails and completes action need not be an introspective or even a subjective genius. *It is performed objectively by publicness.* Its force is manifest in the impact third parties have on particular social roles as those who have assumed a role come into contest or dispute with others. This is why, in political life, secrecy is much more fundamental than lying. Without secrecy, in the light of publicity, lies are not sufficiently durable to serve malicious projects for long.

---

* Note here again that judgment is not a simple faculty but rather situated within a relationship where the object of judgment provides essential cues and frames that constitute the subject of judgment as such.

[†] In the two years following September 11th the Bush administration trumpeted at least 935 lies favoring American military action in Iraq; this number is from a study of public statements conducted by the Center for Public Integrity, available at http://www.publicintegrity.org/WarCard/.

6. The Export of "Moral Clarity"

An arrogant hermit may hold his tongue. The purely social claim to an omnipotence thrives otherwise. It drives an obsession with secrecy towards monocracy. In the case of the administration of George W. Bush, the starkest symptom of such a drive was the combined ideological and psychological impulse to claim absolute certainty.[92] This gesture was sustained by an equation of uncertainty with devastating weakness. The combination of these elements can be brutally restated as a perverted syllogism: *since we will die if we are not right, we are right.* One might say, too, from this same perspective, that *as long as we are threatened, we will be right.* This, it seems, is the real doctrine of George W. Bush and his entourage. They have expressed it time and time again.

Nowhere did this appear with greater precision than in the first presidential debate of the 2004 campaign. That is, once again, where George W. Bush most bluntly asserted what appears to be a founding tenet of his belief: "we have to be right one hundred percent of the time." He elaborates this commonplace, saying that "if America shows uncertainty or weakness in this decade, the world will drift toward tragedy."[93] Here, at the juncture of so-called moral clarity and national security, the President raises the stakes. He invests his belief with shocking public significance; an idea becomes a fact, speculation becomes reality. Exhibited is the way in which individual aspirations to an omnipotence contribute to a systematic and impersonal political pathology of undivided action.

With such words the President paints a picture of the nation and its personification in himself; he literally "represents" us so as to remake the Citizen in his image. He seeks, with these words, reelection, and at the moment we are most directly responsible for him, he presents us as responsible for the world. He appears as the savior of the world. *Our responsibility*, he implies, can only be met by affirming the omnipotence he seeks. "The advance of human freedom," George W. Bush solemnly declared in the days after September 11th, "now depends on us."[94]

Is this not, on its nebulous face, a statement of foreign policy? Approach it then first from that perspective. We have heard said, with wide repetition, that "this is a thoroughly Wilsonian proposition."[95] Woodrow Wilson, we have been told, became "the patron saint of the Iraq war" and "Wilsonian rhetoric has been widely invoked to justify America's current global crusade."[96]

The prominence of this rhetoric is both peculiar and telling. More often than not the epithet *Wilsonian* is used as a synonym for *idealism*. It is supposed to mark a contrast with *realism*, which is to say, to underscore the difference between foreign policy motivated by principles like freedom and democracy and foreign policy driven by pure self-interest. In this very general sense, however, practically all American diplomacy since Wilson—and often before him—has been presented to the American people as Wilsonian.* What, then, did it mean to say that George W. Bush was "becoming the most Wilsonian president since Wilson himself" or to insist that the administration's national security strategy to "bring the hope of democracy . . . to every corner of the world"[97] "almost exactly echoes Woodrow Wilson's pledge to 'make the world safe for democracy'"?[98]

Admit the zeal of the believer: each of these presidents could be described as "a deeply religious man" who supposed "that it was his calling to improve the world along lines revealed to him by the Creator and perfected in the United States," and who drew "great strength in the struggle against opponents" from a "religious conviction" that "also made him inflexible on issues he cared about deeply."[99] But when Wilson used the stark opposition of "good" and "evil" to set forth the tasks of the nation in his first inaugural address in 1913, his purpose was not specifically to demonize others but to point to internal ambiguities of a rapidly changing society and, in a familiar Progressive mode, to propose amelioration of the life conditions of working people.[†] Thus to identify the "Bush Doctrine" as Wilsonian is to ignore more or less subtle but surely crucial differences of context and belief. Wilson's position on foreign affairs was complex but ultimately multilateral; Bush is a unilateralist by temperament, by historical moment, and by way of America's present and vastly augmented military capacity relative to potential foes. Wilson was an architect of a world organization of nations; Bush has attempted to put another nail in its coffin. It may be particularly significant that Wilson conceived foreign interventions as a type of "policing" and thus

---

* The policies promoted by Henry Kissinger are typically offered as paradigmatic "realism." Appropriate scrutiny of this claim would take us too far afield.
† E.g. "The great Government we loved has too often been made use of for private and selfish purposes, and those who used it had forgotten the people. . . . Our duty is to cleanse, to reconsider, to restore, to correct the evil without impairing the good, to purify and humanize every process of our common life without weakening or sentimentalizing it."

essentially guided by law; for Bush the application of armed forces in favor of "principles" is first, foremost, and almost always war, an event at best at the outer limits of the law.

By the time of his second inaugural address in 1917, Wilson was clear about the domestic effects of American foreign policy in ways that seem well beyond Bush's insight. He recognized that "the war inevitably set its mark from the first alike upon our minds, our industries, our commerce, our politics and our social action." Coming to the conclusion of that speech Wilson warned: "We are to beware of all men who would turn the tasks and the necessities of the nation to their own private profit or use them for the building up of private power." Although to cite this here is in no way to ignore the rage of profiteering rampant during the Great War, it would repay us amply today to note that the tone set by the president resonated widely, reaffirmed the democratic struggle against corruption as the orienting principle of Progressivism, and was registered in common sense in ways that would shape the resistance to excess consolidated a decade later in the social and political experience of the Great Depression. To be called *Wilsonian* in this sense, President George W. Bush would have had to issue repeated, stern and public warnings not only to the Enrons, the Bechtels, the Halliburtons, but to every agency that created material for his own electoral campaigns. This is laughable on its face. Rather the president seems to have done little but facilitate in public discourse and institutional fact a heightened culture of opportunism after September 11th.[100]

On the topics of foreign affairs, President Bush is only in the most superficial way comparable with Wilson. When it comes to the domestic articulations and consequences of foreign military activity, that comparison is even weaker. With this in mind, however, it may now be admitted that they share a certain disturbing tone. Concerning one way that war is significant for domestic political life these two presidents do converge. Entering his second term Wilson believed that the ongoing world war had made Americans "citizens of the world." And although we would "remain true to the principles in which we have been bred," these were "not the principles of a province or of a single continent." As America had "known and boasted all along," these "were the principles of a liberated mankind." To this point Wilson's speech clings to the ambiguity just described. Then, however, the president who "kept us out of war" heads towards war with tones that ring today almost more like Bush than George

W. Bush himself.* The reelected president told his assembled public in Washington that these "native" principles are "a platform of purpose and action" where

> it is imperative that we should stand together. We are being forged into a new unity amidst the fires that now blaze throughout the world. In their ardent heat we shall, in God's Providence, let us hope, be purged of faction and division, purified of the errant humors of party and of private interest, and shall stand forth in the days to come with a new dignity of national pride and spirit. Let each man see to it that the dedication is in his own heart, the high purpose of the nation in his own mind, ruler of his own will and desire.[101]

Wilson confronts us with an almost fanatical[†] nationalist drive, where the "imperative" of "unity" is "purged," "purified," and "forged" in worldly but "Providential" "fires," then personalized to make "dedication" to the "nation" one's "own will and desire." Below we will turn our attention towards analogous ideological energies after September 11th. Here the question remains as to what such a vision of political life might entail for foreign policy. And, surprisingly, this brings yet another deep difference between Wilson and Bush to the foreground. In these words of Wilson, it seems to me, there is still substantial ambiguity and thus openness about where the "principles of a liberated mankind" should take root. Whatever imperialist projects came into view in the early twentieth century for the increasingly militarized United States, this speech at least leaves Wilson and his public open to the possibility that cosmopolitanism and a gospel of liberty could be realized on American soil, and that immigration, with the consequent creation of a culturally complex society, could be its major instrument.[102] This pattern had been taken to heart in various ways by Progressives over the preceding half century;[‡]

---

* The second inaugural address was given on March 5, 1917; the president asked Congress to declare war on April 2, and they did so on April 6. How Wilson's tone sounds today and its real contextual significance are again two different matters; the situation in Europe to which Wilson referred was in no important way comparable with the domestic political regime of Saddam Hussein or the jihadist networks of Al Qaeda.

† For reasons that will be given towards the end of this chapter, I use the word *fanatic* in a precise sense informed by its confused historical development as the name for those intolerant of impurity and antagonistic to the inherent plurality of political life.

‡ I of course do not mean to suggest that no "nativism" appeared in Progressive politics.

the massive restrictions on immigration of the interwar period were yet to come.

So while it may be said that President Wilson did not have the deep pluralist vision of a Horace M. Kallen or a Randolph Bourne,[103] even his politics of "Americanization" could be understood within this "new tradition" at the "golden door." Indeed, it was not the policymakers but a poet, Emma Lazarus, who had a decade before inscribed in public culture a Progressive vision of our dedication and duty to liberty, told as the story of the world coming to America and not as America conquering the world. Consider . . .

The New Colossus	*Comment*
Not like the brazen giant of Greek fame,	• The first Colossus, at ancient Rhodes, was one of those original "wonders of the world," and it symbolized defense against invasion with the masculine figure of Helios or Apollo, among other things a patron of the herder of sheep and goats and colonists. Jefferson associated the image of Colossus with "monocrats."[105]
With conquering limbs astride from land to land;	
Here at our sea-washed, sunset gates shall stand	
A mighty woman with a torch, whose flame	• Like the original, the "new Colossus" guards a port and, Lazarus declares, joins together sea and sun, the two great and original moving forces of the earth as a whole.
Is the imprisoned lightning, and her name	
Mother of Exiles. From her beacon-hand	
Glows world-wide welcome; her mild eyes command	• The figure, though, is feminine, and in her modern way tames those elements of nature, redeploying them to give welcome and solace, like a mother, to the rejected and those ejected from elsewhere. This enormous icon, beacon, draws the world towards us, where the ancient statue served to remind that all comers would be repelled.
The air-bridged harbor that twin cities frame.	
"Keep, ancient lands, your storied pomp!" cries she	• For the exceptional modern possibilities of America, history has no models, no lessons; liberty is not something we can wish for *them*, nor export to *them*, but only what *they*, with the intensity of desire typical of those with nothing left to lose, can bring to *us*.
With silent lips. "Give me your tired, your poor,	
Your huddled masses yearning to be free,	
The wretched refuse of your teeming shore.	• "Invade us," Liberty seems to say, and, like a host who lights the path for the welcome guest, we will make *you* a home and thus realize for ourselves the one that is our dream, our destiny, "the gift" wrote E. A. Robinson in the voice of the demos, " that I was bringing when I came."
Send these, the homeless, tempest-tost to me,	
I lift my lamp beside the golden door!"[104]	

The gist of these words is known to every American as a hymn of our mission of freedom.* Notice, however, that this vision is antithetical to George W. Bush's programs of war, from the building of fences against the "homeless tempest-tost" to blustery invitations that call contending powers to "bring it on." Notice, too, that informed by Lazarus, and with some but less vigor by Woodrow Wilson, we would have to directly contradict the forty-third president's missionary program "to advance the cause of freedom around the world" by the imperial and "preventive" force of arms.[106] To call this president a *Wilsonian*, then, is to reduce the complex historical moment of the Great War, the war that made the United States "modern" in a dozen ways, to a selling point for the deep-running monocratic tendencies that guide the decisions of George W. Bush, the president who, barely a week after September 11, 2001, with the eyes of the whole world upon him, declared that "the advance of human freedom . . . now depends on us."[107]

That world, the watching and waiting world, he implied, calls out for us, for our intervention, for us alone. This is the solitude one expects from the suicidal, the narcissistic, or the megalomaniac. Our president seemed, thereby and repeatedly, to assert that *being attacked* separated America from other nations, at the very moment when new and unexpected sympathy and solidarity were streaming in from around the world. Although we made more friends on September 11th than we lost, the Executive imagined us alone. And as fanaticism must turn away the friends it cannot control, it was just this self-image that fathered the fact of isolation and fostered unilateral action.

7. The Cold War Comes Home: The Revival of Reaganism

If there is any one thing that neoconservatives are unanimous about, it is their dislike of the counterculture.

IRVING KRISTOL, "What Is a Neoconservative?" (1976)

"The advance of human freedom . . . now depends on us." Should we hear in the president's words nothing but a nebulous statement of foreign policy? Certainly there is resonance of the so-called Bush Doctrine. But now

---

* The poem was written in anticipation of the Statue of Liberty in 1883 and was mounted on a plaque in the pedestal in 1903.

we must again extricate ourselves from the awkward embrace of foreign affairs to see things from the position of the Citizen. To *start* from *outside* that experience is paradoxically short-sighted. It is precisely against this type, a major type, of mistake that this book is directed.*

If a world-historical movement towards liberty "depends on us," the presidential voice coaxes citizen-auditors to believe, it is not because "we" are merely the centurions of an empire but, like Plato's guardians, exemplars of a virtue it is our destiny to protect. In this, the direction of the American self-image is reversed, and, as we shall see, even as a gift or commodity for export to the world it works from *inside out*.† Wherever it may be applied, this American virtue is not first inculcated or refined by opening or travel or worldly experience but born and bred at the hearth, in the "homeland," more Teutonic Alberich than Aegean Odysseus. Just as the President is not simply the leader in foreign affairs or merely the Commander-in-chief, the "Bush Doctrine" is a moral vision of domestic political order, an image of the πολις, or "city," in which personal and national virtue converge.

This is a perfect Platonism, as in *The Republic* where that old philosopher makes visible the inner workings of Man (ἄνθρωπος) by externalizing hidden but essential qualities of the Good (ἀγαθόν) in the form of a City (πόλις). Or it is a political evangelism of the "new Jerusalem," that puritan and purifying theocratic desire to make the "City of Man" into the "City of God." Wherever the deep historical roots of the president's insistence may lie, however, this convergence of politics and virtue must be decoded here from another angle. For—and this is the essential point—*it is a key ideological presumption of the Cold War*. Against this backdrop certain silhouettes take shape. Just as this is the Plato of Leo Strauss promulgated by a cadre of scholar-bureaucrats, what we see in George W. Bush is a contorted reiteration of John Winthrop's "city upon a hill"—not as John F. Kennedy saw it, a site in full public view where our responsibility to government is to engage it with "courage, judgment, integrity, dedication,"[108] but as it was presented by Ronald Reagan in a "farewell

---

* A strong corrective to this error is offered by general themes pursued in this book concerning the way that, as far as the Citizen is concerned, foreign-policy claims occur within and form a key part of domestic politics in the context of *civic war*.

† This is why John McCain, in the campaign-before-the-campaign of 2008, seeking to avoid a repeat of the trouncing he took from Rove and Bush in 2004, combined in one breath statements like "Rumsfeld . . . is one of the worst secretaries of defense in history" and "Roe vs. Wade . . . should be overturned." Speech at Hilton Head Island, South Carolina, February 19, 2007.

address" in many ways antithetical to the most famous one of that other "father" of our country.* Passing the torch to his protégé George H. W. Bush in January 1989, President Reagan concluded a summary of what he perceived as his accomplishments with some starkly revealing remarks. In "the past few days," he declared, "I've thought a bit of the 'shining city upon a hill.'" He explains himself in this way:

Reagan's Address	*Comment*
"The phrase comes from John Winthrop, who wrote it to describe the America he imagined. What he imagined was important because he was an early Pilgrim, an early freedom man ... and like the other Pilgrims, he was looking for a home that would be free. . . . in my mind [the shining city] was a tall proud city built on rocks stronger than oceans, wind-swept, God-blessed, and teeming with people of all kinds living in harmony and peace, a city with free ports that hummed with commerce and creativity, and if there had to be city walls, the walls had doors and the doors were open to anyone with the will and the heart to get here. . . . And how stands the city on this winter night? More prosperous, more secure, and happier than it was eight years ago. But more than that; after 200 years, two centuries, she still stands strong and true on the granite ridge, and her glow has held steady no matter what storm. And she's still a beacon, still a magnet for all who must have freedom, for all the pilgrims from all the lost places who are hurtling through the darkness, toward home. . . . We've done our part. And as I walk off into the city streets, a final word to the men and women of the Reagan revolution, the men and women across America who for eight years did the work that brought America back. My friends: We did it. We weren't just marking time. We made a difference. We made the city stronger. We made the city freer, and we left her in good hands. All in all, not bad, not bad at all. . . . And so, good-bye, God bless you, and God bless the United States of America.	• The word *shining* is a nice Hollywood touch but is not Winthrop's. • Winthrop would have been dead set against Reagan's equation of "freedom" with "free enterprise." • Is the president expressing here an affinity for the oppressive "cultural unity" of the Pilgrims (with, as he alludes earlier, its particular "civic ritual")? • The characteristic feature of Reagan's city is not that it is visible and thereby under and responsive to the watchful eye of the world, but its impermeable strength. • To immutability Reagan adds a different kind of visibility: the beacon that attracts, rather than the inspection that constrains. • Washington foresaw in retirement the "sweet enjoyment of partaking, in the midst of my fellow-citizens, the benign influence of good laws under a free government, the ever-favorite object of my heart, and the happy reward, as I trust, of our mutual cares, labors, and dangers."[109] Reagan, by contrast, returns to the anonymity of the crowd, private life withdrawn from the city, and the "city," he is proud to believe, is relieved of an oppressive state. Washington, who never gave a "revolution" his own name, ends his term of public life with aspirations to international neutrality, seeking pardon for his failings, and a humility that warns of the dangers of despotism that may arise from vigorous parties; and while our first president aspires to national unity, he comes at it from a point of view opposite to Reagan's: because of what we are, contention is inherent in human affairs, and politics is our way of living with that fact. To Washington's thoroughly political pessimism Reagan opposes a dangerously antipolitical optimism.

The issue here is not presidential virtue. But neither is it primarily a matter of vice, as it may have seemed when, some pages back, I suggested that the Executive today is changing in ways that are comparable to and perhaps grow out from abuses of that office by President Richard M. Nixon. Nixon did indeed contribute mightily to the monocratic tendency sketched in this chapter. President Bush has indeed evinced some comparable traits of public and private personality. Yet the now fairly common assertion that the machinations of the Bush administration are like or "worse than Watergate" should give us pause: Is this the right comparison? Does it serve the Citizen today?[110] For whatever its validity, this analogy also has decisive limitations. It draws attention away from those key features of the Bush administration's movement towards monocracy that remain, unlike Nixon's criminal activities, *within* the constitutional system.† It is not the moral but the political significance of monocracy that is of highest concern for the Citizen.

Indeed, the correspondence that tells more on George W. Bush is not with Nixon, who blended politics with vice, nor even with Goldwater's extravagant "extremism in the defense of liberty is no vice,"[111] but with Reagan, who sought to ground basic power politics on the spectacle of virtue.‡ In this deeper sense, which takes seriously the primacy of relations among citizens over the nation's entanglements with foreign others or enemies, what the Bush administration has professed may be with greater clarity described as a variant of Reaganism than as anything

---

* Ronald Reagan, farewell address from the White House, January 11, 1989. See George Washington's "Farewell Address" from 1796 (first drafted in 1792). It is worth pondering President Bush's shameful invocation of Washington and his analogy between Iraq and the American Revolution on President's Day, February 19, 2007.

† Nixon clearly engaged in criminal activity around the Watergate affair; it is not my purpose to consider which activities of members of the Bush administration have been criminal. Moreover, I will not take up the more general question of whether criminal activity is inside or outside what I refer to as the constitutional system.

‡ N.b. I am not saying Reagan was virtuous, any more than William Bennett's arguments—a mainstay of Reaganism—about virtue should be measured against his gambling addiction. What Reagan did was to open the rhetorical field of "virtue" in a specific way; indeed, he unleashed a whole industry that is of high political significance. This latter fact stands in complex relation to the discourse of "justice" that was for "the Sixties" a symbolic center of gravity.

specific to President Bush himself.* It will take several somewhat tangential steps to see what this means.

Once again, the large topic here is how foreign-policy claims issue from and are woven into domestic political effects. We know well that national political actors may push this or that foreign policy in order to advance a domestic interest or agenda. Some such opportunisms are largely ad hoc.† This common observation, however, plays down the extent to which such connections may be more substantial. Can the stronger argument be made that certain types of foreign-policy claims or demands are not just transient vehicles for domestic interests but also constitute basic forms of and motives for domestic politics?

If by *politics* is meant nothing more than transactions made by elites to circulate money and status among themselves, then it is easy enough to find evidence that points this way: the infamous "revolving door" that links public office and private industry is about as basic a form and as base a motive as one might imagine. But such a limited perspective leaves the Citizen out of the picture altogether. The purpose of this book is the opposite: to relocate the Citizen at the center of political life. Thus I propose that the hypothesis must be tested on rather different ground.

The "Bush Doctrine"—in its more tacit way like the outspoken Reaganism from which it is derived—is not just or primarily an approach to foreign affairs. It is the emblem of a comprehensive ideology that aims to transform American political life. I do not mean just that it pushes towards specific policy goals, although it does that too. Even as a matter of foreign policy the "Bush Doctrine" operates from the outside in on the very possibility of politics. This general fact should surprise no one; it is perfectly consistent with the historical formation of national states.[112] There is, however, a fact of higher urgency for the Citizen. It is that the basic political motives and forms implicated in the "Bush Doctrine" emerge from the inside out. This implicit fact of the Cold War

---

* Libertarians have said, "George W. Bush is no Ronald Reagan" (Boaz 2004), but then they also said that Ronald Reagan was no Barry Goldwater (a comparison in which Goldwater himself concurred). What I introduce here belies, insofar as these various "doctrines" cross paths, the assertion that "neoconservatism" is essentially an orientation to foreign policy; I have more to say about this below.

† Although they would not be seen as such outside the "system of opportunism" sketched above.

was made explicit and programmatic with the refounding of American conservatism by Barry Goldwater at the Republican national convention in 1964. Goldwater's words mobilized the conservative reaction against the "countercultural" and "counter–Cold War" social forces of the 1960s: "This Nation . . . can be freedom's missionaries in a doubting world. But . . . first we must renew freedom's mission in our own hearts and in our own homes." Ronald Reagan picks up on this and, in turn, becomes the proximate inspiration for George W. Bush.

Ronald Reagan spared no opportunity to state the foundations of his beliefs. Let us take to represent the aspects of Reaganism relevant here a striking aphorism that appears, again, in that president's farewell address. "All great change in America," he intoned, "begins at the dinner table"— which is to say, that imagined hearth of tutored Cold War consensus where "Father Knows Best" and the family assembles under paternal direction after the women's work is done and the prayers have been said.[113]

Why is this relevant to the "Bush Doctrine"? Because the view out to the world from George W. Bush's Reaganism—with its "axis of evil," unilateralism, preemptive and preventive warfare, "renditions"—is not merely congenial to the prominent "social issues" owned by his coterie—dogged against taxes, immigration, and feminism; rabid on abortion rights, gay marriage, and gun control; uncomprehending of constitutional secularism, the science of evolution, and a critical press; and so forth—but essentially joined to them.*

To see how this works, consider now again that the "checks and balances" of power are not just a pushing-and-pulling operation between two branches of government. This process is typically mediated by other institutions and practices or, as Madison observed, by partial overlap in the otherwise conflicting branches.[114] In addition, beyond the *government* itself, *society* is always already implicated insofar as each of these contending powers relies on the mobilization of human energies and judgment in order to advance itself.

---

* Once again, a general linkage between foreign policy and domestic affairs was made for conservatives in an influential way by Barry Goldwater in his famous acceptance speech at the Republican national convention in 1964. It should be noted that his views on particular issues eventually diverged sharply from those who claimed his legacy. Just after Reagan came to power with the help of the newly consolidated "Christian Right," Goldwater said: "I am warning them today: I will fight them every step of the way if they try to dictate their moral convictions to all Americans in the name of 'conservatism.'" Cited from *Congressional Record*, September 16, 1981.

A famous example of this general fact appears in the way political parties can operate (both positively and negatively) to offset direct conflict or confluence between the Executive and the Legislature. This is neither a formal aspect of constitutional "separation of powers" nor is it necessarily an instance of "popular sovereignty." It is, however, a potential for transformation of the political system and was recognized as such already in the first years of the Republic. In 1800 John Marshall predicted that if Jefferson acceded to the office of the president he would, by caucusing with fellow partisans and becoming "the leader of that party which is about to constitute the majority of the legislature . . . embody himself in the House of Representatives, and by weakening the office of the President . . . increase his personal power."[115] In retrospect, we can see that Marshall was only half right: Jefferson's networks outside the office also increased the office.[116]

The perspective repeatedly applied in this book reminds us that this is no isolated instance. It is rare indeed that one can increase one's power by acting in a simple unilateral manner. It is much more effective to develop relationships with the counterpowers that could or should, under normal circumstances,* block the enlargement of your projects, or with the counterpowers that could or can be made to impede the path of those who stand in your way. The difference between these two ways of getting what or where you want seems like a difference between direct and indirect action but is really something else. For we need to recognize that the appearance that power "acts directly" is usually misleading. In either case power is not a substance that, like water from a faucet, flows or doesn't. Power is a modality within or inflection of a division of action, and it is always within a complex constellation of (what appear on the surface to be) powers and counterpowers that one's own capacities for action are constituted in the first place.

When it comes to Executive power, this type of indirect engagement with *political* forces by way of direct address to *society* became especially important in the twentieth century.† "Reconstructive" presidents—the

---

* *Normal* here simply means a prior condition of sufficient duration and habit to have lost its crisp edges within the general flow of events; thus, as I have repeatedly said of the political scene of *civic war* in this book, *emergency* is not the same as *exceptional* and can without contradiction become a "normal" state of affairs.

† This process is not limited to the Executive. Consider again how J. William Fulbright used committee hearings as a "publicizing speech act" to facilitate the slow transformation of Congress during the Vietnam War, as discussed earlier in this chapter.

ones who have most transformed the political system by first pushing off hard against their predecessors—have of course reached out to *society*; this is a pivotal feature of how Jefferson and Jackson and eventually Lincoln redefined the position of the presidency.[117] But that peculiarly new and somehow deeper complicity with the people so vital for the success of Reaganism emerged from a wide range of subsequent factors. These included the refined mix of an utterly personal voice and new technologies of communication (think of FDR with the radio, or JFK with the television),* the generalized scope of emergency carefully blended with a paternal theme in claims about security (think of the "fear management" of the civil defense phase of the Cold War and the way it has constantly been recalibrated, e.g. by the symbolism of a protective embrace from a "shield in space" against incoming nuclear weapons), the revolution in the "politics of rights" with and after the GI Bill of Rights and the civil rights movement (keep in mind that the defense of rights is an Executive matter and thus an opportunity for deference to the president, a fact that even Reagan's antientitlement rhetoric took advantage of), and so forth.

Such resources—shaped around social factors like technology, psychology, law, and so forth—facilitated Reagan's transformation of the constitution of power in ways that would provide important models for George W. Bush. While, once again, it is not similarities between Nixon and Bush that clarify developments after September 11th, some of the parallels with Reagan can be further highlighted by contrast with Nixon. Think of Nixon's position in time. He did not merely take over the Vietnam War from Lyndon Johnson. He had been a pivotal player in the first two periods of the Cold War, but what he inherited from that Democratic president was "the Sixties." There is a sense in which having lost the election of 1960 Nixon became president too late. By 1968 the Cold War had been diametrically reshaped—let's say *inverted*, but with its major features intact—by those who suffered most from the future-annulling terror by which it was driven: the young. Nixon presided over times that were pitched against the times for which he stood. In this context Nixon did occasionally take advantage of emergency powers—in the form of

---

* This paradoxical mix of personal and impersonal that derives, especially, from *the microphone* is an important feature of contemporary political culture. N.b. that FDR and JFK were not the first radio or television presidents, just as Reagan was not the first Cold War president.

complex warmaking power derived from Johnson, in declarations of emergency during the postal strike of 1970 and economic downturn of 1971[118]—but this was not the primary vehicle by which he positioned himself in the political field. Nixon personalized his use of the Executive office not by creating an attractive public persona as Reagan would but by operating in secret with close associates as a cabal (from domestic elections to a manipulated coup d'état in Chile). These several differences converge in this last one, which is essential. Within the constitutional system and its specific divisions of action, no cabal can succeed for long "on its own." Even highly motivated and disciplined groups depend on the response they meet: *they advance only where others stand down.*

It is in this regard that Reagan's complicity with society made the crucial difference. What had in the 1950s been a generalized anxiety was in "the Sixties" amplified into widespread social conflict. When Reagan entered upon the stage of national politics, there had been no successful presidency since Eisenhower—with JFK assassinated, LBJ withdrawn, Nixon resigned, Ford appointed, and finally Carter held hostage by students in Teheran. By 1980 the inversion of Cold War themes that characterized "the Sixties" had fully brewed its own reaction. Reagan arrived at just the right moment for his own ambitions.

While Ronald Reagan may be extolled today for "ending the Cold War" the fact is the opposite: he *refounded* it, which is to say—under the rubric of a "new beginning" that drove an interdependent ambition to squeeze out social programs while ramping up military ones, to cut taxes and impose "monetary discipline" while deregulating business[119]—Reagan set the Cold War back on its feet and drove it forward with new and renewed vigor. With the advent of President Reagan, the Cold War system of political culture resumed the postures and tones through which it had operated in the formative years after World War II—which is to say, the period in which Reagan worked actively with the FBI and the House Un-American Activities Committee.[120] After the election of 1980 this new phase of the Cold War grew exponentially, precisely in overcoming what had for the span of an entire generation appeared as its nemesis; Reagan had, of course, with the collaboration of the FBI and the CIA, built his successful campaign to become governor of California around a direct assault on the social movements at Berkeley.[121] These "accomplishments" shine by comparison with the Nixon who had deeper credentials— McCarthy's co-conspirator, heated antagonist of Khrushchev—but ended his career trying to make peace in Vietnam and to construct a strategic alliance with China. As Bill Clinton would later observe, by comparison with Reagan and the Reaganists who followed him, "Nixon was a communist."[122]

The general names common sense has given to these facts of political culture are emblematic of fundamental differences between ways the constitutional system of power was transformed by Nixon and by Reagan. There are no "Nixon years" in the history books; no person or movement subscribes to "Nixonism." By contrast, "Reaganism" is the core ideology of the Bush administration and the 1980s are widely known as the "Reagan years."

A specific difference between these two regimes is the complicity of civil society. In the dynamic balancing of counterpowers that gives shape and motive to each and every identifiable power in the constitutional system, Reagan operated on civil society to undermine those forces that might obstruct his projects. This is how he expanded the Executive power. If in some crucial instances this enlarged power was used against itself, and policies attacked politics, Reagan was by no means the enemy of "big government" that he and later Reaganists would have us believe. What matters here, however, is how Reagan reshaped political culture in a Cold War mold and the impact this had on the constitution of power.

Complicity between the president of the "Reagan years" and civil society was achieved through the massive symbolic machinery of the Cold War. Reagan's revival of the 1950s cultural system, in which a looming "evil empire" is called on stage to win the public over to a wide range of domestic projects, would not have been possible without a context of ongoing *civic war*.* The complicity inherent in *civic war* has a soporific effect on counterpowers that might otherwise hold Executive power in check. Reagan's coup de théâtre, his elaboration of Goldwater's intuition into a presence that haunted the whole American scene, provided the model for and thus illustrates what I meant when, a few pages back, I wrote that the view out to the world from George W. Bush's Reaganism is not merely congenial to the prominent "social issues" owned by his coterie but essentially joined to them.[123]

---

* Indeed, when war became, so to speak, too military for Americans in the late 1960s, it ceased to serve the purposes of domestic political ideology.

Nixon grasped after a "silent majority" within civil society but, as the White House became for him a fortress, he failed to articulate this connection and was overtaken by the predominant social forces of "the Sixties."* By contrast, not only was Reagan able to use the American defeat in Vietnam and the foreign-policy debacles of his predecessor Jimmy Carter as a springboard, but he also built a concomitant complicity with *society* against "the Sixties."† It was this disillusionment with and rejection of *the reaction against the Cold War* that allowed Reaganism to constitute a profoundly different ideological landscape. As we have already seen, the element of nostalgia in this transformation—for the early Cold War, for a fantasy life we share from motion pictures, for a time supposedly before urban violence and domestic deception—was strong. However, it added a powerful new variation on the Cold War theme. Nothing served it more than Reagan's ability to delegitimize the Left in its various forms—electoral (i.e. the "New Deal" or "Great Society" Democrats), cultural (i.e. the critical and ironic public culture of "the Sixties"), movement (i.e. the campaign against the war in Vietnam), and institutional (i.e. the labor unions). President Reagan made resistance to the *expansion* of the powers of his office exceedingly difficult; he did this not just by asserting his own power directly (as in the PATCO strike) but by eroding those sites of resistance from which citizens could have stood against him as they did, for example, against Nixon.‡ In this context it seems clear why Reagan's public persona as a personable and unassuming "regular guy" was so important for both the success of Reaganism and the peculiar tacit enlargement of the presidency that came with it.

---

* I referred above to this period of the Cold War as the Reactivist Sixties because the predominant tendencies were in key respects a mirror image of the civil defense posturing of the 1950s that retained its essential features; the "counterculture" took its cues and symbolic forms from the "culture" of the Cold War and in that way continued it.

† "The Sixties" is not a clear-cut historical fact or chronological period but rather a symbolic form that coordinates many facets of social imagination and makes it an effective part of political beliefs and actions.

‡ It could be illuminating to compare effects of massive demonstrations against the war in Vietnam (e.g. in New York in 1967; the "moratorium" of 1969; in Washington, DC, after Kent State in 1970) with the antinuclear demonstration of June 12, 1982. This is complicated by the perverse way that the antinuclear movement becomes part of the revival of the Cold War, with, perhaps, Jonathan Schell's *Fate of the Earth* (early 1982) functioning, like Hersey's *Hiroshima* (1946b; first published in the *New Yorker*, Hersey 1946a), to reconstitute the "terror" that Reagan then proposes to "manage" for us in, to give the most famous example, the "Strategic Defense Initiative" speech, March 23, 1983.

It has been said that after September 11th George W. Bush came into his own as a leader. This underestimates radically his success in the prior year, starting with the assumption of the presidency itself after a failed election and "judicial *coup d'état*,"* continuing with the creation of a new and dedicated Reaganist and neoconservative cadre within the State, then extending through momentous policy initiatives such as Cheney's secret Energy Task Force, Rumsfeld's first moves to reorganize the military, and one of the largest tax cuts in U.S. history.[124] Before September 11th the president also pushed forward his project of social transformation in a series of fifteen extralegislative executive orders touching on "faith-based initiatives" (3), measures against unions and regulations favorable to labor (8), social security (1), energy policy (2), and veterans affairs (1).†

Be that as it may, something was added from September 11th forward. Bush was able to recapture a kind of complicity with civil society comparable to Reagan's.‡ He quickly deployed through this diminished resistance to advance a domestic agenda the substance of which also borrowed heavily from the comprehensive Reaganist program. Obvious parallels include the transformation of the State through antistate rhetoric and policy,§ the refounding of the Cold War with a return to the repressed fantasy values of the 1950s (as first reconfigured by the "Reagan years" and with an added twist of 1990s supercharged-market-and-single-superpower bluster), and the assertion of a "post-Vietnam-syndrome" national identity through projection of a foreign adversary

---

* Expression used first by Jack Kemp, Ann Coulter, Rush Limbaugh, etc. to attack the vote-count rulings of the Florida Supreme Court and then descriptively with reference to the effect of the Supreme Court's ruling in *Bush v. Gore* (531 U.S. 98 [2000]) on the outcome of the 2000 presidential election; cf. Dionne and Kristol (2001) and more recently Remnick (2007).

† These measures range from establishing commissions to intervention in the Northwest Airlines strike on March 19, 2001 (this was based on the Railway Labor Act [1926]discussed in chapter 3).

‡ N.b. that *complicity* in any important sense cannot be measured by "Presidential Job Approval" polls because it is indirectly related to presidential action and concerns primarily and directly those things that might stand in the president's way. The low informational content of such polls is suggested by the fact that the two highest ratings were for Harry S. Truman in August 1945 when he had just brought the Japanese to surrender (91.87 percent approval) and for George W. Bush in the weeks after September 11th when he had done nothing (89.81 percent approval); cf. http://www.presidency.ucsb.edu.

§ The empirical evidence does not support the claim Reagan made about himself, i.e. that he dismantled the state.

in the Manichaean terms of an "evil empire."* Perhaps the most pronounced institutional outcome of this revived Reaganism was—as in
the original case—convergence of deep tax cuts with sharply increased
military spending,[125] effectively notching up intense fiscal and political
pressure on social programs and continuing to "shift risk" from the State
onto individuals.† Where the president of the "Reagan years" reached an
impasse in this regard, the Bush administration carried the torch farther.
Viewed as a whole, the program of these several phases of Reaganism
has aimed at a comprehensive recomposition of American society, from
the grand scale and minutiae of the federal budget to basic moral assessments of self and others; the careful observer will have seen, too, that
it has been uncannily preoccupied with the organization of gender relations and with pushing back against the social pressure of feminism.‡
As we have seen, the primary symbolic vehicle of the ongoing Reaganist
political movement preceded Reagan himself. It gathered steam from
the original Cold War, but not in the sense we ordinarily have in mind.
Rather it persistently rearticulated the domestic struggle of political culture that Irving Kristol identified as beginning just after World War II.§
Cold Warriors like him were fixated by "critical inquiry into liberalism"
and over the last half century this purportedly intellectual engagement
has (d)evolved into an all-out assault on the "radical . . . agenda of contemporary liberalism," which, in the view of Kristol and his cohort, is to
advance the "rot and decadence" of American society.[126] *This* Cold War
is punctuated by the Bomb and the Bay of Pigs and the Afghan War and
bin Laden at the same time that it stretches from Joseph McCarthy to

---

* It may be worth mentioning that all three tropes would surely have found their way into
Vladimir Propp's *Morphology of the Folk Tale* (1928) had that work been rewritten as an account
of the Hollywood film.
† Increased inequality of income and wealth is another outcome of Reaganism. Although measured through persons or households it, too, is a consequence of institutional changes.
‡ It is worth noting that the founding text of modern feminism, Simone de Beauvoir's *Le deuxième
sexe*, appears at the outset of the Cold War (1949; English trans. 1953); that the "backlash" against
feminism's modest gains corresponds to Reagan's revival of the Cold War; that popular identification of this "backlash" by Faludi (1991) occurs at the same moment as the dissemination of the
topos "culture wars" to replace "Cold War" (Hunter 1991); and that post-9/11 political culture
has bent in a similar way (Flanders 2004; Faludi 2007; Ferguson and Marso 2007).
§ As Kristol personalizes this, he sees his own coming of age as its origin; in fact it had been ongoing long before his arrival under another set of names.

Barry Goldwater to Ronald Reagan to Newt Gingrich to George W. Bush and back again.* Ann Coulter and Dinesh D'Souza and Mona Charen and William Bennett see all this with a weird clarity; the rest of us have ignored it. It is a process astonishingly accelerated by the unfortunate but correct judgment of the Bush administration that contemporary U.S. citizens see their primary stakes even in wartime neither as "life and limb" nor as a broad public interest but as short-term monetary loss or gain. I hold that all this is consistent with and indeed plays into the increasing relative importance of *civic war.*

8. The Breeding Ground of Monocracy

Were parties here divided merely by a greediness for office . . . , to take
a part with either would be unworthy of a reasonable or moral man,
but where the principle of difference is as substantial and as strongly
pronounced as between the republicans & the Monocrats of our country,
I hold it as honorable to take a firm & decided part, and as immoral to
pursue a middle line, as between the parties of Honest men, & Rogues,
into which every country is divided.

THOMAS JEFFERSON TO WILLIAM BRANCH GILES (DECEMBER 31, 1795)

The number of "rogues"—connivers, cheats, looters, and generally slimy bastards—is large. *Civic war* has provided them with fertile ground for *roguing.* Opportunism is rampant, and profit without propriety, now as always, is a moving force.

Does this mean that the extension of an empire, backed by global networks of military bases, constitutes nothing more than a "strategy of plunder" in the service of capital accumulation?[127] Whatever else one may say about the pursuit of empire—it's objectionable, unjust, ultimately self-defeating, or it's admirable, liberating, necessary—I want to point to one simple historical fact: the pursuit of empire is not inherently undemocratic. As this book is not focused on the effects of public and

---

* Gingrich and Armey 1994 and Gingrich 2005 may be taken as paradigmatic documents of the two phases of the Reaganist cultural Cold War revival; that Gingrich has also devoted himself to writing pop novels about war seems significant in ways too complicated to consider here.

private action abroad but on the domestic political conditions under which choices favoring or impeding such action may be made, this political fact must here be given priority over moral assessment.

We have seen that military aggression in Iraq increased the Bush administration's capacity to pursue its agenda inside the United States. Considering now the particular opportunism of the profit motive, one may go farther and say, following Nobel laureate George Akerlof, that this domestic policy agenda amounts to little more than "a form of looting."[128] Frances Fox Piven, recent president of the American Sociological Association, articulated this perspective with great clarity. Piven argues that "in this instance war is also a strategy for domestic predation" that dispossesses "resources and rights from ordinary Americans on an unprecedented scale."[129] In other words, the era of "after 9/11" is characterized by a form of "class war" that is unfolding roughly as follows: strong tendencies within both the State (Johnson's "Great Society") and civil society (a general "cultural" tilt against authority) made "the Sixties" a bad time for profits; in the 1970s "big business responded by mobilizing an army of lobbyists and think tanks to promote a political agenda that would shore up profits by rolling back the public policies of the New Deal and the Great Society"; that agenda "gained considerable traction under Ronald Reagan," and its main planks "were cutting taxes on business and the affluent, reducing government regulation of business, weakening unions, and slashing the public programs that shored up the power of workers, largely by reducing the pain of unemployment."[130] However, "eight years of Reaganism essentially produced a standoff" with regard to "the biggest social programs . . . Social Security and Medicare"[131] and in some important respects the Reagan administration ended in "political failure."[132]

When Ronald Reagan ramped up the federal deficit in the 1980s he had a larger political intention. This intention was expressed with stunning simplicity in the first presidential debate that preceded his election. Facing John Anderson, Reagan referred to the federal government in this allegorical way: "If you've got a kid that's extravagant, you can lecture him all you want to about his extravagance . . . or you can cut his allowance and achieve the same end much quicker."[133] This antistate political program later came to be referred to by others on the Right as "starving the beast."[134]

Pivotal figures in the administration of George W. Bush learned a decisive and dangerous lesson from this aspect of Reaganism. As Vice

President Cheney would later put it, "Deficits don't matter."[135] What he meant was that the enlargement of deficits would not raise a political response. Against this background it is difficult not to conclude that the quick and astounding reversal after 2000 of the unprecedented budget surplus of the Clinton years was not simply a coincidence of fiscally incompatible policies, nor even the issue of mismanagement, but rather an intentional return to Reagan's political program of forcing socially responsible government out of existence through a process that would, as a side effect, minimize debate and impose upon it the appearance of necessity. In other words, the present massive deficit is not an "accident" but a strategy: cut taxes (and shift remaining ones from unearned to earned income), raise military expenditure (while further privatizing services to funnel this tax money to business interests), and in that way squeeze out social programs (which had buffered the market position of salaried employees and thus decreased profits to capital).

Professor Piven is particularly skilled at but hardly unique in offering an analysis of the long-term political scene along these lines. Should we be persuaded by it? That depends in part on how much one thinks it can explain. Are *all* such changes in policy and practice directly driven by lust for profit? That does not seem plausible. Does a pervasive tendency favor excessive profit making and allow that fact to color deeply other motives and actions? That would be difficult to deny.

These are momentous questions. Every person who seeks the position of the Citizen should examine them with care. Many writers have pressed us with arguments one way or the other. This book, however, will offer no direct counsel towards an answer. Instead I touch on this inevitable topic for a purpose tangential to it. I want to emphasize that the Citizen who takes this as the point of departure is likely to come soon to an impasse. The forms of power and their articulation in democracy had better be the first concern for the Citizen; only these political considerations will provide the criteria from which disputes about economic justice can find durable accommodation and appropriate review. Let me be clear. In no way do I wish to rule out of bounds questions about the proper place and extent of profit-seeking and even opportunism in a democratic nation. But I do insist that we had better first set a stage that is apt for considered political judgment and action.

And why shift ground in this particular way? Because I fear that the very way the question itself is formulated may be misleading. Just to ask—

Is the whole scene, the reconfiguration of American national life after September 11th, the continuing juggernaut of Cold War political culture, driven by a dangerously unchecked and unregulated drive for profits?—urges upon us a certain view of politics, in which power and its strategies appear in the narrowest of frames, and all that matters is what an agent wants (let's call this *profit* or *dominance*) and the instrumental means by which that end is achieved (let's call this profit/dominance-*seeking*). These themes are entirely familiar and they are woefully inadequate.[136] To proceed under their banner is to make invisible the real material implication of the Citizen in society and politics just when it should count the most. However accurate the image of profit-seeking opportunists, however much that figure draws attention and mobilizes hot anger, it can little inform effective action. It runs like water from our grasp.

The first invisible implication of the Citizen is very basic: "we" are the substance and the energy through which projects advance or not; all profit-making activities of the scale under consideration here are inherently social endeavors and operate through the division of action; this does not of itself create any obligation of "part" to "part" or "part" to "whole." It simply means that as a matter of practical fact profit seekers cannot achieve their ends without "us."* This raises a somewhat different but more clearly political question. In the processes of interdependence, what forces and combinations remain at the disposal of the Citizen?

The second invisible implication concerns the way the forces at the disposal of the Citizen operate through the constitutional system in its broadest sense. Whatever the profit seeker may attempt or accomplish, especially (although not only) as matters of public policy, the result is delimited and shaped by the counterpowers of the Citizen's own political designs and practices. At the same time, the Citizen's designs and practices take form in interaction with other constitutional powers. Thus the properly pointed topics of inquiry for the Citizen are neither the motives of profit seekers nor the paths along which they achieve their goals, but rather the ways in which profit seekers are able to deflect, bypass, or

---

* It is a typical mistake of political theorists preoccupied with philosophical ethics to assume that connection implies obligation; to see correctly that there is no such obligation is not to deny the fact of the connection. Nor is it to abjure the political process of creating obligations through law that satisfy the claims of democratic justice.

overcome the resistance of those whose energies and lives the profit seekers deploy to their own advantage. The political question is why others do not impede the progress of profit seekers when they transgress the limits between the merely opportune and the clearly opportunistic, or why citizens do not impede "any sort of monocratic authority" when it "tends to cross the boundary line that separates general attentiveness to the well-being of society from the active imposition of authority."*

To see America as an empire or in the throes of domestic plunder—true or false—is not to illuminate these basic political facts. Yet these facts are of utmost importance for the Citizen.

At this point a kind of auxiliary argument could be brought forward. It is easy, and even common, to suppose, in essence, that people are uninformed, ignorant, duped, self-absorbed, or self-deceivers; as a consequence they fail to achieve an authentic civic sensibility or to engage in activism. It is perversely reassuring to imagine that a mask or veil prevents us citizens from seeing our true interests. "If we just had a bit more education, a bit more information," one might say, "everything would improve." Of course, this is not inherently false; sometimes the Citizen lacks an adequate synthetic view of relevant facts. And a claim like this need not be insulting. For example, a recent and neatly drawn version of this kind of argument advanced by Jacob S. Hacker suggests that the "domestic plunder" identified by Piven has been screened behind an extremely successful "crusade" in favor of "personal responsibility" and that when this obfuscation is brought to light it may be counteracted.[137] Evidence strongly favors Hacker's analysis and common sense supports the solution he proposes.

Nonetheless, even such a positive way of thinking may distract our attention from another type of and more specifically political problem. It concerns those practices and dispositions that define the role of Citizen and that are conditions of possibility for politics.

The issue is not beliefs per se. It is how our understandings of the world around us, which are bases of judgment and motives for action, are made public in speech and, as a consequence, are both transformed and manifest as real social forces through the division of action.

---

* As per the epigraph to this chapter.

To be blunt, the political problem after September 11th cannot be reduced to a lack of knowledge or information: everyone knows that the United States is engaged in military operations around the world, and that American corporations have made huge profits abroad and at home from supposedly "idealistic" war, and that the attacks of September 11th became a pretext for lining up congressional majorities behind legislation like the Patriot Act; only those with an interest in covering the tracks of their own complicity with aggression will insist today that the argument that Saddam Hussein had "weapons of mass destruction" was convincing in the eighteen months before the invasion of Iraq.* The more fundamental political problem is that shock, terror, war, emergency, and prevailing representations of violence—which is to say the features of our common life investigated in this book—leave the Citizen speechless, impede processes through which speaking transforms the public, and prevent the integration of speech with power. What we see here is the failure of politics in its most basic sense.

Now, when I write "the integration of speech with power" I do not mean that a good debate will by some necessity of logic produce a good executive action. Rather, my point is to return us to a major theoretical claim that runs in the background of the various exposés and arguments in this book: the way that the constitutional system produces powers is consistent with the facts that all action is divided and every apparently simple power is a resultant of overlapping and contradictory social activities; action therefore does not just take place in time but also makes up a kind of space-among-persons, or a fabric of human relationships; this space is constantly being invoked, inflected, ordered, transformed, and so forth, by the use of language; the convergence of social space, action, and language is what makes *speech* into a form of power and what constitutes the basic field of politics as distinct from violence.† To the field of politics the constitutional system adds relatively formalized channels and boundaries that are themselves *differentials* between the social types and political roles the Constitu-

---

* One thinks here of several candidates who sought to become president in 2008.
† We have, of course, Aristotle—not as a student of Plato but as a reader of that other great student of Socrates, Isocrates—to thank for this insight. This will be the starting point for the argument developed in detail in *The Position of the Citizen*, the second part of *Democracy in America after 9/11*.

tion brings together; this system also maintains a final recourse to the Citizen.

When it comes to politics—as opposed to matters economic, social, cultural, administrative, and so forth—the Citizen enters the power-constituting mix *by speaking in public*.* Woe to the person who thinks this is "just talk." Public speech does much more than simply blow off steam or even add or give access to information; everywhere people come together, press for their own projects, produce tension, and navigate or negotiate through it, public speech ever so incrementally or in one brilliant moment transforms beliefs and actions, thereby rechanneling human energies, and thus amplifying or attenuating powers. I emphasize that this occurs *everywhere people come together* because most readers of this book will have a very schematic view of American democracy and the position of "the people" within it; while it has been necessary in this book to distinguish the Citizen as a social type in order to define that special role, it is also important to keep in mind that any natural person can and often does shift from their other roles—Soldier, Judge, Congressperson, Teacher, Parent, and so forth—to assume the position of the Citizen, and that this does not only occur in special pre-established spaces—the "town meeting" or the "public square"—but can and must spontaneously make its own space *within* every sort of institution and practice; from the family and the gang to the bureaucracy and the White House, human beings with the need to solve the inherent problems of plurality form political relationships by speaking.

This is the context in which the major empirical themes of this book—*terror, war, emergency*—reenter the scene as well. The proximity of war to the constitutional system acts roughly like the proximity of a magnet to iron filings. The whole field and system of relationships among citizens, of political relationships, is realigned in war. I have tried to keep this general fact clearly before us with the peculiar term *civic war*. The combination of *civic war* and the constitutional system produces qualitatively different types of power; these new types nonetheless remain within the realm of everyday civic life and thus cannot be precisely segregated as *war* power, *emergency* power, or, indeed, even *military* power. Taking this

---

* By the phrase *in public* I mean, once again, speaking in such a way as to implicate a third party in a two-way dispute. This is the minimal and primary starting mechanism for political relationships at all levels.

point further, I have suggested that terror and emergency bend this new type of power towards monocracy.

The monocratic tendency is contrary to the basic facts of political life that are made manifest in the constitution. Nonetheless, this tendency may arise within the constitutional system. Thus monocracy is a political pathology that presents real danger to the Citizen: it is the nemesis of plurality, of divided power, of publicness, of skeptical contest, of debunking speech and negotiation, and, finally, of politics. Indeed, the very possibility of politics meets in monocracy obstacles it may not overcome.

As we attempt to decipher the position of the Citizen after September 11th, these elements of politics provide a simple reason to diverge from arguments focused primarily on economic motives and facts: while sometimes the profit seeker is a monocrat, many monocrats are not seeking profit. From the perspective of the Citizen, monocracy is the more fundamental of the two.* Why? Because monocracy *forestalls reaction against* all sorts of opportunisms, including unalloyed profit seeking.† Monocracy takes the field when agents work to enlarge the scope of their operation at any one of a number of levels through the elimination of antagonists, objectors, contradictors, and so forth. When it comes to defining the position of the Citizen today, tendencies to monocracy must be the focus of our attention. Whoever aims to be the *single power*, the *one idea*, the *unique "decider"*—even in passing, even under the momentary demands of collective action and its exigencies—must be met with the skepticism and pessimism that has since the appearance of the first πόλις characterized political relationships.‡ For this aim to concen-

---

* Hobbes (1651, chapter 13) distinguishes "in the nature of man . . . three principal causes of quarrel. First, competition; secondly, diffidence; thirdly, glory. The first maketh men invade for gain; the second, for safety; and the third, for reputation." Monocracy is related most deeply to *glory* in Hobbes's sense, as it points to those who "use violence . . . for trifles, as a word, a smile, a different opinion, and any other sign of undervalue, either direct in their persons or by reflection in their kindred, their friends, their nation, their profession, or their name." We shall see why just below.

† Some monocratic arguments appear as their opposite—the "pure freedom" claims of market ideology seem like the ultimate pluralism but, without order, structure, or distinction, the many individuals are governed by a single principle that trumps all others; in any event, claims about pure markets are always made in the context of disputes and never have the status they purport to describe.

‡ Uruk, founded around 3700 BCE in Mesopotamia, is generally taken to be the first πόλις, although the Anatolian city Çatalhüyük preceded it by some 4,000 years and the Chinese city

trate power is incompatible with the plurality inherent in the position of the Citizen itself. Simply, there cannot be *just one Citizen*. Even when a single effect or action emerges from politics, that result may be assigned or delegated to a single person but it is not their property. The persistent tension between *the one and the many* is, as a social fact, synonymous with the tension between monolithic consensus and the inescapable everyday fact of contending voices and interests. The tendency to monocracy is a cancer for politics. The most fundamental interest of citizens is thus the defense of the conditions of possibility for our own position, for our own role in the constitutional order from which power arises and through which it is modulated and its agencies controlled. Indeed, as deep and destructive as socioeconomic problems may be, only insofar as politics provides a way to stand outside those problems can complicity in them be undercut, resistance to them formulated, and some alternative force brought to bear.

What if Francis Fox Piven is correct in describing the Bush administration as a cabal for the extraction of value from the majority of Americans and its transfer to an ever smaller economic elite? There would still remain for citizens a need, a profound need, to understand ourselves as something greater than victims, or as something less than heroes on a quest to triumph over our own victimhood. There is both more and less to the story of the Citizen. This requires from us a perspective that not only clarifies the normal conditions of our lives and the special conditions added when we adopt the role of Citizen, but one that also shows the leverage those political conditions provide to us in everyday life. I propose that inquiry into the tendency to monocracy takes us in that direction. It draws attention back to the constitution of power as a relationship among several decidedly different social roles. It is in this constitution of power—rather than, for example, in the dynamics of followers and leaders—that the Citizen and the Executive complement one another and exert mutual influence.

I want to insist that within this frame everything I have written in this book about the positions, programs, and powers of the Executive sheds a certain light—as if, perhaps, in a strange mirror—on the power of the

---

Ningbo by about 1,000 years. Cities with political characteristics appeared in the Nile valley around 3150 BCE and in the Indus River valley around 2600 BCE.

Citizen. Our theme has been the back-and-forth between these social roles because neither stands in isolation. Whatever may be the policy content of the programs and practices of the Executive, every undertaking from that office pressures the Citizen to act in particular ways. This is a resource for the Executive, which is constantly adjusting this mode of engagement with the Citizen in the hope that its projects will not meet resistance. Diminished resistance allows for the expansion of its own power.

Direct address will rarely win for the Executive the complicity of contending powers that would otherwise constrain it. How is this complicity fostered, not in the home or the school, but within the constitutional system itself?

The Executive sets a tone. With an extensive capacity to mobilize the division of action in society, the mere orientation of the Executive can invigorate or infect the system. By the way it pursues its own goals the Executive opens some channels and closes others for the Citizen. Some actions are promoted, some practically excluded.

The agent of monocracy and the ultimate enemy of politics is not the profit seeker. Monetary gain in office is taboo; if it occurs in secret, publicizing illicit profit seeking is often sufficient to counteract it by bringing moral and legal prohibitions to bear.

What, then, is it that sets the tone of the Executive towards monocracy? It is the vainglorious strong intolerance of difference—so strong, indeed, that whatever its narcissism cannot incorporate is characterized in some way as "impure" and marked for purification, conversion, conquest, or erasure. It is a motive deeply antagonistic to the inherent plurality of political life.

In the *fanatic* such characteristics are clearly recognizable. Let us not take this word lightly. Consider its root in the Latin *fanum*, or "temple." Trace, as political theorist Dominique Colas has, its complex history. You will discover what Colas demonstrates with acuity. The "issue of fanaticism" is "to be found at the center of current political forms" and "if we persist in thinking about and understanding fanaticism only from a distance, as something that characterizes the 'other,' we may forget that it penetrates all modernity."[138] The basic sense of *fanaticism* is shaped by its stark opposition to the plurality of "civil society." On that dialectical basis arises an intricate dynamic within the historical uses of the term. Colas captures this with chilling clarity. I quote at length from his book *Civil Society and Fanaticism: Conjoined Histories.*

Colas on Fanaticism   *Comment*

Gathered together in the love of a Great Pronouncer of Pure Truth that is the foundation of their community, fanatics believe that his Word is absolute and that they are its only authorized interpreters. Proud to be its servants and instruments, they hate those who ignore or disdain it, and they desire to make the world comply with the commandments of their supreme rector: either an anthropomorphic God, who like a king, loves to command, or a Law, "all-powerful because true," as Lenin said of Marx's theory, that bends the universe to its necessity. That the world has until now slipped the grasp of the supreme injunctions of this ultimate power is [in their view] an accident that must be corrected. Fanatics, fervent vehicles of the words of an order that surpasses and sustains them, are ready for sacrifice. They erase themselves as subjects, as loci of self-conscious subjectivity, to the point of considering of no account their pilgrimage on earth, of no account the lives of those who gather elsewhere than in the love of the master whose absolute authority they wish to impose. Their "egos" are swallowed up in the truth they love and by which they desire to be loved, while those who ignore, reject, or combat their just cause are necessarily doomed to annihilation.... Regardless of the principle that illuminates and animates them, whether their enthusiasm is excited by an omnipotent God or some absolute knowledge, fanatics move to attack the unbearable disorder of an imperfect, impure, inadequate world. They are, therefore, always sacrilegious or, to follow the etymology, the *fan*atic is always pro*fan*ing: attacking the temples, polluting, the relics, defying the taboos, and cursing the gods of the "other."... [T]he fanatic has no need to construct or discover what is true, or to take the mystic's slow and solitary way through the dark night toward God. The fanatic enjoys instead an immediate and unmediated kind of total certitude, which inhabits, possesses, and violently propels him.[139]

• *Love*—as a private sentiment that needs no justification—is wholly out of place in politics; if one starts there, all conflict becomes a matter of *hate* rather than negotiation.

• As *fanaticism* is a social fact, it cannot "live and let live" but must prove itself to itself by proving itself to others, and thus everywhere seeks, without the qualms of the skeptic, compliance.
• Religious and secular manifestations of fanaticism have essentially the same structure.

• Disagreement and nonconformance are, for the fanatic, accidental and not essential characteristics of human relationships.

• If there is only one source of Truth, that source must both lie beyond *me* and be larger than *me*. My self-worth depends on this transcendent being, and anyone who ignores or escapes it does damage to *me*.

• Impurity is an injury and must be erased; this is in itself an injury to anyone who disagrees with the fanatic, which injury in turn becomes another reason for their annihilation.

• Once the Truth has been pronounced, it exists outside time, and this presses the fanatic to ignore the exigencies of time as well; unaccustomed to negotiation and uninterested in it, the fanatic turns easily to violence.

Psychoanalysis may offer clues to personality governed by the fantasy of omnipotence and omniscience. And, we may ask, which is the chicken and which the egg: is a pure sense of certainty the motive to an omnipotence, or is it *libido dominandi* that breeds self-certainty? The result is the same. But what Colas describes here is not merely psychological disorder. Narcissism may be involved, but in a secondary, social way. The fanatic imagines his private feelings and commitments as sufficient rule for imposition on others. Even as his claims depend on the essentially public character of belief, it is precisely this fact and its implications—plurality, difference, judgment, contest, negotiation—that the fanatic denies. This contradictory status of fanaticism suggests its place in political life. Again, Colas makes this clear:

> fanaticism can be something other than an absurd and monstrous pathology provoking only disgust. The moment that the government of a civil society is recognized as having the right to exercise political domination, the moment that civil society becomes the legitimate arena in which each person seeks the personally useful, fanaticism moves into absolute opposition to such society, mobilizing those faithful to a prince not of this world or who, oppressed, proclaim the prophecy of a just realm. For to promote civil society as a positive value is to promote both tolerance and "bourgeois" values . . . and civil society's enemies are of at least two types—although both types may be found united in a single individual. Fanatics, who by definition reject mediation and representation and wish to establish a new world without delay and without institutions, may be disciplined militants marching lock-step at the command of the supreme sovereign or anarchists, iconoclasts revolted by the complacency of the guardians of the temple, whom they see as idol worshipers. They may be servants to an inflexible law or relentless utopians, activist assassins or asocial outcasts moved by impatient hopes.[140]

At the end of the second section of this chapter, I gestured towards a symmetry between the Executive and the Terrorist. What Colas identifies as the modern complementarity between "civil society" and fanaticism suggests a deeper explanation of this symmetry. It is not simply that the Terrorist gauges the way his acts will force the overreaction of an American president, or that the Executive will then freight its projects, if not exactly on the repetition of terrorist attacks then certainly on their constant reiteration through representations. The perverse symmetry arises from a common genealogy in and the logic of *fanaticism*. Since September 11th the Executive—with its Reaganism revived in ways that the original could never achieve—and the Terrorist—with its increasingly acephalous free-floating networks and influx of spontaneous actors—stand, with respect to the Citizen, on the same terrain. They of course differ radically on ideals, on substance, on details. But they both aspire to the same kind of antipolitical politics, which is to say a politics that makes fodder of the

Citizen when we are not excluded altogether, and thus slates for extinction our essential civilizing social role.*

Fanaticism is a capacious vehicle for monocracy. It motivates a reduction of the plurality of citizens and of the contest of powers to *one*. It may begin as a personal trait, but on entering the political realm it becomes a spring within the constitutional system. This occurs, and fanaticism becomes a real social force, when citizens begin to accept the univocal, authoritative, and arrogant claims of the fanatic, allowing these claims to serve as justifications in the public sphere. Only if the judgment and resistance of others stand against it does fanaticism fail to rise to this systematic level. Otherwise a rage becomes social distemper, it becomes *common sense*.

To the overwhelming majority of members of Congress who have since September 11th recoiled at every Executive infringement on their power, Senator Robert Byrd remarked in a not entirely ironic tone that "the President is not God."[141] The President cannot but be susceptible to this unimpeachable logic. And each brutal realization that he is not God must lead the pretender farther and farther under the cover of secrecy and solitude.[142]

Without fanatical drive, spurred as it is by denial of the natural limits on over-reach which normally arise from the "care of the self,"† projects of domestic "plunder" could not be sustained for long. Fanaticism is what joins together into a tightly closed circle, in the long-term context of *civic war*, the Cold War, presumptions of omnipotence ranging from the nuclear to the evangelical, attacks on publicness and unfettered speech, efforts to reduce conflict to questions of loyalty or "moral clarity," and so forth. These are the real political dimensions of George W. Bush's revival of Reaganism. Fanaticism and the tendency to monocracy are the driving forces of the present phase—as of the past phases—of the Cold War as a system of domestic political culture.

---

* Viewed within this terrain, the editors of the January 17, 1920, issue of *The Nation* seem particularly astute in their description of the Palmer Raids: "The unprecedented outburst of terror and terrorism which at the moment is venting itself upon Socialists, Communists, 'Reds,' and agitators of all sorts in this country grows in volume and intensity from day to day. Every morning now brings news of more raids, more scores or hundreds of men and women arrested, more tons of papers seized, more offices and assembly rooms wrecked, more plans for deportation, more promises of purgings yet to come."

† Jean-Jacques Rousseau famously distinguished between productive "care of the self" (amour de soi-même) and destructive pride (amour propre).

What does fanaticism in the Executive mean for the Citizen? Consider this again against the backdrop of basic facts of political life: human beings who must live together every day can address problems with violence or with speech; the political option is speech, and its democratic form is dialogue. Thus did the fanatical character of the president appear with utmost clarity in a candidates' debate on September 30, 2004, where George W. Bush stood before the nation without script, staging, or surrogate. For nearly an entire first term of office he had been sequestered from dialogue at every level and every turn. He had had almost no conferences with the press. Only avid supporters were permitted to attend his stops on the campaign trail. By many reports he brooked no objection, even within his inner circle. Those who viewed the debate witnessed the cumulative consequences of this antipolitical speechlessness, secrecy, and solitude.

We know that when speech extends into dialogue—as it naturally does, as it is evoked by the other—it opens different perspectives. This opening is a manifestation of human plurality. Animating plurality and making it transmissible, dialogue brings us towards new truths consistent with the changing circumstances of life together with others. One reason dialogue is so vital for democracy is that—for anyone who seeks to achieve his or her goals within the division of action—it tends to bring even the most frivolous self-expression into line with equality and dignity. After all, to solicit *others* whom you need for *yourself*, you are likely to get farther if you do not spit on them.

Those who witnessed that first presidential debate gained insight into another connection between dialogue and leadership. For the first aim of human speech is to be heard. Hearing some piece or tone of oneself within the other in their reaction, one speaks again. In the back-and-forth, everything depends on the kind of "fittingness" that Cicero called *decorum*. This decorum is vastly broader than etiquette or even civility. It has no fixed rule book. It refers to the fact that if you do not speak in a "fitting" way in each specific situation, you will not be heard. You won't get the desired reactions; the world will not bend your way.[143]

Whatever the situation—from the funkiest low-down street talk to the high-flown orations of a Lincoln—the civil sensibility of decorum is gathered in the practice of dialogue. As much as one learns about others in dialogue, it is not the information it carries that makes it a key to democracy. As each person seeks decorum he or she must adjust his or her own position. Intertwined with the issue at hand, an unstated negotiation goes on within speech to make speech effective. Our world together grows together as we talk. This growth of the common world, small or large, cool or rambunctious, always in the movement of new needs and projects, is what in the course of human nature and its plurality carries politics away from inflexibility. In this natural development of political relationships the fanatical character is faced with two options: to adapt, or to become even more overreaching, self-certain, secretive, and isolated; the fanatic is forced to become less or more of what he is.

A person with comprehensive or enormous resources—hermetic autonomy, evangelical community, the entourage of the White House, the apparatus of the State, and so forth—can sometimes afford long spells of fanaticism. It helps if the fanatic is liberated by managers who place power above principle. But this will not stop his character from withering. As his basic human capacity for forming political relationships with others atrophies, those around him may be dragged down to each new degraded level. And rising is more difficult than falling.

With each step that leads *the political* into degradation the fanatic will call his position "principled." This may take him some distance farther. For, his auditors today will tend to forget that a principle, as the word *principio* literally tells us, is not a conclusion and must always be applied *here* and *now* and with *us*.* A principle is nothing more and nothing less than a maxim of wide decorum; it is not a—because there is no—universal law that applies itself. Nevertheless we have become accustomed to acting as though principles can and should do our thinking for us and this suits the fanatic just fine. When he assumes a leading office like the Executive, the fanatic leads by attempting to fix *decorum* outside experience, rather than by educating, which is to say, literally, by drawing what is *right* out from those to whom he speaks. The fanatic brings his church with him to the office.†

---

* It was, I have argued elsewhere, the widespread success of the new doctrine of "method" after the sixteenth century that promoted—against a rhetorical culture that understood language as a living fact—the automaticity of thought so congenial to dogmatics. Cf. Meyers 2003.

† Viewed literally as principles, the "ten commandments" may be antithetical to all dogmatic and evangelical uses of them. These are (literally) "words" for people to use in reflecting on their own lives; they were given to the people, not to judges; the "judges" seem in any event more like counselors (Exodus 18), as people come voluntarily to them and (it seems) may come alone (which is to say not only with disputes in need of mediation); again, while judgment is *ex post*, these "words" seem meant to function *ex ante*; insofar as they form—as is often implied—a

Along such lines fanatical traits of character remap the office of the Executive. As the Constitution is a system composed of relations among its parts, changes in one part necessarily transform other parts, and new configurations of the Executive must, in turn, eventually transform the political life of the nation. The Executive reach for omnipotence affirms and promotes undivided action—doubly vain assertions of "will" overcome counsel, deliberation, alliance, multilateralism. Self-certainty and secrecy decline dialogue,* badgering or, lacking interlocution, compelling others into speechlessness.[144] The unitary person, office, group, or nation wants nothing of the plurality of humankind, not merely accepting but rejoicing in a spacelessness beyond the need for negotiation, mutual adjustment, diplomacy, or, finally, politics.† Change over time, following experience, reflection, remorse, or simply the desire to learn and to better oneself or one's companions, has little significance for the fanatic, who lives in a kind of timeless time punctuated only by its eschatological end. Without the natural perspective of growth in the flow of time, the evolution of a position appears, absurdly, as a "mixed message" that is inherently "wrong." The fanatic incessantly repeats statements like "we never change our beliefs," "there must be certainty from the U.S. president," "you've got to be consistent when you're the president . . . there's a lot of pressures and you've got to be firm and consistent," "you can-

---

system of punishable offenses, it is only God who is in the position of judge. N.b. the root in biblical Hebrew is *rbd*, or *dibar*, which is a standard word for "word" (and used in the sentence before in just that way); the phrase "ten commandments" at Exodus 34:28 means simply "the ten words" or "statements"; this is carried over in the Greek translation as *dekalogos*. Cf. Deuteronomy 10:4.

* The depth of this mentality was suggested when Senator Mark Pryor (D-Arkansas) asked the nominee for assistant secretary of homeland security, "If there is a conflict of interpretation between your Department and other departments and other agencies . . . who will have the President's ear?" and received this response from Gordon England, later confirmed by the Senate to this post: "Senator, I guess I would be surprised if there are different conclusions . . . these are people of good faith working together to get the best answer. So I do not see that there is different analysis going on and arriving at different answers. This is the very best people we have working together to get the best answer for the Nation. So hopefully we are not going to have that situation that you are mentioning." Cf. Senate Committee on Governmental Affairs, *Hearing before the Committee on Governmental Affairs on the Nomination of Hon. Gordon R. England to Be Deputy Secretary of the Department of Homeland Security*, 16.

† In a telling lapsus in the debate of October 6, 2004, President Bush transformed the commonplace "reasonable people can disagree" into the claim "this is an issue that divides America, but certainly reasonable people can agree on how to reduce abortions in America," suggesting thereby a false equation between reason and agreement.

not change positions in this war on terror if you expect to win," and so
forth.[145] Even when compelled by an election or the counsel of allies and
others to change, "innovation" for the fanatic often turns out to be a superficial gloss on more of the same.*

We can be as usual inattentive to detail; we can say, although the game
of "what he really meant" has been inexhaustible during this most astonishingly inarticulate presidency, that everyone knew what President
Bush intended when he said, "I don't see how you can lead this country in
a time of war, in a time of uncertainty, if you change your mind because
of politics."[146]

Yet for at least one moment let us take this literally. It reveals a deep
misunderstanding of the conditions of everyday life together among citizens. For exactly what politics involves—always and above all—is changing minds, one's own and another's, in an ongoing process of mutual
negotiation and adjustment in favor of a better life. Do not be mistaken:
I am not saying that politics is a communitarian lovefest; the fact is that
the benefits of politics derive from and return to the incessant conflict
that arises from plurality and the contests of difference.

Now, in the normal course of political relationships, a choice to withdraw from dialogue will brew an incapacity for it. This incapacity may
even, for a while, sustain the fanatic. Dick Cheney has no intention to
explain himself, and George W. Bush seems unable to do so. Eventually,
however, fanaticism must come to be incompatible with the position of
the Citizen. Our life goes one way, and, without the suppleness of character and office that allows for learning and adjustment to new facts, the life
of the Executive goes another way. In the long term, the common sense
of the people advances while the leader lags behind. A fanatic will thus
make the position of the Executive ineffective for want of *decorum*; this is
what happened with President Nixon.

The expectation that decorum and presidential power could be directly proportional arises against the background of a more general fact.
Each power in a system of divided powers depends on the others and this
dependence is an essential feature of that system. *Decorum* is the grammar of signs and corresponding practical judgments that gives living and

---

*As was the case when Bush forced out Rumsfeld but continued to use the language of the
"surge" from Rumsfeld's program to transform the army as the public relations term for the
supposed change of strategy in Iraq coming into 2007.

flexible order to social activities; it is the internal navigational system of the division of action. More specifically, decorum in the back-and-forth between the Executive and Citizen* is a key feature of the constitution of presidential power. And under normal circumstances, insistent pressure from a fanatic, simply by virtue of doing what fanatics do, which is to refuse mediation, adjustment, and negotiation, will force decorum to fail. This failure itself is important for the operation of the system; it results in a divergence between social roles and a corresponding reconfiguration of conflicts.

In the period after September 11th, however, this kind of divergence has been forestalled. The fact that decorum has *not* broken down is particularly destructive.

The issue is not simply that the George W. Bush is inattentive, or that the president does not hear what others are telling him.† What matters much more for politics—with *politics* here meaning the particular sort of relationship that arises among citizens and the way that citizens are linked into the constitutional system of powers through that relationship—is that President Bush was able at almost every level to make democratic decorum irrelevant. I do not mean that he is not polite. I do mean that he disentangled himself from the wide variety of forces, some institutional‡ and many informal, which constitutional design and democratic practice have historically put in place to *make the President adjust to others* and which, in that way, give a particular shape and limits to his power. It may seem odd to suggest that by simply ignoring the needs and interests of other groups within the constitutional system, or by playing effective timing games to at first ignore them and then respond when it's too late, President Bush was able to significantly leverage up his power. Nevertheless, due to one other key factor, this was indeed the case.

The other factor is that almost no one successfully called his bluff. And what inhibited this response? The sermonic power of the President, the regulatory jargon of the Officer, the expert discourse of the Bureaucrat, the legal interpretations of the Attorney, the clamoring for recognition of the Pundit, and a dozen other conformist voices. All these characters

---

* I acknowledge but do not make explicit here the mediating role of Congress in this relation.
† Although one should not discount the extent to which Bush's psychological detachment was reconstructed by his cabalistic "inner circle" into a kind of insularity.
‡ E.g. issuing secret edicts to the NSA or ruling by executive order rather than legislation or using "signing statements" to pull the rug from under legislation.

achieved a remarkable and destructive convergence: they made the position of the Citizen and the position of the Executive appear as identical. With identification complicity "goes without saying." This public complicity had a collateral effect that is of still further advantage to the President: as long as the Citizen and the Executive appear to speak with one voice, Congress will be strongly inclined to support the President no matter where he reaches.*

Indeed, for almost the whole of his time in office an impression prevailed in the "public sphere" that to speak against George W. Bush was to speak against America itself. This symbolic equivalence cannot, after Nixon and especially after Clinton, be chalked up to a tradition of sheer respect for constitutional office. The public image President Bush constructed for himself was not about objective reverence but rather centered by subjective charisma, staged on the model of Reagan, and illuminated by the Cold War imaginary of the Protective Father.†

The vehicle that brought about this convergence of Citizen and Executive and of their constitutionally distinguishable powers, the instrument of America's grotesque and self-defeating single-mindedness, the machinery that has grabbed and narrowed our attention and redirected our energies, the ideology that disavows the political relationships it exploits, is *war*, specifically in the form of *civic war*, now as for decades now with the cultural content of the "Cold War."

In other words, what forestalled the failure of decorum was the displacement of one type by another, the interweaving of a new fabric of symbolic handles and motors, the magnetic realignment of the whole field and system of relationships among citizens: the polyphonic decorum of democracy gave way to the fanatical decorum of monocracy, an order of things within which George W. Bush's eccentric charisma has maximum aptitude.

Terrible war can be the vocation of reasonable and democratic peoples. But the "war on terrorism" that became after September 11th the vehicle of the Executive's fanaticism was from the start framed by the president as a—literally *fan*atic—defense of the temple. Five days after

---

* One might think this would be different for a "lame duck" president; however, even with President Bush's poll ratings drastically down and a midterm vote against him that was said to be based on objections to the war in Iraq, the majority-Democratic 110th Congress had failed utterly to make any substantial inroads against him by the end of 2007.

† This same Reagan-like persona was adopted by candidate John McCain in 2008.

September 11th President Bush summarized what was to come: "This crusade, this war on terrorism is going to take a while."[147]

Throughout the Middle East, this sentence, voiced by an evangelical Christian, was heard as a reference to *the* historical Crusades, as a renewed pitting of Christianity against Islam. If that was what he had had in mind, however, a president incapable of recalling any of his mistakes could not so easily have regretted this allusion.* Rather, Bush displayed quick and vocal sympathy for believers who thought that the terrorists had "hijacked Islam itself."† As the subsequent and often-pronounced parallels of "Communism" and "Islamism" would show, the image of "crusade" marked the continuation of something at least as secular as it was religious. For crusades, unlike defensive actions, are undertaken by true believers, devotees-of-the-one-truth, or, in a word, *fanatics*.[148] The parallel in the president's statement was not events of the dark-age past but of more recent and revivifying memory.

The image of "crusade" brandished by the president invoked a common use of the word in reference to the "fight against Communism" abroad and at home.[149] It was animated by the political evangelism of the Cold War, something larger than but complemented by Christian evangelism, where the word *crusade* had also been a staple since it was adopted in 1947 by the Reverend Billy Graham.‡ Thus did *crusade*, in the mysterious way of all cultural commonplaces, highlight again without declaring the main line of continuity between the political scene in America after September 11th and the world that spawned the character, policy commitments, and perverse legitimacy of the Bush administration.

As we have already seen, the fanatical element in the "Bush Doctrine" works from both sides of a supposed divide between domestic and foreign policy. While the secular missionary theme appears in foreign policy as a gospel of "freedom and democracy," this "good word" is nonetheless directed to believers at home so as to constitute a domestic political

---

* In the "town hall"–style debate of October 6, 2004, a citizen asked President Bush to name three mistakes he had made: Bush failed to do so.

† Whether or not one agrees with the substance of this assessment, it accepts in principle the possibility of a "good" Islam, something that the original "crusaders" could never have done.

‡ N.b. that Reagan and Graham were, according to Graham himself, connected since 1953. The promotion of Graham by William Randolph Hearst, beginning with Los Angeles meetings in 1949, is also important.

environment in which projects often more strictly speaking evangelical and in any event antipluralist can be pushed forward across the wide spectrum of so-called social issues—from abortion to "family values" to the "pledge of allegiance." These fields *of domestic contest* are, once again, established by the call to war. Whatever misplaced common sense tells us, the Right-wing avant-garde of the "culture wars" was able to locate this as the primary fact of September 11th from almost that day itself. "But what about our spirit?" asked William Bennett in his book *Why We Fight*. He then continued this way:[150]

Bennett on "Why We Fight"	*Comment*
To me, that precious and indefinable quality, whose health has been my abiding preoccupation over the last decades, remained, and remains, a cause of worry. A few days after the September attacks . . . I said [to college students in Texas] that, though we had just become, through the deaths of our fellow citizens, a radically diminished country, in some ways we were also a better country: focused on, and thinking about, more important things than had been the case before September 11. At a terrible cost, we have been reminded of what mattered, we had had our perspective restored; this was a necessary and a salutary thing. . . . Still, I said in mid-September, I was concerned about the future. I was afraid that, as a country, . . . having been softened up, we might not be able to sustain collective momentum in what we were now being called upon to do. To be sure, I said, I had every confidence that our president, and our military commanders, would see us through to the end of the larger war on terror, to which the president had committed us. My real worry was whether the American people themselves would persevere, whether they would rise to the full implications of this moment of moral clarity, turn the coming age into an age of moral clarity, and not permit their own magnificent response to September 11, or the magnificent selves they had revealed in those days, to fade into just another distant memory.	• This "abiding preoccupation" has been with moral and cultural purity, particularly as expressed by Reagan and his neoconservative followers. One discovers in reading Bennett's book that the agency of moral degradation is the "peace party," which he identifies with "the terrorists" (e.g. p. 17), with the "relativist ethos of the cultural left" (p. 68), with the movement against the Vietnam War (p. 40), and, recalling the original language of the Cold War, as "unpatriotic" and "anti-American" (p. 141). • Note the familiar tropes of the fanatic: "terrible cost" is "restorative" and "salutary"; this impulse does not occur by chance, but by "necessity." "We" must not be "soft." • Bennett assumes that authorities—like the president and generals—are dedicated to the right cause and are strong, but that the people are weak. This repeats almost verbatim the concerns of elites about the "moral fiber" of Americans that guided public policy during the Civil Defense phase of the Cold War. (See chapter 5 above.) • September 11th is not just an attack, or a criminal act, but a "moment of moral clarity," the consummation of Bennett's "abiding preoccupation," and an apocalyptic sign of the coming "age of moral clarity." • The word "magnificent" here is charged with the glorification of martyrs to the cause, the apotheosis of heroes.

As Bennett comes to the conclusion of his hastily produced polemic book *Why We Fight*, he joins the nominal topic and pretext of the book, which is September 11th and the "war on terrorism," to what is in fact its predominant theme—a recitation of the dogma of "us . . . veterans of the 'culture wars' of the last three or four decades"—by writing that "we must not squander the opportunity."[151] What better than a "crusade" to apprentice novice "culture warriors" and bring the nation back into line?[152]

At the same time, it was the old warriors of the Cold War crusade who drew up new plans, mobilized troops, and sent them into battle. Thus one is inevitably pulled back around to the other side of the relation between foreign policy and domestic politics. The "righteous" seek the "right" war; in it they find a principle; that principle trumps negotiation and alliance, as fanatics rarely find partners and, at critical moments, are apt to reject even their oldest friends. The seductions of unilateralism are burning and impatient.[153] Indeed, "going it alone" is a frighteningly straightforward extension of the domestic posture of this kind of Executive: idealist, self-absorbed, doctrinaire, inflexible.

When Russia's president Putin spoke at the Munich Conference on Security Policy in February 2007, the American representative at the conference, Secretary of Defense Robert Gates,* responded this way: "Speaking," he said, "as an old Cold Warrior . . . one Cold War was quite enough." But what Putin had said, although hostile to the United States, was in a sense just the opposite. He objected to the novelty of the international situation in which U.S. ambition and sway stood unrestrained. This situation, however, had arisen from the return to power in the United States of "Cold Warriors"—which Gates acknowledged himself to be. Thus, Putin slyly observed that "just like any war, the Cold War left us with live ammunition, figuratively speaking."[154]

Whatever the personal traits of the American president or the peculiar insular ethos he brought to the Executive office, another dimension of his place within American political life is both more significant and more surprising. In the almost magical way of political pathology, President George W. Bush continued to gain from the conjunction of the constitutional system with *civic war* a widespread sense of unity and demand for consensus despite the clear contradiction between so many of his positions and the plural nature of humankind. It is again the factor of

---

* Gates replaced the cashiered Donald Rumsfeld on December 18, 2006.

complicity that governs here, the way civil society worked for Bush as it worked for Reagan, and continued to sustain him even as the polls turned against his most unconscionable escapades.* This is, one may imagine, what makes President Bush opaque to leaders from other nations: the difficulty of imagining how a person so uncompromising and incapable of negotiation, so oblivious to the need others will always have for compromise and negotiation, could ever have risen to the top of a democratic political system.

Secular and religious motives have often blended together in fanatical movements—Luther and Calvin showed us this as much as do today's Wahhabism or the "Christian Right" in the United States.[155] The wars of September 11th follow an old pattern in this respect. For the Citizen, the consolidation of several-generations-long patterns of *civic war* and Cold War into the "war on terrorism"—conducted as much across the nation as across the globe—raises not just the issue of the private fanaticism of every stripe of fundamentalism, and not just the issue of how such fundamentalisms influence political groups or public decisions, but the appearance of a kind of *public fanaticism*, a wide and deep and outrageous and self-defeating presumption against plurality.

Public fanaticism—the success of fanaticism as a style of interaction with and justification for others—is the breeding ground for monocracy. While it has infected other periods of American history, in the aftermath of September 11th *public fanaticism* has taken a disconcerting new preeminence in American political culture. It is a strangely demagogic force that shapes the position of the Citizen against democracy by undermining the basic structures of political relationship.

It may be worth asking, How do fanatics move themselves into positions of power? In at least one sense this is obvious: they are monomaniacal and, literally, ruthless. They are willing to take measures that others are not. They profit at the margins of democratic decorum the way market entrepreneurs profit at the edges of the "moral economy." The fanatic will appeal relentlessly to principle to gather followers under his flag and to mobilize their support. But content will always give way to the will to purification through unity because this depends on taking and maintaining control. Thus, whatever they may demand from and for others, fanatics in positions of leadership can rarely afford to let principle have

---

* Of course, people are known to vote against their interests.

the last word in governing their own actions. Dick Cheney made this clear long ago when he said that "principle is okay up to a certain point, but principle doesn't do any good if you lose."[156]

This kind of strategic orientation will often produce morally objectionable results. For the Citizen, however, what really matters is that it poses a political problem. Battling the pluralism of human beings into retreat, fanaticism rigidifies the web of interdependence that constitutes our common life and the division of action. It diminishes not only the fanatic, and not only the object of the fanatic's scorn, but the scope of *the political* itself and the quality of human life that politics makes possible. The fanatic atrophies the position of the Citizen. Without this fundamental "check and balance," even the best constitutional systems may slide down the path towards monocracy.

9. The Constitution of Power and the Corruption of the Citizen after September 11th

Long traditions urge us to think of politics in terms of regimes; democracy is one of several possibilities. Monocracy is not a regime. It is a tendency that occurs within the broader set of political facts. The Citizen's attention had better be trained to see the world in two ways at once. Each living *we* is a fabric of interdependence; within it there is constant tugging every which way. This *tension*, which the ancient Greeks sometimes called *stasis* (στάσις), has occasionally been represented in this book by the word *counterpowers*. Under certain conditions, however, the threads all line up. Running contrary to the inherent plurality of human beings this tendency is what I call monocracy. "Any sort of monocratic authority, when given the central position in a public regime, always tends to cross the boundary line that separates general attentiveness to the well-being of society from the active imposition of authority."[157] Yet it remains that no authority is self-originating or unitary. Thus the monocratic tendency occurs within the symbolic system that gives one form or another to the otherwise amorphous fact of human interdependence. Form becomes vehicle and eventually motive for action.

Notice that monocracy and the division of action are not different in the way appearance differs from reality. The symbolic dimension produces effects and shapes our experience by adding to relationships handles and motors, so to speak, with which interdependence can be turned one way or another. Monocracy is one kind of alignment. Thus while sovereign power may present itself in the form of a monarch, *every* version of it still and always arises from a division of action. Thus monocracy had better be seen as an offspring of groups rather than (as it sees itself) as a manifestation of the preeminent individual. It is comparable to situations in which people in roughly the same position seek the same good. For instance, when, hoping to see more clearly, everyone stands up in the theater, the situation is not improved for anyone. Or it may be more apt to put this dilemma of collective action in a slightly different way: monocracy is advanced when only one person stands up. Then the advantage for the monocrat is not simply his capacity to stand on his own two feet—most everyone can do it—but the fact that, for some mysterious reason of habit and belief and attachment and desire and history, those around the monocrat remain seated. Even the *standing* says *sit down*. Thus the following effect is also constitutive of monocracy: one need not stand up specifically *against it*; it is enough just to stand at all, and the monocrat is diminished thereby.[158]

This book is an admittedly unusual sketch of the American constitutional system of power. It is eccentrically drawn from the perspective or position of the Citizen. One implicit axis of that perspective stretches from the fanatic—the one who would realize the monocratic fantasy of omnipotence—to the full manifold of plurality. The scenes and actors of real situations frequently shift along this scale. To be more precise we could call these changes *modulations*, as when the pianist plays the same tune in a different key.

In politics one does not *by oneself* alter the impact and significance of one's own interdependence with others. Action changes as the fabric of interdependence is bent or inflected this way or that by circumstances.* Indeed, this may be why action in politics is largely indirect—a fact hated by radicals of many stripes—and often aims to alter the context as a way to achieve its goals. We have seen in this book how long-developing and comprehensive some transformative circumstances can be: the pressure from *emergency* is intense and, for whoever can appropriate it, effective; that in itself is a motive to inscribe each readjustment of the social environment with the language of emergency; no emergency is easier to

---

* N.b. the common formulations would have it that circumstances are altered by action or vice versa; I am saying something different.

trigger or more consistent in its outcomes than *war*; Americans—from Hollywood to the Pentagon—have become masters of symbolizing the danger of war so as to bring it into society in a manageable fashion; with powerful emotions evoked and physical danger held at bay, political discourses of all types can attach themselves to *war*; thus is the balance of human energies directed one way or another. The open-endedness of this symbolic system—which gained unprecedented force from the promise of its finality in the image of universal nuclear destruction—has provided a field day for opportunists.

War has always had symbolic dimensions. Nonetheless, the "imaginary war"* took its most fully realized form with the advent of the Cold War in the United States, where no one lived with memories of the rape of the American homeland or the burning of a neighbor's house, yet everyone could picture him- or herself at "ground zero" of a nuclear holocaust—incinerated bones still upright for that instant after the flash or in a little bunker with cans of Spam. The Cold War rubbed together the two sticks of *civic* and *military* war and it was the Citizen that caught fire. As a system of domestic political culture, the Cold War started down its inexorable path when Americans realized that nuclear omnipotence could be turned against us. Those sparks and terror set off the cathartic reaction of "the Sixties," which, because it could only end the genocidal skirmish in Vietnam but not the global conflict from which it arose, because it produced from generalized anxiety more social upheaval than social institutions, because it personalized its attack on a corrupt president but did not effectively address the lack of common purpose in public and private office, came to an impasse. In a moment of cultural despair for both the Left and the Right, Ronald Reagan entered the national scene. He reignited the Cold War that he would later be said to have ended. He reminded Americans that "war is a force that gives us meaning."[159]

This all pertains to the constitutional system of power. A century of *civic war*, for half that time in the guise of the Cold War, has set in place the circumstances that modulate power today. It is not simply *war*, but the specific opportunistic use of war by *fanatics* that has turned the constitutional system of power towards antipolitical monocracy and away from the democratic dynamo of plurality in action.

* Described in chapter 5.

If this has been difficult to see, it is because a primary impulse of the Cold War *as a cultural system* is to deny the fundamental social fact on which all cultural systems depend and which, properly understood, provides the criterion by which the Citizen may measure monocratic tendencies and thereby protect his or her own position against them. This social fact is the *division of action*.

The insistent use of this phrase throughout this book may have seemed an eccentric abstraction. In political experience, however, the Citizen is always at the center and the division of action could not be more earthily fine-grained and urgent. The precise composition of the division of action is, at any given moment, a set of very specific empirical conditions—the combined effect *on someone* ("me" or "you") of the shifting details of *who* depends on *whom* in *what way* and for *how long* and *why*. Every person implicated in the division of action is both its subject—which means that our energies and inclinations compose it, our desires and expressions shape it—and its object—which means that the cumulative outcomes of actions bear upon and constrain what we may achieve or even imagine.

My point here is really about what happens when *civic war*, especially in the form so intimately known to us as the Cold War, modulates the constitutional system. *Civic war* is a particular division of action. It is a wide composition of symbols and institutions that set conditions for one person's or group's use of other persons or groups. This is where politics begins; this is what structures the social role of Citizen; this is the context within which the Citizen must find a position.

In this sense, the division of action is the background against which constitutional processes occur. It is the field within which powers emerge from the interaction among constitutionally generated roles and from the continuity and change within those roles over time.

Americans are told day in and day out that each branch of government, in its own way, represents the people. This may be correct insofar as it delimits a special status for the body of citizens. It is incorrect insofar as it suggests that the *representing*—the connection between the people and government—occurs as a matter of transmittal or delegation. That "space" or mediation we call "representation" *is itself part of the constitution of power*. The image that would suggest that *you* are acting through *them*, the Citizen through the Representative, may be true in some sense but must be viewed in light of a much more fundamental fact that points in exactly the opposite direction. *They*—which is to say presidents, congresspersons, justices, and all the other roles made by institutions of the State—can command, order, legislate, rule, pass judgment, and what have you, but none of this becomes *action* unless it passes through *you*. This is the full significance of the division of action for political life and it is why we must locate the primary pathology of democracy in America after 9/11 just there, in the haunting grounds of *civic war*. All this is normally hidden behind images of both "popular sovereignty" and "representative government," images which assume agents and a type of agency that simply do not exist.

This constitution of powers in the common web of life does not in itself prove any responsibility. It is neither a communitarian ethos nor a moral law. It is simply a fact of democratic politics. For better *and* for worse, everyone in the great fabric of democracy will try to take advantage of it. The effects of this striving contest will be amplified by America's culture of opportunity. The only way for the Citizen to be on guard against the monocratic tendency is to accept and attempt to capture or "own" one's implication in it. This is how complicity is changed back into politics.

Although there is no necessary connection between *terror* and *war*, we have seen that the Executive has many motives to link them together.* Thus what the Citizen had better ask—as we asked earlier in this book—is *Why would anyone expect the Executive to respond to terror in any other way? What forces are in play—what systemic "checks and balances"—that could prevent the Executive's return to the deep well of the Cold War? Why has that cultural system proven so well-suited for joining terror to war and bringing both into the political realm?*

Viewed this way, the Cold War, now returned to us as a "war against terrorism," has been and continues to be a kind of political suicide. I do not refer to a person who ruins his or her chances for reelection. What I mean is that we participate in and feed into a cultural environment where the Citizen is gasping for air. This Cold War pulls a veil over program after program of fanatics. All the more so since this Cold War has ceased to be named as such. Where *civic war* in general has developed around a *normalization of emergency*, this Cold War's version of *civic war* adds a hallucinatory *centering of fanaticism*.

---

* The first point is developed in chapters 1 and 2; the second is broached in the section "Civic War and the Monocratic Tendency" in the present chapter.

Imagine this: a major national network broadcasts on its regular news Ann Coulter, who—as she defends her attempt to slander presidential hopeful John Edwards—adds that the word "faggot . . . has nothing to do with gays."[160] By its sheer absurdity, let this stand as paradigm for the thousands of large and small shifts in the norms of what is objectionable and what is not. Even if "the center" is a dead metaphor in a country where Left and Right have lost their traditional political meaning, this is the astonishing kind of thing that counts today as "not extreme" or even "moderate."

While it may be that Coulter's Alice-in-Wonderland idiocy trivializes whatever it touches, the basic point is this: positions that are extreme in their denial of the division of action and in their aspiration for unchecked expansion of their own field of control now fit comfortably within American common sense. We barely bat an eyelash when George W. Bush declares, "I am the decider." If nonsense like this is occasionally identified as such, we nevertheless typically fail to see where it is carrying us, as when Vice President Dick Cheney's claim to "not [be] part of the executive branch" was ridiculed in the summer of 2007 even while it continued to work as a screen for his involvement in the Plame affair. Even you, my informed and assiduous Reader, are you still outraged and mobilized by such obnoxious events? Are you offended and moved when high officers disguise a continuing policy of deception that led to war in Iraq? That ramped up *civic war* in America?[161]

You see how easily such outlandish propositions pass without resistance. By the standards of truth and logic they may be false and absurd. But viewed from the position of the Citizen they are deeply antipolitical and, for precisely that reason, antidemocratic. This shift in common sense is the spiraling cause and effect of the complicity of civil society that first supported Reagan and now supports Bush's Reaganism and may soon uphold another Reaganism as well, perhaps a Democratic one.

Once we have identified the Citizen as the substance of constitutional powers, another question comes to the foreground: *Why is the Citizen so reticent to take a position against the fanatic?* Where one has fanatical neighbors one can close the door. Public office, however, is an open door; to ask for a vote is to invite inspection and judgment.

Admit that incumbency is a stronghold. Admit that, once a shift to war has been accomplished, the Executive rises to the top of the constitutional system. Admit a dozen other such advantages.

It remains that the fanatic is inherently against plurality. It remains that the fanatic is inherently a threat to political relationships. The fanatic may be measured in several ways as obnoxious, unlawful, immoral, bad, and so forth. Yet, despite all that, it also remains that the fanatic is to be expected. The circumstances of modern American politics—some of which are sketched in this book—are bound to produce persons of this sort.

Thus what really matters most for the Citizen is how fanatics fit into the constitutional system of powers. Or, more precisely, *how they will be made to fit.*

If we say the fanatic pushes that system towards monocracy, it must be added that *any unchecked* tendency can go the same way. What specific problem of constitutional politics, then, arises with the fanatical officeholder? Ask who will drag him back inside the division of action and the answer is some *counterpower*. Yet this, too, is the same for any officeholder.

What differentiates the fanatic appears in this paradox: just the one who the Citizen has the strongest interest in opposing is the one who invokes the least opposition; just the leaders authorized for emergencies and wars and supplied with great resources, weapons, and institutions are the ones we hold most in awe. What inspires awe, it may be said, is the spectacle of their power. Yet they act through us. Awe-inspiring, it should thus be said with more precision, is the pretense and presumption that they act alone. The image of great power is solitude, a lonely deity who never holds a press conference. And yet "the President is not God."

And yet, who will judge him? Who will say of the one to whom the sacred office is entrusted that he has "taken us for a ride"? Before the research for responsibility, or the demand for accountability, there is the mundane fact of standing up. There is the interruption of complicity. There is the retraction of energies lent. There is the withdrawal of funds misappropriated.

Do you see that here judgment fails twice? There is the question of *standards* to apply and there is the question of *where to stand*. For monocracy to hold sway, the second failure is nearly enough. *This is the corruption of the Citizen.*

Corruption is not illegality. Nor is it unethical behavior. Corruption is a particular type of violation of norms that contextualize law and morality. Political corruption of the sort I want to expose here violates the norms that make possible effective behavior in public. I do not mean just any sort of behavior, but the practices and ways of acting that make politics possible. Corruption is an attempt to violate the spirit of the law under the cover of the law itself, the spirit of the maxim under the cover of the maxim, the spirit of publicness in the full daylight of the public square. The corrupt invoke norms to avoid scrutiny, to avoid the judgment of others.

Thus corruption is a failure of judgment in yet a third sense. For in the formation of political relationships one must invite the judgment of others. The Citizen, in office or out, demands to be judged by his or her peers. This is a kind of jeopardy without which no free person could be expected to lend him- or herself to another, and absent cooperation, absent a constant exchange of energies among selves, no polity could survive. The essence of this political fact appears in and is sustained by the first and oldest principle of justice, that "no person should be a judge in their own case."

The corruption that has overcome the Citizen after September 11th is the failure to take on this specifically political, constitutionally necessary, power-controlling responsibility of judgment. Driven by shock, terror, war, and emergency, and bullied incessantly by the fanatics for whom these narrowing machineries are instruments of a "culture war"—"the real Cold War" that has begun "now that the other 'Cold War' is over," as Irving Kristol has said—and vehicles of monocracy, the person—it may be you or me—in the swing of everyday life becomes an "American," a "Patriot," a "Follower of the Commander-in-chief," a "Supporter of the Troops," and perhaps even a "Voter," but not a *Citizen*.

For the fanatic who obtains public office is not simply a person who pushes zealously onwards his particular dogma. He is the one who so completely values his beliefs and the potential of his official position to advance those beliefs that he refuses to present himself for judgment. In the extreme, the fanatic may postpone recall by election;* more typically he will avoid offering clear and public evidence to justify his actions. Secrecy and silence are suspensions of judgment, not abrogation of right.

* Some plans circulated in the fall of 2004 between the Department of Homeland Security and the Department of Justice concerning postponement of the presidential elections; cf. Michael Isikoff, "Election Day Worries," *Newsweek* (July 19, 2004). One might also count election fraud in this general category.

The corrupt Citizen is the one who, faced with a fanaticism that defends the office to advance the cause, fails to demand the ordeal of publicness and the imposition of judgment. The corrupt Citizen hides this failure behind a veil of rectitude and deference and respect. The corrupt Citizen steps forward wrapped in the flag.

There is a fourth and final issue of judgment. It is certain that terror and war and emergency bring their own kinds of disorder. There are disputes over whether this fact is a source of "clarity" or error, insight or blindness. In either case, it is obvious that expanding powers that would ordinarily be balanced by the everyday position taking of citizens have since September 11th been adjudged appropriate and left unchecked.

So ask yourself, Is this judgment correct? What is the measure for it?

It is at this point that a flood of other topics and debates I have held in abeyance throughout this book would like to come crashing in. And this is what I want to say to you now: these topics and debates, for all their vital import, do not touch directly the essence of democracy. Democratic societies make all sorts of bad choices. The motive force of the position of the Citizen, and the real and decisive effect of the Citizen in the constitutional system, concerns power: where it will go, how far, how much.

There is no fixed rule that can tell us when power has reached or passed its proper limit. It is a matter of *judgment*, a faculty that is in every instance complex beyond representation. At this point we are beyond rules. But neither can we be guided by whim or desire. The political option given to us by our human nature calls us onto ground that is neither objective nor subjective. The Citizen gambles on leaving him- or herself open, in the engagement of each new problem that life sets before us, to the judgment of others. This is a gamble one might make before a loving God, but never before one omnipotent stranger. And that is the best case we have against monocracy.

Notes

Port of Entry

1. An early and excellent analysis of the impact of the Bush presidency on civil and political rights is Chang 2002.

One

1. Images and quotes cited here are from the documentary film *9/11* made by Gédéon and Jules Naudet and originally broadcast by CBS in March 2002. I worked from the DVD issued in September 2002, entitled *9/11: The Filmmakers' Commemorative Edition*. I have transcribed the words it records without correcting the grammar.
2. Firefighter Damian Van Cleaf in *9/11*.
3. Opening titles from the DVD *In Memoriam: New York City 9/11/2001*, originally shown on HBO, May 26, 2002.
4. Jamal Braithwaite in *9/11*.
5. *In Memoriam*, chapter 7.
6. Firefighter in *In Memoriam*, minute 30:18.
7. Jules Naudet adds that this fact scared him somewhat, but that is another matter.
8. These descriptions are from Rudolph Giuliani's commentary and the images of *In Memoriam*.
9. Jamal Braithwaite in *9/11*.
10. Estimates from photographs and witness testimony suggest that as many as 200 people fell from the two towers. While it is impossible to know how many chose to jump and how many were pushed out the windows by explosions or other people struggling for air, we do know that some people left the building holding hands with another person. We have also the evidence of their posture during the fall; see Flynn and Dwyer 2004; and *9/11: The Falling Man* by Singer, 2006.
11. One may find this commonplace almost anywhere; here it is cited from Jacqueline Rose's polemic (2003) against Tony Blair's impending participation in the invasion of Iraq.
12. Aristotle *Rhetoric* 1383a. For a general sense of how fear is embedded in the time flow of typical human experiences, see the preceding sections 1382a–b.
13. Aristotle *Rhetoric* 1383a.

14. Spinoza's *Ethics* (1996), part 3, section "Definitions of the Affects," definition 13 and its "explication": "Metus est inconstans Tristitia, orta ex idea rei futuræ, vel præteritæ, de cujus eventu aliquatenus dubitamus." Note that Spinoza includes past things as well as future things; although this point is not central here, I doubt that we fear past things and, if we do, I would argue that that emotion has a different structure. Note also that here and elsewhere Spinoza clearly asserts that "it follows simply from the definition of these affects that there can be no hope without fear, and no fear without hope" (ex solâ, horum affectuum definitione sequitur, non dari Spem sine Metu, neque Metum sine Spe), *Ethics*, part 3, proposition 50.

15. Gédéon Naudet interview in *9/11*.

16. Rudoph Giuliani in *In Memoriam*.

17. Quotes in the preceding two paragraphs are from Damian Van Cleaf interview in *9/11*, except the description of Chief Pfeifer as "calm" after the first building collapsed, which is from Jules Naudet in *9/11*.

18. Recent studies, advanced with 4D echography, show the capacity for and fact of prenatal learning. Experiments with infants suggest that human beings begin to learn fear in conjunction with other cognitive developments around the sixth month. Cf. e.g. Marks 1987b and more generally Marks 1987a. Marks (1987b, 668) affirms the ancient understanding that fear depends on belief: "Fear of strange events requires the prior learning of what is familiar, a process which starts in the womb."

19. Cf. Dewey 1894–95, 1896.

20. Of the many works written on this, most directly relevant here is *The 9/11 Commission Report* (National Commission on Terrorist Attacks upon the United States 2004, chapters 2 and 5).

21. Statements reported from American Flight 11 and United Flight 93, National Commission on Terrorist Attacks, *The 9/11 Commission Report*, 10, 6.

22. The development of cinematic culture in America is detailed in my forthcoming book *Left Speechless*. It involves, among other things, a significant relocation of certain human faculties—animation, imagination—outside the body. A preliminary statement of this argument about modernity may be found in Meyers 2002a.

23. It may be easier for Americans to see how political legitimacy is undermined by recalling examples outside the case we consider here; think, for instance, of the impact of "drug cartels" and the "drug war" on the balance of political forces in Colombia.

24. Cf. Sperber 1985. More of this research program is laid out in Sperber 1996.

25. I acknowledge that there is an element of circularity in this claim since we have increasingly defined the "public sphere" as this realm of circulating images.

26. There is an enormous literature on the historical, sociological, and psychological patterns of personal biography that lead people to commit acts characteristic of contemporary terrorism. See e.g. Sageman 2004; Stern 2006; and the discussion of Scott Atran's essay "Genesis and Future of Suicide Terrorism" (2003) on the Web site http://www.interdisciplines.org, July 2003.

27. Analogous dynamics are present in all identity politics; for a witty and graceful unfolding of the dialectics of identity, cf. *N Word*, the musical dialogue by West and Dyson, 2007.

28. The quote is, of course, from Shakespeare's *As You Like It* (2.7.139). The insightful analogy of dramaturgy in sociology appears in the work of Kenneth Burke (1945) and his famous followers like Goffman (1959).

29. Cf. the reconstruction of events in National Commission on Terrorist Attacks, *The 9/11 Commission Report*, chapter 1.

30. This may be a very general instance of the universal learning capacity that Jean-Jacques Rousseau referred to as *perfectibilité*; see e.g. his *Discours sur l'origine et les fondemens de l'inégalité parmi les hommes* in Rousseau 1959–, originally published in 1754. From another angle, this may suggest that "false memory syndrome" is an exaggerated instance of a normal process.

31. It is interesting that three influential statements of this "traditional" view appeared almost simultaneously at the middle of the first phase of the Cold War concurrent with intensifying mechanisms of secrecy. Cf. Wolin (1960) and Habermas (1962), both of whom were influenced by Arendt (1958).

32. This distinction is, for instance, prerequisite to understanding the motive and effect of the Al Qaeda attacks. Using the American "public sphere," they did not enter into or engage a dispute in the United States, but rather tried to reconfigure alignments in Saudi Arabia and in the "Arab World" more generally.

33. This phrase is from James 1890.

34. Mansbridge (1980) and Barber (1984) were the first political theorists in the recent wave of studies of democratic deliberation to emphasize the aspect of reception.

35. Cf. the long development in the thinking of Jürgen Habermas and his followers that began with Habermas 1976.

36. If you think this is news from the post–World War II "science of communication," cf. Hardman 1934, 576: "The publicity value of the terroristic act is a cardinal point in the strategy of terrorism. If terror fails to elicit a wide response in circles outside of those at whom it is directly aimed, it is futile as a weapon in a social conflict." Other analogous uses of the media are worth considering, such as the attack by the George W. Bush campaign and affiliated groups on John Kerry's war record in the presidential electoral campaign of 2004. An editorial in the *Los Angeles Times* (August 25, 2004) charged "fabrication," and asserted that the "technique President Bush is using against John F. Kerry was perfected by his father against Michael Dukakis in 1988, though its roots go back at least to Sen. Joseph McCarthy. It is: Bring a charge, however bogus. . . . But make sure the supporting details are complicated and blurry enough to prevent easy refutation. Then sit back and let the media do your work for you. Journalists have to report the charges. . . . But the canons of the profession prevent most journalists from saying outright: These charges are false. As a result, the voters are left with a general sense that there is some controversy over . . . Kerry's service in Vietnam. And they have been distracted from thinking about real issues (like the war going on now) by these laboratory concoctions."

37. More precisely, Descartes says our first passion is what he calls *admiration* in *Les Passions de l'âme* (1650, especially sections 53, 59–77), and "astonishment is an excess of admiration" (section 73, my translation). Rightly or wrongly, Descartes is famous for making the most influential modern break from the ancients. Yet his work on the passions is clearly situated in the tradition of such treatises, which lean heavily on book 2 of Aristotle's *Rhetoric*.

38. For a set of historical studies on the relation between curiosity and *libido sciendi*, see Jacques-Chaquin and Houdard 1998.

39. See e.g. Kammen 1986 on the growth of the civic religion of the constitution in the United States. It should be mentioned that universal adherence to the identification of America with the image of Columbus has been declining.

40. Released on May 25, 2001, *Pearl Harbor* is one of a growing number of romanticized celebrations of the American military. The paradigm for this post-Vietnam revival is Steven

Spielberg's *Saving Private Ryan* (national release, July 24, 1998). It should be said that the life of "Pearl Harbor" as a cultural topos follows to some extent generational change: for someone like John F. Kennedy, with direct experience of World War II, analogies to Pearl Harbor had durable force—see May and Zelikow 1997, cited in Gaddis 2004, 131; the image lost some of its effectiveness for those who came to power after other traumatic experience; the image regained force in the wave of nostaglia of the third generation after World War II as images of "good" and "triumphant" wars reentered the "public sphere" to force out images of Vietnam, and the Heroes of Virtuous War were again paraded before us—as in the wildly popular book published by Tom Brokaw in 1998 entitled *The Greatest Generation*.

41. That television provides for many people the same interpretive framework is rather obvious. Gédéon Naudet, walking south towards the World Trade Center on September 11th, reported that "the scene here is just one right out of one of the movies you would see in Hollywood." He was hardly alone in thinking this way. This reflects an important but indirect sense in which television is part of the "public sphere": it is not simply a form of interaction (if it is that at all), but a very rapid generator of commonplaces. It should be said, however, that this function may not derive from the simple fact that people watch television, but from the multitude of ways in which they talk with others about what they watch, and through verbal-social interaction take it to "heart," refigure their own image after it, interpret situations in its light, etc. It seems to me a major sociological error to think that *this* dialogical process that *concerns* television takes place through the medium *of* television. Note that "blockbuster" success is typically and correctly explained this way: when a show like *American Idol* becomes the topic of watercooler conversation in the morning, everyone watches it the night before.

42. In the terms of C. S. Peirce's "logic of relatives," one might say that the viewer is stuck in "firstness."

Two

1. The lovely phrase—"the world turned upside down"—trumpeted recently by people like Victor Davis Hanson (e.g. 2002, 11) was common in the English Civil Wars of the seventeenth century and through the age of revolutions in Europe, famously becoming a term of philosophical art in Hegel's *Phänomenologie des Geistes* (1807). On this phrase in the English context, see Hill 1972; on Hegel, see Gadamer 1982, 35–53. Not surprisingly, it is within this same English context that Thomas Hobbes (*Elements of Philosophy*, 1655, 91) proposed that only by "feigning the world to be annihilated" could it be understood and set right with new order; Hobbes continues to be a favorite source for "realist" approaches to international relations. The phrase also appears as the title of children's books like *Die verkehrte Welt* (1669) and *The World Turned Upside Down; or, The Comical Metamorphoses* (1765), and perhaps this is what Hanson intends to mimic.

2. Instructive on this point is the version of the "quarrel between the moderns and the ancients" that characterized the long nineteenth century.

3. The first view is typical of misreadings of Hegel, perhaps by Hegel himself, which suggested that reason might have such omnipotence. The second view was partially pursued by Freud, although he, too, was infected by the misreading of history we attribute so facilely to Hegel.

4. Consider, for example, the much repeated observation that in the fall of 2001 church attendance increased. It is obvious, however, that the churches were there before: fright-

ened people with a need for religious solace did not go out and invent a new religion. They made use of what they already had—habits, institutions, customs, etc.; in one word, *experience*—to come to grips with the circumstances of the day. That is how it always works. You start from where you are. And that comes from somewhere.

5. Here from Rudolph Giuliani, "Quote of the Day," *New York Times*, September 11, 2004.

6. I refer to the commonplace that flooded conservative political discourse in America after Fukayama (1992) made new use of this Hegelian trope. With respect to the preceding sentence, it may be worth noting that while our lives are not theologically, cosmologically, or mathematically infinite, we live in a sort of secular infinity suggested by Hegel, still little understood and certainly belied by the phrase "the end of history." Cf. Meyers 1989, chapters 3 and 4.

7. Literally hundreds of commentators immediately said that "life would never be the same after September 11th," and this quickly became one of the primary figures in public discussion.

8. Cf. Hanson 2002, chapter 30, for an extended development of this widespread commonplace.

9. The phrase "war president" was most famously used by George W. Bush in an hour-long Oval Office interview with Tim Russert for NBC's *Meet the Press* on February 7, 2004. Bush's entourage was still using this language in late summer of 2007; cf. Karl Rove's remarks on his resignation at www.whitehouse.gov/news/releases/2007/08/20070813-5.html.

10. Hanson 2002, 11. Notice the extent to which this kind of claim makes incoherent peculiar and implausible declarations like "they will not change us." Cf. President Bush's speech on September 20, 2001.

11. E.g. Elliot Abrams, who escaped felony indictments in the Iran-Contra affair with a plea bargain, was later pardoned by George H. W. Bush and served in several capacities in George W. Bush's administration in connection with the National Security Council.

12. Cf. e.g. Mann 2004.

13. One may recall here Zbigniew Brzezinski's declaration to President Carter on the Soviet invasion of Afghanistan: "We now have the opportunity of giving the USSR its Vietnam war." Cf. Brzezinski's interview in *Le Nouvel Observateur*, January 15–21, 1998.

14. The chronology of planning for the invasion of Iraq shows the same kind of long-term development, in which the open letter of the Project for the New American Century to President Clinton (January 26, 1998) promoting "regime change" and then immediate postinaugural planning in the White House as George W. Bush assumed the presidency (described in Suskind 2004, chapter 2; and Woodward 2004, chapter 1) were pivotal moments. As Clarke (2004, 264) writes, "The administration of the second George Bush did begin with Iraq on its agenda."

15. Of course, from the point of view of those who performed them, the attacks of September 11th were part of a jihad. Exactly how this relates to the type of warfare under discussion here is beyond the scope of this book.

16. First quote from *Hamlet* (1.5.27), second from *Romeo and Juliet* (5.3.198). Michael Howard described American military action at the end of 2001 as more like a "hunt" than a war; see Howard 2001, cited in Silver 2004.

17. Presidential proclamation of September 14, 2001, no. 7462: "On Tuesday morning, September 11, 2001, terrorists attacked America in a series of despicable acts of war." Bush's address at the national prayer service, September 14, 2001: "War has been waged against us by stealth and deceit and murder. This nation is peaceful, but fierce when stirred to anger. This conflict was begun on the timing and terms of others. It will end in a way,

and at an hour, of our choosing." On September 15 President Bush spoke of a "long, unrelenting war" and, the next day, of a "crusade" against the evil-doers. In a speech on September 17: "I believe—I know that an act of war was declared against America." Two days later President Bush addressed a joint session of Congress: "On September the 11th, enemies of freedom committed an act of war against our country. Americans have known wars—but for the past 136 years, they have been wars on foreign soil, except for one Sunday in 1941." Congress, as a body, was somewhat more cautious about the use of the word *war*: it is not included in either *Joint Resolution to Authorize the Use of United States Armed Forces against Those Responsible for the Recent Attacks Launched against the United States*, 2001, or *Uniting and Strengthening America by Providing Appropriate Tools Required to Intercept and Obstruct Terrorism*, 2001. It should also be said that influential neoconservative militarists went to work right away; cf. Krauthammer 2001.

18. Cf. Hanson 2002.

19. Toby Keith's best-selling album of 2002 was called *Unleashed*, and the song referred to here is "Courtesy of the Red, White, and Blue (The Angry American)."

20. This oft-repeated phrase was purportedly said to George W. Bush by workers at "Ground Zero" on September 14. It became a mainstay of his campaign to claim a mandate for the war in Iraq, as well as the punch line of his standard "stump speech" and his most-played television ad during the presidential election of 2004.

21. Hanson 2002, chapter 17.

22. The letter from John Ashcroft to President Bush dated February 1, 2002, may be the primary document on this topic. This and other key memoranda, especially implicating the lawyers around Alberto Gonzales, may be found in Greenberg and Dratel 2005. It was indicative of this unhappy moment that the advocates of torture and enemies of the Geneva conventions became the director of homeland security and the attorney general of the United States. Out of such views, it seems, the ambivalent discussion of "just war" was revived in such well-publicized documents as the Institute for American Values' "What We're Fighting For: A Letter from America" (February 12, 2002) and then in a book by Jean Bethke Elshtain (2003), who seems to have been the main architect of the "Letter."

23. Krauthammer continued his support for the war in the face of the evidence; even fellow neoconservatives like Francis Fukuyama began to find him "strangely disconnected from reality . . . [as if] the Iraq war has been an unqualified success, with all of the assumptions and expectations on which the war had been based vindicated," while "Mr. Krauthammer and other supporters of the war mischaracterized Iraq and Islamic radicals as an immediate threat to the existence of the United States, a claim that justified immediate intervention. The Soviet Union arguably threatened the existence of the United States . . . but Iraq never did." Cited or summarized from Fukuyama's article in *The National Interest* by Kirkpatrick (2004).

24. U.S. Constitution, Article 2, §§ 2 and 3.

25. U.S. Constitution, Article 1, § 8, clauses 1 and 11.

26. Fifty-six involved "actual gunfire or imminent threat," sixty-four lasted more than thirty days, sixty-five were outside the Western Hemisphere. These figures from the appendix to the testimony of Senator Barry Goldwater before the Senate Committee on Foreign Relations, April 23, 1971; cited here from Senate Committee on Foreign Relations, *War Powers Legislation*, 359–79.

27. *War Powers Resolution of 1973*, passed by two-thirds majority of the Senate and the House of Representatives over the veto of President Nixon.

28. The fundamental document of the so-called Bush Doctrine issued from the National Security Council under the title *National Security Strategy of the United States*, September

20, 2002. By 2004 it had been declared "a dead letter"; see Rose 2004. Rose is the managing editor of *Foreign Affairs*. See also Reeves 2005.

29. Michael Howard, Stanley Hoffman, and many others argued against applying the interpretive framework of war.

30. Although John Kerry did not publicly express the "crime-not-war" point of view that George W. Bush and Dick Cheney held against him during the 2004 presidential campaign, he eventually did seem to come close to that perspective. Cf. Bai 2004.

31. This fact is considered from a different angle in Silver 2004.

32. Particularly stunning is the August 6, 2001, presidential daily briefing entitled "Bin Laden Determined to Strike in US." By 4 p.m. on September 11th, CNN was reporting that U.S. officials believed there were "'good indications' based on 'new and specific' information developed since the attacks" that Osama bin Laden was involved (September 11 Chronology, http://archives.cnn.com/2001/US/09/11/chronology.attack). Osama bin Laden's three taped public messages in 2001 first celebrate the attacks (October 7, November 3) and then claim responsibility (December 13).

33. Osama bin Laden, fatwa entitled "Declaration of War against the Americans Occupying the Land of the Two Holy Places," first published in the London newspaper *Al Quds Al Arabi*, August 1996.

34. See generally William S. Cohen, prepared statement to the National Commission on Terrorist Attacks upon the United States, March 23, 2004, as well as his testimony before the 9/11 Commission at http://govinfo.library.unt.edu/911/archive, Eighth Public Hearing.

35. Tenet, *Written Statement for the Record of the Director of Central Intelligence*, October 17, 2002. See also Max Cleland's interview with Amy Goodman on *Democracy Now!* March 23, 2004.

36. Cf. Will 2001.

37. See "Clinton Warned Bush of bin Laden Threat," Reuters, October 15, 2003.

38. See National Commission on Terrorist Attacks, *The 9/11 Commission Report*, 256ff., and more generally Clarke 2004; Schlesinger 2004; and Bamford 2004. The language of "acceleration" is brutally clear in Donnelly, Kagan, and Schmitt 2000. One might note with some irony here that it has also been said that FDR waited for Japan to attack the United States.

39. *Saving Private Ryan* was released in 1998, directed by Steven Spielberg and starring Tom Hanks. *We Were Soldiers* was released in 2002, directed by Randall Wallace and starring Mel Gibson. Both Hanks and Gibson have served as boosters for these films and, with their success, as propagandists for "good" American wars; the antipolitical (and thus antidemocratic) image of war advocated in these films continued its infection of American society in 2007 with Ken Burns's film *The War*. Cf. Meyers 1990.

40. Woodward 2004, 24.

41. Cf. Steel 2003, 26.

42. Hanson 2002, chapter 30.

43. Hanson 2002, 168.

44. Hanson 2002, 172.

45. I have altered the verb tense in this sentence. An image favored by Hanson is actually borrowed from the Japanese general Nagumo, who saw Japan as having "awakened a sleeping giant and filled her with terrible resolve" after Pearl Harbor.

46. Hanson 2002, xv.

47. National Commission on Terrorist Attacks, *The 9/11 Commission Report*, xvii.

48. "Impressive" and "good" are not the same; for a withering critique see also DeMott 2004.

49. Posner 2004, 9.
50. Posner 2004, 9.
51. This observation merits more discussion than I can allot here concerning "the general will" and the nature of political representations. For a recent and especially perspicuous "process-oriented" approach to "representation," see Urbinati 2006.
52. Line from the The 9/11 Commission Report cited, with his assessment, in Posner 2004, 9.
53. One may sense similarities here with Friedrich A. Hayek's conception of order in Law, Legislation, and Liberty (1973); for my deep differences with that view, see Abandoned to Ourselves (2006).
54. George W. Bush, address to the nation from the White House, September 11, 2001.
55. Cf. the editorial by Thomas Friedman (2001). "On Sunday I interviewed Jordan's King Abdullah, one of America's real friends. He had three wise messages: We can win if you Americans don't forget who you are, if you don't forget who your friends are and if we work together. 'The terrorists are trying to break down the fabric of the U.S.,' said the Jordanian monarch. 'They want to break down what America stands for. The terrorists actually want to provoke attacks on Arabs or Muslims in the U.S., because if the American communities start going after each other, if we see America fragment, then you destroy that special thing that America stands for. That's what the terrorists want—they want to be able to turn to your friends here and say, 'Look, this is all a myth.' . . . That is why you have to be very careful when you respond—make sure you respond in a way that punishes the real perpetrators, that brings justice, not revenge, because otherwise you will be going against your own ideals, and that is what the terrorists want most."
56. James Mann, author of Rise of the Vulcans, observed on the National Public Radio interview program Fresh Air that bin Laden consistently displayed his plans. He is hardly the only one to notice this.
57. Osama bin Laden, interview taped around October 2001, released by CNN in January 2002.
58. Even landmark cases become decisive only because the system's balance subsequently changes for many reasons that did not adhere at the time they occurred.
59. Cf. Dworkin 2002.
60. George W. Bush, address to a joint session of Congress and the American people, September 20, 2001.
61. The word unchallengeable comes from James Mann's description (2004, 239) of what Paul Wolfowitz, Condoleezza Rice, and the other "Vulcans" wrote into the National Security Strategy of September 2002 (available at http://www.whitehouse.gov/nsc/nss.pdf).
62. Among many and ongoing examples, consider the audiotape entitled Where Is the Honor? which surfaced on the third anniversary of September 11th, in which someone claiming to be Abu Musab al-Zarqawi says, "The holy warriors made the international coalition taste humiliation . . . lessons from which they still are burning"; cited here from Hendawi 2004.
63. "Private war" is the embarrassing topic of a novel meant to "inform the citizen about terrorism through fiction" by Christopher Dickey called The Sleeper (2004). This picks up on an interesting American practice of imagining an individual figure like Rambo as the solution to collective problems; however, Rambo's original rampages were meant, at the same time that they rescued someone and killed others, to prove something to a failing State. Note the criminal conviction of Jonathan Adema and his consorts in an Afghan court (September 15, 2004) for running a private prison and interrogation facility.
64. How the roles of Soldier and Citizen should and should not overlap is a long-standing theme in both descriptive and normative thinking about classical republics and re-

publicanism. At the moment in which this tradition becomes particularly relevant for Americans—the war for our national independence—Adam Ferguson (who was not an American) wrote some most perspicuous lines on this subject (1767). It becomes a major theme in American political sociology when, after World War II, the mingling of Citizen and Soldier roles in the person of the Veteran and the accelerating development of a combined private military industry and public military bureaucracy made it a topic of high civic significance. Cf. Huntington 1957; and Janowitz 1960.

65. Cf. Meyers 1990.

66. Lord Salisbury, from Taylor 1975, cited in Silver 2004.

67. "Der Krieg ist eine bloße Fortsetzung der Politik mit anderen Mitteln." Clausewitz 1976, 87.

68. "War does not belong in the realm of arts and sciences; rather it is part of man's social existence. War is a clash between major interests, which is resolved by bloodshed—that is the only way in which it differs from other conflicts. Rather than comparing it to art we could more accurately compare it to commerce, which is also a conflict of human interests and activities; and it is still closer to politics, which in turn may be considered as a kind of commerce on a larger scale. Politics, moreover, is the womb in which war develops—where its outlines already exist in their hidden rudimentary form, like the characteristics of living creatures in their embryos." Clausewitz 1976, 149.

69. A vast literature is relevant on this point; excellent general sources include the volume edited by Charles Tilly 1975, and Mann 1986, 1993. Specifically on Clausewitz, see Paret 1976.

70. Clausewitz's conception of politics is bound up with many additional features of the "State-centered" version of politics. Most notably, it is firmly rooted in the discourse of the "new model will" (sketched further in Meyers 1995), taking as axiomatic that war is action aimed "to compel our opponent to fulfill our Will," but which applies violence to that end rather than the discursive maneuvering characteristic of normal politics; cf. Clausewitz 1976, 75.

71. Clausewitz 1976, 78; proposition in section 6, refutation in section 7.

72. Clausewitz 1976, 78, 79, 80; proposition in section 6, refutation in sections 8 and 9.

73. Cf. Clausewitz 1976, 80ff. Properly speaking, this places Clausewitz within a tradition of rhetorical inquiry. By this I mean, here and as hinted elsewhere throughout the notes, a systematically perspicuous account of action as it is situated in particular historical cases and coordinated by speech. A categorical distinction between the "certain" and the "probable" is one of the foundations of the rhetorical tradition after the historical emergence of philosophy. It is telling that Clausewitz gives priority to "what seems to be true" (a literal translation of *Wahrscheinlichkeiten*), which philosophers have classified as misleading and unworthy objects for investigation; by contrast, rhetoricians have typically understood that appearances are decisive for politics.

74. Objections to or dismissals of Clausewitz in the American context begin early with admiration for the French theorist of war Antoine-Henri de Jomini, whose works—*Traité de grande tactique* (1805, trans. 1865), although a manuscript translation from 1806 is in the Library of Congress and may have circulated) and *Précis de l'art de la guerre* (1838, trans. 1854)—were widely read in the United States. Cf. Shy 1986. There is debate about how much Clausewitz was known in the United States before his first translation in 1873 and whether his ideas influenced Lincoln; cf. Bassford 1994, chapter 4.

75. One particularly misleading use of Clausewitz I have in mind is by Michel Foucault (1980, "Two Lectures"), who plays on Clausewitz's maxim to give priority to war. He presumes to shed light on politics only by presupposing that we already know the

answer to the question posed here: what is war? Another line of thought—from Carl Schmitt to Giorgio Agamben—sustains a similarly misleading approach that defines politics by "the exception," a notion easily assimilable to war. As I have written in the text, all this points back—sometimes explicitly—to Thomas Hobbes. It is worth noting that something like Foucault's "inversion" of Clausewitz may also be found in Weber, or in thinkers like Walter Lippmann in America in the 1920s. That the modern State was built on the development and use of its warmaking capacity is likewise well-known; see e.g. Tilly 1975. Everyday events may remind us of the continuing relevance of this fact, e.g. "Washington, Feb. 19 [2002]—President Bush has decided to transform the administration's temporary wartime communications effort into a permanent office of global diplomacy to spread a positive image of the United States around the world and combat anti-Americanism, senior administration officials said today." *New York Times*, February 20, 2002.

76. Howard 1979, 1. Howard's synthetic statements are propitious not only by the way they diverge from common sense but also in representing—at least in a superficial way—the self-conception of American military organizations; cf. e.g. U.S. Marine Corps, *Warfighting* (1997, first ed. 1989), which begins with a section, "War Defined," that builds explicitly on Clausewitz and (at p. 3) closely mimics Howard. Indeed, *Warfighting* (1989 ed., 79) simply says of Clausewitz's *On War* that "all Marine officers should consider this book essential reading."

77. Tilly 1975, introduction. This two-way relationship was occasionally the self-conception urged on and adopted by princes even before "the State" was fully formed as a concept and a set of institutions.

78. Cf. e.g. Bensel 1990; Hooks 1991; Skocpol 1992; Sparrow 1996; and Katznelson and Shefter 2002. The symbolic dimensions of this process feature in works like Slotkin 1973, 1985, 1992; and Rogin 1987.

79. N.b. that I am not saying that no Americans have been confronted by military force within our borders; a whole range of public, quasi-public, and private armed forces have been brought to bear many times against rioters, strikers, protesters, and local governmental institutions.

80. Cf. Hobbes 1651, chapter 13: "Hereby it is manifest that during the time men live without a common power to keep them all in awe, they are in that condition which is called war; and such a war as is of every man against every man. For war consisteth not in battle only, or the act of fighting, but in a tract of time, wherein the will to contend by battle is sufficiently known: and therefore the notion of time is to be considered in the nature of war, as it is in the nature of weather. For as the nature of foul weather lieth not in a shower or two of rain, but in an inclination thereto of many days together: so the nature of war consisteth not in actual fighting, but in the known disposition thereto during all the time there is no assurance to the contrary. All other time is peace."

81. "Phatic communion" is the expression introduced by Malinowski (1923).

82. The identification of "phatic communion" by Malinowski (1923) greatly accelerated the recovery of the rhetorical sense of "performativity" in language—our "doing things with words." The fact that language constitutes social groups in general and in war in particular applies to all parties. For example, Marc Sageman (2004, 182) identifies language use as a locus of struggle against *terror networks*—"The global Salafi jihad feeds on anti-Western and anti-American hate speech. Such virulent discourse is a necessary condition for the jihad and provides a justification for it. It is important to eradicate it and encourage civil discourse in Muslim communities."

83. Innumerable studies of "social control" (from John Dewey on) make this clear; cf. e.g. Melossi 1990. This recursive quality of social control in politics may seem similar to, but is in fact completely different from, the claim that "the constitution [is] the highest order system of social rules for making rules." Rawls 1971, 222. Politics is not primarily about rules; cf. Meyers 1998.

84. The immediate appearance of a debate about "just war" in conjunction with the planning of expeditions to Afghanistan and Iraq needs to be understood as part of the political maneuvering to constrain these projects in a particular way—not as a debate about simply confirming or denying them. Many of the positions taken were consistent with older "Cold War liberalism." The symbiotic relation between rules of war and forms of politics is nothing new; cf. e.g. Ober 1996, 53–71.

85. For a general argument on the former point, cf. Manicas 1989.

Three

1. Former Supreme Court Justice Arthur Goldberg, testimony before the Senate Foreign Relations Committee in *War Powers Legislation*, 771. The line in question is from Justice Potter Stewart's concurring opinion in *Jacobellis v. Ohio*, 378 U.S. 184 (1964), in which Justice Goldberg co-authored the opinion of the court.

2. This fact has often been discussed under the term *legitimacy*. Such an assimilation of basic facts of politics to law is, however, deeply misleading. If anything, the reduction should go the other way—law is fundamentally embedded in politics—although this too is misleading for most purposes.

3. The assignment of powers is the basic division between Article 1 and Article 2.

4. Cf. *Federalist* nos. 47 and 48.

5. *Buckley v. Valeo*, 424 U.S. 1, 121 (1976).

6. Justice Jackson in *Youngstown Sheet and Tube Co. v. Sawyer*, 343 U.S. 579, 635 (1952).

7. Emphasis added. This view is a commonplace, here asserted by then-Justice Rehnquist in *Buckley v. Valeo*, 122. The per curiam decision in *Buckley v. Valeo* was unsigned; research into the drafting history has shown that section 4 ("The Federal Election Commission") was written by then-Justice Rehnquist. Cf. Hasen 2002.

8. I am not sure who among the "Framers" knew the frontispiece of Hobbes's *Leviathan*. In any case, one might say, they would have read such images in the manner of Montesquieu. The importance of Hobbes for the Founders is suggested by Gerald Stouzh (1970).

9. *Federalist* no. 51.

10. "Invisible hand" is the metaphor closely associated with a (mis)reading of Adam Smith's view of the order of market systems. The view that the U.S. Constitution was a "machine that would go of itself" developed in the course of the nineteenth century; cf. Kammen 1986. Kenneth Burke (1945) is most perspicacious on the general way of living with language that permits this kind of effective belief.

11. *Federalist* no. 51. This and the preceding quote from Madison are cited by Rehnquist in *Buckley v. Valeo*, 122.

12. Cf. e.g. *Luther v. Borden*, 48 U.S. 1 (1849); *Baker v. Carr*, 369 U.S. 186 (1962); *Powell v. McCormack*, 395 U.S. 486 (1969); and *Goldwater v. Carter*, 444 U.S. 996 (1979) for discussion of "political questions" in constitutional law. More generally, see Fisher and Mourtada-Sabbah 2001. On the political context of *Luther v. Borden*, cf. Mowry 1901.

13. It is also a mistake to conclude from this that power is somehow derivative from the "performative" aspect of the Constitution.

14. Cf. Rossiter 1948. In classical terms, "constitutional dictators" seem to be what Aristotle referred to as αἰσυμνῆται; generally, dictators are chosen and within the law, whereas δεσπόται are not chosen and are not within the law. Nonetheless, see the "fable" of Stesichorus at the head of this chapter, where the oppressor is first chosen as στρατηγός, or commander-in-chief.

15. There is a vast literature on this question and it is not my purpose here to review it; cf. Shane and Bruff 1996. N.b. that "separation of powers" is not the same as "balance of powers," and that the former can be profoundly unbalanced.

16. Compton was one of many individual witnesses who volunteered to speak at the "Hearing on the War in Vietnam, conducted by the Hon. Robert W. Kastenmeier, Member of Congress, 2nd District, Wisconsin," the transcript of which is published in Kastenmeier 1966, 153. Compton added that the war was illegal, too, "because we are in this affair unilaterally without any sanction of the United Nations' Security Council or General Assembly." Of those in this meeting who opposed the war, the most common objections were that it was immoral (Walter Grengg, Louise Smalley, Francis Hole, Gehrta Amlie, Elizabeth Lornitzo, Mrs. Robert Franz, Betty Compton) and that unilateral action without the United Nations was wrong (Henry Berger, Jennie Turner, Edwin Weeks, H. J. Kubiak, Elizabeth Lornitzo, Betty Compton).

17. The American military presence in Vietnam waxed and waned as follows (year/number of persons): 1959/760; 1960/900; 1961/3,205; 1962/11,300; 1963/16,300; 1964/23,300; 1965/184,300; 1966/385,300; 1967/485,600; 1968/536,100; 1969/475,200; 1970/334,600; 1971/156,800; 1972/24,200; 1973/50.

18. Up to 1970, these included *Luftig v. McNamara*, 373 F. 2nd 333 (1966); *Mora v. McNamara*, 389 U.S. 934 (1967); *Velvel v. Johnson*, 287 F. Supp. 846 (D.D.C. 1968); *Velvel v. Nixon*, 415 F. 2nd 236 (Cal. 10, 1970); *MacArthur v. Clifford*, 393 U.S. 1002 (1968); *United States v. Sisson*, 294 F. Supp. 515 (1968); *United States v. Holmes*, 387 F. 2nd 781 (7th Cir.), cert. denied, 391 U.S. 936 (1968); *Pietsch v. President of the United States*, 434 F. 2nd 861 (2nd Cir. 1970); *Davi v. Laird*, 318 F. Supp. 478 (W.D. Va. 1970); and *Massachusetts v. Laird*, 400 U.S. 886 (1970). For a list of challenges to the war that did not raise the overall question of its constitutionality, see Fisher and Mourtada-Sabbah 2001, 48 n. 201.

19. *United States v. Sisson*, 515, cited in Fisher and Mourtada-Sabbah 2001, 48.

20. *DaCosta v. Laird*, 405 U.S. 979 (1972). Douglas cites his own previous dissenting opinions dating back six years.

21. That assertion of the "political question" doctrine was itself a matter of political position-taking was suggested by such anomalies as *Campen v. Nixon*, 56 F.R.D. 404 (N.D. Cal. 1972) in which, as Fisher and Mourtada-Sabbah (2001, 57) summarize it, the California court "ruled that plaintiffs had no standing to challenge the legality of the Vietnam War on the ground that there had been no declaration of war by Congress."

22. *Orlando v. Laird*, 443 F. 2nd 1042 (1971). This same argument was restated by the Second Circuit Court of Appeals in its decision in *DaCosta v. Laird* even though the Tonkin Gulf Resolution had by that time been repealed.

23. Referring to *Commonwealth of Massachusetts v. Laird*, 451 F. 2nd 34 (1st Cir. 1971).

24. Senator John Stennis, testimony before the Senate Foreign Relations Committee, with clarification by the chairman, Fulbright, in Senate Foreign Relations Committee, *War Powers Legislation*, 711. The exact date of Senator Stennis's testimony in 1971 is not indicated.

25. The Tonkin Gulf Resolution was repealed by Public Law 91–672, 84 *Stat.* 2055, section 12 (1971). The word "fraudulent" is from J. William Fulbright's statement as chairman of the hearings before the Senate Committee on Foreign Relations, 92nd Congress, 1st

session (April–May 1971), 21. But see already Fulbright's *Arrogance of Power* (1967), a book he wrote in 1966. Not only Democrats later claimed they were misled by President Johnson in 1964; e.g. Republican senator Charles Mathias said in 1983, "I voted for the Gulf of Tonkin resolution, and I think it is fair to say that most of us who did vote for it felt, as the facts were revealed, that we had been bamboozled and that there was no mechanism by which the Congress could come to grips with the situation once the resolution had been passed." American Enterprise Institute 1984, 4.

26. On instances of clearly illegal warmaking, cf. the so-called Church Committee Report (Senate Select Committee to Study Governmental Operations with Respect to Intelligence Activities, 1976) and U.S. Office of Independent Counsel, *Final Report of the Independent Counsel for Iran/Contra Matters* (1993). Whether or not a *war* is illegal, activities undertaken by or at the behest of the United States may be illegal; e.g. following the post-9/11 detention cases, it may be that some captured in the "war on terror" have not been treated consistent with rights thereby affirmed for citizen-detainees; cf. Baker and Dunham 2005; on the general significance of these cases, cf. Fiss 2005.

27. This presumption guides thinking about constitutions in general; cf. e.g. Ferejohn and Pasquino 2004. In the United States, the predominant view seems to deny "delegation" in principle but accept it in well-defined practice. Acknowledging "delegation," cf. *Wayman v. Southard*, 10 Wheat. (23 U.S.) 1, 42 (1825); denying "delegation," cf. *United States v. Shreveport Grain and Elevator Co.*, 287 U.S. 77, 85 (1932); *United States v. Curtiss-Wright Corp.*, 299 U.S. 304 (1936) touches on the idea that certain congressional powers cannot be "delegated." Again, *Orlando v. Laird* identifies "mutual and joint action" on the part of Congress and the Executive based on a de facto "ratification" of military action by Congress and providing "a discoverable and manageable standard imposing on the Congress a duty of mutual participation in the prosecution of war" with the result that "judicial scrutiny of that duty . . . is not foreclosed by the political question doctrine."

28. While in certain respects we do not agree, my thinking about emergency powers has been greatly informed by conversations with Kim Lane Scheppele and by reading her ongoing work in this area, including early draft material from *The International State of Emergency*, forthcoming; and Scheppele 2004, 2006, 2007.

29. This fact lies behind the democratic critique of expertise; cf. Senator Fulbright's introduction to the first televised hearings on Vietnam policy: "There is no secret information or magical formula which gives Presidential advisors wisdom and judgment on broad policy but which is not available to the intelligent citizen." Senate Committee on Foreign Relations, *The Vietnam Hearings*, xi.

30. Corwin 1957, 171, originally published in 1940.

31. This is what Fulbright aimed to transcend by staging a public scene. Concerning Iraq, we now know all too well how ineffectual were a handful of votes against the *Authorization for Use of Military Force against Iraq Resolution* of 2002 (Public Law 107–243), which had an accelerated legislative life of fourteen days, advanced with 136 co-sponsors, brushed off one vigorous objection by Barbara Lee, and passed in the House (296/133) and in the Senate (77/23). Then was illustrated what Madison wrote in *Federalist* no. 44: "No axiom is more clearly established in law, or in reason, than that wherever the end is required, the means are authorized; wherever a general power to do a thing is given, every particular power necessary for doing it is included." For the legislative history of the Iraq resolution, including lists of those who found the courage to vote against it, see http://thomas.loc.gov/cgi-bin/bdquery/z?d107:HJ00114:@@@L&summ2=m.

32. Relyea 1974, following Corwin 1957, 152ff., cites the "Stewardship Theory" of Theodore Roosevelt and William Taft's staunch opposition to it as paradigms of opposing interpretations

of appropriate "reach." Cf. likewise Woodrow Wilson (1908, 68–69) on the president as leader of his political party: "if he rightly interpret the national thought and boldly insist upon it, he is irresistible. . . . His office is anything he has the sagacity and force to make it."

33. Cf. Strum 1972, 125–26, cited in Relyea 1974, 2. This may be understood as a statement of "legal positivism" or as suggesting a broader sociological "symbolic interactionism."

34. Fulbright's introduction to Senate Committee on Foreign Relations, *Vietnam Hearings*, xii.

35. Quote is from Senator Albert Gore; Senate Committee on Foreign Relations, *Vietnam Hearings*, 44–45. When Johnson said in 1968, "We have set our course and we will pursue it just as long as aggression threatens us; make no mistake about it: America will prevail," Gore responded at the hearings this way: "I would object to the use of 'we' if it includes the elected representatives of the American people [who] have not set this course of a wider war in Vietnam" (38). By 1968 Fulbright was saying of the Tonkin Gulf affair that "there was a high degree of inaccuracy in the presentation of the Administration to this committee, and to the Senate through this committee." Senate Committee on Foreign Relations, *Present Situation in Vietnam*, 5. By 1971 he was calling it "fraudulent"; cf. Senate Committee on Foreign Relations, *Legislative Proposals relating to the War in Southeast Asia*, 21.

36. This view was persistent. Opening the hearings in 1970, Senator Fulbright noted: "It has been said that it is too late now to debate whether we should or should not have gone into Vietnam in the first place. My own feeling is that the continuing exploration of this question is still pertinent, not just for the sake of history, or for the parceling out of praise and blame, but for the purpose of defining our national interests and the best means of upholding them." Senate Committee on Foreign Relations, *Vietnam Policy Proposals*, 3. I share this belief and it animates this book.

37. Johnson's first major justification for the escalation of the war was made in a speech at Johns Hopkins University on April 7, 1965. The testimony was published in Senate Committee on Foreign Relations, *Vietnam Hearings*. Not all the testimony was actually broadcast; CBS turned away its cameras during Kennan's statement, resulting in a protest resignation by Fred Friendly, director of the news.

38. This "discussion" is documented in publications by the Senate Committee on Foreign Relations: *The Vietnam Hearings*, 1966; *Present Situation in Vietnam*, 1968; *Briefing on Vietnam* ("sanitized" public version), 1969; *Vietnam Policy Proposals*, 1970; *Moral and Military Aspects of the War in Southeast Asia*, 1970; and *Legislative Proposals*, 1971.

39. This is the thrust of Senate Committee on Foreign Relations, *Legislative Proposals*.

40. Senate Committee on Foreign Relations, *Moral and Military Aspects*, 89.

41. Senate Committee on Foreign Relations, *Legislative Proposals*, 192.

42. Justice Jackson's concurring opinion in *Youngstown Sheet and Tube Co. v. Sawyer* at p. 653.

43. This structure of power is reflected in the apparent contradiction between John Locke's claim in the second of his *Two Treatises of Government* (1690) that the "legislative power is not only the supreme power of the commonwealth, but sacred and unalterable in the hands where the community have once placed it" (section 134) and his notion of "prerogative" (chapter 14) as the "power to act according to discretion, for the public good, without the prescription of the law, and sometimes even against it" (section 160), a power implicitly given by "the people" and potentially revocable by them (section 161) as they see fit (section 240 and chapter 19, "On the dissolution of government . . . ," passim).

44. It should be said, however, that occasionally the Supreme Court has disagreed. E.g. the Supreme Court found in *United States v. Curtiss-Wright Corp.* (1936) that the President

has, with regard to foreign relations, certain "inherent" powers. Senator Barry Goldwater, e.g., affirmed this view in his testimony before the Senate Committee on Foreign Relations, April 23, 1971, 355. Before the same committee, former Justice Arthur Goldberg rejected "this concept of inherent power," saying that when he served on the Court he had written "that our Constitution was not a suicide pact," yet "this is a far cry from recognizing the President's unfettered power to plunge us into a war without congressional sanction as distinguished from the President's power to repel a surprise attack." In Senate Committee on Foreign Relations, *War Powers Legislation*, 770.

45. Hamilton's own position was more complex. In any event, the balance of history has not gone Cheney's way. Cf. Corwin 1957, 170–226.

46. Cheney's comments are from a discussion held on December 6, 1983; the printed transcript is published in American Enterprise Institute 1984, 24, 3.

47. "Iran Contra Affair: The Final Report: Excerpts," *Los Angeles Times*, November 19, 1987, 16, as cited in Dean 2004b, 182. Emphasis added.

48. Cf. Burke 1945, which is a classic account of constitutional language in everyday discourse; for a more historical viewpoint, cf. Kammen 1986.

49. Mickey Herskowitz, hired in 1999 to write an authorized biography of George W. Bush, did more than twenty interviews and was then fired by the Bush campaign. He attributed these words to Bush in an interview with Russ Baker; see Baker 2004. Only after President Bush's reelection in 2004 did general discussion of his attachment to the phrase "political capital" emerge. The activist spirit conveyed here should have been sufficient warning to those who naively believed a close election and questions of legitimacy would lead to a modest or consensus-oriented administration. Woodward (2004, 28) cites Cheney as saying "a notion of sort of a restrained presidency because it was such a close election, that lasted maybe 30 seconds."

50. Contrast Wolfe 2005, where he claims that George W. Bush is in a "goodness" rather than a "greatness" tradition of American political culture; his categories and their application are more than a little unconvincing.

51. Relyea (2001, 2) sees this Executive power as delegated by the Legislative branch and issuing from Article 1, § 8. Explicitly, it concerns the "privilege of the Writ of Habeas Corpus," which may be suspended if "the public Safety may require it." But it is also, arguably, implicit in the authority to "provide for the common Defense and general Welfare"; in the commerce clause; in the authorizations concerning war, armed forces, and militia; and in the capstone of congressional authority, the final clause of section 8, which grants the power "to make all Laws which shall be necessary and proper for carrying into Execution the foregoing Powers, and all other Powers vested by this Constitution in the Government of the United States, or in any Department or Officer thereof."

52. Locke 1690. That terms for disputes about governmental powers were informed by Locke is suggested by the following argument *against* "prerogative" presented to the Supreme Court by David Dudley Field on behalf of Milligan in *Ex Parte Milligan*, 71 U.S. 2, 30 (1866): "If the President has this awful power [to try by court martial, without jury, and deny habeas corpus], whence does he derive it? He can exercise no authority whatever but that which the Constitution of the country gives him. Our system knows no authority beyond or above the law. We may, therefore, dismiss from our minds every thought of the President's having any prerogative, as representative of the people, or as interpreter of the popular will. He is elected by the people to perform those functions, and those only, which the Constitution of his country, and the laws made pursuant to that Constitution, confer." There is, of course, a vast literature about the "Lockean" character of American democracy. I return briefly to this topic in the next chapter.

53. The National Emergencies Act (1976), here concerning 50 *U.S. Code* 34, sections 1601–51.

54. This paragraph and the quotes it contains are drawn from Relyea 2001, passim. In keeping with the dialectical-composite model of power alluded to earlier in this chapter, one should further note the oppositions within the division of action which give form to Executive emergency powers: "Congress may modify, rescind, or render dormant such delegated emergency authority." Moreover, "disputes over the constitutionality or legality of the exercise of emergency powers are judicially reviewable. Indeed, both the judiciary and Congress, as co-equal branches, can restrain the Executive regarding emergency powers. So can public opinion." Relyea 2001, 2.

55. Corwin 1947, 177–78.

56. Chapters 33 and 34 respectively of Title 50.

57. Consider, e.g., the view expressed in President Monroe's first inaugural address (1817): "The safety of these States and of everything dear to a free people must depend in an eminent degree on the militia" and when "invasions [are] too formidable . . . recourse must be had to the great body of the people . . . so organized and trained as to be prepared for any emergency." With more specific reference to civil liberties in times of war, cf. Stone 2005.

58. Cf. Rossiter 1948, 230. It is interesting that Rossiter looks for support for his views in works written in the 1890s, e.g. Dunning 1898.

59. On Lincoln's balancing act between his expanded reliance on his role as Commander-in-chief and his Executive role, cf. Corwin 1947, 16–22. The shift from the former to the latter, at least with respect to habeas corpus, came on March 3, 1863, when Congress passed *An Act relating to Habeas Corpus, and Regulating Judicial Proceedings in Certain Cases.* The larger balance constituting this power was again altered when the Supreme Court ruled in *Ex Parte Milligan*, (1866). The separate opinion by Chief Justice Chase in this case (see note 95 below) seems to have spurred further congressional action on this score, deriving from and bearing on what might be called the persistence of the Civil War into the "Reconstruction" period; cf. e.g. *An Act Amendatory to* [the habeas corpus act of 1863], 1869, and *An Act to Enforce the Provisions of the Fourteenth Amendment*, 1871.

60. A law passed in 1935 requires publication of "executive orders." On the history of these orders, cf. Senate Special Committee on National Emergencies and Delegated Emergency Powers, *Executive Orders in Times of War and National Emergency: Report of the Special Committee on National Emergencies and Delegated Emergency Powers*, 1974; and Senate Special Committee on National Emergencies and Delegated Emergency Powers, *Summary of Executive Orders in Times of War and National Emergency: A Working Paper*, 1974.

61. Cf. *An Act to Define, Regulate, and Punish Trading with the Enemy*, 1917. The McCarran Act is the *Internal Security Act of 1950*; cf. especially title 2, sections 100 and 102.

62. This genteel Progressive commonplace is from Corwin (1947, 177), but it is, of course, reminiscent of Marx and the presuppositions that led to the appearance of the sociology of class conflict. It was perhaps the central self-observation at all levels of American society for half a century beginning in the 1870s. Note that the general point I develop here—concerning the transformation of Executive power as a function of an increasingly muddied boundary between war and society—overlaps but is not identical with claims made by Schlesinger (1974, 209). He attributes the growth of the "imperial presidency" to two major structural changes: "the decay of the parties left [the president] in command of the political scene, and the Keynesian revelation placed him in command of the economy." However, it is not just by way of macroeconomic policy that the balance of constitutional power shifted within the relationship joining economy and society with the State. In other words, the developments I describe precede the Keynesian

consensus; once that policy orientation was in place, it was the logic of the Cold War (as a focused sort of Keynesian policy?) that took command of the scene.

63. For a general description, see Brecher 1972, chapter 1. For a list of deployments, see government document cited at Relyea 1974, 32 n. 115.

64. Cf. political party platforms from 1884 and 1888 in Schlesinger 1973.

65. *An Act to Regulate Commerce* (1887) set "fair charges" for railroads on interstate runs. The Department of Labor Act (1888) established what seems to have been a short-lived agency with power to report on "controversies and disputes between employers and employees ... which may tend to interfere with the welfare of the people of the different states." In any case it gave no power to mediate. An earlier Bureau of Labor had been established in the Department of the Interior by the Bureau of Labor Act (1884); this eventually became the Bureau of Labor Statistics (after a brief period, from 1903, in the Department of Commerce and Labor) in 1913 with the establishment of the Department of Labor. The creation of powers for mediating railroad disputes is a complex overlay of this institutional development; the Erdman Act, which I discuss in the text below, established a Board of Arbitration for Interstate Commerce that was eventually replaced—by virtue of the Newlands Act of 1913—by the U.S. Board of Mediation and Conciliation; even then, this power changed several times during and after World War I (its jurisdiction was restricted in 1917 with the establishment of the Railroad Administration and the federal seizure of most railroads, and it was eventually abolished by repeal of the Newlands Act and its replacement by the Railway Labor Act (1926). Cf. "Records of the National Mediation Board" in the National Archives (http://www.archives.gov/research/guide-fed-records/groups/013.html) for a summary history of relevant legislation; more generally, cf. Stone 1991.

66. The Sherman Anti-Trust Act of 1890 declared that "every contract, combination in the form of trust or otherwise, or conspiracy, in restraint of trade or commerce among the several States, or with foreign nations, is declared to be illegal" and that "every person who shall monopolize, or attempt to monopolize, or combine or conspire with any other person or persons, to monopolize any part of the trade or commerce among the several States, or with foreign nations, shall be deemed guilty of a felony." It was infamously applied first against unions, which were cited as "combinations in restraint of trade" in 1893, but then successfully against Standard Oil in 1911 and strengthened by the Clayton Antitrust Act and the Federal Trade Commission Acts in 1914. See Thorelli 1954.

67. That the law of 1888 had failed is the conclusion drawn by Justice McKenna in his dissent in *Adair v. United States*, 208 U.S. 161, 185 (1908), who goes on to propose against the court's majority that the mediating powers of the Erdman Act of 1898, struck down here, were an appropriate remedy in the instance of "rights exercised in a quasi-public business"—as railroads had become—"and therefore subject to control in the interest of the public" (190). At issue here was whether unions and union membership could be protected by law against firing according to the unchecked "will" of the property owner.

68. The best history of this remarkable social experiment and the national proportions of its failure is in Lindsay 1942; see also the contemporary account by Carwardine (1894).

69. Governor John Altgeld, *General Order No. 7 to the Militia of Illinois*, May 25, 1894; cited in Barnard 1938, 278.

70. Governor John Altgeld's first telegraph message to President Grover Cleveland, July 5, 1894; cited in Barnard 1938, 295–98.

71. Governor John Altgeld's second telegraph message to President Grover Cleveland, July 6, 1894; cited in Barnard 1938, 304–6.

72. Altgeld, July 5 message.
73. Altgeld, July 6 message.
74. Altgeld, July 6 message.
75. *In re Debs*, 158 U.S. 582 (1895).
76. On the overlapping history of the use of military forces in domestic disorders, see U.S. Army 1997.
77. The Hepburn Act of 1906.
78. The Mann-Elkins Act of 1910.
79. Erdman Act (1898). Provisions in this act that guaranteed rights to union activity were declared unconstitutional in *Adair v. United States*.
80. Cf. *Adair v. United States*, Justice Holmes dissent: "So I turn to the general question whether the employment can be regulated at all. I confess that I think that the right to make contracts at will that has been derived from the word liberty in the amendments has been stretched to its extreme by the decisions; but they agree that sometimes the right may be restrained. Where there is, or generally is believed to be, an important ground of public policy for restraint the Constitution does not forbid it, whether this court agrees or disagrees with the policy pursued. It cannot be doubted that to prevent strikes, and, so far as possible, to foster its scheme of arbitration, might be deemed by Congress an important point of policy, and I think it impossible to say that Congress might not reasonably think that the provision in question would help a good deal to carry its policy along. But suppose the only effect really were to tend to bring about the complete unionizing of such railroad laborers as Congress can deal with, I think that object alone would justify the act. I quite agree that the question what and how much good labor unions do, is one on which intelligent people may differ,—I think that laboring men sometimes attribute to them advantages, as many attribute to combinations of capital disadvantages, that really are due to economic conditions of a far wider and deeper kind—but I could not pronounce it unwarranted if Congress should decide that to foster a strong union was for the best interest, not only of the men, but of the railroads and the country at large."
81. Department of Labor Act, 1913; citation is from section 8.
82. *Arbitration of Controversies with Railway Employees Act*, 1913; this was repealed in 1926.
83. *Fair Labor Standards Act of 1938*, section 206. It should be said that the topic of wages as a legislative issue was not new, even in 1912; e.g. *An Act to Provide for Extra Work in the Government Printing Office, in Cases of Emergency*, 1883, is loosely related to wage controls. The original minimum-wage law in Massachusetts was from the start contested then much as it is now: a Mr. Cole of the Boston Industrial Commission looking into the decreasing rate of population growth in the state found not less immigration but "a prejudice against the industrial laws" of the commonwealth and "cautioned the Minimum Wage Board against further handicapping the industrial growth of the State. . . . The State which now establishes wages by statute once had a Railway Commission with no power except to give advice. . . . Nor is it sure that [the Minimum Wage Board] benefits those whose wages it orders raised. Employment at a wage the employe [*sic*] cannot earn is precarious. An increase of wages at the cost of the loss of the job is a sacrifice, not a benefit. The employer who must pay $8 will not hire those worth less. Possibly some part of the laundry work can be done more cheaply across the State border." *New York Times*, July 17, 1915.
84. The emergency powers authorized in the Adamson Act were within a year affirmed by the Supreme Court in *Wilson v. New*, 243 U.S. 332 (1917). I will discuss both just below. Corwin (1947, 177) claims that *Wilson v. New* was "the first time that the Supreme Court

... ever took cognizance of an emergency short of war or invasion as affording ... a justification for unusual interventions by government, especially in the fields of economic and industrial relations." However, we have already seen that in the last decades of the nineteenth century the federal government had exercised with some frequency extraordinary police and militia power to determine the outcome of industrial conflict. Thus it must be said that Corwin's view of the field of "industrial relations" seems peculiarly narrow: he includes wage controls but excludes social mechanisms for determining wages, like strikes. Corwin seems not to have noticed that *In re Debs* was an early and vivid expression of the Supreme Court's view that the Executive has authority to intervene in "emergency" caused by labor disputes. What Corwin's observation does highlight is how the application of emergency power shifted from one social position to another: in 1894 it bolstered capitalists against workers; in 1917 it weakened capitalists vis-à-vis workers. The difference followed a generation in which the Progressives had further established themselves. The ambivalence of their "progress" in this respect has been noted by historians.

85. I refer to the so-called Coal Strike by the United Mine Workers in Pennsylvania in 1902. Corwin (1957, 153–54) asserts that Theodore Roosevelt was the first to do this. On the strike, cf. Grossman 1975.

86. This description, citing Theodore Roosevelt's *Autobiography*, is from Corwin 1957, 154. I note here the ambivalence of the policy strategy of "receivership" during this period.

87. *Adair v. United States. Lochner v. New York*, 198 U.S. 45 (1905), includes the magnificent dissent by Holmes, consistent with the dissent in *Adair*, pointing in the direction of labor regulation in the Adamson Act and justified in *Wilson v. New*.

88. Cf. Senate Special Committee on National Emergencies and Delegated Emergency Powers, *Summary of Executive Orders*.

89. It has often been noted that the program of "industrial democracy" produced, by virtue of its own aspirations, contradictory consequences; much of this was played out in the centrist politics of Progressives against elements further to the left. This complex picture was elaborated by "revisionist" historians of the 1960s like Gabriel Kolko (1963) and Weinstein (1968). For the context of parallel ideological justifications in the Progressive Era, cf. Lustig 1982.

90. The Adamson Act of 1916.

91. The quote is from *Wilson v. New*. We have already seen a precedent for considering railroads as not entirely private: Justice McKenna dissents in *Adair v. United States*, writing, about railroads, that "we are dealing with rights exercised in a quasi-public business and therefore subject to control in the interest of the public."

92. A recent account of that election may be found in Chace 2004; on Lawrence, see chapter 11, as well as Cahn 1980 and, more generally, Brecher 1972.

93. Characterization of 1916 as the height of Emma Goldman's popularity is from Stansell 2000, chapter 4. One gets a clear sense of the excitement of this moment from Goldman herself in *Living My Life* (1931, volume 1).

94. Ekirch 1974, 153.

95. Note, however, that a separate opinion by Chief Justice Chase and three other justices concurred in the particulars but expressed strong resistance to the broader claim made by Justice Davis that it was not in the power of Congress to authorize military tribunals in Indiana and, perhaps, in general. Thus, wrote Chase, "it may be thought to follow that Congress has no power to indemnify the officers who composed the commission against liability in civil courts for acting as members of it. We cannot agree to this. . . . We think that the power of Congress . . . to authorize trials for crimes against the security and

safety of the national forces may be derived from its constitutional authority to raise and support armies and to declare war. . . . We have no apprehension that this power, under our American system of government, in which all official authority is derived from the people and exercised under direct responsibility to the people, is more likely to be abused than the power to regulate commerce or the power to borrow money" (*Ex Parte Milligan*, 136, 137, 142, 143). Note that, by implication, the objection raises the specter of an emergency power applicable to the kinds of question involved in the Adamson Act and, one might say, the kind of question pressing so oddly on the nation today.

96.   *Wilson v. New.*

97.   *Wilson v. New.* Does this exhibit, to borrow the terms of the Vietnam-era war resistance case *Orlando v. Laird*, a willingness to enter the "political question" of the "method of congressional collaboration" once "joint action by the President and Congress" has been undertaken?

98.   It was common to compare Wilson's assumption of extraordinary power with Lincoln's; cf. Williamson 1925, chapter 4, "Essentials of American Constitutional Government," section 38, "Unity": "The concentration of war powers in the hands of President Lincoln during the Civil War was matched by the temporary dictatorship wielded by President Wilson during the World War. In both cases, the national executive became, for the period of the emergency, as powerful and as efficient as the executive of a highly centralized monarchy." Williamson taught at Smith College and was the author of manuals, civics books, and novels.

99.   The basis for this was the Federal Possession and Control Act (1916, 645), which reads: "The President, in time of war, is empowered, through the Secretary of War, to take possession and assume control of any system or systems of transportation, or any part therefore, and to utilize the same, to the exclusion as far as may be necessary of all other traffic thereon, for the transfer or transportation of troops, war material or equipment, or for such other purposes connected with the emergency as may be needful or desirable." Control over the railroads was ceded back to private ownership with the Esch-Cummins Transportation Act (1920). Cf. Williams 1972 on Wilson's hard line on domestic dissent.

100. The Federal Control of Telegraphs and Telephones Acts (1918) included a joint resolution "to authorize the President, in time of war, to supervise or take possession and assume control of any telegraph, telephone, marine cable, or radio system or systems or any part thereof and to operate the same in such manner as may be needful or desirable for the duration of the war, and to provide just compensation therefor." Control over the means of communication was ceded back in 1919.

101. The independent dynamic of emergency powers pushed forward, notwithstanding very public assertions to the contrary, such as the remarkable State of the Union address by Warren G. Harding delivered on December 6, 1921, including these lines: "I am very sure we shall have no conflict of opinion about constitutional duties or authority. During the anxieties of war, when necessity seemed compelling there were excessive grants of authority and all extraordinary concentration of powers in the Chief Executive. The repeal of wartime legislation and the automatic expirations which attended the peace proclamations have put an end to these emergency excesses but I have the wish to go further than that. I want to join you in restoring, in the most cordial way, the spirit of coordination and cooperation, and that mutuality of confidence and respect which is necessary in representative popular government."

102. *An Act to Limit the Immigration of Aliens into the United States*, 1921. This was followed by the comprehensive legislation of 1924, including the National Origins Quota of 1924.

103. It was never below 240,000 during the 1920s, and then fluctuated between 23,000 and 36,000 from 1932 to 1936; these immigration figures are based on historical statistics from 2003 *Yearbook of Immigration Statistics* of the Department of Homeland Security. That immigration has since the Reagan administration continued to be seen in terms of emergency is exhibited clearly in Senate Subcommittee on Immigration and Refugee Policy of the Committee on the Judiciary, *Immigration Emergency Powers*, an oversight hearing in 1982 to review presidential emergency powers with respect to immigration. The current rhetoric is even more hostile.

104. See e.g. statutes in the period of the Great Depression preceding the election of FDR, such as *Joint Resolution to Provide Additional Appropriations for the Department of Justice for the Fiscal Year 1930 to Cover Certain Emergencies*, 1929; *An Act to Provide Emergency Financing Facilities for Financial Institutions, to Aid in Financing Agriculture, Commerce, and Industry, and for Other Purposes*, 1932; and *Emergency Relief and Construction Act*, 1932.

105. Winsor McCay (1869–1934), famous for his early cartoons like *Dreams of a Rarebit Fiend* and *Little Nemo*, made what has been called the first animated "documentary"—*The Sinking of the Lusitania* (release date 1918)—as part of the propaganda effort of the war.

106. These two diary entries are cited at http://www.spartacus.schoolnet.co.uk/FWWarmistice.htm.

107. I leave out of consideration here the juridical sense of "total war" as war without rules that is aimed at the annihilation of the enemy. It is in this sense that Napoleon stretched "total war" across the map of the Western world; cf. Bell (2007).

108. Corwin 1947, 5.

109. Corwin 1947, 4. On the other sense of "total war," see Neely 2004.

110. The phrase was coined by Erich Ludendorff, famous German chief of staff to von Hindenburg during World War I, who published a book called *Der totale Krieg* in that year.

111. Accounts of situations where the boundaries are presented as clear seem to presuppose a narrow view of all the key terms, from *emergency* itself to *constitution* and *power*. On the one hand, this may reflect the actual situation of a time and place like ancient Rome; even so, that would not justify adoption of the same conceptual procedures for our time. On the other hand, I find implausible that basic "sociological" facts relevant to the constitution of power (which, from an ancient point of view, we may designate as "rhetorical") were categorically different; our view of clear legal boundaries in Rome derives from juristic sources whereas, concerning contemporary America, we have a vastly wider array of information about how law is embedded in social relations and culture, which is to say exactly the sort of facts that muddy the distinction between "norm" and "exception" or between the "inside" and the "outside" of the legal system.

112. I am responding here mainly to Agamben 2005, chapter 1.

113. This influential view is expressed in Schmitt 1985.

114. It seems telling that Carl Schmitt adopts the vocabulary of "either/or" and "decision" from Kierkegaard, who, in turn, did not restrict it to questions of political sovereignty; cf. Kennedy 2004, 47–48. Of course, one need only open the pages of Aristotle to find judgment at the center of political life and the theory thereof.

115. This suggests, contrary to expectation, that the general Lockean "prerogative" is as substantial as anything in Hobbes despite its not being grounded in war as it is for the latter. It counts, however, that it is also constrained in Locke's view by the possibility of resistance.

Four

1. Roosevelt 1938–50. "A year before, Justice Louis D. Brandeis had suggested that the depression constituted 'an emergency more serious than war.'" Cf. Relyea 1974, 56.
2. Act sustaining Franklin Delano Roosevelt's call for declaration of emergency, 1933.
3. On America's "cinematic culture," see a brief statement in Meyers 2002a. This idea will be presented in detail in several forthcoming works.
4. Rossiter 1948, 273. Documentation from the National Archives—under the title "208.2 General Records of the Office of War Information 1941–45"—gives the genealogy of the integration of the Office of Emergency Management into the war effort as follows: "Executive Council established by EO 6202-A, July 11, 1933, to advise on interagency problems of new governmental agencies concerned with economic recovery. National Emergency Council established by EO 6433-A, November 17, 1933, to provide logistical support to Executive Council. Industrial Emergency Committee established by EO 6770, June 30, 1934, to advise the President on problems of relief, public works, labor disputes, and industrial recovery. Executive Council and IEC consolidated into NEC by EO 6889-A, October 29, 1934. United States Information Service established in NEC, March 1934, as a central clearinghouse for information on all phases of governmental activity. NEC abolished by Reorganization Plan No. II of 1939, effective July 1, 1939, and personnel and functions (including USIS) transferred to Office of Government Reports in the Executive Office of the President. OGR made an administrative unit of the EOP by EO 8248, September 8, 1939, to prepare reports and evaluations concerning programs of federal agencies. Office of Emergency Management established in the EOP by administrative order, May 25, 1940, in accordance with EO 8248 to assist the President in clearing information on defense measures and to maintain liaison with national defense agencies. Division of Information established in OEM by Presidential letter, February 28, 1941, with functions relating to public information on the defense effort. Office of Facts and Figures established in OEM by EO 8922, October 24, 1941, to disseminate in the United States information about defense efforts and policies."
5. First War Powers Act is 55 *Stat.* 838; the Second War Powers Act is 56 *Stat.* 176.
6. Cf. Watkins 1939; Burnham 1943; Corwin 1947; Rossiter 1948; Robbins 1950; Andreski 1969; and Melman 1974.
7. Both examples cited in Fisher 2004, 75–80. The rent-control case is *Wood v. Miller*, 333 U.S. 138 (1948).
8. Roosevelt, 1941 volume, 390–91; cited in Fisher 2004, 79. Roosevelt justified this policy to the public in his radio address of September 11, 1941, reprinted in Williams 1970, 2:274.
9. Relyea 1974, 87–116 passim.
10. That four declared states of national emergency were still in effect—FDR's banking emergency, 1933; Truman on Korea, December 16, 1950; Nixon on the postal strike, March 23,1970; Nixon on trade, August 15, 1971—was the first finding and premise of hearings of the Senate Special Committee on National Emergencies and Delegated Emergency Powers in 1973. Repeating, more exhaustively, an effort made by Congress in 1947 to terminate outstanding statutory provisions triggered by emergency (which left in effect 103 such powers; Fisher 2004, 80, citing 61 *Stat.* 449 [1947]), the National Emergencies Act, signed on September 14, 1976, "generally returned all standby statutory delegations of emergency power, activated by an outstanding declaration of national emergency, to a dormant state two years after the statute's approval." Literally speaking, the 1976 law did not cancel the 1933, 1950, 1970, and 1971 national emergency

proclamations but "did render them ineffective by returning to dormancy the statutory authorities they had activated, thereby necessitating a new declaration to activate
standby statutory emergency authorities." Relyea 2001, 12. Cf. Olson and Woll 1999 for
analysis and update before the election of George W. Bush.

11. On the Greek situation in particular, see Ostwald 1969, 1986; on the persistence of the
notion of νομος as culture and as antithesis of nature in social thought, see the extraordinary survey in Kelley 1990.

12. John F. Kennedy, inaugural address, January 20, 1961. The quote is from Romans 12:12.

13. John F. Kennedy, special message to Congress, May 25, 1961. The declaration of the new
space program is preceded in this speech by a long and terrifying articulation of the
Cold War. Nonetheless, one finds in this and other speeches by JFK a sense of the essential implication of the Citizen in politics that is entirely absent from later administrations and which accounts, I think, for some of his strong appeal as a leader.

14. The emerging discussion about class was famously marked and accelerated by Harrington (1962).

15. Zarefsky 1986, 21–22, and chapter 2 generally.

16. Zarefsky 1986, 35.

17. Zarefsky 1986, 31, 36.

18. Frank Church, preface to Relyea 1974, v. Against the background of recently renewed
discussions of German legal theorist, Carl Schmitt, especially following positions set
forth by Giorgio Agamben, one may be inclined to misread this sentence as referring to
the normalization of "exceptional" powers. Perhaps Church, following Rossiter, following Schmitt, does not entirely escape this error, but an error it nevertheless is to reduce
the institutional and cultural integration of "emergency" to a logical puzzle about the
relation between "exception" and "norm." Indeed, the paradox stated as "the exception becomes the norm" simply proves that the content of the practice was in the first
instance incorrectly described as an "exception" and that its principle quality was rather
"emergency." However common it may be to conflate "exception" and "emergency," this
confuses the real issues. See above at chapter 3, pp. 112–19.

19. It has been argued that, concerning these and other matters related to the institution in the United States of government bound by constitutional law, no authors
were more widely read or more influential than Locke and Blackstone; concerning
the former, cf. Hartz 1955 as well as the enormous and ongoing dispute about his thesis; concerning the latter, cf. Boorstin 1941. Blackstone does refer to prerogative as an
"exception."

20. Blackstone writes in the *Commentaries on the Laws of England* (1765–69, book 1, chapter
7, pp. 136–37) that "there cannot be a ſtronger proof of that genuine freedom, which is
the boaſt of this age and country, than the power of diſcuſſing and examining, with decency and reſpect, the limits of the king's prerogative. A topic, that in ſome former ages
was thought too delicate and ſacred to be profaned by the pen of a ſubject, it was ranked
among the arcane imperii; and, like the myſteries of the bona dea, was not ſuffered to be
pried into by any but ſuch as were initiated in it's ſervice; becauſe perhaps the exertion
of the one, like the ſolemnities of the other, would not bear the inſpexion of rational and
ſober enquiry. The glorious queen Elizabeth herſelf made no ſcruple to direct her parlia-
ments to abſtain from diſcourſing of matters of ſtate; and it was the conſtant language
of this favorite princeſs and her miniſters, that even that auguſt aſſembly 'ought not to
deal, to judge, or to meddle, with her majeſty's prerogative royal.'"

21. A brief survey of these issues in the U.S. context can be found in Franklin 1991.

22. Blackstone 1765–69, book 1, chapter 7, p. 232.

23. All this is condensed from Locke, who writes, e.g., in the *Second Treatise of Government* (1690, chapters 13 and 14) that "prerogative being nothing but a power, in the hands of the prince, to provide for the public good, in such cases, which depending upon unforeseen and uncertain occurrences, certain and unalterable laws could not safely direct; whatsoever shall be done manifestly for the good of the people, and the establishing the government upon its true foundations, is, and always will be, just prerogative."

24. A preliminary development of this claim may be found in Meyers 1995. On the nineteenth-century emergence of this topos in American law, see Horwitz 1977.

25. While I have stressed the way we understand "prerogative" today, it should be said that a closer look at Locke and especially at Blackstone would show that both conceive of that power as reined in by major limitations that refer to the good of the people; these details are not essential here, although the spirit expressed by them will command the scene in chapter 6. Cf. Blackstone 1765–69, book 1, chapter 7, p. 244, as follows: "In the exertion therefore of those prerogatives, which the law has given him, the king is irresistible and absolute, according to the forms of the constitution. And yet, if the consequence of that exertion be manifestly to the grievance or dishonour of the kingdom, the parliament will call his advisers to a just and severe account. For prerogative consisting (as Mr Locke has well defined it) in the discretionary power of acting for the public good, where the positive laws are silent, if that discretionary power be abused to the public detriment, such prerogative is exerted in an unconstitutional manner." From this he draws the systematic conclusion: "The enormous weight of prerogative (if left to itself, as in arbitrary government it is) spreads havoc and destruction among all the inferior movements: but, when balanced and bridled (as with us) by its proper counterpoise, timely and judiciously applied, its operations are then equable and regular, it invigorates the whole machine, and enables every part to answer the end of its construction."

26. The reverse proposition continues to vex; cf. 2005 American Sociological Association presidential address by Michael Burawoy and response by Craig Calhoun, the president of the Social Science Research Council (Calhoun 2005).

27. The historical significance of this way of describing the systematic character of constitutional polity is discussed in my forthcoming book on Jean-Jacques Rousseau, *Abandoned to Ourselves* (2006).

28. George W. Bush, Rose Garden comments to press, April 18, 2006.

29. "President is not God" is from Robert Byrd, interview on the National Public Radio show *Fresh Air*, July 27, 2004. The senator's unusually perspicuous views are spelled out in Byrd 2004.

30. The function and effect of this fact can be viewed in widely different ways; I will come to that in a moment. The important point is that even captives and prisoners without enforceable rights are not subject to the "prerogative" of their captors, but rather to powers that are more systematic, are constituted within extensive divisions of action, and, at the same time, are exercises of extremely local and perverted "will."

31. Jackson, *Youngstown Sheet and Tube Co. v. Sawyer* at p. 652.

32. Jackson, *Youngstown Sheet and Tube Co. v. Sawyer* at p. 652.

33. Cf. Lobel 1989.

34. Jackson, *Youngstown Sheet and Tube Co. v. Sawyer* at p. 653. He adds: "The public may know the extent and limitations of the powers that can be asserted, and persons affected may be informed from the statute of their rights and duties."

35. Relyea 2001, 18. He adds: "Furthermore, due to greater reliance upon statutory expression, the range of this authority has come to be more circumscribed, and the options

for its use have come to be regulated procedurally through the National Emergencies Act."

36. That complicity is infrequently studied as such may be a consequence of the way it results from other mechanisms that are, from the point of view of inquiry, unrelated: e.g. issue bandwidth, risk taking, party discipline, incumbency effects, etc.

37. Executive Order no. 10,340, 1952.

38. *New York Times*, April 25, 1952, 1; press conference transcript in *Public Papers of the Presidents: 1952*, 273; both cited here from Fisher 2004, 115.

39. Fisher 2004, 115–16.

40. Justice Black, writing for the Court: "Even though 'Theater of war' be an expanding concept, we cannot with faithfulness to our constitutional system hold that the Commander in Chief of the armed forces has the ultimate power as such to take possession of private property in order to keep labor disputes from stopping production. *This is a job for the nation's lawmakers, not for its military authorities*" (*Youngstown Sheet and Tube Co. v. Sawyer*, emphasis added).

41. Cf. e.g. Shane and Bruff 1996, passim.

42. "What the Court decided was a narrow thing indeed: the steel seizure was illegal because it was inconsistent with any of the procedures which the legislature had especially prescribed for dealing with emergencies of which the steel crisis was a particular instance. Congress had foreseen the possibility that labor disputes might interrupt the production of articles necessary to the nation's survival; it had established by law three distinct modes of dealing with such disputes, each of them inconsistent with the mode the President actually followed; it had reserved to itself the cognizance of all cases requiring the application of an extraordinary remedy—particularly, seizure. In these circumstances, it was not left to the superior wisdom of the President to anticipate the extraordinary remedy by applying it without the authority of a law." This summary and concurring analysis from Wilmerding 1952, 331.

43. Jackson, *Youngstown Sheet and Tube Co. v. Sawyer* at p. 654.

44. Jackson, *Youngstown Sheet and Tube Co. v. Sawyer* at p. 654.

45. Justice Jackson's concurring opinion in *Youngstown Sheet and Tube Co. v. Sawyer*, 653–54. The social, psychological, and rhetorical dimensions of this effect have been dealt with in literature too numerous and varied to list here. I believe that Justice Jackson's observations were deeply informed by his experience as a judge in the trials of Nazi war criminals at Nuremberg.

46. This has been thought of by some—following the terminology of Sieyès that distinguishes between a *pouvoir constituant* and a *pouvoir constitué*—as a "constituent power" from which the constitution itself is founded and arises; contrary to this view, the perspective I develop here assumes that the "power of the people," at least insofar as that power is relevant to the ongoing life of constitutional democracy, is not prior to the constitution but an organic development with it; to put the matter bluntly, the convention did not *found* the Constitution, they *proposed* it, and what they proposed became that social and juridical fact that we call the Constitution over time as a matter of political development. Another important point too complicated to develop here is the asymmetrical fact that all agents who assume positions within the branches of government also position themselves as citizens, whereas few citizens occupy that same dual role to act as Legislator, Executive, or Judge.

47. The changing interpenetration of law into society may, from one point of view, be thought of as "juridification"; cf. Teubner (1987), whose approach is heavily influenced by Niklas Luhmann. Habermas (1987, 359) gives an oft-cited concise statement. For an

attempt to differentiate types of "juridification," cf. Blichner and Molander 2005. All this overlaps with but is narrower than the cultural process I have in mind here.

48. Hannah Arendt (1958) might have referred to this as the "destruction of common sense," but that view reflects an insufficiently rhetorical understanding of the nature of common sense itself.

49. On the changing sources of "critique," cf. Boltanski and Chiappello 1999.

50. Jackson, *Youngstown Sheet and Tube Co. v. Sawyer*, 653–54.

51. As against Hedges's claim (2003) that "war is the force that gives us meaning," I would insist that "war is the meaning that gives us force."

52. Kaldor (1990) suggests that the Cold War was functional in this way for both the United States and the Soviet Union. I come back to this topic below.

53. Jackson, *Youngstown Sheet and Tube Co. v. Sawyer*, 642.

54. Max Weber's famous definition of the State in his 1919 address "Politik als Beruf."

55. Cf. "On the First Principles of Government" in Hume 1742.

56. It is worth noting that none of the subjects in Milgram's famous experiments were forced to harm their supposed subjects; cf. Milgram 1963 and more generally Adorno et al. 1950.

57. This response may take different forms, including the "normal resistance" analyzed by Scott (1985, 1992) or the political practice of electoral abstention.

58. Cf. recently Tyler 1990; generally, I think a careful reading of Hume suggests the best approach to this question.

59. This common phrase was applied, e.g., to the Cold War; I shall have more to say about this in the next two chapters. Cf. Hogan 2000, 134–68; and Medhurst 1994.

60. This ancient view was famously codified and popularized by Conrad Lorenz (1966).

61. Elias 1988, 178.

62. Rosanvallon 1988, 219–20.

63. On "shock and awe" as a larger strategic plan than simply having impressive bombs, see references in Gaddis 2004, 99, 138.

64. This is the vocabulary of Kenneth Burke, who often wrote perspicuously about the cultural politics of war. A watered-down use of the idea of "framing" has been popularized recently by George Lakoff, e.g. 2002, 389ff. He borrows from Goffman (1974), who, in turn, borrows from Burke.

Five

1. Adapting terms from one of the most perspicacious modern political thinkers, Giambattista Vico, we may say that "war" is an "imaginative universal."

2. Quoted here from President George H. W. Bush, CNN interview, October 1997.

3. The term "Cold War" was first used by Bernard Baruch in 1947 (Kaldor 1990, 33). Myths about how the Cold War was supposed to have ended lurk in the words of those who have done most to continue it; consider e.g. Vice President Cheney's remarks at the state funeral of Ronald Reagan on June 9, 2004: "For decades, America had waged a Cold War, and few believed it could possibly end in our own lifetimes. The President was one of those few. And it was the vision and will of Ronald Reagan that . . . ended an evil empire. More than any other influence, the Cold War was ended by the perseverance and courage of one man who answered falsehood with truth, and overcame evil with good."

4. This point is developed by Mary Kaldor (1990) and Guy Oakes (1994).

5. Discussion about the "revolutionary" consequences of nuclear weapons began immediately after World War II—e.g. Einstein 1947; and Brodie 1946—and continued through the 1950s with such far-reaching, widely diverse, and influential interpretations as Moch 1954; Davis 1955; Anders 1956; Kissinger 1957; Teller 1958; Halle 1958; Toynbee 1958; Aron 1958; Sternberg 1959; Burns 1959; Brown 1960; Kahn 1960; and Gallois 1960. N.b. that Anders, a major figure in antinuclear politics, was Hannah Arendt's first husband and clearly a crucial source for her magnum opus of 1958, *The Human Condition*; see the way she sets up the problem in the "Prologue" and then her note to Anders's book on p. 150.

6. For early standard accounts in this perspective, cf. Williams 1972 (originally 1959); Lukacs 1966; Halle 1967; Aron 1973; and Gaddis 1972. That there were three geographically distributed Cold Wars—in Europe, Asia, and Latin America—is a point made by Chalmers Johnson (2004b). This simple point is yet another nail in the coffin of the distinction between a "closed" period of Cold War and an "open" period of "globalization," the language made popular by Thomas L. Friedman (1999).

7. First is from President Truman's address before a joint session of Congress, March 12, 1947; the second is from his inaugural address, January 20, 1949.

8. This view of serial wars, "cold" or otherwise, has been advanced by a wide range of people; cf. e.g. Grieder 2004; Podhoretz 2004; and Elnajjar 2004.

9. On the CIA's education of Osama bin Laden, cf. Coll 2004; on President Bush's foreign-policy group, cf. Mann 2004. Gates (1997) refers to himself as "the ultimate insider."

10. Following this idea to its "logical conclusion," some writers identify 1917 as the beginning of the Cold War; cf. Fontaine 1966.

11. I address briefly the transmission and transformation of the attributes of God in the "new model will" in Meyers 1995.

12. The articulation was made by Kant; the description of industrialization is from Karl Marx (1848); the cultural investments of the "new model will" include, e.g., the mythological figures of the Entrepreneur and the Genius; on the transformation of American law, cf. e.g. Horwitz 1977.

13. Summary of press release by Harry S. Truman, August 6, 1945, available online at http://www.trumanlibrary.org. The passage that I have placed in italics derives from the original draft, not from the document as released to the press. On recommendation of the British government this passage was replaced in the final version with the clause "pending further examination of possible methods of protecting us."

14. The bomb, obviously, compared with Donald Rumsfeld's plan for making the most of the "revolution in military affairs," spelled out in his "Guidance and Terms of Reference for the 2001 Quadrennial Defense Review, June 22, 2001"; this classified document has been widely discussed and was reported by Shanker (2001). The background source for this approach to military organization is Andrew W. Marshall, director of the U.S. Department of Defense's Office of Net Assessment since 1973.

15. Creation of Department of Defense compared to the creation of the Department of Homeland Security.

16. Compare 1948 and 2000. "In the American presidential election of 1948 … foreign policy played no important part." Lukacs 1966, 72. This is also true of the election of 2000.

17. Consider that in 2005, when Michael Newdow won his challenge to the constitutionality of the "pledge of allegiance" in the Ninth Circuit Court of Appeals and a kind of pandemonium ensued with statements from members of Congress and, finally, a Supreme Court ruling against him, the issue was a late-nineteenth-century relic that had gained

legal status in 1942 but into which the offending phrase "under God" had been added only in 1954 (*Joint Resolution to Amend the Pledge of Allegiance to the Flag*). Statements made at the time (cf. H.R. Rep. 83–1693, 3 [1954]) make clear the Cold War motivations. Likewise, note similarities in impulses that drove overheated debates around the issue of same-sex marriage in the election campaign of 2004 (which followed the ruling in May of that year by the Massachusetts Supreme Court that prohibition of same-sex marriage was unconstitutional; cf. *Goodridge v. Department of Public Health*, 440 Mass. 309 [Massachusetts Supreme Court, 2003]), and the central Cold War image of threat to the "sanctity" of the family; cf. discussion of the "nuclear family" in Oakes 1994, chapter 4.

18. The documentary film by Jayne Loader, Kevin Rafferty, and Pierce Rafferty, *Atomic Café* (1982), presents a good sample of some of these cultural products. Cf. Boyer 1985; Weart 1988; and Winkler 1993.

19. President Bush's diary entry for September 11, 2001, is cited in Woodward 2004, 24.

20. Cf. Schrecker 2004.

21. Cf. Woodward 1960 on "free security" and its consequences for American character and culture.

22. Byrnes, cited in Williams 1972, 253.

23. Cf. Oakes (1994), who makes at length the argument summarized in this passage.

24. Oakes 1994, 47.

25. E.g. the *Federal Civil Defense Act of 1950* and *Reorganization Plan no. 1* of 1958.

26. Cf. Oakes 1994 for a well-developed and convincing argument about the culture of "civil defense." Cf. Funkenstein 1986 for a very general and persuasive account of the early modern secularization of the three attributes of God: omnipotence, omniscience, and omnipresence.

27. Cf. e.g. Yergin 1977; and Hogan 1998.

28. N.b. that the Civil Defense Act was effectively militarized; cf. e.g. President Kennedy's executive order "Assigning Civil Defense Responsibilities to the Secretary of Defense and Others" (1961).

29. This was the Citizen's view even as the Pentagon planners spoke blithely in terms of millions killed in a series of ultimately "survivable" exchanges of nuclear weapons. This perspective ultimately had bearing on conventional warfare as well, especially as the spectacle of the battlefield in Vietnam was brought by television into living rooms across the United States.

Six

1. The military budget for FY1950 was $122 billion in 1995 dollars, whereas appropriation made in 1950 for FY1951 was $220 billion. *1995 Military Almanac* (1996). Aron (1974, 48) writes: "It was in 1950 that the United States resigned itself to the European practice of maintaining a large standing army, not merely a navy and air force." Conscription was reinstated in 1947.

2. Gaddis 2004, 10.

3. Even the civil rights movement, which appeared before us as a profound transformation around America's most intractable problem, was modulated by the Cold War. Cf. Dudziak 2000.

4. Preceding a Senate vote to authorize invasion of Iraq, the White House seems to have orchestrated a turn to nuclear imagery. Just before the first anniversary of September 11th, Condoleezza Rice responded to CNN interviewer Wolf Blitzer's questions about

evidence for "weapons of mass destruction" in Iraq by reciting an obvious set line: "We don't want the smoking gun to be a mushroom cloud" (September 8, 2002). Days before the October 11, 2002, vote by which the Senate granted broad authority to invade Iraq (77 for, 23 against), President Bush deployed the same topos: "Facing clear evidence of peril, we cannot wait for the final proof—the smoking gun—that could come in the form of a mushroom cloud." Speech in Cincinnati, Ohio, October 7, 2002.

5. Debate between presidential candidates John Kerry and George W. Bush, September 30, 2004.

6. A position expressed, e.g., by David Frum at the panel "The Future of Neo-Conservatism: Iraq, and America in the World," New Yorker Festival, October 2, 2004, broadcast on C-SPAN. It may be added that the case of people like Henry Kissinger is telling: to deny the importance of domestic politics in one's own country while determining foreign policy is itself a powerful way of taking a position within domestic politics; in the instance of Kissinger this apparently also involved violations of the law. Hitchens 2001, a suggestive but generally unconvincing book, nonetheless provides sufficient evidence to make this point.

7. As of the beginning of the cynically named "'surge'"—it was in fact a straightforward escalation—announced in January 2007, 3,086 American soldiers had been killed in Iraq. As of September 2007, since the invasion of Iraq 27,753 American military personnel had been wounded; the number of documented civilian deaths from violence in the same time period stood between 75,600 and 81,400 (from Iran war statistics, http://www.icasualties.org and http://www.iraqbodycount.org; other organizations give higher or lower figures).

8. To judge from the Pentagon budget ($500 billion for FY2006, not including the wars in Iraq and Afghanistan), "you'd think that we were still fighting the Soviet Union and that the Cold War were [sic] still raging on." Kaplan 2006.

9. *Federalist* no. 11.

10. George W. Bush, address on escalation in Iraq, January 10, 2007.

11. Cf. Castoriadis 1975; Anderson 1991; Taylor 2007, chapter 4; see also Calhoun 1999.

12. A perfect example may be seen in Charles Krauthammer's article for *Time* magazine, "Don't Cash the Peace Dividend."

13. In the same remarkable vein, see Charen 2004. N.b. that the producer of the Fox television show *24*, David Surnow, considered making with Ann Coulter a hagiographic film about Senator McCarthy.

14. The "clash of civilizations" motto first appeared in this new phase of public debate in Bernard Lewis's piece "Roots of Muslim Rage" (1990) and Samuel Huntington's "Clash of Civilizations" (1993). On the internationalization of the Cold War in the form of cultural conflict, cf. Saunders 2001.

15. Remember that the first best-selling book on "globalization"—after, of course, the *Communist Manifesto*—was Barnet and Muller 1974, not Friedman 1999.

16. On the *foreseeable* future, nothing is more enticing than David Hume's *Enquiry concerning Human Understanding* (1748, sections 4.1.20–27, 4.2.28–33).

17. The idea of social structure has, since Marx, produced a great deal of debate in social theory. The wider discursive and methodological conditions for this debate are analyzed in Meyers 1989.

18. Cf. my forthcoming book on Rousseau and the history of social theory, *Abandoned to Ourselves* (2006).

19. To be more precise, we should say that these acts *can no longer be stated in terms of intentions*. Excellent work by Mary Carruthers of New York University illustrates how,

outside the symbolic universe of the modern "will," emotions could be integrated with intention and reason into a view of action. It is worth noting, too, that in the rhetorical tradition that formed this context, *intention* is an attribute of the audience/object/reception of the act, not of the performer/subject/producer of the act. Consider Aristotle (*Rhetoric* 1418a): "And whenever you wish to arouse emotion, do not use an enthymeme, for it will either drive out the emotion or it will be useless; for simultaneous movements drive each other out, the result being their mutual destruction or weakening. Nor should you look for an enthymeme at the time when you wish to give the speech an ethical character; for demonstration involves neither moral character nor moral purpose."

20. One study of such "willing what cannot be willed" is Elster 1983, 44ff.

21. What people in groups believe and how they believe it, and the connections joining belief to emotion and action, are matters of enormous complexity and of supreme significance for political life. This problematic is what motivated the emergence of rhetoric from the life of the polis in ancient Greece and made it the quintessential civic art in Rome. In the moment of rhetoric's modern twilight—the eighteenth century—Giambattista Vico proposed his great synthetic account of public imagination, and Rousseau, unlike the English so-called contract theorists, spelled out the rhetorical constitution of social order in essentially theatrical, musical, and religious terms. With varying degrees of naïveté the topic reappeared in the supposedly "post-rhetorical" twentieth century under the enlarged question, specific to mass democracy, of how to "manufacture consent." Prominent versions include Walter Lippmann's account (1922) of the new conditions of state propaganda, Herman and Chomsky's Marxian twist (1988) on this argument, linking it to the interests of social elites, and the purportedly neutral concept of "discursive Will formation" advanced by Habermas and his followers. For the American scene, Lippmann's voice (1922, end of chapter 15) has been especially influential: "That the manufacture of consent is capable of great refinements no one, I think, denies ... and the opportunities for manipulation open to anyone who understands the process are plain enough. . . . The creation of consent is not a new art. It is a very old one which was supposed to have died out with the appearance of democracy. But it has not died out. It has, in fact, improved enormously in technic, because it is now based on analysis rather than on rule of thumb. And so, as a result of psychological research, coupled with the modern means of communication, the practice of democracy has turned a corner. A revolution is taking place, infinitely more significant than any shifting of economic power. . . . Within the life of the generation now in control of affairs, persuasion has become a self-conscious art and a regular organ of popular government. None of us begins to understand the consequences, but it is no daring prophecy to say that the knowledge of how to create consent will alter every political calculation and modify every political premise. Under the impact of propaganda, not necessarily in the sinister meaning of the word alone, the old constants of our thinking have become variables."

22. This is complicated by the special sorts of opportunism that are symbiotic with other instances of opportunism itself: think here of the spate of 9/11 related movies, especially sensationalist commercial ventures like *United 93* (Paul Greengrass) and *World Trade Center* (Oliver Stone) that parade as history. The lead actor in Stone's film, Nicholas Cage, told the New York Times, "I see it as storytelling which depicts history . . . This is what happened. Look at it. 'Yeah, I remember that.' Generation after generation goes by, they'll have 'United 93,' 'World Trade Center,' to recall that history" (quoted from Halbfinger 2006). Television shows like the Fox Network's *24* have tapped into the "war on terror" with remarkable success, a fact that has not gone unrecognized by the political opportunists who promulgated it: e.g. the Heritage Foundation hosted a symposium

on *24* "and its place in American culture," proposed by the wife of Justice Clarence Thomas (and attended by both), which brought together Michael Chertoff (secretary of homeland security), Rush Limbaugh, and the creators of the show; Chertoff alluded and Limbaugh asserted that Vice President Cheney and Secretary of Defense Donald Rumsfeld are enthusiastic fans of *24*. Everything real appears eventually in the land of shadows, and by February 2007 it had been confirmed by the U.S. Military Academy at West Point "that Brigadier General Patrick Finnegan recently travelled to California to meet producers of the show broadcast on the Fox channel" and "told them that promoting illegal behaviour in the series—apparently hugely popular among the US military—was having a damaging effect on young troops" (The Independent, February 13, 2007). At the same forum in Hollywood, "retired U.S. Army Col. Stu Herrington, who learned interrogation techniques in Vietnam and is an expert asked by the Army to consult on conditions at Guantánamo Bay, said that if Bauer worked for him, he'd be headed for a court-martial," adding that "I am distressed by the fact that the good guys are depicted as successfully employing what I consider are illegal, immoral and stupid tactics, and they're succeeding. . . . When the good guys are doing something evil and win, that bothers me" ("Group Decries Jack Bauer's Use of Torture," Associated Press, February 11, 2007).

23. Accounts of genocide in Bosnia and Rwanda make this clear in vivid detail; cf. e.g. Gourevitch 1999. See more generally on the local circumstances of violence Kalyvas 2006. I suspect that the Palestinian cause, while held together with symbolic formulations like "return," is kept alive by the desperate conditions of everyday life and daily outrages by occupying Israeli forces; it is perhaps cruel but probably true to say that if *only* the wrongs committed against one's ancestors were involved there would be substantially fewer people calling for the destruction of Israel.

24. Generally on the topic, cf. Elshtain 1987 and the "other side" in Addis, Russo, and Sebesta 1994.

25. On the rise of "presidential war" in the antebellum republic, see Schlesinger 1973, 47–77; concerning its resurgence in World War II and then the rapid growth of this phenomenon during the Korean War and the Vietnam War, see chapters 5–7 passim. Violence becomes regenerative through the regulation of fear.

26. For an account of the intricate give-and-take of American intervention in Afghanistan against the Soviet Union and the eventual results, see Coll 2004. The bitter irony of this fact is poignantly expressed in U.S. diplomat John Brady Kiesling's letter of resignation addressed to Secretary of State Colin L. Powell from his post in Athens, Greece, on February 27, 2003, just days before the invasion of Iraq. He writes: "The September 11 tragedy left us stronger than before, rallying around us a vast international coalition to cooperate for the first time in a systematic way against the threat of terrorism. But rather than take credit for those successes and build on them, this Administration has chosen to make terrorism a domestic political tool, enlisting a scattered and largely defeated Al Qaeda as its bureaucratic ally." For his reflections after the fact, see Kiesling 2006.

27. The instrumentalization of human beings by political leaders is famously summed up by Trotsky's comment that "you can't make an omelet without breaking eggs"; in the spirit of Emma Goldman—who responded directly to Trotsky—Hannah Arendt wrote an essay in 1951 under the title "The Eggs Speak Up" (in Arendt 1994).

28. Here Skowronek's distinction (1997) between presidents who "articulate" (Truman, Johnson, George H. W. Bush) and those who "reconstruct" (Eisenhower, Reagan, and George W. Bush) seems apt. For reasons I shall return to later in this chapter, I think it is important to see that in key respects the model for George W. Bush is not his father

but Ronald Reagan, and that the admiration held for him by many in his administration came from their own experience with Reagan and was transferred to Bush.

29. It seems that even supporters of the new type of army advanced by Donald Rumsfeld were caught in related internal conflicts; consider the case of General Kevin Byrnes, former commander of the U.S. Army Training and Doctrine Command and nominal signatory of the pamphlet *The Army Future Force: Decisive 21st Century Landpower* (August 2003), whose subsequent dismissal (in the summer of 2005) seems to have been engineered by neoconservatives at the Department of Defense like Stephen Cambone; Cambone himself was out by early December 2006.

30. This figure is from a talk given by Berkeley political scientist Paul Pierson at the Department of Politics, Princeton University, March 11, 2005. Cf. Hacker and Pierson 2005. This percentage stands for the total of the three Bush tax cuts up to 2006.

31. Thus the highly contested idea of "inherent" presidential power emerges in the discussion of a presumed "very delicate, plenary and exclusive power of the President as the sole organ of the Federal Government in the field of international relations—a power which does not require as a basis for its exercise an act of Congress." *United States v. Curtiss-Wright Corp.*, 319–20. Former Justice Goldberg, thought to support this idea, actually opposed it; cf. his testimony in Senate Committee on Foreign Relations, *War Powers Legislation*, 770.

32. James Madison; conclusion drawn in *Federalist* no. 48.

33. For an analogous approach, see Tulis 1987.

34. Cheney's campaign speech in Des Moines, Iowa, September 7, 2004, as reported by Milbank and Hsu 2004. Hayes (2007, 447ff.) insinuates that what Cheney said was at least ambiguous and probably distorted by the press for political reasons because it (i.e. what I quote in the text here) continued this way: "and that we'll fall back into the pre-9/11 mindset, if you will, that in fact these terrorist attacks are just criminal acts, and that we're not really at war."

35. Although see e.g. Nichols 2004.

36. See chapter 3 (note 49) above on George W. Bush's chilling attachment to "political capital."

37. This favored tactic of Karl Rove (cf. Moore and Slater 2005, chapter 1; generally see also Moore and Slater 2003 and 2006, as well as Cannon, Dubose, and Reid 2003) has been repeated in a wide variety of contexts. Another striking example appears in the political effects eventually issued from the Bush administration's novel definitions and applications of torture. The initial, widespread, but ultimately short-lived public shock produced by the outrages at Abu Ghraib led to investigations, further revelations, debates, and policy adjustments concerning torture by agents of the United States. Of particular interest here are longer-term consequences of the rhetorical stretching undertaken and then broadcast by the White House. For absent the short-sighted ideological reconfiguration of torture by President Bush's lawyers, and the public propaganda effort to support it, one would be hard-pressed to imagine that a nominee for the highest legal office in the United States who refused—blatantly, tauntingly—to renounce the use of torture would ever have passed scrutiny by the Senate. Yet Michael Mukasey was confirmed by that body on November 8, 2007. It is clear that the slip of torture into the zone of legitimate State action has been a complicated cultural process that began even before September 11th and has occurred in part by lassitude, inattention, and habit. However, the acceleration of this process is now largely a function of a pathetic failure of courage and public resistance. That fifty-three senators voted for Mukasey despite his defiance is telling; that all incumbent senators seeking the presidency (Joseph R. Biden

Jr., Hillary Clinton, Barack Obama, Christopher J. Dodd, John McCain) abstained from voting indicates a much broader and more chilling fact about the political scene. On this score, the position of John McCain—former prisoner of war, himself tortured, opponent of torture, author of the McCain amendment (to defense appropriations H.R. 2863, Public Law 109-148) limiting the use of torture in interrogation, the person who forced President Bush to declare that "this government does not torture and . . . we adhere to the international convention of torture" [*sic*] (although, characteristically, Bush again repudiated this in the signing statement)—is particularly astonishing and disgraceful. For documentation of the legal process, see Greenberg and Dratel 2005; on the rhetorical character of the legal debate, see Scheppele 2005; on Abu Ghraib, see Strasser 2004a and Hersh 2005, part 1; on the vote, see Hulse 2007b; on Bush's public concession to McCain and international law, see Knowlton 2005; the signing statement is Bush 2005.

38. Article 2, § 2.1.

39. Cf. Garry Wills's eloquent piece on this obvious but almost entirely overlooked point: "At Ease, Mr. President," *New York Times*, January 27, 2007.

40. *Federalist* no. 8.

41. Article 4, § 4.

42. U.S. Senate, *National Commitments*, 17, cited in Schlesinger 1974, 141. Cf. also Oakes 1994 concerning Acheson's general views of the American public.

43. Kennan 1972, 298, cited in Schlesinger 1974, 128. Ronald Steel (2004) points out that in fairly short order Kennan became an active opponent of the militarized policy of containment he had convincingly conceived. Whether this bears on his view of democracy is another question.

44. Taft speech from 1951 was reprinted in *Congressional Record*, May 19, 1971, S7318–S7323. The second quote is from Vandenberg 1952, 553; both are cited in Schlesinger 1974, 133. Note, too, that apparently Taft's resistance to the lowered scrutiny implied in bipartisanship was matched by an acute sense of how foreign policy produces domestic consequences; cf. Williams 1972, 237.

45. This famous line is from Justice Arthur Goldberg's opinion in *Kennedy v. Mendoza-Martinez*, 372 U.S. 144 (1963), 160. It is worth noting that Goldberg later made clear that he did not mean to sanction all independent warmaking by the president. Cf. his testimony recorded in Senate Committee on Foreign Relations, *War Powers Legislation* (770).

46. President Bush's full answer on NBC's *Today* show (interview with Matt Lauer, August 30, 2004), as reported by the Associated Press in the *New York Daily News*, was "I don't think you can win it. But I think you can create conditions so that the . . . those who use terror as a tool are less acceptable in parts of the world." For an indication of how little attention this remarkable reversal received in the press, see http://mediamatters.org/items/200409020009.

47. E.g. Democratic vice-presidential candidate John Edwards (*ABC Nightline*, August 30, 2004): "The war on terrorism is absolutely winnable"; likewise Senator Joseph Biden (D-Delaware): "To suggest that the war on terror can't be won is absolutely unacceptable." See Allen 2004.

48. Kerry's self-presentation as "war hero" in Vietnam—when in fact the most heroic thing he did was to oppose that war—should likewise be counted as an appropriation of Bush's "culture war" positions.

49. Reporters caught Kerry windsurfing off Nantucket and this was his first word when asked "Can we win the war on terrorism?" cf. "Bush Says U.S. Will Win Terror War" at CNN.Com, August 31, 2004.

50. Cf. "Bush Says U.S. Will Win Terror War." McClellan claimed that Bush "was talking about winning it in the conventional sense . . . about how this is a different kind of war and we face an unconventional enemy."

51. President Bush, remarks to the American Legion, August 31, 2004.

52. Neoconservatives have identified the tendency of power to drain away and propose to respond by embracing empire. Cf. e.g. Kristol and Kagan 1996: "The ubiquitous post–Cold War question—where is the threat?—is thus misconceived. In a world in which peace and American security depend on American power and the will to use it, the main threat the United States faces now and in the future is its own weakness. American hegemony is the only reliable defense against a breakdown of peace and international order. The appropriate goal of American foreign policy, therefore, is to preserve that hegemony as far into the future as possible. To achieve this goal, the United States needs a neo-Reaganite foreign policy of military supremacy and moral confidence." See also Kagan's follow-up piece "The Benevolent Empire" (1998).

53. Cheney's influence was noted early by, e.g., Dean (2004b) and has been further confirmed in the friendly biography by Hayes (2007). Apparently President Gerald Ford advised George W. Bush to drop Cheney from the Republican ticket prior to the election of 2004; cf. DeFrank 2007. Hayes (2007, 435ff.) insinuates on this point as on other ones that the pressure on Cheney was a concoction of the press.

54. Debate of September 30, 2004. President Bush here reasserts his administration's policy of so-called anticipatory defense. Comparable statements were constantly repeated by Donald Rumsfeld and Condoleezza Rice. The recent transformation of Iraq, which had essentially no terrorist activity before the American invasion of 2003, into a hothouse for new terrorists shows the absurdity of this idea. Reflecting on those who in 1950 (e.g. Secretary of the Navy Francis Matthews) talked of "preventive war" and the need to "pay any price," former president Harry S. Truman wrote in his *Memoirs* that "there is nothing more foolish than to think that war can be stopped by war. You don't 'prevent' anything but peace." Cited from Moore 2003.

55. Schlesinger 1974, 212–13.

56. The extreme posturing of the Bush administration may—for a variety of reasons—be counted as an extension of a long-term trend that Arthur Schlesinger, Jr. (1974) called "the imperial presidency." Schlesinger himself related the Bush administration to this thesis in Schlesinger 2003 and then pushed the argument further in Schlesinger 2004. The account I give here is different in a number of respects, in particular as pertains to the historical origins of this trend, the relation between war powers and emergency powers, the imbrication within this process of the changing nature of war, the aspects of the economy that motivate the trend (my view, labor relations; his view, Keynesian monetary policy), etc. You will have noticed that many of the general conclusions he advances, and often states with elegance, appear widely in American political discourse from the Founders forward.

57. First debate of the presidential candidates John Kerry and George W. Bush, September 30, 2004.

58. Schlesinger 1974, 168–69. He also writes that "the separation of powers was in no trouble before the Korean War." I do not agree with this claim.

59. Schlesinger (1974, 144) asserts the commonplace that "where independent power exercised in domestic affairs did not necessarily produce equivalent power in foreign affairs, . . . independent power exercised in foreign affairs was very likely to strengthen and embolden the Presidency at home." My argument in this book suggests the relationship is rather more complex and, as stated, the first side of this equation strongly overstates

the asymmetry. Cf. e.g. Williams's view (1972, 238 et passim) that the Cold War was driven by the desire for export markets and that around this fact converged a political coalition of business, industrial labor unions, and agribusiness.

60. Schlesinger 1974, 397.

61. Notwithstanding suggestive curiosities like Justin A. Frank 2004.

62. Representative Findley, recorded in the *National Gazette*, vol. 2, March 13, 1793, and cited here from Wilmerding 1952, 326. The debate at this point concerned an alleged violation of the appropriation laws by the secretary of the treasury, Alexander Hamilton. The word "financier" means financial officer, and "officer" throughout means approximately what we mean today by "officeholder."

63. *Annals of Congress* 16:570. This proposition was attributed to Broom by John Smilie.

64. Jefferson to Colvin, September 20, 1810, in Jefferson, *Works*, 11:146; cited from Wilmerding 1952, 328.

65. Jefferson to Colvin, September 20, 1810, 148–49; cited from Wilmerding 1952, 329.

66. Bailey 2007, 250–51.

67. *Annals of Congress* 16:516.

68. Wilmerding 1952, 324.

69. Wilmerding 1952, 324.

70. Representative Findley, *National Gazette*, 2:156, March 13, 1793; cited from Wilmerding 1952, 326.

71. This and preceding quotes in this paragraph from a letter of August 12, 1803, to John C. Breckinridge; see Jefferson 1904–5, 8:244, cited in Shane and Bruff 1996, 16. Jefferson did not in fact make this kind of public justification in this instance.

72. This may be why, in the words of Jeffrey K. Tulis (2007), "every American President who has faced emergency, except Jefferson, has interpreted the Constitution as containing prerogative power." Bailey 2007, 16 et passim, elaborates Jefferson's position. Generally, see also Robinson 1996 and Tushnet 2005.

73. As Bailey (2007, 25) suggests, "Jefferson attempted to empower executive administration by connecting it to public opinion." Wilmerding's excellent treatment (1952) of these issues makes two assumptions that draw a skeptical eye. He assumes that the Congress will always be in session after the Executive acts outside the law; this is a topic treated at length by Carl Schmitt and his followers. They certainly refer to a context reigned over by a pathology of undivided action. As I have already suggested, however, in my judgment Schmitt's presumption that an Executive can, in the first phase, obviate the normal state of affairs required for the second phase is not warranted in the instance of the United States. We face problems of a different kind. In addition, when Wilmerding writes (1952, 324), "Imperious circumstances may sometimes require the high officers of government to act *outside* the law; but when such action is taken, the causes of it ought to be truly imperious, and ought to be stated immediately to Congress, who is the only judge of the propriety of the measure, and not the man who has usurped its decision," it seems to me that he unnecessarily diminishes the ultimate role of the people in this process of judgment.

74. Gross and Aoláin 2006, 126. The synthetic statement quoted indicates a key feature of what I discuss here as the Jeffersonian common sense of the early American republic; Gross and Aoláin try to generalize this under the phrase "Extra-Legal Measures model of emergency power" (2006, introduced at 111) and treat this "model" in a serious and interesting way, sharply distinguishing it from other approaches, notably those guided by Carl Schmitt. While I, too, want to extrapolate from Jefferson's original context, I find myself skeptical of if friendly to the approach of Gross and Aoláin. First, it should

be noted that where I cite Gross and Aoláin the treatment of this issue (123–30) is largely a gloss on the extraordinary article by Wilmerding (1952); this, in turn, seems to be the foundation for their generalization. Now, the views collected in Wilmerding and expressed elsewhere that I am aware of tend to terms like acquit, sanction, and indemnify to name the second step in the process. Gross and Aoláin persistently assert as synonym and eventually as theoretical principle the word ratify or ratification (pivotally at 139–42 and 170). Those words are not unprecedented. I speculate that they derive in the thinking of Gross and Aoláin from a reading of Jefferson's letter to John C. Breckinridge of August 12, 1803. We have already seen that the discussion in this letter bears on the issue at hand. However, there Jefferson applies the word *ratify* in a strict and limited way to what Congress must do concerning the legislative obligations entailed by the Louisiana Purchase. Gross and Aoláin err in transferring the term to the general argument about the constitutional status of emergency powers. This is both a semantic and a logical mistake, and it has consequences for jurisprudence and ultimately for political theory. With *ratify* comes the connotation that the illegal act is made legal or at least provides a precedent for future law. Gross and Aoláin diligently recognize and discuss this, but in so doing confront a difficulty of their own making. If instead we stick with Jefferson and his contemporaries, or follow more closely the careful reading and insight of Wilmerding, we may also adhere to the clear connotation of *acquit, sanction, indemnify*, etc. Those words tell us that an individual person who has acted against the law in an emergency may also and at once have acted in a manner understandable from and appropriate to the commitments of the Citizen; he or she should therefore not be made to suffer the costs and punishments that ordinarily accompany transgression of valid law; we judge and act according to our dedication to "the city" and its constitution; nonetheless, the fact that such a person is guilty of having broken the law remains and is an accepted part of our historical self-consciousness; legislators, judges, and citizens alike are not thereby authorized to reconfigure the law; commanders, executives, and "financiers" must still weigh the consequences of their acts and shiver at the prospect of punishment before the uncertain tribunal of public opinion and its coercive agencies.

75. Jefferson to Breckinridge again, cited from Shane and Bruff 1996, 16. N.b. that at this point Jefferson is no longer referring to "ratification" of the treaty by Congress but of "approval" and "indemnity" by the nation.

76. Cf. Tulis forthcoming, where he argues convincingly that impeachment is not a juridical process but a political one that has a place in the separation and balancing of powers of the sort I suggest here, and that it should play a larger role in our political life.

77. Congressman Dan Burton and Phyllis Schlafly, both cited in Dean 2004b, 54, 93.

78. Cf. e.g. John Jay who notes in *Federalist* no. 64 that "perfect secrecy" is "sometimes requisite."

79. Wilson 1913, chapter 6. How long after the election of 1916 Wilson held to this view is another question.

80. In his review essay "The Missionary" (2003), Ronald Steel identifies these as "theological" categories; he echoes the terms and tenor of the great symbolic interactionist Kenneth Burke.

81. This development is surveyed in Moynihan 1998.

82. Schlesinger 1974, 326, and chapter 10 passim. The expression "the secrecy system" is from Schlesinger as well.

83. Cf. entries for *nation, national*, and *national security* in the *Oxford English Dictionary*.

84. Schlesinger 1974, 169.

85. Schlesinger (1974, 159) cites Rogers 1958, 1013, as the first official occurrence of the phrase. On the history of "executive privilege" see also Berger 1974; and Rozell 1994.

86. Schlesinger 1974, 157–58.

87. A good and relevant example would be the exposé on the CIA published in *Ramparts* in 1967, cited in Cox 1975, 100.

88. Cf. Dean 2004a, 2004b, passim.

89. Two quotes from Dean 2004b, 92. "Culture of secrecy" from Kevin Phillips (2004, xi). who argues convincingly (appendix B, 343–48 et passim) that this obsessive secrecy is consistent with the orientation and public behavior of the Bush family as a whole.

90. George W. Bush identified himself this way on February 8, 2004, in an interview with Tim Russert on NBC's *Meet the Press.*

91. This fact is more clearly expressed by the structure of the argument in Hannah Arendt's *Human Condition* (1958) than it is stated explicitly.

92. Cf. Justin A. Frank 2004, 82ff.

93. Cf. President Bush's closing remarks in the debate with John Kerry, September 30, 2004.

94. This use of the first person plural radiates the classical ambiguity of sovereignty described as the "private" and "public" bodies of the king; cf. Kantorowicz 1957.

95. Kaplan 2003.

96. Steel 2003, 26.

97. First quote from Kaplan 2003; second quote from National Security Council, *National Security Strategy of the United States of America,* from the preface signed by George W. Bush, 4.

98. Kaplan 2003, 21–22. Note that after supporting the invasion of Iraq, the editors of the *New Republic* reversed themselves in an editorial entitled "Obligations" in the issue of November 27, 2006. "Safe for democracy" is from Wilson's speech declaring U.S. entrance into World War I, printed in the *New York Times,* April 2, 1917.

99. This is a description of Wilson, from Ronald Steel's gloss (2003) of Brands 2003.

100. Of course, war-profiteering was rampant during the Wilson administration, a fact everywhere underlined by the Left and famously ridiculed in Marc Blitzstein's *The Cradle Will Rock* (1938).

101. Woodrow Wilson, second inaugural address, March 5, 1917.

102. To justify his veto of HR 6060 (*An Act to Regulate the Immigration of Aliens to and the Residence of Aliens in the United States*) on January 28, 1915, Wilson wrote a poignant message to the House of Representatives, asserting that "in two particulars of vital consequence this bill embodies a radical departure from the traditional and long-established policy of this country.... It seeks to all but close entirely the gates of asylum which have always been open to those who could find nowhere else the right and opportunity of constitutional agitation for what they conceived to be the natural and inalienable rights of men; and it excludes those to whom the opportunities of elementary education have been denied, without regard to their character, their purposes, or their natural capacity.... Restrictions like these, adopted earlier in our history as a Nation, would very materially have altered the course and cooled the humane ardors of our politics. The right of political asylum has brought to this country many a man of noble character and elevated purpose who was marked as an outlaw in his own less fortunate land, and who has yet become an ornament to our citizenship and to our public councils.... The literacy test and the tests and restrictions which accompany it constitute an even more radical change in the policy of the Nation ... [proposing] to turn away from tests of

character and of quality and impose tests which exclude and restrict; for the new tests here embodied are not tests of quality or of character or of personal fitness, but tests of opportunity. Those who come seeking opportunity are not to be admitted unless they have already had one of the chief of the opportunities they seek, the opportunity of education. The object of such provisions is restriction, not selection. . . . If the people of this country have made up their minds to limit the number of immigrants by arbitrary tests and so reverse the policy of all the generations of Americans that have gone before them, it is their right to do so. . . . But I do not believe that they have. I respectfully submit that no one can quote their mandate to that effect. Has any political party ever avowed a policy of restriction in this fundamental matter, gone to the country on it, and been commissioned to control its legislation? Does this bill rest upon the conscious and universal assent and desire of the American people? I doubt it. . . . I am not foolish enough to profess to know the wishes and ideals of America better than the body of her chosen representatives know them. I only want instruction direct from those whose fortunes, with ours and all men's, are involved." Excerpted here from John Woolley and Gerhard Peters, "The American Presidency Project," hosted by University of California, Santa Barbara, http://www.presidency.ucsb.edu/ws/?pid=65386.

103. Cf. Kallen 1915; and Bourne 1916.
104. Lazarus 1889; on Lazarus, cf. Schor 2006.
105. Cf. Thomas Jefferson to Thomas Mann Randolph, Jr., November 16, 1792 (Jefferson 1950, volume 24); he uses the image to praise Washington in 1796, although this is also when he fears the president is under the sway of Hamilton; see epigraph to section 4 of this chapter.
106. George W. Bush, President's Day speech at Mount Vernon, Virginia, February 19, 2007; essentially the same line may be found in dozens of other speeches by this president.
107. George W. Bush, speech in Washington, DC, September 20, 2001.
108. John F. Kennedy, speech at Massachusetts General Courthouse, January 9, 1961.
109. George Washington, "Farewell Address," drafted in 1792 and rewritten in 1796.
110. Cf. John Dean (2004b), who was Richard M. Nixon's White House counsel.
111. Goldwater nomination acceptance speech, Republican national convention, San Francisco, July 16, 1964.
112. In Charles Tilly's concise formulation, "war made the state and the state made war" in his introduction to Tilly 1975.
113. The effect of this fantasy on real families has been disastrous; cf. e.g. Hacker 2006.
114. Madison writes in *Federalist* no. 47 that "on the slightest view of the British Constitution, we must perceive that the legislative, executive, and judiciary departments are by no means totally separate and distinct from each other. The executive magistrate forms an integral part of the legislative authority. He alone has the prerogative of making treaties with foreign sovereigns, which, when made, have, under certain limitations, the force of legislative acts." Adding to this a long list of similar confluences, he concludes that "from these facts, by which Montesquieu was guided, it may clearly be inferred that, in saying 'There can be no liberty where the legislative and executive powers are united in the same person, or body of magistrates,' or, 'if the power of judging be not separated from the legislative and executive powers,' he did not mean that these departments ought to have no PARTIAL AGENCY in, or no CONTROL over, the acts of each other. His meaning, as his own words import, and still more conclusively as illustrated by the example in his eye, can amount to no more than this, that where the WHOLE power of one department is exercised by the same hands which possess the WHOLE power of another department, the fundamental principles of a free constitution are subverted."

115. Beveridge 1916–19, 2:537, cited in Corwin 1957, 18.
116. It is a commonplace to see Jefferson's presidency as a station on the path of increasing power for that office; cf. e.g. Shane and Bruff 1996, 16. That argument is made in more depth within the framework laid out by Skowronek 1997, 61–85. One may think first of his famously willful acts in this regard—such as the Louisiana Purchase—but these were, I suspect, related to the enlargement of the office through precisely the kinds of relationships of *civil society* that parties bring to the constitutional process as a whole; this must be what facilitated his principled commitment to the idea of "political indemnification." See again section 4 of this chapter, "Two Poles of Power."
117. This terminology and the corresponding assessment of Jefferson and Jackson are borrowed from Skowronek 1997.
118. Cf. discussion in Relyea 1974.
119. The rhetoric of the "new beginning" appears immediately in Reagan's first inaugural address, January 20, 1981; Skowronek (1997, 417) puts it together with these large policy themes but does not connect this to the Cold War.
120. See "The Campus Files: A Chronicle Special Report," *San Francisco Chronicle*, June 9, 2002, on the outcome of a seventeen-year-long Freedom of Information Act suit.
121. "Campus Files." Reagan's tactics ranged from "character assassination" against Clark Kerr—aided by FBI director Hoover—to the declaration of a state of emergency and the use of the National Guard to suppress student demonstrations.
122. Cited in Remnick 2006, 45.
123. Buchanan 2004 argues from the Right against this view.
124. For other strong moves early in the Bush administration, see e.g. the special report of the Center for Responsive Politics 2001.
125. On the relative size of defense budgets and tax cuts over time, *Budget of the United State Government, Fiscal Year 2007*, http://www.gpoaccess.gov/usbudget/fy07/index.html.
126. Kristol 1993, 144. It is important that Kristol repeatedly insists that anticommunism "ceased to interest" him (142, 144) and that he identified the real threat to American society as "liberalism." The effect of this is to elide the two while denying the elision, and thus to paint liberals as communists. The immediate context and consequences of Kristol's perspective are discussed in Brock 2002, chapter 3.
127. The quote is from Piven 2004, but the argument is developed in, e.g., Johnson 2004a, 2006.
128. Interview with George Akerlof, *Der Spiegel* online, August 1, 2003.
129. Piven 2004, 38; see also 11, 12, 88. This should come as no surprise, as it is consistent with more general historical facts described, e.g., in many writings by Charles Tilly. Cf. the brief statement in Tilly 1985. Piven has long argued that a "new class war" advanced during the Reagan administration; see Piven and Cloward 1982.
130. Piven 2004, 39; cf. Skowronek 1997, 427.
131. Piven 2004, 40.
132. Skowronek 1997, 429.
133. Debate between Ronald Reagan and John Anderson, September 21, 1980.
134. The phrase first appeared in public in a book by Reagan's director of the Office of Management and Budget, David A. Stockman (1986).
135. This mantra of neoconservatism was said by Vice President Dick Cheney to Secretary of the Treasury Paul O'Neill, as reported in Suskind 2004, 291.
136. I refer here not only to economistic and rational-choice theories of power but also to "will"-oriented instrumentalist conceptions of power, from Max Weber to Bertrand Russell to Steven Lukes; see Meyers 1989.

137. Hacker 2006.
138. Colas 1997, 6.
139. Colas 1997, 5, 6.
140. Colas 1997, 6.
141. Robert Byrd, interview with Terri Gross, *Fresh Air*, August 2004. Cf. Byrd 2004.
142. Which is to say, too, into a world where lies don't count. On the centrality of lies to the Bush administration, see Corn 2003.
143. This capacity to connect with the particular circumstances at hand is the absolute center of rhetoric; cf. Aristotle *Rhetoric* (1355b 25–26), where he writes, "Let rhetoric then be a capacity [δύναμις] of discovering [θεωρῆσαι] in each case the available means of persuasion."
144. Cheney's influence over the decision-making process leading to the invasion of Iraq and the suppression of dissenting views in the intelligence community has been widely documented; see e.g. Suskind 2004, chapter 2; and Isikoff and Corn 2006.
145. All quotes from the presidential candidates' debate of September 30, 2004, except the third one, which is from the debate of October 6, 2004. By 2008, the same line of attack was being directed against Barack Obama.
146. This line is from the presidential candidates' debate of October 6, 2004; President Bush made almost identical statements three times in the debate on September 30, 2004.
147. Cf. "Bush Enters Mideast's Rhetorical Minefield," Reuters, September 22, 2001.
148. Cf. D'Souza (2007, especially chapter 7) for a breathless and perverse inversion of this idea, in which "Muslims" are presumed to be correct in seeing the supposed attack on religion ("traditional morality") by "secularists" of the "West" as a "crusade."
149. Cf. e.g. Aron 1973, chapter 2.
150. Bennett 2002, 168–69.
151. Bennett 2002, 133, 155.
152. It may be that what I am calling secular evangelism never really escapes its religious paradigm. This is suggested in another neat turn of phrase from Garry Wills: "the odd euphoria of war resembles the jubilant confession of sinfulness at the Great Awakening. We are afraid and exhilarated. The multiple items of population are drawn together into a People, God's People." Wills 2003, 29.
153. Although consider Immanuel Wallerstein's argument (2004) about how easily the value of and possibility for multilateralism can be overstated when viewed within the structure of the world system.
154. In his remarks at the 43rd Munich Conference on Security Policy, delivered February 10, 2007 (translation transcript from *Washington Post*, February 12, 2007), the Russian president said that the effect of "unilateral and frequently illegitimate actions" today is "an almost un-contained hyper use of force—military force—in international relations" with the result that "finding a political settlement also becomes impossible," and that this has brought "greater and greater disdain for the basic principles of international law." "One state," he added, "... the United States, has overstepped its national borders in every way," a fact that "is visible in the economic, political, cultural and educational policies it imposes on other nations."
155. Recent documentation concerning the latter may be found in Hedges 2006.
156. Dick Cheney, as reported in Nessen 1978, 230; cited in Dean 2004b, 45.
157. As per the epigraph to this chapter. This quote is borrowed from *Le Trésor de la Langue Française Informatisé*, which mistakenly refers to *tome* 2, p. 427.
158. An effect incomparably described by Vaclav Havel (1985).

159. I mean this in a sense significantly different from the recent book by Chris Hedges with the title *War Is a Force That Gives Us Meaning*.

160. Fox News broadcast, March 5, 2007.

161. In June 2007 the vice president, who had previously claimed "executive privilege" so as to protect his dealings with energy corporations from public scrutiny, sought to escape oversight related to security matters by arguing that, as president of the Senate, "he's not part of the executive branch, so he doesn't have to comply" (Representative Henry A. Waxman interviewed in Shane 2007). Representative Rahm Emanuel responded to this provocation by sponsoring an amendment to, as he put it, "no longer fund the executive branch of his office, and he can live off the funding for the Senate presidency" ("National Briefing Washington," *New York Times*, June 27, 2007). While Cheney's assertion that he was of neither branch of government did not take hold (Rutenberg 2007) it was integrally linked to extraordinarily far-reaching effects in another area. Less than one week after the invasion of Iraq an executive order (March 25, 2003) had given the vice president's office greater leeway in the classification of documents (Executive Order amending Clinton's public access EO 12,958 of 1995 at http://www.whitehouse.gov/news/releases/2003/03/20030325-11.html). This had provided a basis from which the vice president could impede efforts to verify the justifications provided to Congress and the people for the war. It was under this cover that now convicted perjurer and then vice-presidential chief of staff I. Lewis Libby—we cannot say "perversely" because we do not know the original intention of this adjustment to the rules—leaked information with the aim of discrediting arguments against the war that were based on the suspicion that false claims had been made by Cheney and the president. The link between these two sordid affairs was sorted out by Frank Rich (in Rich 2007), but beyond that rare piece of investigative journalism Cheney's "screen play" met no serious reaction, as if it were just an everyday occurrence, "more of the same." This was hardly coincidental. Cheney's persistent efforts to escape not just accountability but all forms of scrutiny have been widely documented; cf. for example the fact sheet issued in June 2007 by Representative Henry A. Waxman, Chairman of the Committee on Oversight and Government Reform, entitled "The Vice President's Efforts to Avoid Oversight and Accountability." Libby, who took the fall, had his sentence commuted by the president two days after his conviction. It is worth noting here that the last convictions comparable to Libby's were a result of the Iran-Contra affair, during which the soon-to-be-fired and convicted Oliver North was praised by then Representative Dick Cheney; cf. Wilentz 2007.

Works Cited

The topic of this book is the transformation of everyday civic life. Thus a moderately curious person who had read just one newspaper five days per week since September 11, 2001, could refer to more than 2,000 individual items. The researcher who has followed events, examined their context, and sought to frame them in relation to larger history has necessarily cast his eyes on many times that number. The following information is therefore and by necessity limited to documents and works directly cited in this book, showing more of the ebb and flow of the argument than its entire background.

In my way of thinking different sources often carry different types of meaning. To reflect this I have divided the materials into several sections. The first section contains documents produced by actors in the course of action, which is to say public speeches, statements, declarations, letters, and interviews; these are listed according to the author's name, although debates between equals are listed under the word "debate." The second and third sections contain visual, audio, and Internet materials, which, it seems to me, differ more from printed matter than among themselves; these are listed alphabetically by title and, for Web sites (section 2) I found myself consulting regularly, by description. The fourth section lists in chronological order all laws cited in this book. Judicial rulings are cited in the fifth section alphabetically by the name of the petitioner. Government documents are cited according to the issuing agency in section 6. All this is followed by the familiar alphabetical list of print materials.

Public Speeches, Statements, Declarations, Letters, and Interviews

Akerlof, George. 2003. Interview in *Der Spiegel* online, August 1.

Altgeld, John. 1894. General order no. 7 to the militia of Illinois, May 25.

Ashcroft, John. 2002. Letter to President George W. Bush, February 1. http://news.findlaw.com/wp/docs/torture/jash201021tr.html.

bin Laden, Osama. 1996. Fatwa entitled "Declaration of war against the Americans occupying the land of the two holy places." First published in *Al Quds Al Arabi* (London), August.

———. 2001. Public message, October 7. Broadcast by Al-Jazeera.

———. 2001. Public message, November 3. Broadcast by Al-Jazeera.

———. 2001. Public message, December 13. Released by the U.S. Department of Defense.

———. 2002. Interview recorded around October 2001. Released by CNN, January.

Brzezinski, Zbigniew. 1998. Interview in *Le Nouvel Observateur*, January 15–21.

Burawoy, Michael. 2005. Presidential address, Annual Meeting of The American Sociological Association.

Bush, George H. W. 1997. Interview on *Larry King Live*, CNN, October 5.

Bush, George W. 1999. Interview with David Horowitz in *Salon*, May 6.

———. 2001. Statement by the president in his address to the nation from the White House, September 11.

———. 2001. National day of prayer and remembrance. Presidential Proclamation 7462, September 14.

———. 2001. Remarks by the president to police, firemen, and rescue workers, New York City, September 14.

———. 2001. Address at the national day of prayer and remembrance, National Cathedral, Washington, DC, September 14.

———. 2001. Radio address to the nation, the White House, September 15.

———. 2001. Remarks by the president to employees at the Pentagon, September 17.

———. 2001. Address to a joint session of Congress and the American people, U.S. Capitol, September 20.

———. 2002. Remarks by the president on Iraq, Cincinnati, OH, October 7.

———. 2003. Speech aboard the USS *Abraham Lincoln*, May 1.

———. 2004. Interview in the Oval Office with Tim Russert, *Meet the Press*, NBC, February 7.

———. 2004. Interview with Matt Lauer, *Today*, MSNBC, August 30.

———. 2004. Remarks to the American Legion, Nashville, TN, August 31.

———. 2005. President's statement on signing of HR 2863, December 30.

———. 2006. Comments to the press in the Rose Garden, April 18.

———. 2007. Address escalating the war in Iraq, White House Library, January 10.

———. 2007. Interview with Scott Pelley on *60 Minutes*, CBS, January 12.

———. 2007. President's Day speech, Mount Vernon, VA, February 19.

Byrd, Robert. 2004. Interview with Terri Gross on *Fresh Air*, National Public Radio, July 27.

Cheney, Dick. 2004. Remarks at the state funeral of Ronald Reagan, June 9.

———. 2004. Campaign speech in Des Moines, IA, September 7.

Cleland, Max. 2004. Interview with Amy Goodman, *Democracy Now!* March 23.

Cohen, William S. 2004. Prepared statement to the National Commission on Terrorist Attacks upon the United States, March 23.

Debate of presidential candidates Ronald Reagan and John Anderson, September 21, 1980.

Debate of presidential candidates John Kerry and George W. Bush, September 30, 2004.

Debate of presidential candidates John Kerry and George W. Bush, October 6, 2004.

Edwards, John. 2004. Interview on *Nightline*, ABC, August 30.

Frum, David. 2004. Comments at the panel "The Future of Neo-Conservatism: Iraq, and America in the World," New Yorker Festival, October 2. Broadcast by C-SPAN.

Gates, Robert. 2007. Response to Vladimir Putin at the Munich Conference on Security Policy, February 10.

Goldwater, Barry. 1964. Nomination acceptance speech, Republican national convention, San Francisco, July 16.

———. 1971. Testimony before the Senate Committee on Foreign Relations, April 23.

———. 1981. Comments concerning Ronald Reagan recorded in the *Congressional Record*, September 16.

Harding, Warren G. 1921. State of the Union address, December 6.

Johnson, Lyndon B. 1964. State of the Union address, January 8.

———. 1965. State of the Union address, January 4.

———. 1965. First major statement of Vietnam policy, April 7.

Kennedy, John F. 1961. Speech at Massachusetts General Courthouse, January 9.

———. 1961. Inaugural address, January 20.

———. 1961. Special message to Congress, May 25.

Kiesling, John Brady. 2003. Letter of resignation addressed to Secretary of State Colin L. Powell from his post at the U. S. Embassy in Athens, Greece, on February 27.

McCain, John. 2007. Speech at Hilton Head Island, SC, February 19.

Monroe, James. 1817. First inaugural address.

Murray, Patty. 2006. Press release from Senator Murray's office, December 6.

Petraeus, David H. 2007. Testimony before congressional hearings, September 11.

Powell, Colin L. 2003. Speech to the Security Council of the United Nations, February 5.

Project for the New American Century. 1998. Open letter to President Clinton, January 26. http://www.newamericancentury.org/iraqclintonletter.htm.

Putin, Vladimir. 2007. Remarks at the 43rd Munich Conference on Security Policy, February 10. Translated by *Washington Post*, February 12, 2007.

Reagan, Ronald W. 1981. Inaugural address, January 20.

———. 1983. "Strategic Defense Initiative" speech, the White House, March 23.

———. 1989. Farewell address, the White House, January 11.

Roosevelt, Franklin Delano. 1941. U.S. will shoot at sea, radio address, September 11.

Rove, Karl. 2007. Public remarks on his resignation, the White House, August 13.

Rumsfeld, Donald H. 2001. Prepared testimony to the Senate Armed Services Committee, U.S. Senate, Capitol Hill, Washington, DC. Prepared statement accompanying the classified document "Guidance and terms of reference for the 2001 quadrennial defense review, June 22, 2001." U.S. Department of Defense, http://www.defenselink.mil/speeches/2001/s20010621-secdef.html.

——. 2006. Address to 42nd Munich Conference on Security Policy, February 4.

Taft, Robert. 1951. Speech in Congress, reprinted in *Congressional Record*, S7318–S7323, May 19, 1971.

Tenet, George. 2002. Written statement for the record of the director of central intelligence before the Joint Inquiry Committee, October 17. http://www.cia.gov/cia/public_affairs/speeches/2004/tenet_testimony_03242004.html.

Truman, Harry S. 1945. Hiroshima press release, August 6.

——. 1947. Address before a joint session of Congress, March 12.

——. 1949. Inaugural address, January 20.

Washington, George. 1796. Farewell Address, originally drafted in 1792, rewritten in 1796.

Wilson, Woodrow. 1915. Letter justifying his veto to the House of Representatives, January 28.

——. 1917. Second inaugural address, March 5.

——. 1917. Declaration of U.S. entry into World War I, *New York Times*, April 2.

Web Sites

Call-in discussion programs, http://www.cspan.org.

Demographic statistics, http://www.census.gov.

Iraq war statistics, http://www.icasualties.org.

Iraq war statistics, http://www.iraqbodycount.org.

Legal documents, http://memory.loc.gov/ammem/amlaw/lwsl.html.

Legislative information, http://thomas.loc.gov.

Presidency of George W. Bush, http://www.whitehouse.gov.

President Truman papers, http://www.trumanlibrary.org.

Public opinon polling data, http://www.presidency.ucsb.edu.

September 11 chronology, http://archives.cnn.com/2001/US/09/11/chronology.attack.

Statute law database, http://heinonline.org/HOL/Index?collection=statute.

The United States Code online, http://uscode.house.gov.

World War I documents, http://www.nationarchives.gov.uk.

World War II documents, http://www.archives.gov.

Other Nonprint Media

Atomic Café. Documentary film by Jayne Loader, Kevin Rafferty, and Pierce Rafferty, released 1982. Archives Project.

"Courtesy of the Red, White, and Blue (The Angry American)." Song by Toby Keith, released on the CD *Unleashed*, 2002. Dreamworks.

Dreams of a Rarebit Fiend. Animated film by Winsor McCay, released 1921, on "Winsor McCay: The master edition," DVD produced by Anke Mebold, released 2004. La Cinémathéque Québecoise and Milestone Film and Video.

In Memoriam: New York City 9/11/2001. Documentary film produced by John Hoffman, originally broadcast on HBO, May 26, 2002. HBO Documentary Films, Brad Grey Pictures.

9/11. Documentary film by Gédéon and Jules Naudet, released 2002. Goldfish Productions.

9/11: The Falling Man. Documentary film by Henry Singer, released 2006. Darlow Smithson Productions.

N Word. Musical dialogue between Cornel West and Michael Eric Dyson, released on *Never Forget: A Journey of Revelations*, 2007. Hidden Beach Productions.

Pearl Harbor. Motion picture directed by Michael Bay, released 2001. Touchstone Pictures.

Saving Private Ryan. Motion picture directed by Steven Spielberg, released 1998. Dreamworks.

The Sinking of the Lusitania. Animated film by Winsor McCay, released 1918, on "Winsor McCay: The master edition," DVD produced by Anke Mebold, released 2004. La Cinémathéque Québecoise and Milestone Film and Video.

24. Television series created by Joel Surnow and David Cochran, 2001–7. FOX TV.

United 93. Motion picture directed by Paul Greengrass, released 2006. Universal Pictures.

The War. Documentary film directed by Ken Burns, released 2007. Public Broadcasting Service.

We Were Soldiers. Motion picture directed by Randall Wallace, released 2002. Paramount Pictures.

Whatever It Takes. Television ad for Bush-Cheney campaign, 2004.

Where Is the Honor? Audio tape recording of Abu Musab al-Zarqawi, broadcast on September 11, 2004.

World Trade Center. Motion picture directed by Oliver Stone, released 2006. Paramount Pictures.

Laws

1798 Alien and Sedition Act. *An Act to Establish an Uniform Rule of Naturalization.* 5th Cong., 2nd sess., chap. 54 (June 18).

1798 Alien and Sedition Act. *An Act concerning Aliens.* 5th Cong., 2nd sess., chap. 58 (June 25).

1798 Alien and Sedition Act. *An Act respecting Alien Enemies.* 5th Cong., 2nd sess., chap. 66 (July 6). Still in effect as 50 *U.S. Code,* sections 21–24.

1798 Alien and Sedition Act. *An Act for the Punishment of Certain Crimes against the United States.* 5th Cong., 2nd sess., chap. 74 (July 14).

1863 *An Act relating to Habeas Corpus, and Regulating Judicial Proceedings in Certain Cases.* 37th Cong., 3rd sess., chap. 81 (March 3).

1869 *An Act Amendatory to* [the habeas corpus act of 1863]. 40th Cong., 3rd sess., chap. 13 (January 22).

1871 *An Act to Enforce the Provisions of the Fourteenth Amendment.* 42nd Cong., 1st sess., chap. 22; 17 *Stat.* 13 (April 20).

1883 *An Act to Provide for Extra Work in the Government Printing Office, in Cases of Emergency.* 47th Cong., 2nd sess., chap. 23; 22 *Stat.* 402 (January 13).

1884 *Bureau of Labor Act.* 48th Cong., 1st sess., 23 *Stat.* 60 (June 27).

1887 Interstate Commerce Act. *An Act to Regulate Commerce.* 49th Cong., 2nd sess., chap. 104; 24 *Stat.* 379 (February 4).

1888 *Department of Labor Act.* 50th Cong., 1st sess., chap. 389; 25 *Stat.* 182 (June 13).

1890 *Sherman Anti-Trust Act.* 51st Cong., 1st sess., chap. 647; 26 *Stat.* 209 (July 2).

1898 Erdman Act. *An Act concerning Carriers Engaged in Interstate Commerce and Their Employees.* 55th Cong., 2nd sess., chap. 370; 30 *Stat.* 424 (June 1).

1906 *Hepburn Act.* 59th Cong., 1st sess., chap. 3591; 34 *Stat.* 584 (June 29).

1910 *Mann-Elkins Act.* 61st Cong., 2nd sess., chap. 309; 36 *Stat.* 539 (June 18).

1913 Department of Labor Act of 1913. *An Act to Create a Department of Labor.* Public Law 62-426; 62nd Cong., 3rd sess., chap. 141; 37 *Stat.* 736 (March 4).

1913 Newlands Act. *An Act Providing for Mediation, Conciliation, and Arbitration in Controversies between Certain Employers and Their Employees.* Public Law 63-6; 63rd Cong., 1st sess., chap. 6; 38 *Stat.* 103 (July 15). Repealed in 1926.

1914 Federal Trade Commission Act. 63rd Cong., 2nd sess.; 38 *Stat.* 717 (September 26).

1914 *Clayton Antitrust Act.* 63rd Cong., 2nd sess., chap. 323; 38 *Stat.* 730 (October 15).

1916 *Adamson Act.* 64th Cong., 1st sess., 39 *Stat.* 721 (September 3).

1916 *Federal Possession and Control Act.* Public Law 64-242; 64th Cong., 1st sess., chap. 418; 39 *Stat.* 619 (August 29).

1917 Immigration Act. *An Act to Regulate the Immigration of Aliens to and the Residence of Aliens in the United States.* HR 10384; 64th Cong., 2nd sess., chap. 29 (February 5).

1917 Trading with the Enemy Act. *An Act to Define, Regulate, and Punish Trading with the Enemy.* 65th Cong., 1st sess., chap. 106; 40 *Stat.* 411; 12 *U.S.Code*, section 95a (October 6). Includes the Espionage Act of June 15.

1918 *Sedition Act of 1918, Amending the Espionage Act of 1917.* 65th Cong., 2nd sess., chap. 75 (May 16).

1918 *Federal Control of Telegraphs and Telephones Act.* Pub. Res. 65, 38; 65th Cong., 2nd sess., chap. 154; 40 *Stat.* 904 (July 16).

1920 *Esch-Cummins Railroad Transportation Act.* Public Law 66-152; 66th Cong., 3rd sess.; 41 *Stat.* 456.

1921 Emergency Quota Act. *An Act to Limit the Immigration of Aliens into the United States.* 67th Cong., 1st sess., chap. 8; 42 *Stat.* 5 (May 19).

1924 National Origins Quota. *Immigration Act of 1924.* Public Law 68-139; 68th Cong., 1st sess. (May 26).

1926 *Railway Labor Act.* 69th Cong., 1st sess.; 44 *Stat.* 577 (May 20).

1929 *Joint Resolution to Provide Additional Appropriations for the Department of Justice for the Fiscal Year 1930 to Cover Certain Emergencies.* 71 Pub. Res. 28; 71st Cong., 2nd sess., chap. 10; 46 *Stat.* 52 (December 20).

1932 *An Act to Provide Emergency Financing Facilities for Financial Institutions, to Aid in Financing Agriculture, Commerce, and Industry, and for Other Purposes.* 72nd Cong., 1st sess., chap. 8; 47 *Stat.* 5 (January 22).

1932 Emergency Relief and Construction Act. *An Act to Relieve Destitution, to Broaden the Lending Powers of the Reconstruction Finance Corporation, and to Create Employment by Providing for and Expediting a Public-Works Program.* Public Law 72-302; 72nd Cong., 1st sess., chap. 520; 47 *Stat.* 709 (July 21).

1933 *An Act to Provide Relief in the Existing National Emergency in Banking . . .* [sustaining FDR's call for declaration of emergency]. HR 1491; Public Law 1, 73rd Cong., 1st sess. (March 9).

1938 *Fair Labor Standards Act.* Codified as 29 *U.S.Code* 8, sec. 206 (June 25).

1941 *First War Powers Act.* 55 *Stat.* 838 (December 18).

1942 *Second War Powers Act.* 56 *Stat.* 176 (June 5).

1947 *National Security Act.* Public Law 235; 80 Cong., 1st sess.; 61 *Stat.* 496 (July 26).

1950 *Internal Security Act of 1950 (McCarran Act).* 81st Cong., 2nd sess., chap. 1024 (September 23).

1950 *Federal Civil Defense Act of 1950.* 81st Cong., 2nd sess., chap. 1228; 64 *Stat.* 1245 (January 12, 1951).

1952 Executive Order no. 10,340. Directing the Secretary of Commerce to take possession of and operate the plants and facilities of certain steel companies. *Federal Register* 17, no. 71 (April 8; published April 10).

1954 *Joint Resolution to Amend the Pledge of Allegiance to the Flag of the United States of America.* Public Law 396, 83rd Cong., 2nd sess., chap. 297; 68 *Stat.* 249 (June 14).

1958 *Reorganization Plan No. 1.* 72 *Stat.* 1799–1801 (April 24; effective July 1).

1961 Executive Order no. 10,952. Assigning civil defense responsibilities to the Secretary of Defense and others. *Federal Register* 26, no. 140:6577 (July 20; published July 22).

1964 *Tonkin Gulf Resolution.* H.J. Res. 1145, Public Law 88-408; 88th Cong., 2nd sess. (August 7).

1971 *An Act to Amend the Foreign Military Sales Act, and for Other Purposes (Repeal of Tonkin Gulf Resolution).* Public Law 91-672; 91st Cong., 2nd sess.; 84 *Stat.* 2055, sec. 12 (January 12).

1973 *War Powers Resolution.* H.J. Res. 542, Public Law 93-148; 93rd Cong., 1st sess., (November 7).

1976 *National Emergencies Act.* Public Law 94-412; codified at 50 *U.S. Code* 34, 1601–51 (September 14).

2001 *Joint Resolution to Authorize the Use of United States Armed Forces against Those Responsible for the Recent Attacks Launched against the United States.* S.J. Res. 23, Public Law 107-40; 107th Cong., 1st sess.; 115 *Stat.* 224 (September 18).

2001 *Uniting and Strengthening America by Providing Appropriate Tools Required to Intercept and Obstruct Terrorism (USA PATRIOT ACT).* HR 3162, Public Law 107-56; 107th Cong., 1st sess.; 115 *Stat.* 272 (October 26).

2002 *Joint Resolution to Authorize the Use of United States Armed Forces against Iraq.* Public Law 107-243; 107th Cong., 2nd sess.; 116 *Stat.* 1498 (October 16).

2003 Executive Order no. 13,292. Amending Clinton's public access Executive Order no. 12,958 of 1995 to give the vice president's office greater leeway in classification. *Federal Register* 68, no. 60:15313–34 (March 25; published Mary 28).

2006 *Department of State Authorities Act.* HR 6060, Public Law 109-472; 109th Cong., 2nd sess. (September 19).

Court Decisions

Adair v. United States, 208 U.S. 161 (1908).

Baker v. Carr, 369 U.S. 186 (1962).

Buckley v. Valeo, 424 U.S. 1 (1976).

Bush v. Gore, 531 U.S. 98 (2000).

Campen v. Nixon, 56 F.R.D. 404 (N.D. Cal. 1972).

Commonwealth of Massachusetts v. Laird, 451 F. 2nd 26 (1st Cir. 1971).

DaCosta v. Laird, 405 U.S. 979 (1972).

Davi v. Laird, 318 F. Supp. 478 (W.D. Va. 1970).

Ex Parte Milligan, 71 U.S. 2 (1866).

Goldwater v. Carter, 444 U.S. 996 (1979).

Goodridge v. Department of Public Health, 440 Mass. 309 (Massachusetts Supreme Court, 2003).

In re Debs, 158 U.S. 564 (1895).

Jacobellis v. Ohio, 378 U.S. 184 (1964).

Kennedy v. Mendoza-Martinez, 372 U.S. 144 (1963).

Lochner v. New York, 198 U.S. 45 (1905).

Luftig v. McNamara, 373 F. 2nd 333 (1966).

Luther v. Borden, 48 U.S. 1 (1849).

MacArthur v. Clifford, 393 U.S. 1002 (1968).

Massachusetts v. Laird, 400 U.S. 886 (1970).

Mora v. McNamara, 389 U.S. 934 (1967).

Orlando v. Laird, 443 F. 2nd 1042 (1971).

Pietsch v. President of the United States, 434 F. 2nd 861 (2nd Cir. 1970).

Powell v. McCormack, 395 U.S. 486 (1969).

United States v. Curtiss-Wright Corp., 299 U.S. 304 (1936).

United States v. Holmes, 387 F. 2nd 781 (7th Cir.); cert. denied, 391 U.S. 936 (1968).

United States v. Shreveport Grain and Elevator Co., 287 U.S. 77 (1932).

United States v. Sisson, 294 F. Supp. 515 (1968).

Velvel v. Johnson, 287 F. Supp. 846 (D.D.C. 1968); affirmed 415 F. 2nd 236 (10th Cir. 1969); cert. denied, 396 U.S. 1042 (1970).

Velvel v. Nixon, 415 F. 2nd 236 (Cal. 10, 1970).

Wayman v. Southard, 10 Wheat. (23 U.S. 1) (1825).

Wilson v. New, 243 U.S. 332 (1917).

Wood v. Miller, 333 U.S. 138 (1948).

Youngstown Sheet and Tube Co. v. Sawyer, 343 U.S. 579 (1952).

Government Documents

Budget of the United States Government, fiscal year 2007. Government Printing Office, http://www.gpoaccess.gov/usbudget.

General Services Administration. Federal Register Division. National Archives and Records Service. *Public papers of the presidents of the United States: 1952*. Washington, DC: Government Printing Office.

General Services Admistration. Office of the Federal Register. National Archives and Records Service. *Codification of presidential proclamations and executive orders*. Washington, DC: U.S. Government Printing Office, 1989.

National Archives. Records of the Office of War Information. http://archives.gov/research/guide-fed-records/groups/208.html.

National Commission on Terrorist Attacks upon the United States. *The 9/11 Commission report: Final report of the National Commission on Terrorist Attacks upon the United States*. Authorized ed. New York: Norton, 2004.

———. Transcripts of public hearings. http://govinfo.library.unt.edu/911/archive.

National Security Council. *National security strategy of the United States of America (September, 2002)*. With a preface signed by George W. Bush. Washington, DC: National Security Council, 2002.

1995 Military Almanac. Washington, DC: Center for Defense Information, 1996.

Presidential Daily Briefing, August 6, 2001, entitled "Bin Laden determined to strike in US." Declassified April 10, 2004. http://news.find-law.com/hdocs/docs/terrorism/80601pdb2.html.

U.S. Army. *The army future force: Decisive 21st century landpower*. Pamphlet authorized by Kevin Byrnes. August 2003.

———. *The role of federal military forces in domestic disorders, 1877–1945*. By Clayton D. Laurie and Ronald H. Cole. Army Historical Series. Washington, DC: Center of Military History, 1997.

———. *United States Army Field Manual FM 100-5*. June 1993.

U.S. Congress. *Annals of Congress: The debates and proceedings in the Congress of the United States . . . compiled from authentic materials* [by Joseph Gales]. 42 vols. Washington, DC: Gales and Seaton, 1834–56.

———. Biographical directory of the United States Congress. http://bioguide.congress.gov.

———. *United States statutes at large*. Washington, DC: Government Printing Office. 1845–.

U.S. Department of Defense. *Base structure report*. 2003. http://www.defenselink.mil/news/Jun2003/basestructure2003.pdf.

U.S. House. Committee on Government Operations. *Executive orders and proclamations: A study of a use of presidential powers*. Washington, DC: U.S. Government Printing Office, 1957.

———. *The vice president's efforts to avoid oversight and accountability*. Fact sheet written for House Committee on Oversight and Government Reform, from the office of Henry A. Waxman. June 2007.

U.S. Marine Corps. *United States Marine Corps Manual FMFM-1*. 1989.

———. *Warfighting: United States Marine Corps Manual MCDP 1*. 1997. First ed. 1989.

U.S. Office of Independent Counsel. *Final report of the independent counsel for Iran/Contra matters, Lawrence E. Walsh, independent counsel*. 3 vols. Washington, DC: The Office, 1993.

U.S. Senate. *National Commitments*. 90th Cong., 1st sess., Senate Report 797, 1967.

U.S. Senate. Committee on Foreign Relations. *Briefing on Vietnam* ["Sanitized" public version]: *Hearings before the Committee on Foreign Relations.* 91st Cong., 1st sess., November 18 and 19, 1969. Washington, DC: U.S. Government Printing Office, 1969.

———. *Legislative proposals relating to the war in Southeast Asia: Hearings before the Committee on Foreign Relations.* 92nd Cong., 1st sess., April–May 1971. Washington, DC: U.S. Government Printing Office, 1971.

———. *Moral and military aspects of the war in Southeast Asia: Hearings before the Committee on Foreign Relations.* 91st Cong., 2nd sess., May 7 and 12, 1970. Washington, DC: U.S. Government Printing Office, 1970.

———. *Present situation in Vietnam: Hearings before the Committee on Foreign Relations.* 90th Cong., 2nd sess., March 20, 1968. Washington, DC: U.S. Government Printing Office, 1968.

———. *The Vietnam hearings.* Introduction by J. William Fulbright. New York: Vintage Books, 1966.

———. *Vietnam policy proposals: Hearings before the Committee on Foreign Relations.* 91st Cong., 2nd sess., February 3–5 and March 16, 1970. Washington, DC: U.S. Government Printing Office, 1970.

———. *War powers legislation: Hearings before the Committee on Foreign Relations.* 92nd Cong., 1st sess., on S. 731, S.J. Res. 18, and S.J. Res. 59; March 8, 9, 24, and 25, April 23 and 26, May 14, July 26 and 27, and October 6, 1971. Washington, DC: U.S. Government Printing Office, 1972.

———. Committee on Governmental Affairs. *Hearing before the Committee on Governmental Affairs, on the nomination of Hon. Gordon R. England to be deputy secretary of the Department of Homeland Security.* 108th Cong., 1st sess., January 24, 2003. Washington, DC: U.S. Government Printing Office, 2003.

———. Committee on the Judiciary. *Immigration emergency powers: Hearing before the subcommittee on immigration and refugee policy of the Committee on the Judiciary.* 97th Cong., 2nd sess., serial no. J-97-147, September 30, 1982. Washington, DC: U.S. Government Printing Office, 1982.

———. Select Committee to Study Governmental Operations. "Church committee report." *Final report of the Select Committee to Study Governmental Operations with Respect to Intelligence Activities.* 94th Cong., 2nd sess., April 26, 1976. Washington, DC: U.S. Government Printing Office, 1976.

———. Special Committee on National Emergencies and Delegated Emergency Powers. *Executive orders in times of war and national emergency: Report of the Special Committee on National Emergencies and Delegated Emergency Powers.* June 1974. Washington, DC: U.S. Government Printing Office, 1974.

———. *Summary of executive orders in times of war and national emergency: A working paper.* August 1974. Washington, DC: U.S. Government Printing Office, 1974.

———. Special Committee on the Termination of the National Emergency. *Emergency powers statutes: Provisions of federal law now in effect delegating to the executive extraordinary authority in time of national emergency: Report of the Special Committee on the Termination of the National Emergency.* September 1973. Washington, DC: U.S. Government Printing Office, 1973.

Print Material

Addis, Elisabetta, Valeria E. Russo, and Lorenza Sebesta. 1994. *Women soldiers: Images and realities.* New York: St. Martin's Press.

Adler, David Gray, and Larry N. George, eds. 1996. *The Constitution and the conduct of American foreign policy.* Lawrence: University Press of Kansas.

Adorno, Theodor W., et al. 1950. *The authoritarian personality.* New York: Harper.

Agamben, Giorgio. 2005. *States of exception.* Chicago: University of Chicago Press.

Allen, Mike. 2004. Bush tones down talk of winning terror war. *Washington Post*, August 31.

American Enterprise Institute. 1984. *War powers and the Constitution.* Washington, DC: American Enterprise Institute.

Anders, Günther. 1956. *Die Antiquiertheit des Menschen.* Munich: Beck.

Anderson, Benedict. 1991. *Imagined communities.* London: Verso.

Andreski, Stanislav. 1969. *Military organization and society.* London: Routledge and Kegan Paul.

Apel, Karl-Otto, ed. 1976. *Sprachpragmatik und Philosophie.* Frankfurt am Main: Suhrkamp.

Arendt, Hannah. 1958. *The human condition.* Chicago: University of Chicago Press.

———. 1994. *Essays in understanding, 1930–1954.* New York: Harcourt, Brace and Co.

Aristotle. 1947. *The "art" of rhetoric.* Cambridge, MA: Harvard University Press.

Aron, Raymond. 1958. *On war: Atomic weapons and global diplomacy.* London: Secker and Warburg.

———. 1974. *The imperial republic.* Cambridge: Winthrop. Originally published as *La république impériale.* Paris: Calman-Lévy, 1973.

Atran, Scott. 2003. Genesis and future of suicide terrorism, followed by a discussion. http://www.interdisciplines.org, July.

Bai, Matt. 2004. Kerry's undeclared war. *New York Times Magazine,* October 10.

Bailey, Jeremy D. 2007. *Thomas Jefferson and executive power.* Cambridge: Cambridge University Press.

Baker, Luke, and Will Dunham. 2005. U.S. citizen held in Iraq as suspected insurgent. Reuters. April 1.

Baker, Russ. 2004. Two years before 9/11, candidate Bush was already talking privately about attacking Iraq, according to his former ghost writer. GNN.TV, October 28.

Bamford, James. 2004. *A pretext for war: 9/11, Iraq, and the abuse of America's intelligence agencies.* New York: Doubleday.

Barber, Benjamin R. 1984. *Strong democracy.* Berkeley: University of California Press.

———. 2003. *Fear's empire: War, terrorism, and democracy.* New York: Norton.

Barnard, Harry. 1938. *Eagle forgotten: The life of John Peter Altgeld.* Indianapolis: Bobbs-Merrill.

Barnet, Richard J., and Ronald E. Muller. 1974. *Global reach: The power of the multinational corporations.* New York: Simon and Schuster.

Bassford, Christopher. 1994. *Clausewitz in English: The reception of Clausewitz in Britain and America, 1815–1945.* New York: Oxford University Press.

Beauvoir, Simone de. 1949. *Le deuxiéme sexe.* Paris: Gallimard.

Bell, David A. 2007. *The first total war: Napoleon's Europe and the birth of warfare as we know it.* Boston : Houghton Mifflin.

Bennett, William. 2002. *Why we fight.* New York: Doubleday.

Bensel, Richard F. 1990. *Yankee leviathan: The origins of central state authority in America, 1859–1877.* Cambridge: Cambridge University Press.

Bentham, Jeremy. 1791. *Political tactics*. New York: Oxford University Press, 1999.

Berger, Raoul. 1974. *Executive privilege: A constitutional myth*. Cambridge, MA: Harvard University Press.

Beveridge, Albert J. 1916–19. *The life of John Marshall*. Boston: Houghton Mifflin.

Blackstone, William. 1765–69. *Commentaries on the laws of England*. Oxford: Clarendon Press.

Blichner, Lars Chr., and Anders Molander. 2005. *What is juridification?* Working Paper no. 14. ARENA, Centre for European Studies, University of Oslo.

Blitzstein, Marc. 1938. *The cradle will rock*. New York: Random House.

Boaz, David. 2004. *Cato policy report*. Washington, DC: July/August.

Boltanksi, Luc, and Eve Chiappello. 1999. *Le nouvel ésprit du capitalisme*. Paris: Gallimard.

Boorstin, Daniel J. 1941. *The mysterious science of the law: An essay on Blackstone's commentaries showing how Blackstone, employing eighteenth-century ideas of science, religion, history, aesthetics, and philosophy, made of the law at once a conservative and a mysterious science*. Cambridge, MA: Harvard University Press.

Bourne, Randolph. 1916. Trans-national America. *Atlantic Monthly*, July, 86–97.

Boyer, Paul S. 1985. *By the bomb's early light: American thought and culture at the dawn of the atomic age*. New York: Pantheon.

Brands, H. W. 2003. *Woodrow Wilson*. New York: Time Books.

Brecher, Jeremy. 1972. *Strike!* San Francisco: Straight Arrow Books.

Brock, David. 2002. *Blinded by the Right*. New York: Crown.

Brodie, Bernard, ed. 1946. *The absolute weapon: Atomic power and world order*. New York: Harcourt.

Brokaw, Tom. 1998. *The greatest generation*. New York: Random House.

Brown, Harrison. 1960. *Community of fear*. Santa Barbara, CA: Center for the Study of Democratic Institutions.

Buchanan, Patrick J. 2004. *Where the Right went wrong: How neoconservatives subverted the Reagan revolution and hijacked the Bush presidency*. New York: St. Martin's.

Burke, Kenneth. 1945. *A grammar of motives*. New York: Prentice Hall.

Burnham, John. 1943. *Total war: The economic theory of a war economy*. Boston: Meador.

Burns, Arthur Lee. 1959. *Power politics and the growing nuclear club*. Princeton, NJ: Center of International Studies, Woodrow Wilson School of Public and International Affairs.

Bush says U.S. will win terror war. 2004. CNN.Com, August 31.

Bush enters Mideast's rhetorical minefield. 2001. Reuters, September 22.

Byrd, Robert C. 2004. *Losing America: Confronting a reckless and arrogant presidency*. New York: Norton.

Cahn, William. 1980. *Lawrence 1912: The bread and roses strike*. New York: Pilgrim Press.

Calhoun, Craig. 1999. Charles Taylor on identity and the social imaginary. *Cahiers du PEQ* (Programme d'études sur le Québec) 19 (June): 2–9.

———. 2005. The promise of public sociology. *British Journal of Sociology* 56, no. 3: 355–63.

Calhoun, Craig, Paul Price, and Ashley Timmer, eds. 2002. *Understanding September 11*. New York: New Press.

Cannon, Carl M., Lou Dubose, and Jan Reid. 2003. *Boy genius: Karl Rove, the architect of George W. Bush's remarkable political triumphs*. New York: Public Affairs.

Carwardine, William H. 1894. *The Pullman strike*. Chicago: Charles H. Kerr.

Cassin, Barbara. 1995. *L'effet sophistique*. Paris: Gallimard.

Castoriadis, Cornelius. 1975. *L'institution imaginaire de la société*. Paris: Seuil.

Center for Responsive Politics. 2001. President Bush's first 100 days (April 26, 2001). http://www.opensecrets.org/bush/100days/index.asp.

Chace, James. 2004. *1912: Wilson, Roosevelt, Taft, and Debs: The election that changed the country*. New York: Simon and Schuster.

Chang, Nancy. 2002. *Silencing political dissent*. New York: Seven Stories Press.

Charen, Mona. 2004. *Useful idiots: How liberals got it wrong in the Cold War and still blame America first*. Washington, DC: Regnery.

Clarke, Richard A. 2004. *Against all enemies*. New York: Free Press.

Clausewitz, Carl von. 1976. *On war*. Edited and translated by Michael Howard and Peter Paret. Princeton, NJ: Princeton University Press.

———. 1873. *On war*. Trans. J. J. Graham from the 3rd German ed. London: N. Trubner.

Clinton warned Bush of bin Laden threat. 2003. Reuters, October 15.

Coben, Stanley, ed. 1972. *Reform, war, and reaction, 1912–1932*. New York: Harper and Row.

Colas, Dominique. 1997. *Civil society and fanaticism: Conjoined histories.* Stanford, CA: Stanford University Press.

Coll, Steve. 2004. *Ghost wars: The secret history of the CIA, Afghanistan, and bin Laden, from the Soviet invasion to September 10, 2001.* New York: Penguin Press.

Corn, David. 2003. *The lies of George W. Bush: Mastering the politics of deception.* New York: Crown Publishers.

Corwin, Edward Samuel. 1947. *Total war and the Constitution.* New York: A. A. Knopf.

——. 1957. *The president, office and powers, 1787–1957: History and analysis of practice and opinion.* 4th rev. ed. New York: New York University Press.

Coulter, Ann. 2003. *Treason: Liberal treachery from the Cold War to the war on terrorism.* New York: Crown Forum.

Cox, Arthur Macy. 1975. *The myths of national security.* Boston: Beacon Press.

Davis, Elmer Holmes. 1955. *Two minutes till midnight.* Indianapolis: Bobbs-Merrill.

Dean, John. 2004a. Worse than Watergate. *Salon,* June 11.

——. 2004b. *Worse than Watergate: The secret presidency of George W. Bush.* New York: Little, Brown and Co.

DeFrank, Thomas. 2007. *Write it when I'm gone.* New York: Putnam Adult.

DeMott, Benjamin. 2004. Whitewash as public service: How the 9/11 Commission report defrauds the nation. *Harper's Magazine,* December.

Descartes, René. 1650. *Les passions de l'âme.* Amsterdam: Chez L. Elzevier.

Dewey, John. 1894–95. A theory of the emotions. In *The early works, 1882–1898,* vol. 4. Carbondale: Southern Illinois University Press, 1967–72.

——. 1896. The reflex arc concept in psychology. *Psychological Review* 3:357–70.

Dickey, Christopher. 2004. *The Sleeper.* New York: Doubleday.

Dionne, E. J., and William Kristol, eds. 2001. *Bush v. Gore: The court cases and the commentary.* Washington, DC: Brookings Institution Press.

Donnelly, Thomas, Donald Kagan, and Gary Schmitt. 2000. *Rebuilding America's defenses: Strategy, forces, and resources for a new century.* Washington, DC: Report of the Project for the New American Century, September.

D'Souza, Dinesh. 2007. *The enemy at home: The cultural Left and its responsibility for 9/11.* New York: Doubleday.

Dudziak, Mary. 2000. *Cold War civil rights: Race and the image of American democracy*. Princeton, NJ: Princeton University Press.

Dunning, W. A. 1898. *Essays on the Civil War and Reconstruction*. New York: Macmillan.

Dworkin, Ronald. 2002. The threat to patriotism. *New York Review of Books*, February 28, 44–49.

Einstein, Albert. 1947. Atomic war or peace. *Atlantic Monthly*, November.

Ekirch, Arthur A. Jr. 1974. *Progressivism in America: A study of the era from Theodore Roosevelt to Woodrow Wilson*. New York: New Viewpoints.

Elias, Norbert. 1988. Violence and civilization: The state monopoly of physical violence and its infringement. In John Keane, ed., *Civil society and the state: New European perspectives*. London: Verso.

Elnajjar, Hassan A. 2004. September 11th, 2001, and Cold War II: Communism is dead, long live Islamism. *Al-Jazeerah*, August 20.

Elshtain, Jean Bethke. 1987. *Women and war*. New York: Basic Books.

———. 2003. *Just war against terror: The burden of American power in a violent world*. New York: Basic Books.

Elster, John. 1983. *Sour grapes: Studies in the subversion of rationality*. Cambridge: Cambridge University Press.

Emanuel, Rahm. 2007. Comments on National Briefing Washington. *New York Times*, June 27.

Evans, Peter, Dietrich Rueschemeyer, and Theda Skocpol, eds. 1985. *Bringing the state back in*. Cambridge: Cambridge University Press.

Faludi, Susan. 1991. *Backlash: The undeclared war against American women*. New York: Crown.

———. 2007. *The terror dream: Fear and fantasy in post-9/11 America*. New York: Metropolitan Books.

The Federalist. 1961. Ed. by Jacob E. Cooke. Middletown, CT: Wesleyan University Press.

Ferejohn, John, and Pasquale Pasquino. 2004. The law of exception: A typology of emergency powers. *International Journal of Constitutional Law* 2, no. 2 (April): 210–39.

Ferguson, Adam. 1767. *An essay on the history of civil society*. Edinburgh: printed for A. Millar and T. Caddel in the Strand, London, and A. Kincaid and J. Bell.

Ferguson, Michaele L., and Lori Jo Marso, eds. 2007. *W stands for women: How the George W. Bush presidency shaped a new politics of gender*. Chapel Hill, NC: Duke University Press.

Fisher, Louis. 2004. *Presidential war power*. 2nd ed. rev. Lawrence: University Press of Kansas.

Fisher, Louis, and Nada Mourtada-Sabbah. 2001. *Is war power a political question?* Huntington, NY: Novinka Books.

Fiss, Owen M. 2005. The war against terrorism and the rule of law. Paper presented to the Program in Law and Public Affairs, March 28, Princeton, NJ.

Flynn, Kevin, and Jim Dwyer. 2004. Falling bodies: A 9/11 image etched in pain. *New York Times*, September 10.

Fontaine, André. 1966. *Histoire de la guerre froide*. Paris: Fayard.

Foucault, Michel. 1980. *Power/knowledge*. New York: Pantheon.

Frank, Justin A. 2004. *Bush on the couch: Inside the mind of the president*. New York: Regan Books.

Frank, Thomas. 2004. *What's the matter with Kansas? How conservatives won the heart of America*. New York: Metropolitan Books.

Franklin, Daniel P. 1991. *Extraordinary measures: The exercise of prerogative powers in the United States*. Pittsburgh, PA: University of Pittsburgh Press.

Friedman, Thomas L. 1999. *The Lexus and the olive tree*. New York: Farrar, Straus, Giroux.

———. 2001. The big terrible. *New York Times*, September 19.

Fukuyama, Francis. 1992. *The end of history and the last man*. New York: Free Press.

Fulbright, J. William. 1967. *The arrogance of power*. New York: Random House.

Funkenstein, Amos. 1986. *Theology and the scientific imagination from the Middle Ages to the seventeenth century*. Princeton, NJ: Princeton University Press.

Gadamer, Hans-Georg. 1982. *Hegel's dialectic*. New Haven: Yale University Press.

Gaddis, John Lewis. 1972. *The United States and the origins of the Cold War, 1941–1947*. New York: Columbia University Press.

———. 2004. *Surprise, security, and the American experience*. Cambridge, MA: Harvard University Press.

Gallois, Pierre Marie. 1960. *Stratégie de l'âge nucléaire*. Paris: Calman-Lévy.

Gates, Robert. 1997. *From the shadows: The ultimate insider's story of five presidents and how they won the Cold War*. New York: Simon and Schuster.

Gingrich, Newt. 2005. *Winning the future: A 21st century contract with America*. Washington, DC: Regnery.

Gingrich, Newt, and Dick Armey. 1994. *Contract with America*. New York: Times Books.

Giuliani, Rudolph. 2004. Quote of the day. *New York Times*, September 11.

Goffman, Erving. 1959. *The presentation of self in everyday life*. Garden City, NY: Doubleday.

———. 1974. *Frame analysis: An essay on the organization of experience*. New York: Harper and Row.

Goldman, Emma. 1931. *Living my life*. 2 vols. New York: Knopf.

Gourevitch, Philip. 1999. *We wish to inform you that tomorrow we will be killed with our families: Stories from Rwanda*. New York: Picador.

Greenberg, Karen J., and Joshua L. Dratel, eds. 2005. *The torture papers: The road to Abu Ghraib*. New York: Cambridge University Press.

Grieder, William. 2004. Under the banner of the "war" on terror. *Nation*, June 21.

Gross, Oren, and Fionnuala Ní Aoláin. 2006. *Law in times of crisis: Emergency powers in theory and practice*. Cambridge: Cambridge University Press.

Grossman, Jonathan. 1975. The coal strike of 1902: Turning point in U.S. policy. *Monthly Labor Review*, online at the U.S. Bureau of Labor Statistics, http://www.bls.gov/opub/mlr/mlrhome.htm.

Habermas, Jürgen. 1962. *Strukturwandel der Öffentlichkeit: Untersuchungen zu einer Kategorie der bürgerlichen Gesellschaft*. Berlin: Luchterhand.

———. 1976. Was heißt Universalpragmatik? In Karl-Otto Apel, ed., *Sprachpragmatik und Philosophie*. Frankfurt am Main: Suhrkamp.

———. 1987. *The theory of communicative action*. Vol. 2. Boston: Beacon Press.

Hacker, Jacob S. 2006. *The great risk shift: The assault on American jobs, families, health care, and retirement and how you can fight back*. New York: Oxford University Press.

Hacker, Jacob S., and Paul Pierson. 2005. *Off center: The Republican revolution and the erosion of accountability*. New Haven: Yale University Press.

Halbfinger, David. 2006. Oliver Stone's "World Trade Center" seeks truth in the rubble. *New York Times*, July 2.

Halle, Louis Joseph. 1958. *Choice for survival*. New York: Harper and Row.

———. 1967. *The Cold War as history*. New York: Harper and Row.

Hanson, Victor Davis. 2002. *An autumn of war: What America learned from September 11 and the war on terrorism*. New York: Anchor.

Hardman, J. B. S. 1934. Terrorism. In *Encyclopaedia of the Social Sciences*, 14:575–80. New York: Macmillan.

Harrington, Michael. 1962. *The other America: Poverty in the United States*. New York: Macmillan.

Hartz, Louis. 1955. *The liberal tradition in America*. New York: Harcourt Brace.

Hasen, Richard L. 2002. The untold drafting history of *Buckley v. Valeo*. *Loyola-LA Public Law Research Working Paper*, July 15.

Havel, Vaclav. 1985. *Living in truth*. London: Faber.

Hayek, Friedrich. 1973. *Law, legislation, and liberty*. Chicago: University of Chicago Press.

Hayes, Stephen F. 2007. *Cheney: The untold story of America's most powerful and controversial vice-president*. New York: HarperCollins.

Hedges, Chris. 2002. *War is the force that gives us meaning*. New York: Public Affairs.

———. 2003. *What every person should know about war*. New York: Free Press.

———. 2006. *American fascists: The Christian Right and the war on America*. New York: Free Press.

Hegel, Georg Wilhelm Friedrich. 1807. *Phänomenologie des Geistes*. Hamburg: Meiner, 1952.

Hendawi, Hamza. 2004. Explosions rock Baghdad near U.S. offices. Associated Press Wire, September 12.

Herman, Edward S., and Noam Chomsky. 1988. *Manufacturing consent: The political economy of the mass media*. New York: Pantheon Books.

Hersch, Seymour M. 2005. *Chain of command: The road from 9/11 to Abu Ghraib*. New York: Harper Perennial.

Hersey, John. 1946a. Hiroshima. *New Yorker*, August 31.

———. 1946b. *Hiroshima*. New York: Knopf.

Hill, Christopher. 1972. *The world turned upside down: Radical ideas during the English revolution*. London: Temple Smith.

Hitchens, Christopher. 2001. *The trial of Henry Kissinger*. London: Verso.

Hobbes, Thomas. 1651. *Leviathan*. Ed. C. B. McPherson. Baltimore: Penguin Books, 1968.

——. 1655. *Elements of philosophy*. In William Molesworth, ed., *The English works of Thomas Hobbes of Malmesbury*. London: John Bohn, 1839.

Hofstadter, Richard, ed. 1963. *The Progressive movement, 1900–1915*. Englewood Cliffs, NJ: Prentice Hall.

Hogan, Michael. 1998. *A cross of iron: Harry S. Truman and the origins of the national security state, 1945–1954*. Cambridge: Cambridge University Press.

Hogan, Michael. 2000. The science of Cold War strategy: Propaganda and public opinion in the Eisenhower administration's "war of words." In Martin J. Medhurst and H. W. Brands, eds., *Critical reflections on the Cold War*. College Station: Texas A&M University Press.

Hooks, Gregory. 1991. *Forging the military-industrial complex: World War II's battle of the Potomac*. Urbana: University of Illinois.

Horwitz, Morton J. 1977. *The transformation of American law, 1780–1860*. Cambridge, MA: Harvard University Press.

Howard, Michael. 1979. *Restraints on war*. Oxford: Oxford University Press.

——. 2001. Mistake to declare this a war. *Royal United Services Institute for Defense Journal*. December.

Hulse, Carl. 2007a. Congress censures Limbaugh. *New York Times,* October 3.

——. 2007b. Mukasey wins vote in Senate, despite doubts. *New York Times*, November 9.

Hume, David. 1742. On the first principles of government. In *Essays, moral and political*. Edinburgh: R. Fleming.

——. 1748. *Philosophical essays concerning human understanding*. London: printed for A. Millar.

Hunter, James Davison. 1991. *Culture wars: The struggle to define America*. New York: Basic Books.

Huntington, Samuel P. 1957. *The soldier and the state: The theory and politics of civil-military relations*. Cambridge, MA: Harvard University Press.

——. 1993. The clash of civilizations. *Foreign Affairs* 72, no. 3: 22–49.

Institute for American Values. 2002. What we're fighting for: A letter from America. http://www.americanvalues.org/html/wwff.html.

Isikoff, Michael. 2004. Election Day worries. *Newsweek*, July 19.

Isikoff, Michael, and David Corn. 2006. *Hubris: The inside story of spin, scandal, and the selling of the Iraq War*. New York: Crown.

Jacques-Chaquin, Nicole, and Sophie Houdard, eds. 1998. *Curiosité et libido sciendi de la Renaissance aux lumières.* Fontenay/Saint-Cloud: ENS Editions.

James, William. 1890. *Principles of psychology.* 2 vols. New York: Henry Holt.

Janowitz, Morris. 1960. *The professional soldier: A social and political portrait.* Glencoe, IL: Free Press.

Jefferson, Thomas. 1904–5. *The works of Thomas Jefferson.* Collected and edited by Paul Leicester Ford. New York: Putnam's Sons.

———. 1950–. *The papers of Thomas Jefferson.* Princeton, NJ: Princeton University Press.

Johnson, Chalmers. 2004a. *The sorrows of empire: Militarism, secrecy, and the end of the Republic.* New York: Metropolitan Books.

———. 2004b. The three Cold Wars. In Ellen Schrecker, ed., *Cold War triumphalism: The misuse of history after the fall of Communism.* New York: New Press.

———. 2006. *Nemesis.* New York: Metropolitan Books.

Jomini, Antoine Henri. 1805. *Traité de grande tactique.* Paris: Giguet et Michaud.

———. 1838. *Précis de l'art de la guerre.* Paris: Anselin.

Judis, John. 2004. *The folly of empire: What George W. Bush could learn from Theodore Roosevelt and Woodrow Wilson.* New York: Scribner.

Kagan, Robert. 1998. The benevolent empire. *Foreign Policy,* summer, 24–33.

Kahn, Herman. 1960. *On thermonuclear war.* Princeton, NJ: Princeton University Press.

Kaldor, Mary. 1990. *The imaginary war: Understanding the East-West conflict.* Oxford: Blackwell.

Kallen, Horace M. 1915. Democracy versus the melting-pot: A study of American nationality. *Nation,* February 25.

Kalyvas, Stathis N. 2006. *The logic of violence in civil war.* Cambridge: Cambridge University Press.

Kammen, Hayden Michael G. 1986. *A machine that would go of itself: The Constitution in American culture.* New York: Knopf.

Kantorowicz, Ernst H. 1957. *The king's two bodies: A study in mediaeval political theology.* Princeton, NJ: Princeton University Press.

Kaplan, Fred. 2006. Rumsfeld surrenders: The QDR dashes his dreams of military transformation. *Salon,* February 3.

Kaplan, Lawrence. 2003. Regime change. *New Republic*, March 3.

Kastenmeier, Robert W. 1966. *Vietnam hearings: Voices from the grass roots.* Garden City, NY: Doubleday.

Katznelson, Ira. 2003. *Desolation and enlightenment.* New York: Columbia University Press.

Katznelson, Ira, and Martin Shefter. 2002. *Shaped by war and trade: International influences on American political development.* Princeton, NJ: Princeton University Press.

Keane, John, ed. 1988. *Civil society and the state: New European perspectives.* London: Verso.

Kelley, Donald R. 1990. *The human measure: Social thought in the Western legal tradition.* Cambridge, MA: Harvard University Press.

Kennan, George F. 1972. *Memoirs, 1950–1963.* Boston: Atlantic/Little, Brown and Co.

———. 1975. The meaning of Vietnam. *New York Review of Books*, June 12.

Kennedy, Ellen. 2004. *Constitutional failure: Carl Schmitt in Weimar.* Durham, NC: Duke University Press.

Kiesling, John Brady. 2006. *Diplomacy lessons: Realism for an unloved superpower.* Washington, DC: Potomac Books.

Kirkpatrick, David D. 2004. War heats up in the neoconservative fold. *New York Times*, August 22.

Kissinger, Henry. 1957. *Nuclear weapons and foreign policy.* New York: Council on Foreign Relations/Harper.

Knowlton, Brian. 2005. Bush and McCain reach deal on treatment of terror suspects. *New York Times*, December 15.

Kolko, Gabriel. 1963. *The triumph of conservatism: A re-interpretation of American history, 1900–1916.* New York: Free Press.

———. 1985. *Anatomy of a war: Vietnam, the United States, and the modern historical experience.* New York: Pantheon.

———. 1994. *Century of war: Politics, conflict, and society since 1914.* New York: New Press.

———. 2002. *Another century of war?* New York: New Press.

Krauthammer, Charles. 1990. Don't cash the peace dividend. *Time*, March 26.

———. 2001. This is not crime, this is war. *Jewish World Review*, September 12.

Kristol, Irving. 1976. What is a neoconservative? *Newsweek*, January 19.

———. 1993. My Cold War. *National Interest*, no. 31 (spring): 141–44.

Kristol, William, and Robert Kagan. 1996. Toward a neo-Reaganite foreign policy. *Foreign Affairs*, July–August.

Lakoff, George. 2002. *Moral politics*. 2nd ed. Chicago: University of Chicago Press.

Lazarus, Emma. 1889. *The poems of Emma Lazarus*. Boston: Houghton, Mifflin and Co.

Lewis, Bernard. 1990. Roots of Muslim rage. *Atlantic Monthly*, September.

Lindsey, Almont. 1942. *The Pullman strike*. Chicago: University of Chicago Press.

Lippmann, Walter. 1922. *Public opinion*. New York: Harcourt, Brace and Co.

Lobel, Jules. 1989. Emergency power and the decline of liberalism. *Yale Law Journal* 98, no. 7 (May): 1385–1433.

Locke, John. 1690. *Two treatises of government*. London: printed for Awnshan Churchill.

Lorenz, Konrad. 1966. *On aggression*. New York: Harcourt, Brace, and World.

Ludendorf, Erich. 1937. *Der totale Krieg*. Munich: Ludendorff Verlag.

Lukacs, John. 1966. *A new history of the Cold War*. Garden City, NY: Anchor Books.

Lustig, R. Jeffrey. 1982. *Corporate liberalism*. Berkeley: University of California Press.

Malinowski, Bronislaw. 1923. The problem of meaning in primitive languages. In C. K. Ogden and I. A. Richards, *The meaning of meaning: A study of the influence of language upon thought and of the science of symbolism*. London: Kegan Paul and Trench, Trubner.

Manicas, Peter. 1989. *War and democracy*. Cambridge, MA: Blackwell.

Mann, James. 2004. *The rise of the Vulcans: The history of Bush's war cabinet*. New York: Viking.

Mann, Michael. 1986, 1993. *The social sources of power*. 2 vols. New York: Cambridge University Press.

Mansbridge, Jane. 1980. *Beyond adversary democracy*. New York: Basic Books.

Marks, I. M. 1987a. The development of normal fear: A review. *Journal of Child Psychology and Psychiatry* 28, no. 5: 667–97.

———. 1987b. *Fear, phobias, and rituals*. New York: Oxford University Press.

Marx, Karl. 1848. *Manifest der Kommunistischen Partei*. London: Gedruckt in der Office der "Bildungs-Gesellschaft für Arbeiter" von J. E. Burghard.

May, Ernest R., and Philip D. Zelikow, eds. 1997. *The Kennedy tapes: Inside the White House during the Cuban missile crisis*. Cambridge, MA: Harvard University Press.

Medhurst, Martin J. 1994. *Eisenhower's war of words: Rhetoric and leadership*. East Lansing: Michigan State University Press.

Medhurst, Martin J., and H. W. Brands. 2000. *Critical reflections on the Cold War*. College Station: Texas A&M University Press.

Melman, Seymour. 1974. *The permanent war economy: American capitalism in decline*. New York: Simon and Schuster.

Melossi, Dario. 1990. *The state of social control: A sociological study of concepts of state and social control in the making of democracy*. Cambridge: Polity Press.

Meyers, Peter Alexander. 1989. *A theory of power: Political, not metaphysical*. Ann Arbor: UMI.

———. 1990. War and anti-war at the movies. In *Critical Relations*. Williamstown, MA: Highgate Art Trust.

———. 1995. Theses on the genealogy of the modern will. Paper presented at the Meetings of the American Political Science Association, Chicago.

———. 1998. The "ethic of care" and the problem of power. *Journal of Political Philosophy* 6, no. 2: 142–70.

———. 2001. Defend politics against terrorism. Social Science Research Council, http://www.ssrc.org/sept11/essays/meyers.htm.

———. 2002a. Le "musée vivant" raconte sa propre histoire: Une première lecture de l'United States Holocaust Memorial Museum. *Cités* 11:159–83.

———. 2002b. Terrorism and the assault on politics. In Craig Calhoun, Paul Price, and Ashley Timmer, eds., *Understanding September 11*. New York: New Press.

———. 2003. *Method and civic education*. Humanitas XVI, no. 2: 4–47.

———. 2006. *Abandoned to ourselves*. Manuscript.

———. Forthcoming. *Left speechless: America in the light of its Holocaust Museum*.

Milbank, Dana, and Spencer S. Hsu. 2004. Cheney: Kerry victory is risky: Democrats decry talk as scare tactic. *Washington Post*, September 8.

Milgram, Stanley. 1963. Behavioral study of obedience. *Journal of Abnormal Social Psychology* 67:371–78.

Moch, Jules Salvador. 1954. *La folie des hommes*. Paris: R. Laffont.

Moore, James, and Wayne Slater. 2003. *Bush's brain: How Karl Rove made George W. Bush presidential*. Hoboken, NJ: John Wiley and Sons.

———. 2005. *Rove exposed: How Bush's brain fooled America*. Hoboken, NJ: John Wiley and Sons.

———. 2006. *The architect: Karl Rove and the master plan for absolute power*. New York: Crown.

Moore, Mike. 2003. Truman got it right. *Bulletin of the Atomic Scientists* 59, no. 1 (January–February): 20–33.

Mowry, Arthur May. 1901. *The Dorr war; or, The constitutional struggle in Rhode Island*. New York: Johnson, 1968.

Moynihan, Daniel Patrick. 1998. *Secrecy: The American experience*. New Haven: Yale University Press.

Neely, Mark E. 2004. Was the Civil War a total war? *Civil War History* 50, no. 4 (December): 434–58.

Nessen, Ron. 1978. *It sure looks different from the inside*. Chicago: Playboy Press.

Nichols, John. 2004. Ten questions for Dick Cheney. *Nation*, online edition, October 5.

Oakes, Guy. 1994. *The imaginary war: Civil defense and American Cold War culture*. New York: Oxford University Press.

Ober, Josiah. 1996. Rules of war in classical Greece. In *The Athenian revolution: Essays on ancient Greek democracy and political theory*. Princeton, NJ: Princeton University Press.

Ogden, C. K., and I. A. Richards. 1923. *The meaning of meaning: A study of the influence of language upon thought and of the science of symbolism*. London: Kegan Paul and Trench, Trubner.

Olson, William J., and Alan Woll. 1999. Executive orders and national emergencies. *Policy Analysis*, no. 358. Washington, DC: Cato Institute.

O'Neill, Tip. 1994. *All politics is local and other rules of the game*. New York: Random House.

Ostwald, Martin. 1969. *Nomos and the beginnings of Athenian democracy*. Oxford: Oxford University Press.

———. 1986. *From popular sovereignty to the sovereignty of law: Law, society, and politics in fifth-century Athens*. Berkeley: University of California Press.

Paret, Peter. 1976. *Clausewitz and the State*. New York: Oxford University Press.

———, ed. 1986. *Makers of modern strategy*. Princeton, NJ: Princeton University Press.

Phillips, Kevin. 2004. *American dynasty: Aristocracy, fortune, and the politics of deceit in the house of Bush*. New York: Viking.

Piven, Frances Fox. 2004. *The war at home*. New York: New Press.

Piven, Frances Fox, and Richard A. Cloward. 1982. *The new class war: Reagan's attack on the welfare state and its consequences*. New York: Pantheon.

Podhoretz, Norman. 2004. World War IV: How it started, what it means, and why we have to win. *Commentary*, fall.

Porter, Gareth. 2008. How the Pentagon planted a false Hormuz story. Inter Press Service, January 15.

Posner, Richard A. 2004. The 9/11 report: A dissent. *New York Times Book Review*, August 29.

Rawls, John. 1971. *A theory of justice*. Cambridge, MA: Harvard University Press.

Reeves, Richard. 2005. The end of superpower. http://richardreeves.com, October 21.

Relyea, Harold C. 1974. *A brief history of emergency powers in the United States*. Washington, DC: U.S. Government Printing Office.

———. 2001. *National emergency powers*. Congressional Research Service Report for Congress, order code 98-505 GOV. Updated September 18, 2001.

Remnick, David. 2006. The wanderer. *New Yorker*, September 18.

———. 2007. Talk of the town: Al Gore. *New Yorker*, March 5.

Rich, Frank. 2007. When the vice president does it, that means it's not illegal. *New York Times*, July 1.

Robbins, Lionel. 1950. *The economic problem in peace and war*. London: Macmillan.

Robinson, Donald L. 1996. Presidential prerogative and the spirit of American constitutionalism. In David Gray Adler and Larry N. George, eds., *The Constitution and the conduct of American foreign policy*. Lawrence: University Press of Kansas.

Robinson, Edwin Arlington. 1920. Demos. In *The three taverns: A book of poems*. New York: Macmillan.

Rogers, William P. 1958. Constitutional law: The papers of the executive branch. *American Bar Association Journal* 44 (October): 941–44, 1007–14.

Rogin, Michael. 1987. *"Ronald Reagan," the movie, and other episodes in political demonology*. Berkeley: University of California Press.

Roosevelt, Franklin D. 1938–50. *The public papers and addresses of Franklin D. Roosevelt*. Ed. Samuel I. Rosenmen. New York: Harper and Brothers.

Rosanvallon, Pierre. 1988. The decline of social visibility. In John Keane, ed., *Civil society and the state: New European perspectives*. London: Verso.

Rose, Gideon. 2004. The empire strikes out. *Washington Monthly*, September.

Rose, Jacqueline. 2003. We are all afraid, but of what, exactly? *Guardian*, March 20.

Rossiter, Clinton. 1948. *Constitutional dictatorship: Crisis government in the modern democracies*. Princeton, NJ: Princeton University Press.

Rousseau, Jean-Jacques. 1959–. *Oeuvres complètes*. 5 tomes. Paris: Gallimard.

Rozell, Mark. 1994. *Executive privilege: The dilemma of secrecy and democratic accountability*. Baltimore: Johns Hopkins University Press.

Rutenberg, Jim. 2007. White House drops vice president's dual-role argument as moot. *New York Times*, June 28.

Sageman, Marc. 2004. *Understanding terror networks*. Philadelphia: University of Pennsylvania Press.

Saunders, Francis Stonor. 2001. *The cultural Cold War*. New York: New Press.

Schell, Jonathan. 1982. *The fate of the earth*. New York: Knopf.

Scheppele, Kim Lane. 2004. Law in a time of emergency: States of exception and the temptations of 9/11. *University of Pennsylvania Journal of Constitutional Law* 6:1001–83.

———. 2005. Hypothetical torture in the war on terrorism. *Journal of National Security Law and Policy* 1:285–340.

———. 2006. Small emergencies. *Georgia Law Review* 40:835–62.

———. 2007. Legal and extra-legal emergencies. Manuscript, September 15.

———. Forthcoming. Introduction to *The international state of emergency*. Manuscript.

Schlesinger, Arthur M. Jr. 1967. *The bitter heritage: Vietnam and American democracy, 1941–1966*. Greenwich, CT: Fawcett.

———, ed. 1973. *History of U.S. political parties*. 4 vols. New York: Chelsea House.

———. 1974. *The imperial presidency*. New York: Popular Library.

———. 2003. The imperial presidency redux. *Washington Post*, June 28.

———. 2004. *War and the American presidency*. New York: Norton.

Schmitt, Carl. 1985. *Political theology: Four chapters on the concept of sovereignty*. 2nd ed. Trans. George D. Schwab. Cambridge, MA: MIT Press. Original ed. 1922, 2nd ed. 1934.

Schor, Esther. 2006. *Emma Lazarus*. New York: Schocken.

Schrecker, Ellen, ed. 2004. *Cold War triumphalism: The misuse of history after the fall of Communism*. New York: New Press.

Scott, James C. 1985. *Weapons of the weak: Everyday forms of peasant resistance*. New Haven: Yale University Press.

———. 1992 *Domination and the arts of resistance: Hidden transcripts*. New Haven: Yale University Press.

Shakespeare, William. 1943. *Complete works*. London: Oxford University Press.

Shane, Peter M., and Harold H. Bruff. 1996. *Separation of powers law: Cases and materials*. Durham, NC: Carolina Academic Press.

Shane, Scott. 2007. Agency is target in Cheney fight on secrecy data. *New York Times*, June 22.

Shanker, Thom. 2001. Rumsfeld sees discord on size of military. *New York Times*, July 19.

Shy, John. 1986. Jomini. In Peter Paret, ed., *Makers of modern strategy*. Princeton, NJ: Princeton University Press.

Silver, Allan. 2004. America's wars: Perfect and imperfect. Paper presented in the Donner Foundation Series, University of Toronto, September. Manuscript.

Skocpol, Theda. 1992. *Protecting soldiers and mothers: The political origins of social policy in the United States*. Cambridge, MA: Harvard University Press.

Skowronek, Stephen. 1997. *The politics presidents make: Leadership from John Adams to Bill Clinton*. Expanded ed. Cambridge, MA: Harvard University Press, Belknap Press.

Slotkin, Richard. 1973. *Regeneration through violence: The mythology of the American frontier, 1600–1860*. Middletown, CT: Wesleyan University Press.

———. 1985. *The fatal environment: The myth of the frontier in the age of industrialization, 1800–1890*. New York: Atheneum.

———. 1992. *Gunfighter nation: The myth of the frontier in twentieth-century America*. New York: Atheneum.

Sparrow, Bartholomew H. 1996. *From the outside in: World War II and the American state*. Princeton, NJ: Princeton University Press.

Sperber, Dan. 1985. Anthropology and psychology: Towards an epidemiology of representations. *Man* 20:73–89.

———. 1996. *Explaining culture: A naturalistic approach*. Cambridge, MA: Blackwell.

Spinoza, Benedict de. 1988. *Ethica/Éthique*. Paris:Éditions du Seuil.

———. 1996. *Ethics*. London: Penguin Books.

Stansell, Christine. 2000. *American moderns: Bohemian New York and the creation of a new century*. New York: Metropolitan Books.

Steel, Ronald. 2003. The missionary. *New York Review of Books*, November 20.

———. 2004. George Kennan at 100. *New York Review of Books*, April 29.

Stern, Jessica. 2006. *Terror in the name of God: Why religious militants kill*. New York: HarperCollins.

Sternberg, Fritz. 1959. *The military and industrial revolution of our time*. New York: Praeger.

Stockman, David A. 1986. *The triumph of politics: How the Reagan revolution failed*. New York: Harper and Row.

Stone, Geoffrey R. 2005. *Perilous times: Free speech in war time*. New York: Norton.

Stone, Richard D. 1991. *The Interstate Commerce Commission and the railroad industry: A history of regulatory policy*. New York: Praeger.

Stouzh, Gerald. 1970. *Alexander Hamilton and the idea of republican government*. Stanford, CA: Stanford University Press.

Strasser, Steven, ed. 2004a. *The Abu Ghraib investigations*. New York: Public Affairs.

———. 2004b. *The 9/11 investigations: Staff reports of the 9/11 Commission*. New York: Public Affairs.

Strum, Philippa. 1972. *Presidential power and American democracy*. Pacific Palisades, CA: Goodyear.

Suskind, Ron. 2004. *The price of loyalty: George W. Bush, the White House, and the education of Paul O'Neill*. New York: Simon and Schuster.

Taylor, Charles. 2007. *A secular age*. Cambridge, MA: Harvard University Press.

Taylor, Robert. 1975. *Lord Salisbury*. New York: St. Martin's Press.

Teller, Edward. 1958. *Our nuclear future: Facts, dangers, and opportunities.* New York: Criterion Books.

Teubner, Günther, ed. 1987. *Juridification of social spheres: A comparative analysis in the areas of labor, corporate, antitrust, and social welfare law.* Berlin: Walter de Gruyter.

Thorelli, Hans B. 1954. *The federal antitrust policy: Origination of an American tradition.* Baltimore: Johns Hopkins University Press.

Tilly, Charles, ed. 1975. *The formation of national states in Western Europe.* Princeton, NJ: Princeton University Press.

———. 1985. War-making and state-making as organized crime. In Peter Evans, Dietrich Rueschemeyer, and Theda Skocpol, eds., *Bringing the state back in.* Cambridge: Cambridge University Press.

Toynbee, Philip. 1958. *The fearful choice: A debate on nuclear policy.* London: V. Gollancz.

Tulis, Jeffrey K. 1987. *The rhetorical presidency.* Princeton, NJ: Princeton University Press.

———. 2007. On constitutional statesmanship. Paper presented at Alpheus T. Mason Lecture in Constitutional Law and Political Thought, February 22, Princeton, NJ.

———. Forthcoming. Impeachment in the constitutional order. In Joseph M. Bessette and Jeffrey K. Tulis, eds., *The constitutional presidency,* Baltimore: Johns Hopkins University Press.

Tushnet, Mark. 2005. Emergencies and the idea of constitutionalism. In Mark Tushnet, ed., *The Constitution in wartime.* Durham, NC: Duke University Press.

Tyler, Tom R. 1990. *Why people obey the law.* New Haven: Yale University Press.

Urbinati, Nadia. 2006. *Representative democracy: Principles and genealogy.* Chicago: University of Chicago Press.

Vandenberg, Arthur H. 1952. *The private papers of Senator Vandenberg.* Boston: Houghton Mifflin.

Wallerstein, Immanuel. 2004. Soft multilateralism. *Nation,* February 2.

Watkins, Frederick Mundell. 1939. *The failure of constitutional emergency powers under the German Republic.* Cambridge, MA: Harvard University Press.

Weart, Spencer R. 1988. *Nuclear fear: A history of images.* Cambridge, MA: Harvard University Press.

Weber, Max. 1919. *Politik als Beruf.* 2nd ed. 1926. Munich: Duncker und Humbolt.

Weinstein, James. 1968. *The corporate ideal in the liberal state.* Boston: Beacon Press.

Wieseltier, Leon. 2003. Editorial. *New Republic,* September 22.

Wilentz, Sean. 2007. Mr. Cheney's minority report. *New York Times,* July 9.

Will, George. 2001. War without catharsis. *Washington Post,* September 20.

Williams, William Appleman. 1970. *The shaping of American diplomacy.* 2 vols. Chicago: Rand McNally.

———. 1972. *The tragedy of American diplomacy.* 2nd rev. ed. New York: Dell. 1st ed. 1959.

Williamson, Thames Ross. 1925. *Problems in American democracy.* Boston: Heath.

Wills, Garry. 2003. With God on his side. *New York Times Magazine,* March 20.

———. 2007. At ease, Mr. President. *New York Times,* January 27.

Wilmerding, Lucius. 1952. The president and the law. *Political Science Quarterly* 67, no. 3 (September): 321–38.

Wilson, Woodrow. 1908. *Constitutional government in the United States.* New York: Columbia University Press.

———. 1913. *The new freedom.* Chicago: Doubleday.

Winkler, Allan M. 1993. *Life under a cloud: American anxiety about the atom.* New York: Oxford University Press.

Wolfe, Alan. 2005. *Return to greatness.* Princeton, NJ: Princeton University Press.

Wolfowitz, Paul. 1992. Draft of "Defense planning guidance." Excerpted in *Washington Post,* March 11, 1992. http://www.yale.edu/strattech/ 92dpg.html.

Wolin, Sheldon S. 1960. *Politics and vision.* Boston: Little, Brown.

Woodward, Bob. 2004. *Plan of attack.* New York: Simon and Schuster.

Woodward, Carl V. 1960. The age of reinterpretation. *American Historical Review* 66 (October): 1–19.

Yergin, Daniel. 1977. *Shattered peace: The origins of the Cold War and the national security state.* Boston: Houghton Mifflin.

Zarefsky, David. 1986. *President Johnson's war on poverty.* N.p.: University of Alabama Press.

Index